Thinking Through Communication

An Introduction to the Study of Human Communication

Sarah Trenholm
Ithaca College

Allyn and Bacon
*Boston   London   Toronto   Sydney
Tokyo   Singapore*

Vice President, College Division and
Editor-in-Chief, Humanities: Joseph Opiela
Series Editor: Carla Daves
Editorial Assistant: Mary Visco
Cover Administrator: Linda Knowles
Composition Buyer: Linda Cox
Manufacturing Buyer: Louise Richardson
Marketing Representative: Lisa Kimball
Production Coordinator: Deborah Brown
Editorial-Production Service: Susan McNally
Text Designer: Denise Hoffman
Photographer: Adriana Rovers
Cover Designer: Susan Paradise

This book is printed on
recycled, acid-free paper.

Library of Congress Cataloging-in-Publication Data

Trenholm, Sarah, 1944–
    Thinking through communication : an introduction to the study of
human communication / Sarah Trenholm
        p.   cm.
    Includes bibliographical references and index.
    ISBN 013-486374-7
    1. Communication.   I. Title.
P90.T72   1994
302.2—dc20   94-40276
                                                               CIP

Printed in the United States of America

10 9 8 7 6 5 4 3 2 1   99 98 97 96 95

Contents

Part II   Listening and Language

Chapter 3
Decoding Messages: Perception and Listening   53

Chapter 4
Encoding Messages: Spoken Language   81

Chapter 7
Group Communication   195

Chapter 8
Public Communication   231

Chapter 9
Communication and the Mass Media   275

Chapter 10
Intercultural Communication   313

Preface

To the Instructor

This text is designed to introduce your students to basic concepts in speech communication. In writing the text and the instructional materials that accompany it, I've tried to provide you with as much flexibility as possible. The text itself contains core material for the student to read and study. The instructional supplement contains additional materials that allow you to tailor the course to your own interests and to your students' particular needs.

Whether you take a theory or a skills approach to teaching the course, the material in the text should give your students a better understanding of communication as a field of study and should help them think about communication in systematic ways. It should also provide a conceptual foundation for discussing communication and its effects.

Whereas the text itself provides a general overview, the materials in the supplement allow you to fill in details in your own way. I have added suggestions for supplementary lectures, handouts, discussion questions, observation guides, exercises, and assignments. I hope that these materials will allow you to take the course in the direction you want, either in the direction of theory or skills.

To the Student

This book asks you to think about a process that you can do without thinking. It asks you to take a look at behaviors that most of us overlook. In short, it asks you to rediscover communication.

When we get too close to things, we often take them for granted. People, places, and everyday processes become invisible to us. We no longer see their complexity or appreciate their uniqueness. We simply accept them without giving them much thought.

Although there are some advantages to taking things as they come, there are also disadvantages. If we were to see the world fresh every day, if we were required to make conscious decisions about our every action, we would pay a price in time and mental effort. We are often much more efficient when we don't think too much, yet we give up something in exchange for efficiency. When we act without thinking, we lose control of our behavior. We are no longer in a position to make conscious decisions about our actions.

This book was written to make you more aware of the invisible process called communication. It was written in the belief that the first step in mastering communication lies in becoming more conscious of it—in taking the time to think it through.

It is important that we think communication through because we think through communication. The way we see the world and the ways we formulate our plans and act out our social roles are determined by communication practices. When we communicate, we do more than reflect beliefs about the world: we create them. We construct our social world as we talk about it with others. We think through communication.

This book is an introduction to the study of human communication. It is designed to give you the basic concepts you need in order to understand how communication works and to introduce you to some of the most important contexts in which communication occurs. It is also designed to make you more critical of your own communication behavior as both a message sender and a message receiver.

Plan of the Text

The formal study of communication stretches back thousands of years. Like students of today, students in ancient Greece signed up for courses in communication. The first chapter of this book examines the history of communication study. The second chapter provides basic definitions and models of communication. It offers a number of answers to the question "What is communication?" and demonstrates that the way we approach communication determines what we see in it.

Chapters 3, 4, and 5 look at basic encoding and decoding processes. They discuss how we construct and interpret messages. Because understanding how people respond to messages is key to constructing messages effectively, we start by considering message reception. In chapter 3 we look at how receivers process and understand messages. In chapter 4 we turn our attention to the basic material out of which most messages are constructed: spoken language. Chapter 4 examines the structure and function of language and uncovers some of the pragmatic rules that affect the use of language. It also considers how people who ostensibly speak the same language (for example, men and women) may use it in such different ways that misunderstandings occur. Of course, meaning is not conveyed only through words. Time and space, movement and appearance also convey meaning. In chapter 5 we look at the nonverbal messages that sometimes enhance, but often undermine, our spoken messages.

Beginning with chapter 6, we look at the contexts in which communication occurs. Although communication is a unitary process, it is extremely sensitive to environmental constraints. The ways we create meaning and exchange messages are affected by the audience with whom we are communicating and the location in which the communication takes place. In each of the five chapters on context, we look at the unique properties of a given context, at common problems that communicators experience in that context, and at ways to improve communication effectiveness.

In chapter 6 we look at interpersonal communication, the informal, face-to-face interaction that is the most common form of communication. In chapter 7 we move on to group communication, considering the constraints that speaking in groups places on interaction. Chapter 8 moves us from the private to the public realm by looking at face-to-face public address. Chapter 9 considers an increasingly important context, mass communication, paying special attention to the functions and effects of different media. Chapter 10 addresses problems that occur when people from different cultures communicate.

Chapter 11 concludes our examination of communication by giving you a glimpse into the way communication scholars make discoveries about communication. Because communication is such an essential part of our lives, the study of communication does not stop when a book ends or a course concludes. Chapter 11 discusses ways we can continue to think through communication throughout our lives.

Acknowledgments

I am grateful to all my friends and colleagues at Ithaca College for their help and support. In particular, I would like to thank Laurie Arliss, Miriam Brody, Jodi Cohen, Bruce Henderson, Cathy Penner, and Scott Smith whose intelligence, wit, and humor made coming to work a pleasure. Thanks, too, to Steve Dalphin at Prentice-Hall who convinced me to do this book and to Carla Daves at Allyn and Bacon for seeing it to completion. I would also like to extend my appreciation to the expert reviewers who read and criticized the manuscript along the way and whose suggestions vastly improved the final product:

Virginia Kidd, California State University
Julie Yingling, Humboldt State University
Teresa Nance, Villanova University
Jo Young Switzer, Indiana University Purdue University at Fort Wayne
Robin Vagenas, University of Delaware
Ferald Bryan, Northern Illinois University

I would also like to acknowledge the creative work of photographer Adriana Rovers, who designed and shot all of the photos for this book. Finally, I offer special thanks to the great group of students who acted as models:

Aprile Age, Bard College
Kesha Atterberry, Ithaca College
Scott Berger, Ithaca College
Nate Dennis, Ithaca College
David Jung, Ithaca College
Jana Losey, Ithaca College
Keith Mayfield, Ithaca College
Jeremy Allan McCooey, Ithaca College
Anne Penner, Amherst College
Marie Van de Mart, Ithaca College
Amy Selco, Ithaca College
René Williams, Ithaca College
Doualy Xaykaothao, Ithaca College

You guys were fabulous!

S. T.

1

The Communication Tradition

It is in the constant interplay between communication and experience that our world is shaped.

Harvey Shands once said that "people, in cultures, speaking to each other in the local tongue and following the rules and regulations of the group, are playing a great game, the central game of the human condition."[1] This book is about that game. It's about how the game is played and how playing it affects us and the world we live in. It's about the rewards that come from playing the game well, and it's also about the costs of losing. It's about a game that affects us deeply, both on a cultural and on an individual level.

No society has existed, or ever could exist, without a well-ordered system of communication, and no individual could survive for long without knowing how that system operates. Without the ability to communicate, we could not form relationships with others, nor could we understand the world around us, for it is in the constant interplay between communication and experience that our world is shaped.

1

In the following pages we look at how communication affects us as individuals and how it affects us as a culture. We look at the verbal and nonverbal skills that make communication possible and at the many contexts in which it occurs. In short, we'll examine the knowledge and skills necessary to operate successfully in an age that has often been labeled the "age of communication."

In the Time of Aristotle:
A Brief History of Communication Study

Before we begin our study of contemporary communication, it is useful to look at the development of the field—the history of communication study. Communication has been studied seriously for many centuries. In fact, many of the communication principles we believe today were taught in ancient Greece over twenty-five hundred years ago. In the remainder of this chapter, we'll see how the formal study of communication began in fifth-century Sicily and developed in ancient Athens; we'll trace it through the medieval period and the Renaissance, discover how it evolved in the modern period, and look at some recent trends (see Table 1-1 for a summary). This brief tour should help you appreciate the importance of the subject you are about to study and should give you a sense of the way it has changed over the years.

> *Many of the communication principles we believe today were taught in ancient Greece over twenty-five hundred years ago.*

Studying Rhetoric in Ancient Greece

If by some mysterious twist of fate you were to wake up tomorrow and find yourself in ancient Greece, you could still pursue your education, although it's unlikely you'd be able to put together the same class schedule you have today. Many of the courses and majors you now take for granted wouldn't exist. If, however, you were interested in studying communication, if you wanted to learn public speaking, oral interpretation, argumentation and debate, or communication theory, you'd have no problem, for in Athens, Greece, about three hundred years before the birth of Christ, communication was as popular a subject as it is today. It would be quite easy for you to find a school, for there were many famous teachers willing to take on new students. You'd simply have to keep in mind that in those days the study of communication was called **rhetoric,** and teachers of communication were known as **rhetoricians.**

If you were looking for a place to study rhetoric in Athens around 335 B.C., your best bet would be a school called the Lyceum. The Lyceum was

The desire to understand human connectedness is timeless. By studying communication, we enter into a tradition that is centuries old.

founded by **Aristotle,** whose writings on rhetoric are considered by many to be the single greatest source of rhetorical theory. Born in 384 B.C., Aristotle was a student of the other great Greek philosopher, **Plato,** and attended Plato's Academy. Before starting the Lyceum, Aristotle served as tutor to the young son of Philip of Macedon, the child who grew up to be Alexander the Great.

Those of you who are male would have no difficulty attending the Lyceum, for the school was open to any young man who showed an interest in education. Those of you who are female would, unfortunately, have more of a problem. Although historical records show that two women managed to attend Plato's school, it was not Athenian custom for women to receive higher education. Indeed, Axiothea, one of the women who attended the Academy, resorted to the strategy of disguising herself as a man.[2]

If you were to attend Aristotle's public lectures (whether or not in disguise), you would have to rise early. Accompanied by your *paidagogos*—the attendant hired by your parents to make sure you didn't cut classes—you would make your way through the busy *agora*, or central marketplace, to the great wall surrounding the city. Outside the wall you would enter the wooded sanctuary of Apollo the Wolf Slayer, site of the Lyceum. As you would pass the huge gymnasium, you might see young men practicing the discus or wrestling. If it were during one of the many periods in which Athens was at war, you could observe troops, clad in bronze breastplates and shields, taking part in military drills on the open parade ground. In Athens, as in other Greek city-states, physical activity was important to education, and teachers of philosophy and rhetoric shared space in the public gyms with teachers of physical culture and the military arts. As you would near the school library (one of the first of its kind), you would undoubtedly meet friends, and together you would look for seats in front of the colonnaded portico from which Aristotle customarily spoke.

Aristotle held his public lectures in the mornings, covering philosophy, science, and logic.[3] In the afternoons he walked along the shaded walkways known as *peripatos,* stopping from time to time to sit in one of the roomy recesses and talk with his students about ethics, politics, and rhetoric. Because much of his private instruction took place in this way, his school became known as the **Peripatetic School.**

TABLE 1-1

A Short History of Rhetoric and Communication Theory

Cave paintings attest to the universal human need to record and communicate experience. Written records in all ancient civilizations (Egypt, Babylon, India, China) show that communication has long been an object of study.

Classical Period   (500 B.C.–400 A.D.)

With the rise of Greek democracy, public communication became an important tool for problem solving. Rhetoric, the study of "the available means of persuasion," was a respected discipline taught by the great philosophers. The first known communication model, the canons of rhetoric, divided rhetoric into five parts: invention, arrangement, style, memory, and delivery. Classical rhetoric emphasized credibility, ways to ground arguments, and audience analysis. Major figures included Plato, Isocrates, Aristotle, Cicero, and Quintilian.

Medieval Period and the Renaissance   (400–1600)

In response to the rise of monolithic Christianity, rhetoric became secondary to theology. Major rhetorical acts were letter writing and preaching. Parts of the classical paradigm were kept alive, but the focus was prescriptive, not theoretical. Rhetoricians emphasized methods of embellishing and amplifying rhetorical style. Major figures included Augustine, Cassiodorus, John of Salisbury, Erasmus, and Francis Bacon.

If you were to study with Aristotle, your focus would be on persuasive rhetoric. Aristotle considered the science of rhetoric to be that of "observing in any given case the available means of persuasion."[4] He lectured about the ways in which successful arguments can be built, and he described methods of arriving at truthful conclusions. He also talked a great deal about proof. Aristotle believed that a speaker could sway an audience in three ways: through personal character, or **ethos;** through the ability to arouse emotions, or **pathos;** and through the wording and logic of the message, or **logos.** In discussing ethos, Aristotle became one of the first communication specialists to point out the importance of source credibility. If you were fortunate enough to study with him, you would leave school knowing the most frequently encountered types of speaking situations, rules for effective reasoning, the part that human emotions play in persuasion, the necessity for audience analysis, ways of improving style and delivery, and the place of rhetoric in maintaining and discovering truth.

Modern Period   (1600–1900)

Once again, public rhetoric was a major force in determining public policy. The written word became an important medium as books and newspapers became more available. Rhetoric followed four paths: Classical rhetoric revived the work of the ancients. Psychological/epistemological rhetoric investigated receivers' psychological responses to persuasive messages. Belletristic rhetoric saw written and spoken communication as art and developed theories of rhetorical criticism. Elocutionists focused on developing elaborate rules for delivery. Major figures were Fénelon, Lord Kames, George Campbell, Joseph Priestley, and Thomas De Quincey.

Contemporary Period   (1900–present)

Modern departments of communication were formed. Communication study took two paths: Rhetoricians used humanistic methods to analyze rhetorical effects of public discourse. Communication theorists used scientific methods to analyze communication behavior as a social science. Communication study expanded to include interpersonal and group, as well as public, communication. The rise of electronic media signaled additional changes in communication study.

The Classical Period: Enchanting the Mind by Arguments

Although he was arguably the greatest of the early Western rhetoricians, Aristotle was not the first. That honor is shared by two Sicilian Greeks, **Corax** and **Tisias,** who lived a century before Aristotle. The story of Corax and Tisias illustrates clearly that the study of communication is always prompted by practical problems.[5]

In 466 B.C. Sicily experienced a political upheaval when the populace overthrew the existing tyrant and established a democratic constitution. People who had been exiled under the previous regime came back to Sicily and demanded the return of their land and property. This, of course, led to intricate legal problems (similar in some respects to those now occurring in the formerly socialist countries of Europe). Corax recognized that many of the litigants were ill-equipped to argue their own cases persuasively. He and his pupil Tisias systematized their ideas of the art of communication, paying special attention to how speakers could effectively order their ideas. From these early attempts to address practical problems the rhetorical tradition emerged, with each subsequent rhetorician asking new questions and adding new understandings.

In the next one hundred years, the study of rhetoric expanded rapidly as the great orators and philosophers of ancient Greece added their insights and theories about the art of public speaking. Indeed, the rhetoric taught by the Greek philosophers is directly linked to the rhetoric taught in modern communication courses. Much of the advice a modern teacher of public communication gives a student (advice on building audience rapport, organizing one's thoughts, arguing to friendly or hostile audiences, and delivering a speech) was given by Greek and Roman teachers more than two thousand years ago.

The rhetoric taught by the Greek philosophers is directly linked to the rhetoric taught in modern communication courses.

The **classical period** lasted for about nine hundred years, from the fifth century B.C. to the fourth century A.D. It flowered under Athenian democracy, lasted through the years of the Roman Empire, and closed with the advent of Christianity. Communication study was important in classical Greece for a number of reasons. First, Greece was a society that revered the spoken word. Although many Athenians could read and write, the stone, wood, or wax tablets they used were unwieldy. There was no light reading, no books or magazines. Oral expression, in the form of storytelling, poetry reading, dramatic performance, or conversation, was the major source of entertainment. Individual actors, interpreters, and orators were admired and respected, and training in these arts was considered essential.

In addition to the study of artistic or ornamental speech, the Greeks put a great deal of emphasis on persuasion and argumentation. Because Athens was a democracy, would-be politicians achieved office through their ability to speak thoughtfully and persuasively. Important political issues were defined and resolved through public debate, and individual politicians gained public notice as a result of their skills in argumentation.

A final factor contributing to the rise of rhetoric as a field of study was the ban on professional lawyers for so many years. Like their Sicilian counterparts, Greek citizens who wished to bring suit in a court of law had to have the forensic skills to argue their cases successfully. These conditions provided practical reasons for studying communication.

In response to this practical need, a group of itinerant teachers called **Sophists** began to ply their trade. The Sophists were the first professional speech teachers. They advertised their services by posting notices in public places and by turning up wherever they could find an audience. Soon the gymnasia became important locations for learning: the Sophists knew they could find a large and receptive audience in the Athenian version of today's health clubs.

The major concern of the Sophists was teaching the "tricks" of persuasive speaking for use either in the law courts or in political life. Often the Sophists supplemented their income by acting as professional speechwriters and political consultants. Philosophers such as Plato and Aristotle held the Sophists in great contempt, for the philosophers believed that the goal of communication is to discover the truth, not merely to win arguments. The Sophists seemed undaunted by this criticism, however, and bragged that they were so skillful that they could make weak arguments defeat strong ones.

The Greek and Roman philosophers such as Plato, Aristotle, Cicero, and Quintilian were more theoretical (and more ethical) than were the Sophists. **Cicero** (106–43 B.C.), a prominent Roman politician, was considered to be Rome's finest orator. He met his death when he joined the forces opposing Mark Antony after the assassination of Julius Caesar. During his lifetime he delivered many famous speeches and wrote extensively on communication theory. By the time his works were published, the study of rhetoric had stabilized into five major topic areas, the famous **canons of rhetoric.** Cicero did much to elaborate on this, the earliest of communication models.

The canons divided communication into five parts: invention, style, arrangement, memory, and delivery (see Table 1-2). The first, **invention,** was the process of deciding on the subject matter of one's speech and of discovering information and arguments that would lead to sound conclusions. Classical rhetoricians shared Aristotle's belief that through communication one could decide which of several possible "truths" was the most correct. In their writing

Aristotle

TABLE 1-2

Invention

The speaker must begin by discovering what can be said about a given topic and by finding arguments that will allow others to understand it. Classical theory emphasized methods for analyzing audience, subject, and occasion to find material that would move people to belief and action. Through logical thinking and clear topical analysis, the speaker could find grounds for effective arguments. Major speech occasions were three: forensic, deliberative, and epideictic (ceremonial). Modes of proof were three: ethos, pathos, and logos.

Arrangement

The speaker must arrange ideas for maximum impact. Classical theory divided a speech into several parts, which correspond roughly with introduction, body, and conclusion. Theorists agreed that the audience must be put into the proper frame of mind for receiving the message, the subject must be set forth clearly, a case must be built, and the speech must end with a summary and conclusion. Writers recognized that order of elements depends on the nature of the audience (whether hostile or friendly) and on the seriousness of the occasion.

Style

The speaker must select and arrange the wording of the message carefully. Style was thought to differ in relationship to speech purpose: it could instruct, please, or persuade. Classical writers believed language should be clear, lively, and appropriate for the audience. Using figurative language was thought to be a way of increasing audience response.

Memory

The speaker must find a way to keep the message firmly in mind. Classical writers suggested several mnemonic devices to help orators memorize speeches. Theorists also discussed factors that make speech material memorable, including novelty.

Delivery

The speaker must present the speech in a natural, varied, and appropriate way. Voice should convey interest and emotion, and gestures should match the major ideas in the speech.

and teaching they argued that the student of communication should have a wide knowledge of current affairs as well as the ability to think clearly. Theories of invention emphasized modes of argumentation appropriate to major communication contexts.

Style was the second canon. It described the process of selecting the proper words to convey one's message. Classical rhetoricians emphasized correct use of language and cataloged major figures of speech. Cicero believed there were three styles of speaking that corresponded with Aristotle's three modes of speech. The **plain style** built ethos by convincing the audience of the speaker's good character, good sense, and trustworthiness; it was logical, clear, and restrained. The **middle style** emphasized logos by impressing the audience with the soundness of the speaker's position; it consisted of intricate argumentation and careful philosophical distinctions. Finally, the **vigorous style** was based on pathos and was designed to overwhelm the audience; it "pulled out all the stops" and was eloquent and emotional. Cicero, like the other classical rhetoricians, mistrusted emotional appeals and warned speakers not to use the vigorous style without some elements of the other two styles.[6]

The next canon, **arrangement,** theorized how to order one's materials most effectively. Here, for the first time, speakers were taught that a speech must open with an introduction, follow with a statement of purpose, lead into presentation of arguments, and end with a conclusion. Classical rhetoricians also emphasized the necessity of organizing material according to audience needs and goals.

In an oral society, **memory,** the ability to hold content, style, and arrangement in one's mind, was exceedingly important. The science of mnemonics was developed during this time to help speakers keep track of complex arguments. One of the most popular mnemonic systems suggested that the speaker visualize a house or villa with main ideas situated in each room. During the speech, the speaker could then mentally proceed through the rooms, making each argument in the correct order. The method was developed by a rhetor named Simonides who, after reciting a poem at a banquet, was called away from the banquet hall. This circumstance was fortunate, because no sooner did he leave than the hall collapsed, killing many of the guests. When asked to help identify the dead, Simonides realized that he could remember quite easily where each person had been sitting. The incident brought home to him the power of visual memory and set him to wondering whether visualization might be used to recall other kinds of information. The method he devised was used throughout antiquity and is still useful today.

The final canon was **delivery.** Delivery was considered necessary for success because if the speaker did not use a pleasing voice and graceful gestures, the effect of the rest of the process would be undermined. Although they considered delivery less important than the other canons, the Greeks and Romans evidently had an early sense of the importance of nonverbal communication and its effects on speech presentation. Cicero, for example, illustrated the need for nonverbal expression when he warned speakers that they would never be able to make an audience feel indignation, terror, or compassion until these emotions were "visibly stamped or rather branded on the advocate himself."[7]

For classical rhetoricians, communication was a highly important area of study, the "queen of disciplines." Because it was through communication that a

> *For classical rhetoricians, communication was a highly important area of study, the "queen of disciplines."*

society determined policies in its own best interest, rhetoric carried heavy ethical weight. In fact, **Quintilian** (35–95 A.D.), the last of the great classical theorists, defined rhetoric as the study of "the good man speaking well." While the focus of communication study during this time was on legal and political discourse, classical theorists also expressed a concern for all forms of communication. As Plato says in the *Phaedrus,*

> *Is not rhetoric, taken generally, a universal art of enchanting the mind by arguments; which is practised not only in courts and public assemblies, but in private houses also, having to do with all matters, great as well as small, good and bad alike?*[8]

Medieval and Renaissance Communication: Truth Armed Against Falsehood

With the fall of the Roman Empire and the rise of Christianity, rhetorical study declined. During the next two important historical periods, the **medieval period** (which lasted from 400 to 1000 A.D.) and the **Renaissance** (1000 to 1600 A.D.), little insight was added to classical thought. Only at the very beginning of the medieval period, when Augustine wrote, and at the very end of the Renaissance, with the work of Francis Bacon, do we find much original work. During the twelve hundred years following the classical period, most rhetorical works were fragmented versions of earlier thought or handbooks on rhetorical style.

The medieval period and the Renaissance were characterized by the rise to political power of the Christian clergy and the decline of "pagan" theories of rhetoric. With the advent of monolithic Christianity, the goal of communication was no longer to discover possible truth through discussion and debate but to instruct the faithful in certain truth, the revealed "will of God." Classic ideas of rhetoric, therefore, fell into disrepute, and "rhetoric ceased to be a vital, developing discipline."[9]

There was, nevertheless, a practical need for training in communication. The two most important communication activities were letter writing and preaching. The first was of great importance because, in a world of independently held feudal kingdoms, it was necessary to communicate over large distances. In the so-called Dark Ages, most people were illiterate, and even kings and queens were forced to hire professional "dictators" who composed and wrote the political decrees, legal mandates, and religious dispensations that connected feudal society.

Preaching was also of great importance, because it was the duty of the Christian clergy to teach the word of God. **Augustine** (354–430), a major Christian theorist, argued that it would be foolish for truth "to take its stand unarmed against falsehood." To neglect the art of rhetoric would lead to disaster, for if evil speakers were to sway an audience by their eloquence and false arguments and the good were to "tell the truth in such a way that it is tedious to listen to, hard to understand, and, in fine, not easy to believe in," then wicked and worthless causes would triumph.[10]

Augustine

The preacher's goal was to interpret the word of God. He (rarely she) had to study the scriptures, determine their meaning, and pass this meaning on. As a communication theorist, Augustine tried to understand this process. He believed that people communicate through signs. A sign, he said, is something that "causes something else to come into the mind as a consequence of itself."[11] **Natural signs** (for example, smoke, which causes one to think of fire) are created by God, Augustine reasoned. **Conventional signs** (for example, the spoken or written word) are arbitrarily created by humans, and their interpretation is more difficult. For Augustine, communication was a process of "drawing forth and conveying into another's mind what the giver of the sign has in his own mind."[12] This view of communication as a process whereby a sender transmits symbols to a receiver who interprets and acts on them is not far from the view many modern theorists express.[13] And language and the problem of meaning are still important subjects today.

After Augustine, little original theorizing about communication was done. Although the classical paradigm was kept alive, rhetoric became secondary to theology, its subject matter was dispersed throughout the liberal arts, and what remained was prescriptive rather than theoretical. Most rhetorical works were compilations of form letters the writer might copy or manuals on preaching style. Although the study of rhetoric never died out, it became fragmented, and the vigor and originality that had characterized it during the classical period were gone.

The Modern Period:
A Rational Science of Rhetoric

The three centuries from 1600 to 1900 are known as the **modern period.** During this time new attitudes toward knowledge revitalized the study of rhetoric. As the power of the Church declined, secular studies were no longer regarded with suspicion. Nationalism and the rise of democratic forms of government led to increased public debate on important issues of the day. Once again, people believed that political and moral problems could be solved through the exercise of free speech.

Once again, people believed that political and moral problems could be solved through the exercise of free speech.

In his analysis of modern rhetoric, Douglas Ehninger identifies four directions of rhetorical study during the modern period.[14] Those who took the **classical approach** set out to recover the insights of the great classical rhetoricians, adapting them to modern times. Others took a **psychological/epistemological approach.** They investigated the relationship of communication and thought, trying to understand in a "scientific" way how people could influence one another through speech. The **belletristic approach** focused on writing and speaking as art forms, developing critical standards for judging drama, poetry, and oratory. Finally, those who took an **elocutionary approach,** dismayed at the poor delivery of public speakers, designed elaborate systems of instruction to improve speakers' verbal and nonverbal presentation.

No matter what their ultimate goal was, rhetoricians of the modern period were well-versed in the ideas of classical rhetoric. Whether their primary interest was understanding the nature of human thought, developing standards of artistic judgment, or understanding delivery, they built on the insights of the ancients. They coupled these insights, however, with a thoroughly modern belief in the importance of **empiricism** (the process of grounding theory in observation).

Those who took a psychological approach were particularly concerned with finding a scientific basis for the study of human communication, although their science emphasized "armchair introspection" over experimentation. They wanted to understand the process by which human action could be influenced by speech and to describe the thought processes of receivers listening to persuasive messages. More than any previous writer, **George Campbell** (1719–1796) stressed that receivers were active participants in the persuasion process and that the effective communicator studies the inner workings, or "faculties," of the human mind. Contemporary theorists still emphasize the importance of understanding the experiences of individual receivers, and the psychological approach remains one of the major approaches to communication today.

The rhetoricians who took a belletristic view were interested less in the psychology of communication than in problems of style. **Thomas De Quincey** (1785–1859), for example, tried to define the nature of emotional and persuasive discourse, which he called poetic speech. He believed there were three ways of influencing others poetically. The first was eloquence, which received its force through the creation of emotional involvement in listeners; the second was rhetoric, which was more reasonable and intellectual; the third, called Corinthian rhetoric, combined the best of both the emotional and intellectual worlds, using "both analogy and imagery and appeals to both the understanding and the passions."[15]

In general, modern theorists with a classical, psychological, or belletristic bent felt that speakers should be widely read and well educated; should use clear, lively, and concise language; should follow a motivational or psychologically based order of arguments; and should speak with a natural, extemporaneous style, matching gestures and voice to the feeling expressed in their texts.

The elocutionists focused their study of communication on the canon of delivery. Although their initial task was to describe the gestures and vocal characteristics naturally associated with different emotional states, their zeal for systematizing soon led to sets of artificial rules for delivery. They developed elaborate charts detailing the appropriate ways to show major emotions such as pride, shame, horror, and admiration (see Figure 1-1). By using the "self-help" books they published, speakers could mechanically map out the nonverbal behaviors that would make their delivery most effective. Unfortunately, this approach led to a florid style that was anything but natural and spontaneous and that gave a bad name to the study of oral communication for many years.

Communication Today: Contemporary Departments of Rhetoric and Communication Theory

Throughout the history of communication study, new technologies have continually affected our ideas of what communication is. During the modern period, the new technology was printing. As written communication became increasingly important, rhetoricians turned their attention from the study of the spoken word to the study of literary works. Therefore, when American universities and colleges organized themselves into departments, rhetoric was assigned to English departments. Not until the early years of the twentieth century did contemporary teachers of public speaking and rhetoric form their own professional organization and develop their own departments of speech communication. Today these departments are among the most popular on campuses everywhere, but in the early days this was not the case. At that time,

FIGURE 1-1

The Geometric Properties of Easy and Graceful Movement

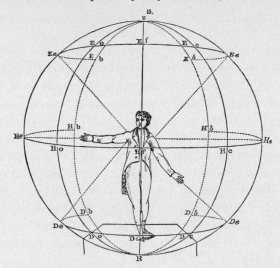

Diagrams Showing the Speaker How to Express Appropriate Emotion

Aversion is expressed by two gestures; first the hand . . . is retracted toward the face . . . then suddenly the eyes are withdrawn, the head is averted, the feet retire, and the arms are projected out extended against the object, the hands vertical.

Veneration crosses both hands on the breast, casts down the eyes slowly, and bows the head.

Horror . . . is seldom capable of retreating, but remains petrified, in one attitude, with the eyes riveted on its object, and the arm held forward to guard the person. . . .

From *A Manual of Elocution: Embracing Voice and Gesture, Designed for Schools, Academies and Colleges as Well as for Private Learners* (pp. 248, 808, 310) by M. Caldwell, 1845, Philadelphia: Sorin and Ball.

the serious study of communication was focused on literary communication, whereas public speaking was associated with the simplistic systems of the elocutionists. Many people considered speech too simple to be studied seriously.[16]

Communication: Science or Art?

As modern departments began to emerge, two approaches to the study of communication developed. Many scholars wanted to pursue traditional rhetorical methods. Like rhetoricians before them, they studied the way symbolic activity shaped public response to political and ethical issues. Proud of their tradition, they were eager to retain their identity as rhetoricians, yet they also recognized the need to address contemporary communication problems. For these scholars, rhetoric remained a humanistic discipline.

A second school of thought took a more scientific approach to the study of communication. At the turn of the century, many disciplines were influenced by the **scientific method**, a belief in controlled laboratory experimentation and careful, objective measurement. Scholars in the natural sciences believed that one could understand a phenomenon only by reducing it to its most basic elements or variables, manipulating these variables in a controlled situation, and observing the results.

Scholars in the emerging disciplines of psychology, sociology, and anthropology embraced this scientific view and sought ways of applying the methods of the "hard" scientists to the study of human behavior. Because many students of communication were convinced that human communication should join the social sciences, in the 1920s communication researchers began publishing empirical research on oral communication. One of the most popular subjects for study was audience psychology and attitude change: early communication scientists used experimental and statistical methods to study source credibility, speech organization, use of evidence, the effects of rational and emotional appeals, and "audience variables such as sex, dogmatism, ego involvement in the subject of the message, and so forth."[17] Since then, social scientists have investigated many more forms of human communication behavior, including interpersonal and group interaction.

Whether you view rhetoric as an art or a science, you will find support in contemporary communication departments, for most departments today teach courses both in rhetoric and in communication theory. Although the methods used by rhetoricians and communication scientists differ, the questions they address are similar. Both types of communication scholars want to understand how communicators affect each other as they interact.

> *Both types of communication scholars want to understand how communicators affect each other as they interact.*

What Do Rhetoricians and Communication Scientists Do?

People with degrees in rhetoric and communication theory apply their interests in many communication-related professions. They may become speechwriters, political consultants or politicians, legal consultants or lawyers, advertising executives, public relations experts, counselors, organizational training and development specialists, professional negotiators, personnel managers, specialists in information storage and retrieval, radio or television performers, media consultants, and the like.

Communication specialists may also teach and do academic research. Those who do so have an almost limitless supply of subjects to investigate and, as we shall see in chapter 11, a variety of ways to study those subjects. In the past, rhetoricians have studied the rhetoric of films, television, social movements, political speeches, political newscasting, cartoons, popular music, psychotherapy, painting, architecture, and even science.[18] Communication sci-

New technologies are continually emerging. During the modern period, the new technology was printing; today it is the computer that is changing our notions of human interaction.

entists have studied how communication affects the development and maintenance of one's self-image, how message variables affect the way we process and
understand information, what factors lead to attitude change,
how interpersonal relationships form and dissolve, how small
groups make effective and ineffective decisions, how complex
organizations use communication to function effectively, how
the media affect audience responses, and the like.[19] New topics arise continuously, for as the shape of society changes, so
too does communication. And it's communication professionals who help us
keep up with our changing world.

> *As the shape of society changes, so too does communication.*

Into the Future: Twentieth-Century Communication and Beyond

Earlier in this chapter, you were asked to imagine yourself in ancient Greece.
Now try taking a step into the future by thinking about what communication
may entail in the twenty-first century. Imagine the following scenario: You've
graduated with honors and now work for a large and successful company. On
the day we're describing, you're a bit behind schedule. As you rush into your
ultramodern office and sink into your plush chair, your computer senses your
arrival and turns itself on. "Hi. You're late. Traffic bad today?" a friendly,
attractive voice asks you. "While you were busy, I took a message from Mr.
Jones. It's about the annual report," the computer continues. "I also took a
message from your friend Claire. It's about the party tonight. Whom shall I
dial for you?"

"I'll call them all later," you say. Then you ask the computer, "When can I
see Mr. Smith today?" The computer checks Mr. Smith's schedule and answers,
"Smith won't be in until this afternoon. I can make an appointment for 3 P.M."
By punching up your schedule, you can see all of your appointments for the
day, including the 3 P.M. appointment that your computer and Smith's have
just arranged.

You and your computer continue to interact throughout the day. The
computer answers the phone, avoiding the calls you tell it to avoid and giving
priority to those you want to accept. It checks important information for you,
reminds you of upcoming projects, and even nags you, insisting that you take
your vitamins and call your mother.

After a hard day at the office (at least hard for your computer), you want
to settle down and read the paper. So, the first thing you do when you get to

your apartment is turn on your personal semiautomatic electronic newspaper. During the day, your newspaper has been hard at work assembling items it "thinks" you'll like from the major news services and information networks. Now it displays on its monitor a menu of topics: finance, people, national news, international news, sports. You touch the last topic, and a number of headlines are displayed. "Five Islanders Ejected in Year's Biggest Brawl" captures your attention. As the screen fills with print, you begin to read about last night's hockey game. As you read, you're curious about the league standings, so you punch in a code to check where the Islanders stand. Then you turn back to the description of last night's game. A still photo shows the melee on the ice. Suddenly it comes to life, and a film clip shows you exactly how the fight began. You continue to browse through a newspaper that's been personally programmed to pick up stories you're interested in.

Now you have an hour before you have to leave for Claire's party, just time enough to invite your neighbor over to eat dinner and to watch a condensed version of the president's speech, which was delivered during the afternoon. After placing two dinners in the microwave, you turn on the television. When you tell it you only have a half hour to look at the film, it automatically runs through the speech and selects the highlights for you and your neighbor. Had you had more time, the TV could have given you an expanded version.

Sound fantastic? Well, this scenario is not as far in the future as you might believe. Similar information technologies already exist.[20] How will this new interactive technology affect the way we communicate? How will it change the way we live our lives? It's hard to say, although it's clear that the change will be profound and that we'll learn to adapt to it. Later on in this book, we'll consider the effects of technology on communication. For now, it is enough to note that the shape of communication—and with it the shape of our personal lives—is changing.

Summary

The study of communication is not a modern invention. We can trace many of today's ideas about communication to earlier periods, in particular ancient Greece and Rome. Although the first Western rhetoricians to be recognized as such were the Sicilian Greeks Corax and Tisias, the study of rhetoric became fully developed only after the Athenian philosophers, including Plato and Aristotle, turned their attention to the art of communication. Early rhetorical systems met a practical need: they provided practical training for individuals who needed to express their thoughts clearly and eloquently in political and legal contexts.

Aristotle and Plato wrote during the classical period (fifth century B.C.–fourth century A.D.). As a result of their work and that of others such as Cicero and Quintilian, by the end of this period a full-fledged communication model had developed. This model, called the canons of rhetoric, divided the process of public communication into five parts: invention, style, arrangement, memory, and delivery. This model has remained vital over the centuries, and much of the information we now study in public speaking classes originated in these canons.

During the medieval period (400–1000) and the Renaissance (1000–1600), the focus of rhetoric shifted, due in part to the political power of the Christian clergy. Particularly important forms of communication were letter writing and preaching. The medieval philosopher Augustine viewed communication as a symbolic process, a view we shall examine in detail in the chapter on spoken language.

In the modern period (1600–1900), the study of rhetoric followed one of four paths. The classical approach revived ancient Greek and Roman models. The belletristic approach focused on communication as art. The elocutionist approach consisted of elaborate, artificial systems of presentation. And the psychological/epistemological approach investigated the relationship between communication and thought, placing special emphasis on the receiver as an active participant in the creation of meaning.

By the twentieth century, a new method of inquiry, the scientific method, became popular. Communication scholars began to see the importance of experiment and objective measurement, and they used these methods to investigate audience response and attitude change. During the same period, a more humanistic, philosophical approach was also used. Contemporary departments of communication acknowledge the importance of communication science yet also honor the rhetorical tradition.

Communication study has a rich tradition. Although methodologies and concerns have changed over the centuries, what hasn't changed is the fundamental importance of understanding communication.

Key Terms

Listed below are the key terms used in this chapter, along with the number of the page where each is explained.

Review Questions

1. What is rhetoric? Where and when did the study of rhetoric first receive systematic attention?

2. Who was Aristotle? What was the name of his academy, and what subjects were studied there? Why was the term *peripatetic* attached to his teaching?

3. According to Aristotle, a speaker could sway an audience in three ways. What are they? Under which does the modern concept of speaker credibility fall?

4. When was the classical period? What social and political conditions caused much of classical rhetoric to focus on persuasion and argumentation?

5. Who were the Sophists, and what approach did they take to rhetoric? Who are the Sophists' modern counterparts?

6. What are the five canons of rhetoric? What basic advice did each give the public speaker?

7. When were the medieval period and the Renaissance? What forms of communication were particularly important during these times? Why?

8. How did Augustine view communication? What important concept did he emphasize?

9. When did the modern period take place? What political changes were instrumental in changing communication practices during this period? What four paths did the study of rhetoric take?

10. What was the major concern of the psychological/epistemological approach? of the belletristic approach? of the elocutionists? How did the latter tarnish the reputation of communication study?

11. In contemporary departments, what two approaches are taken toward communication? What kinds of subjects are studied under each approach?

Suggested Readings

Bizzell, Patricia, & Herzberg, Bruce. (1990). *The rhetorical tradition: Readings from classical times to the present*. Boston: St. Martin's, Bedford Books.

This volume presents readings from the works of the great rhetoricians. Its general introduction and the introductions to each period present excellent summaries of the history of rhetorical thought. If you want to go to the original sources, this book may be the place to start.

Conley, Thomas M. (1990). *Rhetoric in the European tradition*. New York: Longman.

Conley offers commentary on and summaries of important rhetorical works from Plato to Habermas.

Foss, Sonja K., Karen A. Foss, & Robert Trapp. (1985). *Contemporary perspectives on rhetoric*. Prospect Heights, IL: Waveland.

This text focuses on the works of some of the most important contemporary rhetoricians and provides an excellent bibliography.

Harper, Nancy. (1979). *Human communication theory: The history of a paradigm*. Rochelle Park, NJ: Hayden Book Company.

Harper presents an excellent discussion of the history of rhetoric from the Greeks to the nineteenth century.

Notes

1. Shands, Harvey C. (1968). Crystallized conflict: Semiotic aspects of neurosis and science. In Carl E. Larson, & Frank E. X. Dance (Eds.), *Perspectives on communication*. Milwaukee: The University of Wisconsin, Milwaukee, Speech Communication Center, 128.

2. Lynch, John Patrick. (1972). *Aristotle's school, A study of a Greek educational institution*. Berkeley: University of California Press, 57, 93.

3. Bryant, Donald C. (Ed.). (1968). *Ancient Greek and Roman rhetoricians: A biographical dictionary*. Columbia, MO: Artcraft, 15–16.

4. Aristotle. (1954). *Rhetoric and poetics* (W. Rhys Roberts, Trans.). The Modern Library. New York: Random House, 1355b 26.

5. The material on the history of rhetoric is taken from two sources: Thonssen, Lester, A. Craig Baird, & Waldo W. Braden. (1970). *Speech criticism* (2nd ed.). New York: The Ronald Press; and Harper, Nancy. (1979). *Human communication theory: The history of a paradigm*. Rochelle Park, NJ: Hayden Book Company.

6. Cicero. (1939). *Orator* (H. M. Hubell, Trans.). Cambridge: Harvard University Press, 101. For a summary of Cicero's attitudes toward style, see Harper, 46–47.

7. Cicero, II. xliii, 182.

8. Plato. (1952). *Phaedrus, Gorgias* (Benjamin Jowett, Trans.). Oxford: Clarendon, 261.

9. Harper, 70.

10. Augustine. (1952). *On Christian doctrine* (J. F. Shaw, Trans.). Great Books of the Western World: Vol. 18. Chicago: Encyclopaedia Britannica, IV.2.

11. Ibid., II.1; Capes, W. W. (1877). *University life in ancient Athens*. London: Longmans, Green, and Co.

12. Augustine, II.2.

13. Arnold, Carroll C., & Kenneth D. Frandsen. (1984). Conceptions of rhetoric and communication. In Carroll C. Arnold, & John Waite Bowers (Eds.), *Handbook of rhetorical and communication theory*. Boston: Allyn and Bacon, 27.

14. Ehninger, Douglas. (1952, September). Dominant trends in English rhetorical thought, 1750–1800. *Southern Speech Journal*, 3–11.

15. Harper, 153; Cicero. (1949). *De oratore* (H. Rackham, Trans.). Loeb Classical Library. Cambridge: Harvard University Press.

16. Leff, Michael C., & Procario, Margaret Organ. (1985). Rhetorical theory in speech communication. In Benson, Thomas W. (Ed.), *Speech communication in the twentieth century*. Carbondale: Southern Illinois University Press, 4.

17. Bormann, Ernest G. (1980). *Communication theory*. New York: Holt, Rinehart and Winston, 10.

18. From the reference list accompanying Gregg, Richard B. (1985). "Criticism of symbolic induce- ment: A critical-theoretical connection. In Benson, 380–83.

19. From the table of contents of Arnold and Bowers, v–vi.

20. Brand, Stewart. (1987). *The media lab*. New York: Penguin. See especially chapter 3, "Terminal Garden."

2

Definitions, Models, and Perspectives

There are many ways to define and explain communication.

As we saw in chapter 1, communication has had a long history. For thousands of years, scholars have debated the nature of communication, and students have worked to improve their communication skills. Even before the Greeks, people were interested in defining communication and explaining its role in human affairs. We know that the Babylonians and Egyptians thought and wrote about communication, and we can assume that other, less familiar cultures also built theories and models of communication.

Given such interest, one might think that defining communication is a simple matter. Unfortunately, it isn't. As we shall see, there are many ways to define and explain communication. In this chapter we look at some of the issues that arise when people try to describe this complex and important process. We examine what it means to create definitions and build models, and we explore some of the underlying philosophical perspectives and assumptions that affect our understanding of communication.

Defining Communication

A definition is a useful and logical place to start our exploration of communication. The term **definition** comes from a Latin word meaning "to determine, bring to an end, or settle." When we create definitions, we try to pin down concepts by indicating their boundaries. Definitions focus our attention on one category of entities or events to the exclusion of others. Thus, a definition of communication should tell us what kinds of processes may be called communication and what may not, and it should provide us with an understanding of the essential characteristics of communication. What, then, is the definition of communication?

Unfortunately, no single definition of communication is acceptable to everyone. In fact, in the early 1970s, Frank Dance identified 126 published definitions.[1] In the last twenty years, communication scholars have been busily adding to that list, so that now there are a good many more. Why has the concept of communication produced so many definitions? To understand the reasons for this diversity, we have to look first at what it means to create a definition and then at the specific issues that arise when people try to define communication.

Definitions: Discovery or Construction?

One way to think about the world is to assume it is made up of phenomena that exist independently of human knowledge. By carefully observing objects and actions, we can discover their essential features and express them in the form of an objective definition. According to this view, a good definition accurately records and describes something that already exists. Understanding the world and expressing that understanding in a definition are objective processes of *discovery;* theoretically, a single correct definition exists for everything we wish to understand.

A second, and quite different, way to think about the world is to assume that many of its most important phenomena are human constructions. Whatever the world inherently is, it is knowable only through human thought. As we think, we are as likely to create new phenomena as we are to discover old ones. According to this view, a definition is a *construction* rather than a discovery, and it is quite possible for people (having different needs and experiences) to have different understandings of a single phenomenon. If we adopt this approach, then the test of a good definition is not its absolute truth (for that is undiscoverable) but its practical use. Different

> *A definition is a construction rather than a discovery, and the test of a good definition is not its absolute truth but its practical use.*

definitions focus our attention on different aspects of a given phenomenon. A definition is useful if it helps us understand an aspect more fully.

The second approach not only takes a more realistic view of human perception and cognition but also explains how even the most mundane of objects can have a number of equally valid definitions. Even an everyday object such as a telephone can be defined in many ways. If we were to ask an American teenager, a telemarketer, and a telecommunications engineer to tell us what a telephone is, we might get quite different definitions. The teen would be likely to define the telephone in terms of its social functions, seeing it as a way of maintaining relationships. The telemarketer would probably view the telephone as a consumer delivery system, whereas the engineer might concentrate on its structure and mode of operation. Each would visualize and explain the instrument in a different way. And each would be right. All three definitions are useful, because they clarify important aspects of the telephone.

When it comes to social phenomena such as communication, multiple definitions become even more likely. Defining an activity rather than an object introduces even more latitude for subjectivity. Each of a number of definitions is correct insofar as it helps us (and others) understand a significant aspect of the social world.

Deciding What Communication Is

Table 2-1 lists a number of definitions of communication. Before you read any further, look them over and choose the definition that comes closest to your understanding of communication. If none of them appeals to you, try your hand at creating your own definition. Ask yourself what the essential differences are between the definitions listed.

Each of the definitions in Table 2-1 results from a different decision about a basic question. As we shall see, the definitions vary in breadth, intentionality, the relative weight they give to sender and receiver, and the importance they place on symbolic behavior.

TABLE 2-1

Definition 1 Communication is a process of acting on information.

Definition 2 "Communication is the discriminatory response of an organism to a stimulus."[a]

Definition 3 "Communication . . . is an 'effort after meaning,' a creative act initiated by man in which he seeks to discriminate and organize cues so as to orient himself in his environment and satisfy his changing needs."[b]

Definition 4 "Speech communication is a human process through which we make sense out of the world and share that sense with others."[c]

Definition 5 "In the main, communication has as its central interest those behavioral situations in which a source transmits a message to a receiver(s) *with conscious intent to affect the latter's behaviors.*"[d]

Definition 6 Communication is a process whereby people assign meanings to stimuli in order to make sense of the world.

Definition 7 Communication is "the transmission of information, ideas, emotions, skills, etc., by the use of symbols—words, pictures, figures, graphs, etc."[e]

Definition 8 *Spoken symbolic interaction* is the process by which people use words and other symbols to create meaning and to affect one another.

Definition 9 *Nonverbal interaction* is the unspoken, often unintentional behavior that accompanies verbal communication and helps us fully interpret its meaning.

[a]Stevens, S. S. (1950). A definition of communication. *The Journal of the Acoustical Society of America, 22,* 689–90, 689.

[b]Barnlund, Dean. (1968). *Interpersonal communication: Survey and studies.* Boston: Houghton Mifflin, 6.

[c]Masterson, John T., Steven A. Beebe, & Norman H. Watson. (1983). *Speech communication: Theory and practice.* New York: Holt, Rinehart & Winston, 5.

[d]Miller, Gerald A. (1966). On defining communication: Another stab. *Journal of Communication, 16,* 88–98, 92.

[e]Berelson, Bernard, & Gary Steiner. (1964). *Human behavior.* New York: Harcourt, Brace, & World, 254.

How Broad Is Communication?

One of the first questions to ask is how broad or narrow we want communication to be; that is, we must resolve the issue of **breadth.** What kinds of behaviors do you call communication? No doubt you include people talking to one another; that's easy. But what do you make of a situation in which one person draws conclusions about another person without the second person's knowledge? Do you call that communication? And how do you class the bond between a pet and its owner, or the signals that animals send to one another? What about someone "communing" with nature; is he or she communicating? Is it possible for people to communicate with computers or for computers to communicate with one another?

If we wish the concept of communication to include all of the activities mentioned above, we need a very broad definition. Definitions 1 and 2 in Table 2-1 are the broadest and most inclusive. Definition 1 ("Communication is a process of acting on information") includes all of the examples given above, whereas definition 2 ("Communication is the discriminatory response of an organism to a stimulus") excludes machine communication but includes behaviors of living organisms.

Whereas some people prefer to view communication in its broadest sense, others want a more limited definition, one that focuses more directly on human behavior. Arguing that there are essential differences between humans, animals, and machines, these people define communication as a uniquely human process. People who hold this view prefer definition 3 ("Communication . . . is an 'effort after meaning,' a creative act initiated by man in which he seeks to discriminate and organize cues so as to orient himself in his environment and satisfy his changing needs") or definition 4 ("Speech communication is a human process through which we make sense out of the world and share that sense with others"). These definitions set different boundaries for communication.

Is Communication Intentional?

If one of the questions to be resolved about communication is its breadth, another is whether or not it involves **intentionality.** Let's consider the example of unobtrusive observation. Assume that Brennan comes across Brianne, who is unaware that she is being watched. Brianne does something revealing; perhaps she frowns and looks annoyed. As a result, Brennan draws a conclusion about her mood. Is this communication? According to definition 5 in Table 2-1 ("In the main, communication has as its central interest those behavioral situations in which a source transmits a message to a receiver(s) *with conscious intent to affect the latter's behaviors*"), it is not communication, for Brianne did not mean to send a message.

Still other people argue that we can never determine whether or not a message is intentional. The important factors are that Brianne's behavior created meaning in Brennan's mind and that Brennan's future actions will be affected by this meaning. People who take this view prefer that the definition of communication include unintentional as well as intentional behaviors. Definition 6 ("Communication is a process whereby people assign meanings to stimuli in order to make sense of the world") includes both unintentional and intentional behaviors.

Is Communication Sender- or Receiver-Based?

If we accept the situation involving Brennan and Brianne as an instance of communication, we are faced with yet another question. Which of them is communicating? Some people would argue that it is Brianne who is communicating, because it is her behavior that is the source of information. Others would contend that it is Brennan who is communicating, since it is he who assigns meaning. Those people who locate communication in Brianne's behavior take a **sender-based** view of communication, whereas those who see Brennan as the communicator take a **receiver-based** stance. Definition 5 in Table 2-1 ("Communication has as its central interest . . . situations in which a source transmits a message with conscious intent") is sender-oriented, as is definition 7 ("Communication is the transmission of information, ideas, emotions, skills, etc., by the use of symbols—words, pictures, figures, graphs, etc."). Definition 4 ("Speech communication is a human process through which we make sense of the world and share that sense with others") includes both sender and receiver, and the rest of the definitions appear to be receiver-oriented.

Is All Communication Symbolic?

A final question concerns the extent to which a definition of communication emphasizes symbolic or verbal behavior. As we shall see in more detail in ensuing chapters, humans have two code systems at their disposal. We can express ourselves symbolically through words, numbers, and graphic designs. We can also convey meaning nonverbally through facial expressions, body movements, and physical appearance. Many people believe that it is the ability to use **symbols** (arbitrary and conventionalized representations) that makes humans unique and that we should focus our study of communication on the way humans use words to convey meaning. For these people, nonverbal behaviors are only a secondary concern. Definition 7 ("Communication is the transmission of [meaning] by the use of symbols") clearly limits communication to symbolic behavior, whereas the other definitions seem to include both symbolic and nonsymbolic behavior.

Multiple Definitions: Communication as a Family of Concepts

As you move from one definition to another, the boundaries of communication shift, and you focus your attention in a slightly different direction. In choosing one definition over another, consider how that definition expands or

Communication is often viewed as a meeting of minds. To the extent that partners share experiences and try to see things from one another's point of view, communication succeeds.

contracts the domain of communication. A broad definition is useful when you want to emphasize commonalities between human and nonhuman information processing. A narrow definition is useful when you want to focus on a particular kind of communication, say human communication or symbolic communication. There is no right or wrong way to make your choice, nor is it necessary to choose a single definition. Indeed, Frank Dance has suggested that instead of talking about communication as a single concept, it may be more useful to talk about several kinds of communication, for example, animal communication, nonverbal communication, spoken symbolic interaction, and so on. Dance asks us to think of communication as a family of interrelated concepts, each of which has its own utility.[2]

If communication is a family of concepts rather than a single concept, then the two family members receiving the most attention in this book are spoken symbolic interaction and nonverbal interaction. Our discipline has focused from its beginning on **spoken symbolic interaction,** the way people use symbols (primarily words) to create common meaning and to share that meaning with one another. In keeping with this tradition, most of the chapters in this book are devoted to understanding verbal communication. Nevertheless, people are often affected by unintentional behaviors that accompany the spoken word. Therefore, we will also direct attention to **nonverbal interaction,** the unspoken, often unintentional behavior that accompanies verbal communication and helps us fully interpret its meaning. Although animal and machine communication are valid subjects of study and can add to an understanding of communication in its broadest sense, these topics will receive less attention simply because our goal is to understand human communication.

How Models Help Us Understand Communication

In addition to defining communication, scholars also build models of it. A **model** is an abstract representation of a process, a description of its structure or function. Models are useful because they help us understand how a process works. As Cassandra Book and her colleagues point out, models can help us organize our thinking, generate research questions, and make predictions.[3] And just as there are many definitions of communication, so there are many models. Models are representations; they cannot capture a process in its entirety. Instead, each model describes certain aspects of the total process.

Modeling a social process helps us think carefully about the form and function of that process. To create a model, we divide the whole process into its basic parts and consider how these parts are connected. Models stimulate creativity; by building models, we may find out interesting things that previously have been overlooked.

Models stimulate creativity; by building models, we may find out interesting things that previously have been overlooked.

In this section we'll continue our examination of communication by looking at several models. We'll describe each carefully, consider its assumptions, and discover its strengths and weaknesses. We'll also look at how each model characterizes good communication.

The Forms and Functions of Models

Almost any object or process can be modeled, and models can take many forms. Before we consider ways of modeling communication, consider how you might model another kind of entity, a city. A model of a city could be any of the following: a street map, an organization chart of the city's government, a computer simulation of traffic flow, a scale model of the city's architecture, a sociological description of changing neighborhoods, even a board game. Each is an abstraction, a simplified version of the city. Each focuses on only a small part of the process. Yet each helps us answer the questions, what is a city? and how does it work?

Models aid us by describing and explaining a process, by yielding testable predictions about how the process works, or by showing us ways to control the process. A good model does all these things. Models fulfill an **explanatory function** by dividing a process into constituent parts and showing us how the parts are connected. The city's organizational chart does this by explaining how city government works. The sociological description allows us to see the economic and social factors that caused the city to become what it is today.

Models often fulfill a **predictive function.** The traffic simulation and population growth projections function in this way. They allow us to answer "if . . . then" questions. If we add another traffic light, will we then have eliminated gridlock? If the population keeps growing at the current rate, then what will housing conditions be in the year 2000? Models help us answer questions about the future.

Finally, models fulfill a **control function.** A street map not only describes the layout of the city but also allows you to find out where you went wrong if you get lost, and (if you're good at map reading) it keeps you from getting lost in the first place. Models help us recognize and diagnose problems. They show us how to control important conditions.

The Drawbacks of Models

Models are useful in the ways we've discussed, but they also have drawbacks. In building and using models, we must be cautious. First, we must realize that *models are necessarily incomplete.* They are simplified versions of very complex processes. When a model builder chooses to include one detail, he or she invariably chooses to ignore hundreds more. Models can be misleading if they focus on inconsequential parts of a process.

> *Models are simplified versions of very complex processes.*

Second, we must keep in mind that *there are many ways to model a single process.* Most of us like certainty. We've grown up believing that every problem has one right answer. Unfortunately, when we study complex processes, we can never be one hundred percent certain we understand them. There are many "right answers," all equally valuable but each distinct. Although this may be confusing at first, try thinking of it positively.

> *Looking for single answers limits you intellectually; accepting multiple answers opens you to new possibilities.*

Looking for single answers limits you intellectually; accepting multiple answers opens you to new possibilities.

Finally, we musn't forget that *models make assumptions about processes.* It's always important to look "below the surface" of any model to detect the hidden assumptions it makes. Communication models, being abstract, make many

For some, communication is a process of world building. Through communication we agree to abide by collective values and visions of reality.

assumptions. In the next section we'll look at two of the most important types of assumptions a model makes. We'll examine where each model locates communication; for example, does a given model imply that communication occurs in the minds of human interactants, in social norms and rules, or in patterns of moves and countermoves? We'll also examine what value judgments the model makes; we'll try to discover what good communication is from the standpoint of each model. As we shall see, the answers to these questions are often hidden below a model's surface.

It All Depends on Your Point of View: Three Perspectives

Many interesting communication models exist. In this section we'll look at three, each of which takes a different theoretical perspective. In the next section we'll look at a fourth model that will provide us with a practical way to observe communication behavior.

A **perspective** is a coherent set of assumptions about the way a process operates.[4] The first three models we will look at are built on different sets of assumptions. The first model takes what is known as a **psychological perspective.** It focuses on what happens "inside the heads" of communicators as they transmit and receive messages. The second model takes a **social constructionist perspective.**[5] It sees communication as a process whereby people, drawing on the tools provided by their culture, create collective representations of reality. It emphasizes the relationship between communication and culture. The third model takes what is called a **pragmatic perspective.**[6] According to this view, communication consists of a system of interlocking, interdependent "moves," which become patterned over time. This perspective focuses on actual interaction, on what people say and do as they communicate. As we look at each of these models, you'll begin to understand how these perspectives differ in their emphasis on individual psychology, cultural constructs, or actual behaviors.

Communication as Message Transmission

We'll begin with the most familiar approach to communication. Most models and definitions of communication derive from the psychological perspective. They locate communication in the human mind and see the individual as both the source of and the destination for messages. Figure 2-1 visually represents this point of view.

Elements of a Psychological Model

The model in Figure 2-1 depicts communication as *a psychological process whereby two (or more) individuals exchange meanings through the transmission and reception of communication stimuli.* According to this model, an individual is a **sender/receiver** who encodes and decodes meanings. Person A has an idea he wishes to communicate to Person B. A **encodes** this idea, that is, he translates it into a **message,** a form he believes B can understand. The encoded message travels along a **channel,** its medium of transmission, until it reaches its **destination** in B's mind. Upon receiving the message, B **decodes** it and decides how she will reply. In sending the reply, B gives A **feedback** about her response to A's message. A uses this information to decide whether or not he was successful in transmitting his meanings to B.

During encoding and decoding, A and B filter messages through the mental sets they have acquired. A **mental set** consists of a person's beliefs, values, attitudes, feelings, and so on. Because each message is composed and interpreted in light of an individual's past experience, each encoded or decoded message has its own unique meaning. Of course, partners' mental sets can some-

Communication is most successful when individuals are "of the same mind"—when the meanings they assign to messages are similar or identical.

times lead to misunderstandings. The meanings A and B assign to a message may vary in important ways. If this occurs, A and B may miscommunicate. Communication can also go awry if noise enters the channel. **Noise** is any distraction that interferes with or changes a message during transmission. Communication is most successful when individuals are "of the same mind"—when the meanings they assign to messages are similar or identical.

Let's look at how this process works in a familiar setting, the college lecture. Professor Smith wants to inform his students about the history of rhetoric. Alone in his study, he gazes at his plaster-of-Paris bust of Aristotle

FIGURE 2-1

A Psychological Model of Communication

In a psychological model, messages are filtered through an individual's store of beliefs, attitudes, values, and emotions.

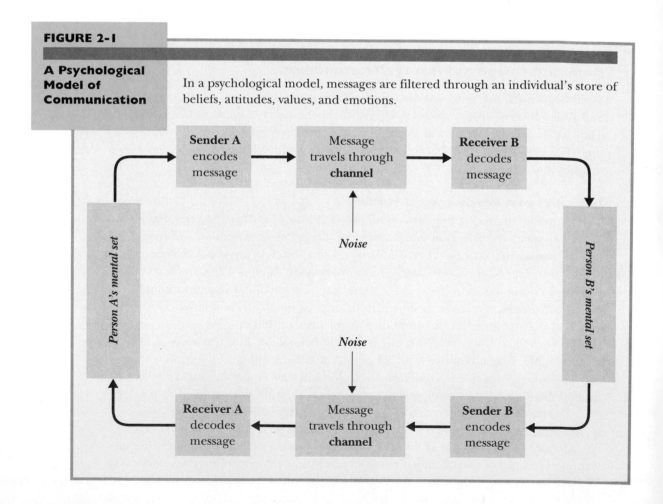

and thinks about how he will encode his understanding and enthusiasm in words. To encode successfully, he must guess about what's going on in the students' minds. Although it's hard for him to imagine that anyone could be bored by the history of rhetoric, he knows students need to hear a "human element" in his lecture. He therefore decides to include examples and anecdotes to spice up his message.

Smith delivers his lecture in a large, drafty lecture room. The microphone he uses unfortunately emits shrill whines and whistles at inopportune times. That he also forgets to talk into the mike only compounds the noise problem. Other sources of distraction are his appearance and nonverbal behavior. When Smith enters the room, his mismatched polyester suit and hand-painted tie are fairly presentable, but as he gets more and more excited, his clothes take on a life of their own. His shirt untucks itself, his jacket collects chalk dust, and his tie juts out at a very strange angle. In terms of our model, Smith's clothes are too noisy for the classroom.

Despite his lack of attention to material matters and his tendency toward dry speeches, Smith knows his rhetoric, and highly motivated students have no trouble decoding the lecture. Less-prepared students have more difficulty, however. When Smith's words go "over their heads," these students guess at his meanings. As the lecture progresses, all of the students give Smith feedback in the form of nonverbal messages. Their smiles and nods, their frowns of puzzlement, and their whispered comments to one another give Smith a sense of how he is doing.

Smith's communication is partially successful and partially unsuccessful. He reaches the students who can follow his classical references. He bypasses the willing but unprepared students who don't have the background to decode his messages. And he completely loses the seniors in the back row who are taking the course pass/fail and have set their sights on a D minus. Like most of us, some of the time Smith succeeds in transferring his meanings accurately, and some of the time he fails.

Improving Faulty Communication

According to the psychological model, communication is unsuccessful whenever the meanings intended by the source differ from the meanings interpreted by the receiver. This occurs when the mental sets of source and receiver are so far apart that there is no shared experience; when the source uses a code unfamiliar to the receiver; when the channel is overloaded or impeded by noise; when there is little or no opportunity for feedback; or when receivers are distracted by competing internal stimuli.

Each of these problems can be solved. The psychological model points out ways to improve communication. It suggests that senders can learn to see things from their receivers' points of view. Senders can try to encode messages in clear, lively, and appropriate ways. They can use multiple channels to ensure that their message gets across, and they can try to create noise-free environments. They can also build in opportunities for feedback and learn to read receivers' nonverbal messages.

Receivers can prepare themselves for a difficult message by studying the subject ahead of time. They can try to understand "where the speaker is coming from" and anticipate her points. They can learn to control internal distractions by focusing their listening skills, and they can ask questions and check their understanding. All of these methods of improving communication are implicit in the model in Figure 2-1.

Problems With the Psychological Perspective

Although the psychological perspective is by far the most popular view of communication, it has its problems. As all models are bound to do, it distorts communication. Earlier in this chapter, we saw that all models have hidden assumptions. What are some of the assumptions hidden in the psychological model?

First, the psychological model locates communication in the psychological processes of individuals, whereas it almost totally ignores the social context in which communication occurs, as well as the shared roles and rules that govern message construction. This model makes individuals appear more independent than they actually are.

Second, in incorporating the ideas of channel and noise, the psychological model is quite mechanistic. It treats messages as though they are physical objects that can be sent from one place to another and occasionally get lost along the way. Noise is treated not as a message, but as a separate entity that "attacks" messages. The model also assumes that it is possible not to communicate, that communication can break down. All of these are mechanical ideas that may distort the way communication actually works.

Finally, the psychological model implies that successful communication involves a "meeting of the minds." The model suggests that communication succeeds to the extent that the sender transfers what is in his or her mind to the mind of the receiver. Thus, the model implies that good communication is more likely to occur between people who have the same ideas than between those who have different ideas. Think about this for a moment. Is accuracy the only value we should place on communication? Is it always a good idea to seek out people who are similar rather than different? Some critics believe the psychological model diminishes the importance of creativity and makes receivers appear to be empty receptacles waiting to be filled with other people's ideas.

Asking Questions From the Psychological Perspective

Models can be used not only to identify potential communication problems and to suggest ways of overcoming them but also to generate research questions. The psychological perspective is usually associated with what is called a **laws approach** to research. Communication scientists who take this approach describe cause-and-effect laws that connect communication variables. A researcher looking for lawful relationships between parts of the communication process might ask the following questions: Are multiple channels more effective than single channels for transmitting complex messages? Does attitude similarity enhance or inhibit communication accuracy? Because the psychological model is linear, it lends itself to this kind of question and to related research methods. Chapter 11 takes up this topic in more detail.

Communication as World Building

The second model takes a very different view of communication. In this model communication becomes a means of world building. Figure 2-2 shows this idea. According to this model, communication is not something that goes on between individuals; instead, communication is something that surrounds people and holds their world together. Through communication, social groups create collective ideas of themselves, of one another, and of the world they inhabit.

> *Communication is something that surrounds people and holds their world together. Through communication, social groups create collective ideas of themselves, of one another, and of the world they inhabit.*

Elements of a Social Constructionist Model

According to the social constructionist model, communication is *a process whereby people in groups, using the tools provided by their culture, create collective representations of reality.* The model specifies four of these cultural tools: languages, or **symbolic codes;** the ways we've been taught to process information, or **cognitive customs;** the beliefs, attitudes, and values that make up our **cultural traditions;** and the **sets of roles and rules** that guide our actions. These tools shape the ways we experience and talk about our world.

The social constructionist perspective maintains that we never experience the world directly. Rather, we take parts of it that our culture makes significant, process them in culturally recognized ways, connect them to other "facts" that we know, and respond to them in ways our culture considers significant. According to this perspective, we construct our world through communication.[7]

FIGURE 2-2

A Social Constructionist Model of Communication

In a social constructionist model, people exist within, and perceive themselves and others through, the communicative practices of their cultures.

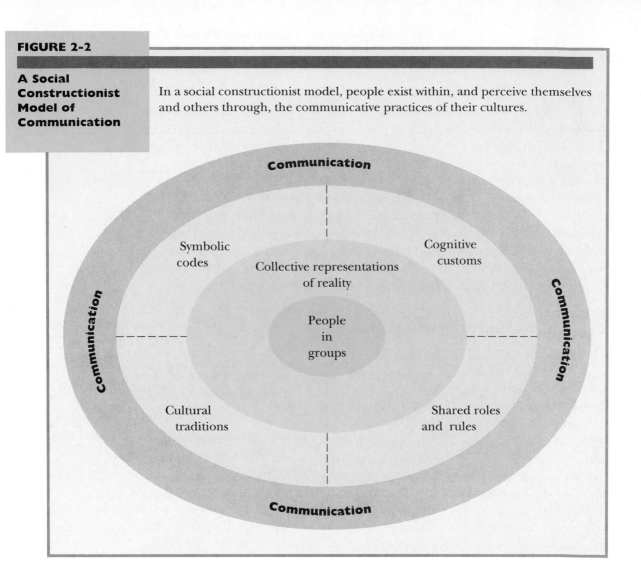

Stop and think about how much of what you know and believe is directly experienced and how much comes to you through words. Consider the topic "prehistoric life." Many of us know a little bit about prehistoric life, but few of us have studied it in great detail. Imagine the life of a prehistoric cave dweller. Do you have an idea of what he or she looked like and how he or she lived? If you're like most people, images and ideas will spring to mind easily. These ideas are probably a strange mixture of scientific inference, romantic myth, and cartoon images from TV and comics. None of these ideas comes from direct experience; instead, they all come from words and images and reflect social understandings. They are the products of stories you read as a child, "facts" your grammar-school teacher taught you, cartoons such as "The Flintstones," movies such as *Clan of the Cave Bear* and *One Million B.C.,* and perhaps details you learned in an anthropology class. Very few of us have seen the actual evidence from which these representations are created. Instead, we've seen collective representations filtered through the conventions of our culture.

Assumptions of Social Constructionism

The social constructionist model draws our attention to two assumptions. First, it shows us that we live in a world made up not of physical but of symbolic objects. It tells us that we see the world through cultural blinders. Second, it emphasizes that in order to communicate, individuals must follow cultural rules. It suggests that communication exists in the language practices and rules of the group. These important insights have some practical value. Let's look at each of them in turn.

The reality we see is essentially a constructed reality. This is the first assumption of the social constructionist model. To get a feel for the importance of culture as a filter for experience, consider the following: First, think about the ways our culture characterizes people of different nations or races. Our culture predisposes us to see such people in ways that embody our values and beliefs but are often dangerously simplistic and patently unfair. Second, think about some of our cultural ideals. As modern-day Americans, we spend a good deal of time thinking and talking about prestige, ambition, and success. Although these are cultural abstractions, they have a great deal of power over the way we lead our lives. As we shall see in chapter 10, in some cultures concepts such as these are not of great importance. In fact, in some cultures they are completely meaningless.

It is important to recognize the constructed nature of reality because our constructions often distort. As communicators, we often accept cultural myths and stereotypes without thinking. Given the fact that symbols have such power to control us, it is useful to develop the critical ability to "see through" cultural constructions and to avoid creating them through our own talk. In the world we live in, we are constantly bombarded with messages. The ability to decipher their biases is a useful skill.

If it is true that we live in a world constructed through words, it is also true that we are not free to talk about anything we wish in any way we wish. The second major assumption of the social constructionist model of communication is that communication is constrained by culture in important ways. When we are born into a culture, we are born into a social group that already has a language, preferred ways of thinking, traditional values, and strict rules for communicating. We could make up our own communication

If it is true that we live in a world constructed through words, it is also true that we are not free to talk about anything we wish in any way we wish.

It is possible to view communication as a kind of game two people play as they create a relationship.
The basic unit is the dyad, not the individual.

rules, but the cost would be severe. Not only would no one understand us, but we might even be considered dangerous lunatics.

Whereas the psychological model suggests that individuals create communication, the social constructionist model suggests the opposite, that communication creates individuals. To be successful communicators, it maintains, we must be willing to follow cultural rules and norms. We must take our parts in the social drama our culture has laid out for us.

In a sense, being a good communicator according to the social constructionist model means recognizing the rules for appropriate conduct that allow social groups to operate. It also means constructing versions of reality that are livable and just. Accuracy is not at issue here, because, according to the social constructionists, we never have direct access to reality. The goal, instead, is to achieve social consensus about the kind of world we wish to create.

Problems With the Social Constructionist Model

For many of you, this model may seem to depart radically from commonsense ideas about communication. To say that we live in a symbolic, rather than a physical, world seems to contradict our most basic notions about the nature of reality. For if we can never gain access to reality but can only experience constructions of it, then how can we tell the difference between truth and illusion? The social constructionist model raises important philosophical questions as it emphasizes a relationship recognized since ancient times: the relationship between rhetoric and truth.

Another troublesome aspect of the social constructionist position is that it defines good communication as socially appropriate communication. Scholars who take this perspective often talk of humans as social performers. To communicate successfully, one acts out a social role over which he or she has little control. For many, this view implies that the good communicator is a social automaton rather than a sincere and spontaneous self. Many people criticize the social constructionist perspective because it places too much emphasis on the social self and not enough on the individual self. They feel that in emphasizing the social and cultural nature of humans, the aspects that make humans unique and individual are forgotten.

Asking Questions From the
Social Constructionist Perspective

When social constructionists do research, they pay particular attention to the implicit rules that guide social action. Researchers who are social constructionists often take what is known as a **rules approach** to understanding communication. Rules researchers believe that human behavior is not so much caused as chosen: In order to accomplish their goals, people choose certain lines of action and follow certain rules laid down by their cultures. We can understand communication behavior by understanding the rules people follow as they act. A rules researcher might ask questions such as these: How do individuals within a given culture use symbols to make sense of the world? Do men and women follow different rules to accomplish their goals? What are the major forms of communication in a given culture, and how are they valued?

Communication as Patterned Interaction

The third model takes yet another view of communication. Instead of focusing on individual selves or on social roles and rules, this perspective centers on systems of behavior. It suggests that the way people act when they are together is of primary importance, and it urges us to look carefully at patterns that emerge as people play the communication game.[8]

Elements of a Pragmatic Model

According to the pragmatic view, communication consists of *a system of interlocking, interdependent behaviors that become patterned over time.* Scholars who take a pragmatic approach argue that communicating is much like playing a game.

Each player responds to his or her partner's moves. As play progresses, patterns of interaction emerge. These patterns help explain the game and its final outcome. This analogy is illustrated in Figure 2-3, which compares communication to a game of chess.

The analogy between chess and communication holds in a number of ways. First, the game itself, not what goes on around it, is the central concern. Although it is possible to find books on chess that analyze the personality of individual players, most books focus on the structure of the game itself. Who white and black represent is not nearly as important as how they respond to one another. To understand chess, you need to understand the present

FIGURE 2-3

A Pragmatic Model of Communication

In a pragmatic model, communication is seen as a game of sequential, interlocking moves between interdependent partners. Each player responds to the partner's moves in light of his or her own strategy in and anticipation of future action. Some moves are specific to this game, and others are common gambits or strategies. Moves make sense only in the context of the game.

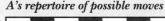

A's repertoire of possible moves

move	A's moves	B's moves
21	. . . . . .	B offends A
22	A ignores B	B repeats offense
23	A challenges B	B ignores A
24	A reissues challenge	B offers apology
25	A accepts apology	B thanks A
26	A changes subject	. . . . . .

B's repertoire of possible moves

Note: Squares on the board represent joint outcomes for each player. Outcomes or payoffs are a result of patterned "play" between partners.

state of the board and the series of moves that produced it. To understand communication, pragmatists argue, you need to do much the same thing: understand the "moves" people use as they work out their relationship to one another.

> *To understand communication, you need to understand the "moves" people use as they work out their relationship to one another.*

Note that in Figure 2-3 the moves are listed sequentially. At every turn, you can see what black did and how white responded. Chess books always list moves in this way, using the exact sequence in which they occurred in the game. It would make no sense to list all the moves of the game randomly. The game consists of ordered, interlocking moves and makes sense only when we follow the sequence. In the same way, an individual **act,** or isolated behavior, makes sense only in context, that is, when we see it in relationship to previous acts. According to the pragmatic viewpoint, the smallest significant unit of communication is the **interact,** which consists of two sequential acts. If you merely hear me cry, you know very little about what is happening. To understand what my crying means, you need to know, at the very least, what happened immediately before I cried. I may have become sad or angry, or I may have laughed so hard I began to cry. My crying may be a sincere expression of sorrow, or it may have been a move designed to make you feel sorry for me. The more you know about what happened before I cried, the more you understand the communication game I'm playing.

One of the factors that makes the game analogy appropriate is the **interdependence** of game players. Each player is affected by what another player does. Players need each other if they are to play. The same is true of communication: A person can't be a sender without someone to be a receiver, and it's impossible for a receiver to receive a message without a sender to send it. The dyad, not the individual, is important. Individuals don't play the communication game; **partners** (or opponents) do.

In a game every action is important. Every move I make affects you, and every move you make affects me. Even if I refuse to move, I am still playing: I am resigning from or forfeiting the game. This is even more significant in communication, where any response counts as a move. According to the pragmatic perspective, *we cannot not communicate.* If a friend promises to write to you and doesn't, his or her silence speaks louder than words. You realize that your friend doesn't want to continue the relationship. It is impossible not to communicate, just as it is impossible not to behave.

Finally, communication resembles a game in that both result in interdependent **outcomes,** or **payoffs.** In chess the payoff is the thrill of victory or the agony of defeat. Communication also has payoffs. Sometimes they are competitive; for example, someone "wins points" by putting down someone else. But more often than not, the payoffs are cooperative. Each person gets something out of playing. In fact, one way to view relationships is as cooperative improvised games. As people get to know one another, they learn to avoid unproductive moves, and they begin to work out **patterns** of interaction that satisfy both of them. This is what we mean when we say that two people are "working out the rules" of their relationship. They are learning to play the relationship game with style and grace.

Therapy and the Pragmatic Approach

According to the pragmatic approach, the best way to understand and improve communication is to describe the forms or patterns that the communication takes.[9] If these patterns are destructive, then the players should be encouraged to find more productive ways of playing the communication game. Let's say that George and Martha are having problems communicating and decide to go to a communication counselor for help. If the counselor takes a pragmatic approach, she will be interested in uncovering the communication patterns that are the root of George and Martha's problems.

In the beginning, George may explain the problem by blaming Martha. "Her need for attention is so great," he may say, "that I'm forced to spend all my time catering to her. This makes me so mad that I have to get out of the house. She can't seem to understand that I need my privacy. She's demanding and irrational." Of course, Martha has her own version of events, which goes something like this: "He's so withdrawn, I can't stand it. He never pays any attention to me. I have to beg to get a moment of his time, and when he does give it, he gets angry. George is cold and unreasonable." Without help, George and Martha will each continue to blame the other. They may even look for explanations in each other's personality or background. Martha may blame George's mother for making him the way he is. George may decide that Martha has a personality flaw.

The pragmatic therapist isn't interested in exploring background issues. Instead, she tries to identify the behavior pattern that is causing the problem. In this case, George's and Martha's responses to one another are ineffective and are exacerbating the problem. The therapist will help George and Martha work out a more effective set of moves that will make them both happy.

Perhaps the most important thing the pragmatic theorist tells us is that to understand communication, we should focus on interaction rather than on personality. When you get into an interpersonal conflict (and it's in the interpersonal and small-group arena that the pragmatic model seems to fit best), how often do you examine the pattern of events that led up to the conflict? Chances are, you don't do so very often; instead, you look for a personality explanation. When you and your roommate have problems communicating, you probably don't ask yourself, "What do I do that causes her to respond the way she does?" Instead, you try to figure out what's wrong with her. This is not the most productive solution to the problem.

Problems With the Pragmatic Perspective

The principal problem with the pragmatic viewpoint is that it holds that both personality and culture are irrelevant. Pragmatists steadfastly refuse to ask why people act as they do. They dismiss factors such as intentions, desires, needs, and so on. They are interested only in how sets of interacts pattern themselves. They also have little to say about the cultural context surrounding interaction. Look again at Figure 2-3, and notice that only what happens on the board is important. What happens outside the world of the game is never considered. Who the players are, where the game is played, and what other players are doing are all irrelevant questions.

Asking Questions From the Pragmatic Perspective

Communication researchers who subscribe to the pragmatic perspective do not take a laws or a rules approach. The approach most compatible with the pragmatic perspective is the **systems approach.** Systems researchers are concerned with describing interdependent patterns of behavior rather than individual behavior. A systems researcher looks at the structure, function, and evolution of a communication system, asking how communicators within the system organize their behavior, how patterns of behavior affect the way the system works, and how communication changes over time. A systems researcher might ask the following questions: How do the members of a dyad become interdependent over time? What effect do different patterns of dominance have on long-term relationships? Do small-group discussions go through standard phases?

Summary and Comparison

In the opening discussion of models, we saw that many different models can describe a single process. The three communication models we've reviewed, although they are different, all contribute to our understanding of communication. They show us that to understand communication, we must look at three factors: the individuals with whom communication originates, the social context within which communication arises, and the interaction through which communication is realized. The psychological approach centers on the first of these factors, the social constructionist perspective focuses on the second, and the pragmatic point of view emphasizes the third. Only by taking all three points of view will we have a clear understanding of how communication works.

What to Look for
When You Look at Communication

Before we move on, we have one more model to consider. This model, developed by Del Hymes, is a kind of field guide for describing communication.[10] One of the ways you can develop sensitivity to communication is to look at the way communication works in various speech communities. Communication teachers often assign papers in which they ask students to describe special kinds of communication. Students may be asked to describe "dorm talk" or "locker room talk" or "children's playground talk." Or they may be asked to compare the rules governing female speech with those governing male speech. These assignments put the student in essentially the same situation as anthropologists who try to explain a strange culture; the student must do what is called an **ethnography of communication.** Hymes presents a systematic way to undertake this kind of observation. Figure 2-4 presents Hymes's model.

Hymes begins by giving a general overview of the context in which communication occurs. When a group of people share common ways of thinking about communication and develop a common style of talk, they have formed a **speech community.** These communities may be large (as when we describe "women's speech") or small (as when we examine the way athletes on a particular team engage in locker room talk). The first step in doing an ethnography is identifying an interesting speech community. Let's say you are studying the communication patterns of members of the Unification Church, who are popularly known as Moonies. You believe that when a member joins the Moonies, he or she becomes socialized into the speech practices of the community, and you want to understand what this process entails. The Moonies, then, are your speech community.

When a group of people share common ways of thinking about communication and develop a common style of talk, they have formed a speech community.

Next, you need to catalog a variety of speech situations within the community. A **speech situation** is a clearly marked occasion that calls for a specific type of speech. By observing church members carefully, you begin to get a sense of what these situations are in this community. Recruitment, weekend retreats, study sessions, and flower sales are four speech situations that call for distinct forms of communication.

Each of these situations consists of a series of **speech events,** or identifiable sequences of speech. The Moonies build cohesion during weekend retreats by playing simple, competitive games. Recruits are invited to play and are warmly accepted by their teams. As play progresses, excitement builds, and group cheering and chanting often lead to an almost ecstatic state. Another weekend workshop activity is called "love bombing." A "love bomber," or

FIGURE 2-4

What to
Look at When
Observing
Communication

Contexts for Observing Communication

Speech Community
People who share common attitudes toward speech

Speech Situations
Clearly marked occasion that calls for speech

Speech Events
Identifiable sequence of speech activity

Speech Act
Purpose served by forms of talk

Elements of Communication

S ituations	Setting and scene of interaction
P articipants	Who speaks, who is addressed
E nds	Goals and outcomes of interaction
A ct Sequences	Content, means of expression
K eys	Tone or spirit of interaction
I nstrumentalities	Channels, or media of transmission
N orms	Rules regulating interaction
G enres	Type of communication enacted

Adapted from *Foundations in Sociolinguistics: An Ethnographic Approach* by Dell Hymes, 1974, Philadelphia: University of Pennsylvania Press.

church member, follows each recruit everywhere and lavishes attention on him or her. Chanting and love bombing are two different speech events that take place in this retreat setting.

Speech events can often be broken down into **speech acts,** or individual, purposeful acts of communication. During love bombing, Moonies may engage in one or more of the following speech acts: showing concern, expressing regard, helping a recruit, and so on.

A complete description of all the speech acts and events included in major speech situations of the Unification Church gives us a good idea of the way current members use communication to persuade and influence prospective members. By observing the way communication works in this context, we can also develop a better understanding of persuasive communication in general.

Hymes lists a series of specific items that an ethnographer of communication observes (see Figure 2-4). Conveniently, the first letters of these items spell the word *speaking.* Hymes believes it is important to describe the specific **situation,** or the environment in which communication takes place (including the time, place, and physical circumstances), as well as the psychological weight a given situation carries. He also believes it is important to describe the **participants** who take part in a given form of speech, as well as their goals, or **ends.** In describing **act sequences,** the ethnographer carefully records communication content and form, noting not only what is said or done but also how it is expresssed.

Key is the tone or spirit (for example, joking, aggressive, or ecstatic) in which a given activity is undertaken. **Instrumentalities** are the channels of transmission used (for example, verbal or nonverbal, written or spoken). In looking at **norms,** the observer indicates the values and beliefs attached to a given form of communication, as well as the rules that regulate its use. Finally, a **genre** is a specialized type of encoded message. Examples of genre include prayers, orations, curses, and so on. Hymes believes the conventions governing each genre should be carefully described to gain a true understanding of communication in a given speech community. Observing communication behavior often seems to be an overwhelming task. By breaking communication down into smaller units, Hymes helps make that task more manageable.

Communication can be understood and modeled in a variety of ways, five of which we've looked at so far (the four models discussed in this chapter and the canons of rhetoric discussed in chapter l). Although the methods are quite different, each helps to explain a small part of a very complex process.

Summary

Through the years, rhetoricians and communication scientists have not always agreed about what communication is and how it works. This chapter looks at a variety of definitions, models, and perspectives, each of which offers different insights into communication.

Definitions help explain and limit concepts. The process of defining can be thought of as either an objective act of discovery or a creative act of construction. According to the second view, the test of a good definition is not its absolute truth but rather its usefulness, and several definitions of a concept may be valid.

One way definitions of communication vary is in breadth. Narrow definitions limit the domain of communication, whereas broad definitions expand it. Another way definitions differ is in the importance they place on intentionality. Further, definitions may be either sender- or receiver-based. Finally, they differ in whether they treat all communication as symbolic. If we take the view that definitions are constructions, we don't have to choose just one definition. Instead, we can think of communication as a family of related concepts. The two members of the family most important in this book are spoken symbolic interaction and nonverbal communication.

Whereas definitions express the essence of a concept, models explore the concept in more detail, focusing on its structure or function. A good model explains a phenomenon, allows us to predict the future and gives us control over future events. Although models are useful, they are always incomplete; there is no perfect model. Models are based on assumptions. The set of assumptions we hold in regard to a given concept is called a perspective. This chapter discusses three perspectives (psychological, social constructionist, and pragmatic) and offers a model based on each one.

The psychological perspective views communication as a process of message transmission. A typical psychological model uses concepts such as sender/receiver, encoding and decoding, message, channel, feedback, and noise. It locates communication in the mental sets of individual communicators. Although the psychological perspective is the most widely used in our field, it has drawbacks: It ignores social context, it is mechanistic, and it places more value on accuracy than on creativity. Researchers who follow this perspective often use a laws approach to research.

According to the social constructionist perspective, communication is the collective creation of meaning. It is not something that goes on between people but, rather, something that surrounds them and holds their world together. Social constructionist models stress concepts such as symbolic codes, cognitive customs, cultural traditions, roles, and rules. Critics of this view argue that its emphasis on truth as a construction can lead to relativism and that its emphasis on cultural appropriateness leaves out individual action. Researchers who follow this perspective often use a rules approach to research.

The pragmatic perspective views communication as a system of interlocking behaviors that become patterned over time. Pragmatists use concepts such as acts, interacts, outcomes or payoffs, and patterned moves. Critics regard the pragmatic perspective as a form of naive behavioralism and argue that it treats communication as context-free. Pragmatic researchers often use a systems approach to research.

The chapter closes with a final model that focuses on what to look for as we observe communication behavior. Rather than describing how communication works, this model directs our attention to factors such as situation, participants, ends, act sequences, key, instrumentalities, norms, and genre. It also situates communication within speech communities and gives special emphasis to the identification of speech acts.

Key Terms

Listed below are the key terms used in this chapter, along with the number of the page where each is explained.

definition   24
breadth   26
intentionality   27
sender-based communication   28
receiver-based communication   28
symbols   28
spoken symbolic interaction   29
nonverbal interaction   29
model   30
explanatory function   31
predictive function   31
control function   31
perspective   33
psychological perspective   33
social constructionist perspective   33
pragmatic perspective   33
sender/receiver   33
encoding   33
message   33
channel   33
destination   33
decoding   33
feedback   33
mental set   33
noise   34
laws approach   37

symbolic codes   37
cognitive customs   37
cultural traditions   37
sets of roles and rules   37
rules approach   41
act   43
interact   43
interdependence   43
partners   43
outcomes or payoffs   43
patterns   44
systems approach   45
ethnography of communication   46
speech community   46
speech situation   46
speech event   46
speech act   47
situation   48
participants   48
ends   48
act sequences   48
key   48
instrumentalities   48
norms   48
genre   48

Review Questions

1. Definitions can be viewed as processes of discovery or as constructions. What is the difference between these two points of view? Which holds that a single correct definition exists for every concept? What is the test of a good definition under the discovery approach? under the construction approach?

2. This chapter identifies four ways in which definitions of communication differ. What are they? Of the definitions given in Table 2-1, which is the narrowest? Which definitions are sender-based and which receiver-based? Which imply that communication is intentional? Which restricts communication to symbolic codes?

3. Dance suggests that communication is not one concept but a family of concepts. What does he mean?

4. What is a model? What are some of the forms that models can take? What are the three functions of models? What are three drawbacks to models?

5. What is a perspective? What are the three perspectives discussed in this chapter? How do they differ? Which focuses on the personality and thought processes of the individual communicator? Which focuses on the way culture affects communication? Which stresses patterns of behavior?

6. What are the basic elements of the psychological model shown in Figure 2-1? Using the example of the professor lecturing, identify sender, receiver, encoding, message, channel, destination, decoding, feedback, mental set, and noise.

7. Using the psychological model, point out some of the factors that can cause communication problems. Derive at least one rule for improving communication based on this model.

8. What are some criticisms of the psychological perspective?

9. How does the social constructionist perspective view communication? What are some of the elements of the social constructionist model shown in Figure 2-2? Think of an example of how your communication is constrained by cultural traditions and shared roles and rules.

10. What criticisms can be leveled against the social constructionist perspective?

11. How does the pragmatic perspective view communication? What are some of the elements of the pragmatic model shown in Figure 2-3? Do you agree that it is possible to think of communication as a game? Give an example of your own, including some specific moves.

12. What criticisms can be leveled against the pragmatic perspective?

13. What is the difference between laws, rules, and systems approaches to research? Which approach asks questions about causes? Which tries to uncover social conventions? Which focuses on describing interdependent behavior?

14. What is an ethnography of communication? Consider your class as a communication situation. What speech events go on in this situation? What speech acts occur regularly? Apply the SPEAKING model to the classroom.

Suggested Readings

Fisher, B. Aubrey. (1978). *Perspectives on human communication*. New York: Macmillan.

   In this book on communication theory, Fisher discusses the nature of perspectives. In the chapter on the pragmatic perspective, he discusses the importance of seeing communication as patterned interaction.

Hymes, Dell. (1974). *Foundations in sociolinguistics: An ethnographic approach*. Philadelphia: University of Pennsylvania Press.

   Hymes lays out his project for an ethnography of communication.

Shweder, Richard A. (1991). *Thinking through cultures: Expeditions in cultural psychology.* Cambridge: Harvard University Press.

> Shweder's work embodies many of the ideas of the social constructionists, including the idea that the self is a cultural product. For Shweder, nothing "just is"; rather, "realities are the product of the way things get re-presented, embedded, implemented, and reacted to" in various contexts. This book is not easy reading, but it is full of fascinating anthropological examples, and it confronts some of the major philosophical problems that the social constructionist view raises.

Sigman, Stuart J. (1992). *Introduction to human communication: Behavior, codes and social action.* Needham Heights, MA: Ginn.

> A collection of readings on a variety of communication topics, including interpersonal deception, the use of visuals on television news, communication about AIDS, dance and social structure, the political consequences of television, and the paintings of van Gogh. These articles are good examples of new approaches to the study of communication. They tend to take social constructionist and pragmatic approaches to understanding social interaction.

Trenholm, Sarah. (1991). *Human communication theory* (2nd ed.). Englewood Cliffs, NJ: Prentice-Hall.

> Chapter 3, on perspectives, assumptions, and methodologies, provides a detailed discussion of perspectives and several additional models of communication.

Watzlawick, Paul, Janet Beavin Bavelas, & Jackson, Don D. (1967). *Pragmatics of human communication.* New York: Norton.

> This classic exposition of the pragmatic perspective is written by three family therapists who believe that understanding communication patterns is the key to diagnosing and changing problem behaviors.

Notes

1. Dance, Frank E. X. (1970). The "concept" of communication. *Journal of Communication, 20,* 201–210.

2. Dance, Frank E. X., & Larson, Carl E. (1972). *Speech communication: Concepts and behavior.* New York: Holt, Rinehart & Winston, 1–16.

3. Book, Cassandra, et al. (1980). *Human communication: Principles, contexts, and skills.* New York: St. Martin's, 31–34.

4. For a general discussion of communication perspectives, see Fisher, B. Aubrey (1978). *Perspectives on human communication.* New York: Macmillan.

5. Gergen, Kenneth J., & Davis, Keith E. (1985). *The social construction of the person.* New York: Springer-Verlag.

6. Fisher, B. Aubrey. (1982). A view from system theory. In Frank E. X. Dance (Ed.), *Human communication theory: Comparative essays.* New York: Harper & Row.

7. Watzlawick, Paul, Bavelas, Janet Beavin, & Jackson, Don D. (1967). *Pragmatics of human communication.* New York: Norton.

8. Hymes, Dell. (1974). *Foundations in sociolinguistics: An ethnographic approach.* Philadelphia: University of Pennsylvania Press.

3

Decoding Messages: Perception and Listening

Different people

exposed to a single

message can come away

with very different

understandings.

In the last chapter, we saw that theorists often disagree on a definition of communication. They do agree, however, that communication is a way of making sense of the world and that during the process of communication we create and exchange messages. In this and the next two chapters, we will look at how this sense-making process works. In this chapter we will describe how people assign meaning to the messages that come their way. In chapters 4 and 5, we will turn our attention to the verbal and nonverbal codes people use when they send messages to others. In all three of these chapters, we will see that communication affects thought and action—in other words, that we think through communication.

We begin by considering message **decoding,** the creative, highly selective process by which people assign meanings to communicative messages. This process is not as simple or as automatic as you might think. Decoding is often highly subjective. Different people exposed to a single message can come away with very different understandings, as the following true story shows.

A group of scientists attending a professional conference was waiting for a meeting to begin when a door opened and two men, one wearing a clown's costume and the other wearing a black jacket, red tie, and white trousers, rushed in. The two men yelled at each other and scuffled briefly. Suddenly a shot rang out, whereupon both men rushed out of the room. The chairperson immediately asked everyone in the room to write a complete description of what had happened. The scientists did not know that the incident had been staged to test the accuracy of their perceptions.

How accurate were their perceptions? Of the forty scientists who responded, none gave a complete description of the incident. Twelve reports missed at least fifty percent of what had happened, and only six reports did not misstate facts or add details that simply were not accurate. The eyewitnesses could not even identify the color of the second man's suit; it was variously described as red, brown, striped, blue, and coffee-colored. In relating this story, William D. Brooks comments on the limitations inherent in perception:

> *The experiment demonstrated dramatically the fallibility of vision and hearing as avenues of information. Similar demonstrations have been made in numerous college speech and psychology classes since the original incident was carried out. Man does not* perceive *all he sees, nor does he necessarily perceive* accurately *what falls on the eye's screen; and yet his intrapersonal communication is limited to and based on the information he has via the process of perception from all the senses.*[1]

Despite the fact that decoding may be a fallible and risky business, accurate communication *is* possible. By understanding how perception and information processing work, you can improve your sending and receiving skills. In the following pages, we'll look at ways to design messages more clearly and to listen more accurately. Before we do, however, we need to understand some general principles of decoding. And perception is the place to start.

What Is Perception?

Perception is a social, cognitive process whereby individuals assign meaning to raw sense-data. It is cognitive because it involves mental effort, and it is social because the categories used to process information are shared with others and are validated by social consensus. People engaged in perception use social knowledge to make sense of the world.

People engaged in perception use social knowledge to make sense of the world.

Perception is subjective and creative. We are automatically attracted to novel or ambiguous scenes because they allow us to supply our own meanings.

Imposing Order and Meaning on the World

Perception is a very active process. As we perceive, we do more than simply record the world: we actively organize it. The world comes to us first as an undifferentiated stream of sensations. We ignore some of these sensations and attend to others. When stimuli capture our attention, we label and categorize them, giving them stability and structure and relating them to past experiences.[2]

You can see how this process works by considering what you do when you watch television. When you turn on the TV, what you actually sense are a series of flickering lights and a jumble of undifferentiated sounds. You quickly **structure** these sounds and shadows into images and words; for example, you perceive two people talking to one another in what appears to be a living room. As the show progresses, you also impose **stability** on what you see. When the camera moves in for a close-up on one character, you are not disoriented. You understand that you are viewing a single character from a new perspective. When the camera pans across the living room, you know the charac-

55

ter still exists even though he or she is no longer in view. Finally, you give the scene **meaning.** You might infer, for example, that the male character is a Cuban bandleader (because of his accented speech and references to his night-club), and you might understand that the female character, the bandleader's wife, is begging him to let her perform in his act. If you have seen the show before (perhaps in reruns), you identify the characters as Lucy and Ricky Ricardo and the program, the old "I Love Lucy" show. All of this happens so quickly that you may not realize that complicated social knowledge is involved. Yet without this knowledge to guide you, you could not organize your sensations in any meaningful way.

Using Cognitive Schemata

Psychologists agree that in order to recognize objects and follow sequences of actions, we must possess internal representations of these objects and sequences. These mental guidelines are called **schemata,** and they help us identify and organize incoming information. When we encounter a perceptual object, we store its characteristics in short-term memory while we search for a schema that makes sense of it. I, for example, have an "I Love Lucy" schema. Having seen the show many times, I know who the characters are and what the typical plot involves. If you have never seen the show, you must work out your own understandings, although a general situation-comedy schema can help you make sense of the format. If you were from a culture without TV, how-ever, you would lack the interpretive schemata needed to understand the con-ventions we take for granted. Schemata make processing rapid and effortless, although, as we shall see, they can sometimes distort perception.

Some events or objects are easily encoded into existing schemata, where-as others force us to create new schemata or to modify old ones. We have schemata for physical objects, types of people (including ourselves), personal traits, relationships, and sequences of actions. The three most important types of schemata are person prototypes, personal constructs, and scripts. (See Table 3-1 for an overview of these schemata.)[3]

Person Prototypes

We often use schemata to form impressions of other people. **Person proto-types** are idealized representations of a certain kind of person. For example, you may have a prototypical image of a TV evangelist, a professor, an extro-vert, and a beauty queen. These images allow you to identify whether or not a given person belongs in one of these categories.

TABLE 3-1

Cognitive Schemata

Person Prototypes

Person prototypes are idealized representations of a certain kind of person. We use prototypes to identify and classify people. If you can form a mental image of any of the following types of people, you are using a person prototype: cowboy, beauty queen, stand-up comic, housewife, politician, or type A personality. Although prototypes give us a "quick take" on someone, they ignore details that make people individuals, and they can lead to stereotyped responses.

Personal Constructs

Personal constructs are the characteristics we habitually notice in others. They are the specific descriptors we use to answer the question, what is he or she like? Often used unconsciously, they affect the judgments and decisions we make about others. Part of the mental apparatus of the observer, they appear to be characteristics of the observed. Like other schema, they can make perception easier and more efficient, but they can also be inaccurate and unfair.

Scripts

Scripts are representations of sequences of actions. By following a script, we know what to do next in a given situation. Well-learned scripts free us from having to make conscious decisions about our actions and give us the confidence that comes from knowing what to do next. Scripts, however, can lull us into mindless and repetitive routines. When communication is scripted, we can rattle off a routine without thinking about it.

The human need to categorize others is very strong. When we encounter someone who doesn't fit neatly into a category, we feel off balance. In 1992 a popular skit on the TV program "Saturday Night Live" concerned an androgynous character called Pat whose equal blend of male and female traits made it impossible to determine her/his gender. Characters in the Pat skits were constantly thwarted in their attempts to figure out whether Pat was male or female. The Pat skits demonstrate the uncertainty most people feel when certain "sacred" social categories, such as gender, are violated.

> *The human need to categorize others is very strong. When we encounter someone who doesn't fit neatly into a category, we feel off balance.*

The information contained in prototypes consists of traits, patterns of behavior, and role relations that fit our idea of a certain type of person. If a person appears to have a sufficient number of these traits, and if he or she exhibits no incompatible traits, then that person is easily recognized and understood.[4]

Prototypes affect communication. We are likely to communicate openly with people who fit positive prototypes and to reject those who fit negative prototypes. Although prototypes are absolutely necessary if we are to process information about people, they can be unfair and simplistic. If our prototypes are inaccurate or incomplete, we misjudge those around us. Only if we are willing to revise prototypes and to keep an open mind can we prevent these perceptual mechanisms from leading to prejudice.

> *We are likely to communicate openly with people who fit positive prototypes and to reject those who fit negative prototypes.*

Personal Constructs

In our daily interactions we often use another kind of schema called a personal construct.[5] **Personal constructs** are the characteristics we notice on a daily basis about others. Whereas prototypes are global categorizations, constructs are specific descriptors. Personal constructs belong to us rather than to the person we are judging. Lori and Tom, for example, have a mutual friend Jean. To Lori, Jean is generous, easygoing, and somewhat insecure. To Tom, Jean is sloppy, a lazy thinker, and somewhat mean-spirited. The adjectives each uses to describe Jean are examples of personal constructs. And examining these constructs tells us not only about Jean but about Lori and Tom as well.

Personal constructs are called personal because we carry them around and use them to describe our social worlds. Out of the hundreds of characteristics that can be attached to another human being, we tend to use only a few. Sometimes we use a construct because it has recently been "primed." For example, if we have just been talking about Mother Teresa, the construct "kindhearted" may be uppermost in our minds, and we may judge others according to their generosity and concern for others. If, on the other hand, we have been studying the latest political scandal, constructs such as "manipulative" may occur to us.

> *Out of the hundreds of characteristics that can be attached to another human being, we tend to use only a few.*

In addition to constructs that we use temporarily because they are suggested to us by events, we also have habitual ways of judging others. Constructs that are important to us and that we frequently use, regardless of circumstances, are called **chronically accessible constructs,** and these constructs are likely to color and bias our judgments. Psychologist John Bargh tells us that there are wide personal differences in construct accessibility and that this accessibility does not often overlap between individuals. Thus, two people may "pick up very different information about a third person, and interpret the same information in very different ways."[6] Chronically accessible constructs often automatically affect the judgments and decisions we make about other people. I may judge others in terms of their physical appearance, you may judge others in terms of their openness and honesty, and yet a third person may notice only how successful or ambitious others are. Each of us sees what is important to us, and we may miss what others see. We may therefore be biased in our perceptions. Chronic constructs can lead to perceptual problems:

> *Because they operate outside of our control and potentially outside of our awareness altogether, we cannot adjust for them through some intentional and controlled process. We cannot say, for example, "Oh, maybe Carol didn't mean it that way," and decide that we can still be friends with her, because as with the color of the sky, we do not question the validity of automatically produced perceptions.*[7]

To examine your own personal constructs, consider a number of people you know and write down adjectives to describe them. Looking at your completed list, you'll see the kinds of judgments you habitually make about others. Are the constructs you listed based on physical or psychological characteristics? Are they fair or unfair? What do they tell you about how you evaluate people?

When individuals use only simple, undifferentiated constructs based mainly on physical characteristics, we say that they lack cognitive complexity. **Cognitive complexity** occurs when an individual has a large, rich, and varied set of personal constructs.[8] The cognitively complex person is willing to combine seemingly contradictory characteristics in creative ways, realizing that people are not all good or all bad. The person who lacks cognitive complexity tends to use one or two simple constructs, ignoring contradictory information. Cognitive complexity is a mark of maturity and is necessary for good communication. Incidentally, the idea of cognitive complexity is itself a personal construct, one used by communication scholars to explain the perceptual behavior of others.

Scripts

A third kind of schema is called a script. **Scripts** are schemata for action sequences.[9] If we experience a situation repeatedly, we abstract its essential features and identify the order in which things happen. We have scripts for all kinds of simple actions: eating in a restaurant, greeting people in passing, working out at a gym, walking to class. Scripts allow us to behave effortlessly, without having to think much about what to do next. When we find ourselves in highly scripted situations, we feel confident. When we encounter unusual or novel situations for which we have no script, we feel uncomfortable and unsure of ourselves.

> *We have scripts for all kinds of simple actions: eating in a restaurant, greeting people in passing, working out at a gym, walking to class. Scripts allow us to behave effortlessly, without having to think much about what to do next.*

Scripts, then, allow us to interact mindlessly, almost as though we were on automatic pilot. When we perform familiar, well-practiced behaviors such as driving to work, we need not pay close attention to what we are doing. As we drive, we can think of the day ahead or work out a personal problem, and we may find ourselves at the office without really knowing how we got there. (Occasionally, in fact, we may end up at the office even though we had intended to go somewhere else, simply because we were following a script.)

Mindless Processing

As the example of driving to the office shows, we often process information automatically, without much conscious thought. We frequently act like "lazy organisms" or "cognitive misers," saving our conscious attention for important situations and spending much of our time in what is called **mindless** or **automatic processing**.[10] We process mindlessly when we rely on old routines and mental habits to give us information about the world.

Mindless processing has its advantages. If our schemata match reality, mindless processing can be adaptive and efficient. Indeed, without some kind

Of all the objects we perceive, people are the most complex and interesting. The schemata we use to guide person perception can help us connect with one another or can separate us.

of automatic processing, the amount of attention we would have to use for simply getting through a day would overwhelm us. Mindless processing frees us to attend to "the new, the unusual, the potentially dangerous, the most informative, and the most important events going on around us at any given time."[11] On the other hand, mindlessness has serious disadvantages. When we accept familiar schemata uncritically, we give up control over our decisions and behaviors. We can be easily influenced to do things we might not do otherwise and see things that aren't there.

The opposite of mindless processing is **mindful processing.** According to psychologist Ellen Langer, when we are mindful we are in a state of "alert and lively awareness."[12] We actively think about our world, controlling it rather than being controlled by it. When we act mindfully, we can overcome automatic assumptions and biases. By expending a little effort, we may be able to override automatic processing and achieve more control over perception.

Information Processing: Communicating for Clarity

Communication effectiveness depends on realistic message processing. Yet perception, as we have seen, is open to distortions and biases. If we often see and hear what we wish rather than what exists in fact, how can we communicate accurately and fairly? In the rest of this chapter, we will look at some answers to this difficult question. In this section we will discuss ways in which message senders can make it easier for receivers to process information. Then, in the final part of the chapter, we will look at ways in which receivers can improve their perceptual skills and become more mindful listeners. Our starting point will be a simple three-step model of information processing.

Steps in Information Processing

Information processing is an active process of creating and storing meaning. Although we never completely shut off this process (even when asleep, we make sense of the world through dreams), we may close down our processing of a particular message, especially if the message is poorly designed. Our attention can wander, we can misinterpret the message, or we can forget it almost before it is over. Because there are so many points at which processing can break down, it is important to understand factors that make messages vulnerable to distortion. One way to examine these factors is to divide information processing into three steps and look at each in turn, keeping in mind, of course, that the steps are interrelated.[13]

The first step in information processing is **attention.** Here receivers filter out extraneous stimuli and focus on the elements that are central to a message. This step is important: if attention fails, receivers will focus on unimportant details and miss vital information. The second step, **interpretation,** consists of two parts: comprehension and acceptance. When receivers **comprehend** a message, they understand its meaning and intent, and they relate it to other information. If comprehension fails, receivers are confused and uncertain about the point of the message. **Acceptance** occurs when receivers evaluate the message and decide it is worth further processing. As a result of acceptance, receivers incorporate message elements into their own belief systems and, in the case of persuasive messages, act on this information. Comprehension and acceptance are interrelated. Without some degree of acceptance, receivers will dismiss a message without bothering to comprehend it. Conversely, without comprehension full acceptance is impossible.

The third step is **retention.** If messages are to be of any use, receivers must store them accurately and retrieve them at appropriate times. All three of these steps must occur if a message is to be effectively processed, and good communicators design their messages so that all three steps occur. Table 3-2 summarizes these steps and offers suggestions for designing easily processed messages.

Capturing Attention

Scholars who study information processing often distinguish between two kinds of attention: voluntary and involuntary.[14] **Voluntary attention** occurs when we willfully focus our attention on a stimulus; it is attention guided by personal plans and goals. **Involuntary attention** is attention spontaneously attracted by the intrinsic properties of a stimulus; it lies outside our control. When we listen to a debate to find out a candidate's position on a particular issue or pore over a map to make sure we are going in the right direction, we are engaging in voluntary attention. When we have no particular plan but simply scan our surroundings and focus on interesting or unusual stimuli, we are engaging in involuntary attention.

A skilled communicator must consider both kinds of attention when designing messages. Voluntary attention can be increased by providing receivers with motivation for focusing on the message. If a receiver's needs and desires are already strong, the message sender need merely let the receiver know that relevant information is available. To an unemployed person, for example, a speech on how to get a good job is inherently interesting. The receiver attends to the message because it connects to his or her immediate needs and goals. To someone with a perfectly good job, however, the same speech is less interesting, and the speaker may have to create motivation, perhaps by showing the receiver that the information will be useful in the future or can lead to job advancement now. In either case, *voluntary attention can be increased by relating message elements to receivers' goals, needs, or plans.*

Involuntary attention works differently. *To increase involuntary attention, one must create vivid and compelling message elements that cannot be ignored.* Humans are "prewired" to take note of novel stimuli. As Marvin Zuckerman explains, an involuntary attention mechanism is part of our biological makeup:

> *Humans are "prewired" to take note of novel stimuli.*

> One of our hominid ancestors in a relatively relaxed state on a plain in Africa might have little engagement of attention by the environment, but the sound of something moving in the brush, the sight of something moving in the distance, or a new smell wafting about must have

---

TABLE 3-2

Design Elements for Easy Message Processing

Elements That Capture Attention
- Increase voluntary attention by tying messages to receivers' goals, needs, and plans.
- Increase involuntary attention by creating intense, novel, complex, or incongruous message elements; when speaking, present concrete, easily visualized ideas.

Elements That Enhance Interpretation by Increasing Comprehension
- Relate new material to familiar material.
- Adapt messages to the learning and interest levels of your audience.
- Provide opportunities for feedback.
- Use repetition.

Elements That Enhance Interpretation by Ensuring Acceptance
- Relate proposals to receivers' current beliefs.
- Offer receivers an incentive for accepting your proposals.
- Encourage audience members to make positive cognitive responses; increase their active involvement in processing your message.

Elements That Increase Retention
- Use active rehearsal and repetition.
- Make information personally relevant to receivers.
- Associate recall with appropriate triggers.
- Provide a simple, vivid summary of main ideas.

had the instant capacity to engage attention and arouse the brain. Novel stimuli do have this intrinsic capacity to stop ongoing activity and to engage the attention mechanism.[15]

What kinds of stimuli have the potential to arouse involuntary attention? Stimuli that are intense, novel, complex, surprising, and incongruous.[16] Vivid colors, loud sounds, and sharp contrasts instantly capture our attention. In addition, evidence suggests that we prefer visual over other sensory modalities—that a picture is worth a thousand words. In terms of verbal material, therefore, vivid, concrete, easily visualized information draws our attention more easily than does drier, more abstract information.[17] We also pay special attention to information that is surprising or that violates well-established schemata.[18]

> *Stimuli that are intense, novel, complex, surprising, and incongruous. Vivid colors, loud sounds, and sharp contrasts instantly capture our attention.*

Public speakers may add special "attention getters" to their speeches. By using humor, startling statements, or vivid descriptions, a sender can make a message immediately appealing. Similarly, in a print ad, color, contrast, and unusual images capture our interest even when we are not particularly motivated to attend.

Of course, vivid stimuli are not always desirable. If audience members are anxious, intense stimuli may make them feel uncomfortable. And competing stimuli in the speaking environment can draw attention away from a message. When deciding where to speak, it's important for communicators to choose environments that are interesting enough to keep receivers alert but not so interesting that involuntary attention take receivers away from the intended message.

Controlling Interpretation

Message elements can be vivid and compelling, but if the message as a whole is unintelligible or unacceptable, it will not be effective. Receivers interpret and evaluate messages, and sometimes their responses are not those the sender intended. Senders can overcome this problem by making sure that the message is easy to understand and that the information it contains is valuable and relevant.

Increasing Comprehension

A sender can increase message comprehension in a number of ways. The first is to *relate new information to old*. Our discussion of schemata has suggested that we make sense of messages by relating them to what we already know. When we encounter new information, we search for schemata that will make sense of it. A skillful message sender helps the receiver find such schemata by using analogy, comparison, and contrast—methods that help receivers interpret new experience in terms of prior meaning structures.

We all have different levels of experience to draw upon, so we all process information at different levels. A fundamental principle of good communication is that *effective senders adapt to the learning level of their listeners, using familiar, concrete, and clear language and appropriate and unambiguous images.* This does not mean that speakers should talk down to an audience, but it does mean that they must make a reasonable assessment of audience members' intellectual ability, degree of expertness, and past experience with the topic.

> *Effective senders adapt to the learning level of their listeners.*

When complex information is presented, it is often necessary to link ideas and to construct interconnected arguments. *Use of a clear-cut organizational pattern that guides a receiver through a message enhances comprehension.* Whether we are reading an article, listening to a story, or hearing a joke, we expect the message to be delivered in a logical order. Organization is as important in a comedy routine as it is in a persuasive speech. The organizational patterns used are relatively informal in some kinds of communication (such as everyday conversation) and relatively formal in others (such as a news broadcast), yet some degree of structure is always necessary. All communication must exhibit coherence.

Relatively informal, interactive discourse such as conversation depends less on formal structure because direct feedback is possible. Indeed, *message comprehension can be increased by providing opportunities for feedback.* A good communicator watches receivers for signs of understanding. If possible, he or she encourages receivers to state their understandings explicitly. A person asks a friend, "Do you understand what I mean? Have you ever felt like that?" and encourages the friend to respond. A person on duty in an information booth offers directions and then listens to make sure they are clear as they are repeated back. A teacher asks, "Who can tell me what feedback is?" quizzing students to see whether or not the class understands. In each case a communicator uses feedback to test comprehension and is prepared to offer more information if the original message was unclear.

> *A good communicator watches receivers for signs of understanding.*

Ensuring Acceptance

A receiver may understand what is said but may still block out or dismiss a message. Effective senders do their best to ensure that receivers accept message content as worthwhile or relevant. *One way to increase acceptance is to show receivers how the information presented fits with other elements in their belief systems.* Most of us find it difficult to accept information that contradicts prior beliefs, attitudes, and values. Often our first response is to discount that information. If you were to hear something shockingly negative about a close and respected friend,

> *To accept radically new information, receivers often must abandon or reorganize old beliefs and values.*

you probably wouldn't believe it—at least not initially. If you were to take a course with a professor who contradicts everything you have been taught, you would not know whom to believe. To accept radically new information, receivers often must abandon or reorganize old beliefs and values; this is usually a difficult process. Senders can make this process easier by showing how new information is supported by old beliefs or, when cognitive realignment is necessary, by helping receivers reorganize belief structures.

Acceptable messages offer receivers an incentive. It is important that receivers see value in a message. Therefore, message content should offer some reward to receivers; receivers should understand why the information conveyed is useful to them. After all, message processing takes time and effort, and receivers see no reason to expend that time and effort on irrelevant or erroneous messages.

Persuasion theorists called **cognitive response theorists** point out that people accept messages not on the basis of what a speaker says but on the basis of their own responses to the speaker's message.[19] When I listen carefully to a speaker, I hold a kind of internal conversation with myself. I

> *What people find out for themselves is often more powerfully convincing than what they are told.*

agree or disagree, supplying supporting examples or counterarguments. These cognitive responses ultimately convince me to accept or reject the speaker's message. The cognitive response principle suggests that *senders who wish to increase acceptance should encourage favorable cognitive responses.* This is often achieved by asking receivers to become actively involved in message processing. Teachers, for example, may give students "hands-on" experience with experiments or exercises, because what people find out for themselves is often more powerfully convincing than what they are told. Therapists may use role-playing for the same reason. Public speakers may ask audience members rhetorical questions to make them think about a topic.

Enhancing Retention

Have you ever listened with interest to a message, understood it, and accepted it, yet later found that you had completely forgotten it? This experience is a common one, and it points to one final step in message processing: retention.

By retention we mean that the message must be accurately stored for retrieval at some later date. How can messages be made more memorable?

First, *active rehearsal and repetition make a message more memorable.* Senders can encourage message retention by using repetition within the message, by asking questions during a message that encourage receivers to repeat message elements mentally, or by providing follow-up activities or exercises that reinforce information rehearsal. Another way to increase message recall is to make information relevant to receivers' experiences. *Information related to self-perceptions appears to be stored more readily than less relevant information.* Information relevant to receivers will also be retrieved more easily.

Message retrieval is often "triggered" by some external stimulus. We pass a restaurant and suddenly remember that we were supposed to meet a friend for lunch. We see an acquaintance jogging and suddenly recall our good intentions to exercise more often. *If senders tie message proposals to appropriate triggers, information retrieval can be increased.* Let's look at an example. A speaker wants children to refuse rides from strangers. To make sure the children remember to say no and run away, the speaker gets the children to role-play. He or she may ask the children, "What should you do when you see a strange car drive up?" and may rehearse their reply or may even take the children outside and have a partner pretend to be a stranger. In this way, the response of saying no and running away is tied to a specific stimulus trigger. The children know when and under what circumstances to remember the desired response.

Finally, *in order to increase retention, messages should be summarized in simple but vivid style.* When we remember information, we do not remember it exactly as it was said. We remember it in our own ways. Often we simplify it, cutting out inessential details, until what we retain is the essence of the message. Of course, when left to do this ourselves, we may choose the wrong information to remember. Effective senders can take advantage of our tendency to summarize while cutting down on distortion, if they themselves supply us with simple points to take away with us. The simpler and more vivid these summaries are, the better we will retain them. Slogans, jingles, and alliterative lists, for example, are easily stored and retrieved, as are emotionally charged examples and vivid images. To ensure retention, ending on a strong note is particularly important.

Information processing is a risky business. Human perceivers are distractable, and we often hear what we want to hear, rather than what was said. Over time we add creative details and forget important points. As communicators, we must be aware of the fallibility of perception. So far, we have looked at this problem from the point of view of the sender, and we have reviewed ways to make messages interesting, clear, convincing, and memorable. These methods are not foolproof, of course. If a receiver decides not to listen, even a great speaker is powerless. Communication is a cooperative enterprise, after all, and both partners bear responsibilities. In the final section of this chapter, we'll consider what receivers can do to increase their ability to perceive messages accurately. We'll look at one of the most important communication skills: listening.

Listening: How Receivers Can Improve Decoding

When we think of communication, we almost always think about message sending. We picture people conversing or giving public speeches or perhaps writing letters. We neglect the other, equally important half of communication: listening. Yet studies show that we spend more time listening than engaging in any other form of communication. And studies also show that most of us have very poor listening skills.

Why do we listen so poorly? One answer lies in our cultural values. As Americans, we value activity and independence. We tend to believe that actively expressing our own ideas is more valuable than passively attending to others' messages. This view reveals a fundamental misunderstanding of listening. Although listening may *seem* passive, it is not. While we listen, we actively create meaning and construct our own versions of reality. Seen in this light, listening is one of the most important forms of communication.

Because of the low value our culture places on listening, most of us have learned to be poor listeners. Parents and teachers make sure we develop skill in reading, writing, and speaking. Listening, however, is usually something we have to learn on our own, and the models we learn from are often not very good. Florence Wolff and her colleagues tell us that our parents often train us to be "nonlisteners." When parents tell a child, "Don't pay any attention to that," or, "I don't want to hear that in this family," they model nonlistening. By not paying attention or by interrupting each other in mid-sentence, parents tell us that it's not important to hear others out.[20] In school, the situation is almost as bad. Teachers, themselves untrained in listening, make up for students' listening deficiencies by patiently repeating themselves. By failing to demand high levels of listening performance, they too may be reinforcing nonlistening.[21]

Because of the low value our culture places on listening, most of us have learned to be poor listeners.

Luckily, listening can be improved. Just as we have learned to be poor listeners, we can learn to be more effective ones. By becoming more aware of the listening process and by practicing listening skills, we can improve our listening effectiveness enormously.

What Is Listening?

For our purposes, we can define **listening** as the process whereby orally communicated messages are attended to, recognized and interpreted in light of needs and experiences, and stored for future use. This definition emphasizes that when we listen we assign meaning to stimuli and that in assigning meaning we are influenced by prior habits, expectations, and desires. Listening, then, is an active, creative process governed by the listener's inner state.

Listening and Hearing

Although hearing is a necessary part of listening, it is only one part of this complex process. **Hearing** is a physiological process that occurs when sound waves are translated into electrical impulses that are then processed by the central nervous system. Hearing is the sensing of external aural data. Listening, on the other hand, goes much further. First, it involves selecting those sensations that are sent on for further processing and filtering out those that are extraneous. Second, it involves labeling, organizing, and assigning meaning to stimuli that have captured our attention. Finally, listening involves storing these created meanings in retrievable form. If any of these processes is short-circuited, listening fails.

We listen for a variety of reasons: to understand, to evaluate, to appreciate, and to share another's experiences.

Ability and Performance

Listening takes skill and mental effort. Unfortunately, many of us fail to make that effort. Years ago, Ralph Nichols and Leonard Stevens conducted a revealing study. They asked teachers at various grade levels to interrupt their lectures and ask students, "What was I talking about before I called time out?" In Grade 1, 90% of the students were able to answer the teacher's question. By junior high, only 43.7% were listening, and the percentage fell to 28% by high school.[22] Although our ability to process information should improve with age, this and similar studies show that actual listening performance worsens over time. A serious gap exists between what we can do as listeners and what we actually do.

Ways to Listen

Speakers are generally purposeful about talk. We speak for specific reasons: to inform, to persuade, to entertain, to make contact, to build relationships, and so on. Listeners are also purposeful about listening. We listen for a wide variety of reasons: to understand, to evaluate, to appreciate, and to empathize.

Often our goal is to understand and retain information. When we listen to someone giving us directions, or when we listen to a college lecture, our goal is to comprehend the message accurately and remember it when we need it. We know we have been successful at this kind of listening when we can process, store, and retrieve exactly what the speaker means for us to understand. We call this form of listening, **listening for understanding.**

Although listening for understanding is the basis of most other forms of listening, it is not the only form of listening. Often we must go beyond comprehension to evaluate message content. Here the goal is to judge the message and decide whether or not it is accurate, complete, or fair. This kind of listening requires critical ability, the ability to consider the speaker's intent, the internal logic of the message, and the adequacy of its evidence. As listeners, we must avoid being swept away by our own emotions or needs, and we must guard against using simple processing heuristics. This kind of **evaluative listening** is extremely important when we encounter persuasive situations.

At times, our concern is neither to memorize information nor to evaluate a message but simply to respond to or enjoy communication. In such cases it may be important to recognize the sender's intent, but it is just as important to experience in our own way what we hear. When we listen to a poem being read aloud, or when we attend a concert, our goal is to find meaning and enjoyment in the performance. Often, understanding the internal structure of a performed piece adds to our appreciation, as does the ability to make connections between the ideas and images we hear and our own knowledge and experience. What happens during this kind of listening is related to, but different from, what happens when we are listening for information. We call this form of listening **appreciative listening.**

Finally, we may listen for relational reasons: to make contact, to understand another's experiences, or to offer comfort or help. This form of listening is called **empathic listening.** Our concern is directed not toward ourselves but toward others. We listen to demonstrate that we care. Because this form of listening is relational, we must be especially concerned with feedback. Our goal is not only to understand but also to indicate our understanding and to respond in ways that help others. Here it is important to avoid being judgmental and to offer clarification and support.

Improving Listening Performance

Although each form of listening requires a different focus and a slightly different set of skills, some general principles can help us improve our overall listening performance. To the extent that we improve attention, interpretation, and storage, we become better listeners. Table 3-3 summarizes some of the ways we can improve our listening.

Improving Attention

In the earlier section on message effectiveness, we looked at two kinds of attention: involuntary and voluntary. Involuntary attention occurs when strong extraneous stimuli capture our attention. Voluntary attention occurs when we willfully focus our attention on a particular subject. Because attention occurs in short bursts and because external stimuli are constantly vying for our involuntary attention, we must make a special effort to ensure that our voluntary attention stays focused. In other words, we continually have to remind ourselves to pay attention.

One way to improve attention is to *recognize how easy it is to be diverted by extraneous details and make an effort to stay focused.* A speaker's clothes or mannerisms, unusual environmental details, competing sounds or movements, or our own concerns and feelings can divert voluntary attention. If we get caught up in these matters, our attention will fade out. Other sources of distractions are self-consciousness (focusing so much on how you are coming across that you miss what the other person is saying) and competitive turn taking (planning and plotting what you will say next, rather than attending to the other person). Luckily, it is possible to override these distractions and refocus attention.

Because voluntary attention is guided by goals and plans, it is especially important to *have a clear purpose in mind upon entering a listening situation.* In other words, know what you want to accomplish by listening, and remind yourself of your purpose whenever you find your attention straying. If, for example, you are listening to a lecture, your purpose may be to understand and remember the speaker's main points as well as supporting examples. Knowing what to listen for when you enter the situation will help you stay focused. In an interpersonal situation, your goal may be to understand as clearly as possible what is bothering a friend and to give him or her feedback. This goal can then direct your attention.

One of the interesting aspects of listening is that we can listen much faster than we can speak. The normal rate of speaking is approximately 150 words per minute, but studies have shown that we can process messages at rates of 300 words per minute or even higher. This means that as we listen, we have plenty of time to think—or to drift off into daydreams. We can *use the time*

TABLE 3-3	
Ways to Improve Listening Performance	***To Improve Attention*** — Focus only on relevant details. — Have a clear purpose for listening. — Use extra time to summarize content and review structure. — Keep a positive attitude; don't assume you'll be bored. ***To Improve Interpretation by Increasing Acceptance*** — Control your emotions. — Acknowledge your biases and delay final evaluation. ***To Improve Interpretation by Increasing Comprehension*** — Pay attention to content, not peripheral cues. — Separate inference from observation. — Prepare yourself by knowing about the topic. ***To Improve Retention*** — Decide what information needs to be stored. — Mentally rehearse and review material to be stored. — Use mnemonic devices or special memory aids. — Seek out feedback; paraphrase or ask questions.

differential between speaking and processing to think about message content and structure rather than to daydream or let attention drift to extraneous details. In public speaking situations, fill time by identifying main ideas, recalling supporting details, and looking for transitions that will identify the structure of the speech. In interpersonal contexts, focus on identifying your partner's feelings and checking nonverbal leakage cues. Most listening situations include spare time. Use it to paraphrase content, relate what is said to what you already know, add your own details, and review and summarize the main ideas of the message.

Finally, you can improve attention by giving yourself reasons to listen. *Don't dismiss a message ahead of time because you assume it will be boring.* If you enter a listening situation expecting the worst, nonlistening becomes inevitable.

Improving Interpretation

Listening is more than attending to a message. It also involves assigning meaning to the stimuli that have captured our attention. When we process stimuli, we react both emotionally and logically. That is, we assign to incoming data positive or negative emotional values at the same time that we use our storehouse of schemata to make sense of these data. We improve listening, then, by controlling our emotional reactions and by finding appropriate schemata for classifying the data.

First, it is important to *control our emotions.* Whether positive or negative, intense emotional reactions can short-circuit the listening process and destroy the objectivity we need to be evaluative listeners. Negative reactions to a speaker or topic, for example, can cause us to close down the perceptual process or to reinterpret what is said according to our own biases. This reaction often occurs when we feel stress or fear; for example, a patient with a serious illness may become so anxious while listening to a doctor that he or she is unable to interpret what the physician is saying or may be so awed by the doctor's expertise and power that important questions are left unasked. The ability to control emotions is also important in empathic listening situations. Such situations call for nonjudgmental acceptance. If we betray strong emotions by our nonverbal reactions, we will destroy the trust necessary for relational development.

> *Intense emotional reactions can short-circuit the listening process and destroy the objectivity we need to be evaluative listeners.*

Individual biases also distort the listening process. It is extremely hard to process information objectively when we disapprove of a speaker's views. It is, therefore, important to *be aware of your biases and delay final evaluation until you have had time to think about what is said.* This principle holds true for positive as well as negative biases. Not only are we likely to reject the views of speakers we dislike, but we are also likely to accept uncritically those messages that reinforce our prejudices. It is important to identify areas in which we hold strong biases. When encountering these areas, we should be especially critical, questioning those views we approve of and giving an objective hearing to those we dislike.

Receivers are often lazy processors who focus on peripheral cues rather than on the content of a message. For example, one's reaction to a speech may be based on the speaker's credentials or on audience reactions rather than on what is actually said. Uncritical audience members may say to themselves, "I'm not sure what he's talking about, but he's important, so the speech must be good." This kind of peripheral processing ignores message content, allowing the receiver to suppose that listening has taken place, when very little has actually happened. It is important to *pay attention to message content rather than peripheral cues when processing information.* This means concentrating on what is actually said, evaluating the logic, evidence, and completeness of the arguments in the message.

We must also *question the adequacy of perceptual schemata and separate inference from observation.* When we listen, we use perceptual schemata to help us make sense of messages. If these schemata are simplistic, then our interpretations are simplistic as well. In addition, schemata often serve to distort perception. Studies show that schemata have embedded within them **schematic default options,** details that are supplied when information is missing. Assume that you witness a car crash. Later, when a lawyer asks you whether or not glass from broken headlights was on the ground, you may answer affirmatively, even if the headlights were not actually broken. Your schema for car accidents supplies details that exist in your mind rather than in the actual situation.[23] Evidence shows that after a period of time, people have trouble distinguishing inferred from observed information.[24]

Although schemata can confuse us, they can also orient us toward a topic, making it easier to process. Consider the following description taken from a study on comprehension and recall:

> *The procedure is actually quite simple. First you arrange items into different groups. Of course one pile might be sufficient depending on how much there is to do. If you have to go somewhere else due to lack of facilities, that is the next step; otherwise, you are pretty well set. It is important not to overdo things. That is, it is better to do too few things at once than too many. . . . After the procedure is completed one arranges the material into different groups again. They then can be put into their appropriate places. Eventually they will be used once more and the whole cycle will then have to be repeated. However that is part of life.*[25]

The passage is fairly incomprehensible until you know the topic. When you find out that it is about washing clothes, it suddenly makes sense. The passage becomes intepretable because you can draw on information in your clothes-washing schema. This phenomenon suggests a final way to increase your listening ability: *Prepare ahead of time by knowing as much as possible about the topic; do your homework.*

Improving Retention

It is impossible to put everything we hear into long-term memory exactly as we hear it. Luckily, we do not need to remember everything exactly. The first principle in improving retention is to *decide what needs to be stored.* In most cases, it is important to store main ideas rather than specific phrasing. In fact, if we concentrate too specifically on wording or descriptive details and not enough on ideas, we'll miss the meaning of the message. A good listener can separate major ideas from extraneous information and can connect ideas and examples to one another.

Once we decide that something should be remembered, we must actively work to retain it. One way is to *mentally rehearse and review ideas that need to be stored.* Remembering is not automatic; it takes special effort. Occasionally, you may want to take notes to ensure that you have a permanent record of a spoken message. Although this is a good idea, special problems can arise with note taking. The first is that as we struggle to write something down, we tune out the rest of the message. Students who try to write down a lecture verbatim generally get lost. If you feel you have to take notes, jot down main ideas along with brief examples. Be sure you understand the idea before you start writing. In addition, notes are of little use if they are not reviewed. The information ultimately has to go into memory, and writing it in a book does not guarantee that you will remember it later. Experts on note taking suggest that you go over your notes as soon as possible after taking them, filling in details and making sense of them.

In special cases, you may wish to use mnemonic devices or special memory aids. Often, simple repetition serves to fix things in memory. However, other devices can help you accomplish message storage. If you tend to be visually oriented, you may find it easier to memorize something (say, a list) by visualizing its parts or items placed in a familiar setting (such as a series of rooms)—a technique we discussed in chapter 1. Another way to remember items is to link them visually to one another. For example, if you have to shop for a lightbulb, suntan lotion, a quart of orange juice, and pencils, visualize a cartoon of a lightbulb wearing sunglasses, lounging in the sun, using a pencil to write a postcard, and drinking a cool glass of orange juice. This unusual image will stay with you as you pick up each item at the store. Acronyms, or made-up words each letter of which stands for an idea you want to remember, are also useful, as are rhymes, such as "*I* before *e,* except after *c.*" Whatever aid you choose, you must spend time and effort to ensure that what you have attended to and interpreted will come back to you when you need it.

Finally, listeners should *seek out feedback whenever possible.* **Paraphrasing** (repeating a message in your own words so that the speaker can check your understanding) and asking questions are important ways not only to clarify your interpretation but also to involve yourself in a message.

Because listening is the forgotten part of communication, we seldom spend much time or effort on it. Yet being able to listen well is one of the most essential communication-related skills.

Remember that listening is an active process that takes attention and energy. Like other goal-directed behaviors, it can be improved with practice. Because listening is the forgotten part of communication, we seldom spend much time or effort on it. Yet being able to listen well is one of the most essential communication-related skills.

Summary

As the psychological model in chapter 2 shows, communicators constantly encode and decode messages. If these processes are faulty, miscommunication can occur. This chapter examines decoding and suggests ways in which both senders and receivers can improve decoding accuracy. To understand decoding, we must understand perception, the social, cognitive process by which people assign meaning to stimuli. As we perceive, we make sense of incoming stimuli by imposing structure, stability, and meaning on them. We use mental guidelines called schemata to carry out this process.

One type of schema is the person prototype, which allows us to label and categorize people. Another is the personal construct, which allows us to describe others' characteristics and make judgments about others accordingly. A third schema is the script, a framework that maps out simple actions and allows us to act in a mindless, automatic way.

Effective messages have three characteristics: they are attention-getting, easy to interpret, and easy to retain. Generally speaking, attention can be increased by providing receivers with incentives for processing and by making message elements vivid and compelling. Message interpretations can be enhanced by making sure messages are easy to understand (thereby increasing comprehension) and by showing receivers that message content is worthwhile (thereby increasing acceptance). Retention can be improved if senders provide simple summaries and link message content to environmental triggers.

Of course, not all the responsibility for effective communication lies with the sender. A major cause of faulty decoding is poor listening. Americans, on the whole, are poor listeners, perhaps because we falsely view listening as a passive process. Although we often equate listening and hearing, listening goes beyond hearing. It is an active process involving a great deal of interpretation.

Just as we speak for different reasons, so we listen with different purposes in mind: to understand, to evaluate, to appreciate, or to share another's experiences empathically. It is important to enter a listening situation with a definite purpose in mind, because the skills and abilities associated with each kind of listening are different.

Receivers can do a number of things to improve listening. To improve attention, they should listen with a positive attitude and a clear purpose; they should also review and summarize important message content while ignoring extraneous detail. To improve interpretation, receivers should control emotions and biases, distinguish what is important from what is not, and research topics ahead of time. Finally, to improve retention, receivers should decide what needs to be stored, use a variety of memory aids to make sure information is stored properly, and become actively involved in messages by asking for feedback.

Key Terms

Listed below are the key terms used in this chapter, along with the number of the page where each is explained.

Review Questions

1. What does the example that opens the chapter—scientists were waiting for a meeting to begin when two men rushed into the room—illustrate about decoding processes?

2. Perception is defined as a social, cognitive process. Why is perception considered social? How do social practices and cultural conditions affect perception?

3. What three things do perceivers do to make sense of stimuli? Give your own examples of each.

4. What are schemata? How do they affect perception? What three kinds of schemata are discussed in the text?

5. What kind of information is contained in a person prototype? How do prototypes affect communication?

6. What are personal constructs? What are chronically accessible constructs, and how are they related to biases? What kinds of personal constructs do cognitively complex people have?

7. What is a script? How are scripts related to mindless processing?

8. What are the three steps in information processing mentioned in your text?

9. What is the difference between voluntary and involuntary attention? What can a sender do to design a message that will capture voluntary attention? involuntary attention? What can receivers do to improve their attention to messages? (Check Tables 3-2 and 3-3.)

10. What can a sender do to increase receiver acceptance and comprehension? What can a listener do to ensure interpretation is as accurate and as rich as possible?

11. How can senders create memorable and retrievable messages? How can receivers improve their ability to retain information?

12. What is listening? What is hearing? Why do Americans listen so poorly?

13. What did Nichols and Stevens find when they examined listening in schools?

14. One listening goal is to listen for understanding. For what additional purposes do we listen? What skills and abilities does each form of listening call for?

Suggested Readings

Baddeley, Alan. (1991). *Your memory: A user's guide.* New York: Macmillan.

In a fascinating introduction to the way human memory works, Baddeley explains the interlocking systems that make up memory. This field guide to human memory includes topics such as: amnesia, why we forget information, the relationship between organization and memory, and the effect of emotions on message storage and retrieval. This intelligent book can help you use your memory more effectively.

Bolles, Edmund Blair. (1991). *A second way of knowing: The riddle of human perception.* New York: Prentice-Hall.

> Bolles provides a readable and intelligent discussion of the science of perception and illustrates that the way we construct our perceptual worlds affects the way we live our lives.

Langer, Ellen J. (1989). *Mindfulness.* Reading, MA: Addison-Wesley.

> In this lively and entertaining book, Langer discusses the personal and social costs of taking perception for granted and suggests ways we can become more accurate, creative, and mindful processors.

Williams, Donna. (1992). *Nobody nowhere.* New York: Avon.

> This extraordinary autobiography explores what happens when the ability to perceive and interpret human interaction is blocked. With great grace and courage, Williams tells us what it is like to be cut off from the "normal" world because of autism.

Wolvin, Andrew D., & Coakley, Carolyn Gwynn. (1982). *Listening.* Dubuque, IA: William C. Brown.

> This text covers a range of kinds of listening and gives practical advice on how to improve listening ability.

Notes

1. The original study is reported in O'Brien, Brian. (1959). How much can we see? In Robert S. Daniel (Ed.), *Contemporary readings in general psychology.* Boston: Houghton Mifflin, 270. It is retold and related to communication in Brooks, William D. (1974). *Speech communication* (2nd ed.). Dubuque, IA: William C. Brown, 23–24.

2. Schneider, David L., Hastorf, Albert, & Ellsworth, Phoebe C. (1979). *Person perception* (2nd ed.). Reading, MA: Addison-Wesley.

3. For a brief description and comparison of social cognitive schemata, see chapter 3 in Trenholm, Sarah, & Jensen, Arthur. (1992). *Interpersonal communication* (2nd ed.). Belmont, CA: Wadsworth. For a fuller discussion of some of the issues in schema theory as applied to media perception, see Wicks, Robert H. (1992). Schema theory and measurement in mass communication research: Theoretical and methodological issues in news information processing. *Communication Yearbook, 15,* 115–145. See also Garramone, Gina M. (1992). A broader and "warmer" approach to schema theory. *Communication Yearbook, 15,* 146–154.

4. Cantor, Nancy, & Mischel, Walter. (1979). Prototypes in person perception. In Leonard Berkowitz (Ed.), *Advances in experimental social psychology* (Vol. 12). New York: Academic Press. See also Pavitt, Charles, & Haight, Larry. (1985).

The "competent communicator" as a cognitive prototype. *Human Communication Research, 12,* 225–40.

5. For the original expression of construct theory, see Kelly, George A. (1955). *The psychology of personal constructs, I: A theory of personality.* New York: Norton.

6. Bargh, John A. (1988). Automatic information processing: Implications for communication and affect. In Lewis Donohew, Howard E. Sypher, & E. Tory Higgins (Eds.), *Communication, social cognition, and affect,* Hillsdale, NJ: Lawrence Erlbaum Associates, 18.

7. Ibid., 18.

8. Crockett, Walter H. (1965). Cognitive complexity and impression formation. In Brendan A. Maher (Ed.), *Progress in experimental personality research, II.* New York: Academic; Delia, Jesse G., Clark, Ruth Anne, & Switzer, David E. (1974). Cognitive complexity and impression formation in informal social interaction. *Speech monographs, 41,* 299–308; and Hale, Claudia, & Delia, Jesse. (1976). Cognitive complexity and social perspective-taking. *Communication monographs, 43,* 195–203.

9. Schank, R., & Abelson, Robert. (1977). *Scripts, plans, goals, and understanding: An inquiry into human knowledge structures.* Hillsdale, NJ: Lawrence Erlbaum Associates.

10. Petty, Richard E., Cacioppo, John T., & Kasmer, Jeff A. (1988). The role of affect in the elaboration likelihood model of persuasion. In Donohew, Lewis, Sypher, Howard E., & Higgins, E. Tory, 119. See also McGuire, William. (1985). Attitudes and attitude change. In G. Lindzey, & E. Aronson (Eds.), *The handbook of social psychology* (3rd ed., Vol. 2). New York: Random House, 233–346: and Taylor, S. E. (1981). The interface of cognitive and "social" psychology. In J. H. Harvey (Ed.), *Cognition, social behavior, and the environment.* Hillsdale, NJ: Lawrence Erlbaum Associates.

11. Bargh, John A. (1988), 28.

12. Langer, Ellen J. (1989). Minding matters: The consequences of mindlessness—mindfulness. In Leonard Berkowitz (Ed.), *Advances in Experimental Social Psychology, 23.* New York: Academic, 137–73.

13. The discussion of information processing is based in part on steps in the Yale Attitude Approach to the study of persuasion, although the steps have been modified to apply to information processing in general. For an example of the Yale approach, see Hovland, Carl I., Janis, Irving L., & Kelley, Harold H. (1953). *Communication and persuasion.* New Haven: Yale University Press.

14. James, William. (1890). *Principles of psychology.* New York: Holt; Neisser, Ulrich. (1967). *Cognitive psychology.* New York: Appleton-Century-Crofts.

15. Zuckerman, Marvin. (1988). Behavior and biology: Research on sensation seeking and reactions to the media. In Donohew, Lewis, Sypher, Howard E., & Higgins, E. Tory, 173.

16. Ibid., 174.

17. Bargh, John A. (1984). Automatic and subconscious processing of social information. In Robert S. Wyer, Jr., & Thomas K. Srull (Eds.), *Handbook of social cognition* (Vol. 3). Hillsdale, NJ: Lawrence Erlbaum Associates.

18. Nisbett, R., & Ross, L. (1980). *Human inference: Strategies and shortcomings of social judgement.* Englewood Cliffs, NJ: Prentice-Hall.

19. An early statement of the cognitive response model can be found in Petty, Richard E., Ostrom, Thomas M., & Brock, Timothy C. (1981). *Cognitive responses in persuasion.* Hillsdale, NJ: Lawrence Erlbaum Associates.

20. Wolff, Florence I., Marsnik, Nadine C., Tacey, William S., & Nichols, Ralph G. (1983). *Perceptive listening.* New York: Holt, Rinehart and Winston, 29.

21. Whitman, Richard F. and Boase, Paul H. (1983) make a similar point in their discussion of listening in *Speech communication: Principles and contexts.* New York: Macmillan, 100.

22. Nichols, Ralph G., & Stevens, Leonard. (1957). *Are you listening?* New York: McGraw-Hill, 12–13.

23. Sypher, Howard E., Donohew, Lewis, & Higgins, E. Tory. (1988). An overview of the roles of social cognition and affect in communication. In Donohew, Lewis, Sypher, Howard E., & Higgins, E. Tory, 35.

24. Bower, G. H., Black, J. B., & Turner, T. J. (1979). Scripts in memory for text. *Cognitive Psychology, 11,* 177–220; Loftus, E. F., & Zanni, G. (1975). Eyewitness testimony: The influence of the wording of a question. *Bulletin of the Psychonomic Society, 5,* 86–88; and Picek, J. S., Sherman, S. J., & Shiffrin, R. M. (1975). Cognitive organization and encoding of social structures. *Journal of Personality and Social Psychology, 31,* 758–768.

25. Baddeley, Alan. (1991). *Your memory: A user's guide.* New York: Macmillan, 82.

4

Encoding Messages: Spoken Language

Language gives us the power to affect and persuade others. But language also exerts power over us.

"It was a bright cold day in April, and the clocks were striking thirteen." These words usher us into the bleak world of *1984*, George Orwell's chilling anti-utopia. Written in 1949, the novel describes a future world where freedom of thought has vanished—a world where Big Brother is always watching.

In *1984*, the Party, or government, controls the masses through the use of a special kind of language: "Newspeak." Newspeak is designed so that any idea that diverges from party principles is literally unthinkable. All words that threaten political unity, words such as *honor, justice, morality, internationalism, democracy, science,* and *religion,* have ceased to exist, and words such as *free* have been stripped of troublesome connotations. The architects of Newspeak have reduced the number of words in the language because "the smaller the area of choice, the smaller the temptation to take thought."[1]

Orwell's novel illustrates a truth we often overlook: we think through language. This is as true of the everyday English we speak as it is of Newspeak. Language gives us the power to affect and persuade others. But language also exerts power over us. In this chapter we look at what we do with language and what language does to us.

We'll begin by defining language and discussing its structure. We'll then move on to consider how we use language during interaction. We'll look at some pragmatic rules that govern language use, and we'll see how language is tied to group identity. Finally, we'll discuss how everyday language choices can sometimes result in unintended effects.

What Is Language?

Newspeak is frightening because it is dehumanizing. It is language "designed not to extend but to *diminish* the range of human thought, to make only 'correct' thought possible and all other modes of thought impossible."[2] Like other thinkers before him, Orwell understood that an important connection exists between language, thought, and humanity. This connection can be found in the stories, myths, and religions of many cultures. Linguist Victoria Fromkin tells us that language is often experienced as the source of human life and power:

> *To some people of Africa, a newborn child is a* kuntu, *a "thing," not yet a* muntu, *a "person." Only by the act of learning does the child become a human being. According to this tradition, we all become "human" because we all come to know at least one language.*[3]

There are many kinds of languages. The most common are those built around the spoken word. Spoken languages are called "natural languages," emphasizing the close link between language and its expression in speech. Not all languages, however, depend on speech. "Artificial" languages, such as computer languages, employ electrical signals, and sign languages use gestures. In this chapter we'll focus on understanding spoken languages. In the next we'll widen our discussion by looking at nonlinguistic codes.

In its most general sense, **language** can be defined as a rule-governed symbol system that allows its users to generate meaning and, in the process, to define reality. As we shall see, spoken language has four important characteristics: it is made up of symbols, it is a kind of knowledge, it is rule-governed and productive, and it affects the way we experience the world.

Human language is closely related to thought. Although it is possible to think in images, most thought is filtered through language.

Language Is Symbolic

To communicate, people must find a way to express the ideas that originate in their minds. A **sign** is the vehicle for this expression. It consists of two parts: the private idea located solely in the mind of a communicator (known as the **signified**); and the form in which the idea is expressed (or the **signifier**). In natural languages, the signifier is a sequence of spoken sounds. In artificial languages, the signifier may consist of electrical pulses, gestures, plastic shapes, marks on a page, or any of the other ingenious ways humans use to express meanings. In each case, the sign connects content and form. The French linguist Ferdinand de Saussure compared the sign to a sheet of paper, the front of which is the signifier and the back, the signified. Creating a word is like cutting a shape out of the paper, a shape that is both conceptual and representational.[4]

The sign relationship can be natural, or it can be produced by humans. An example of a natural sign is the smoke that indicates fire. In this case, the relationship between signifier (smoke) and signified (fire) does not depend on human intervention; it is a natural connection. In other cases, humans create signs. For example, English speakers use the sound sequence "dog" to represent a domesticated canine. The word *dog* is a special kind of sign called a symbol. A **symbol** differs from other signs in that it is arbitrary and conventional. The symbol *dog* is **arbitrary** because there is no natural connection between the idea of dog and the signifier *dog*. There is nothing particularly doglike about the word *dog*. In fact, in northern China, the signifier *gou* is used to represent the same idea. The symbol *dog* is **conventional** because its meaning depends on social agreement. Speakers of English have agreed to use the word *dog* in certain ways that speakers of other languages have not. In our language, the sound sequence "dog" has meaning; in Chinese it does not.

The fact that symbols call up similar thoughts in the minds of communicators even though no natural relationship between sounds and ideas exists has fascinated scholars for thousands of years. Aristotle recognized that symbols were ways of making inner thoughts discernible through sound, and (as you may recall from chapter 1) Augustine thought and wrote about the nature of symbols. The Port-Royal grammarians of the seventeenth century also recognized this connection, describing language as

> *The fact that symbols call up similar thoughts in the minds of communicators even though no natural relationship between sounds and ideas exists has fascinated scholars for thousands of years.*

the marvellous invention of composing out of 25 or 30 sounds that infinite variety of words, which tho' they have no natural resemblance to the operations of the mind, are yet the means of unfolding all its secrets, and of disclosing unto those, who cannot see into our hearts, the variety of our thoughts, and our sentiments upon all manner of subjects.[5]

Language Is a Kind of Knowledge

Language is mental rather than physical. Language is a body of knowledge stored within our brains. As such, it can never be examined directly but must be inferred from speech. Speech is the external, physical side of language, and language is the internal, mental side of speech. When we are born, we have not yet acquired the knowledge we call language. As we grow, we listen to the speech of those around us and figure out the rules that make up language. Every infant has the potential to learn the sounds, words, and sentence structures of any language. Had you been born into a language community other than the one in which you were raised, you would have mastered its language quite easily.

Language Is Rule-Governed and Productive

One of the most amazing things about linguistic knowledge is that it lets us understand sentences we have never heard before. It is unlikely that you have ever before read this sentence: "The large, gray pachyderm wearing the pink tutu ate rainforest crunch ice cream and dreamed of Africa." Yet you know what the sentence means. Your ability to understand and create unusual sentences like this one is called **linguistic productivity,** and it shows that language learning is more than a matter of trial and error. When we learn language, we don't learn a set of specific word combinations; instead, we learn rules that allow us to generate meanings. Of course, most of us can't consciously explain the rules we follow as we speak and listen, but we can use them to make ourselves understood. These rules are complex and interrelated. They tell us how to make the sounds of our language, how to combine those sounds into words, how to order those words into sentences, and how to use sentences in interaction.

Language Affects the Way We See the World

Human language is closely related to thought. Although some thought is purely visual, most is filtered through language. You can see this connection if you watch very young children think: they invariably talk or whisper at the same time. As we grow, overt verbalization gives way to silent, inner speech, but we still do a lot of our thinking through language.

Not only do we think in language, but we also store many memories in words. This phenomenon was demonstrated in a classic experiment performed in the 1930s. Carmichael and his colleagues asked people to view a set of twelve ambiguous figures (see Figure 4-1). Those taking part in the study were told to reproduce the figures as accurately as possible. As each figure was flashed before the subjects, it was labeled. A figure consisting of two circles connected by a short line, for example, was alternately labeled "eyeglasses" or "dumbbell." Results showed that subjects distorted the ambiguous figure to better fit the verbal label. Those shown the "eyeglasses" drew a picture in which the line connecting the circles was rounded to look like the bridge of a pair of glasses. Those shown the "dumbbell" thickened the center piece, making it look like a training weight. Evidently, people stored the verbal labels and then produced matching images, rather than storing the images themselves. As linguist Dan Slobin points out, verbal memory is thus a two-edged sword: It enables us to store and retrieve information, but in the process it can distort perception.[6]

FIGURE 4-1

Figures Carmichael Used to Illustrate the Effect of Language on Memory

Figures in the middle column are the stimuli Carmichael presented to subjects. Figures in both outer columns show how verbal labels distorted subjects' recall.

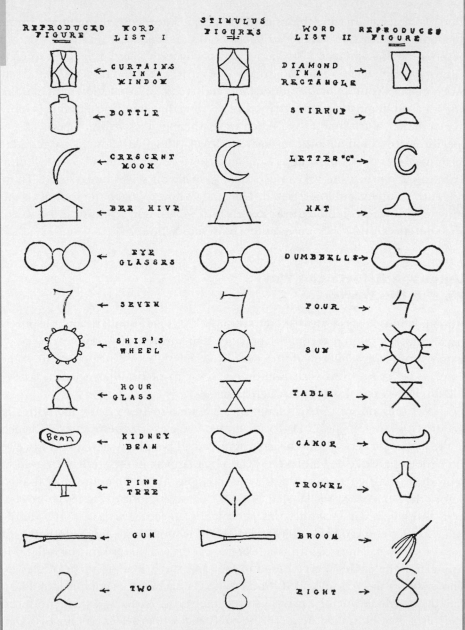

From "An Experimental Study of the Effect of Language on the Reproduction of Visually Perceived Forms" by L. Carmichael, H. P. Hogan, and A. A. Walter, February 1932, *Journal of Experimental Psychology*, 15, pp. 73-86.

If we think and remember linguistically, then it stands to reason that the nature of our language affects the nature of our thought. The **Sapir-Whorf hypothesis** expresses this idea. Named after the linguist Benjamin Lee Whorf and his teacher Edward Sapir, the hypothesis consists of two corollaries: linguistic determinism and linguistic relativity. **Linguistic determinism** is the theory that language determines thought. Sapir believed that we are at the mercy of our language:

> the "real world" is to a large extent unconsciously built up on the language habits of the group. . . . We see and hear and otherwise experience very largely as we do because the language habits of our community predispose certain choices of interpretation.[7]

Linguistic relativity follows from linguistic determinism. It theorizes that people from different language communities perceive the world differently.

Linguists cite many examples of the Sapir-Whorf hypothesis. If you have ever studied a foreign language, you know that some concepts and ideas that are easily expressed in one language are difficult to translate into another. Languages divide the world in different ways. In fact, some people argue that a glance at the most frequently occurring words in a language will give you an idea of what is especially important to speakers of that language. Thus, we are told that Arabic has many words for horses and that the Eskimos have many ways to talk about snow.

> *Some concepts and ideas that are easily expressed in one language are difficult to translate into another. Languages divide the world in different ways.*

Grammatical distinctions also draw our attention to different aspects of the social world. French speakers have two ways to say "you": a polite and a familiar form. Whenever a French speaker addresses someone, he or she must decide which form to use. Speakers of English are not required to think about relationships in the same way. As Slobin points out,

> If we suddenly all switched to French, we would find our attention focussed on many aspects of social relations which were previously not of central concern. . . . in speaking French, or some other language, we would almost certainly have to pay more daily attention to such matters.[8]

Another example of the connection between language and thought is discussed by psychologist Carol Cohn, who studied the ways that "defense intellectuals" discuss nuclear strategy. In her year-long study at a nuclear think tank, Cohn found that policy makers used a specialized language to talk about life and death. As Cohn learned to use this language, she found her own attitudes and feelings changing.

Cohn found that the language of defense strategists is highly euphemistic. **Euphemisms** are inoffensive words used instead of highly charged terms. Although euphemisms allow us to avoid talking about painful or offensive situations, they can also act as blinders. Cohn tells us that defense strategists often used terms "so bland that they never forced the speaker or enabled the listener to touch the realities of nuclear holocaust that lay behind the words."[9] For example, a nuclear expert "sanitizes" bombs that are one thousand times more powerful than the one that destroyed Hiroshima by calling them "clean bombs." When civilian deaths are called "collateral damage," they become easier to dismiss. And when "accidental delivery of ordnance equipment" results in "friendly casualties," the fact that American troops are being killed by American bombs goes almost unnoticed.[10]

Technostrategic language is a form of **jargon,** a specialized language known only to members of an in-group. Cohn reports that gaining access to this jargon gave her a feeling of power. Knowing the jargon also made talking about defense strategy fun, in part because the language used many short, snappy words. Referring to a missile guidance system as a "shoot and scoot" made it easy to forget the darker and more serious side of nuclear scenarios.

The better Cohn got at speaking the language, the more difficult it became to express her own ideas and values. As she accepted a new way of talking, she also came to accept a new way of thinking:

> As I learned to speak, my perspective changed. . . . Speaking the language, I could no longer really hear it. And once inside its protective walls, I began to find it difficult to get out. . . . I had not only learned to speak a language: I had started to think in it. Its questions became my questions, its concepts shaped my responses to new ideas. Its definitions of the parameters of reality became mine.[11]

Language, then, has powerful effects on the ways that we think about and experience the world. Although we are not completely prisoners of language, it is easy to overlook the extent to which our language habits affect our views of the world.

The Subsystems of Language

To know a language, we must first have several other kinds of knowledge. In this section we'll look briefly at how language is put together, and we'll examine what it means to master the sounds, the words, the sentences, and the social context of language. Table 4-1 summarizes our discussion.

The Sounds of Language

When you first experience a foreign language, all you hear is a string of unintelligible sounds. As you learn the language, however, you learn how to pronounce these sounds and how to combine them with one another. When you have accomplished this, you have mastered the first subsystem of language: the sound system. We humans have a rich and varied repertoire of sounds that we combine in countless ways to make up the lexicon of our language. Without this ability, we would be limited to the meanings that can be conveyed through undifferentiated cries and calls. Because we can articulate distinct sounds, we can build a sophisticated system for expressing meaning. The ability to articulate the sounds of our language is a vitally important part of being able to communicate.

The study of the significant sound patterns of language is called **phonology.** Of all the possible sounds we humans can make, only a small portion enter our language. In any language, some sounds are important and others are not. In English, for example, only one kind of "b" sound is significant. Different English speakers pronounce that "b" differently, but these variations can be overlooked. In Hindi, however, there are two kinds of "b" sounds: one is aspirated (accompanied by a short puff of air), and the other is unaspirated. Hindi speakers hear an aspirated and an unaspirated "b" as very different sounds, whereas we hear no difference at all. English, of course, contains some sounds not found in other languages. French speakers, for example, often pronounce the English words *this* and *that* as "zis" and "zat." Their language does not have a sound comparable to our "th."

The significant sound distinctions in a given language are called its **phonemes.** In English, "b" and "th" are phonemes; they are used to construct words, and no English speaker will confuse "bat" and "that." All English speakers have learned how to pronounce the English phonemes and know their basic characteristics. They also know how to use pitch, intonation, and word stress in acceptable ways. All of these skills are part of their knowledge of the sound system of language.

The Words of Language

In every spoken language, sounds are combined into meaningful sequences called words. The study of the structure of the units of meaning in a language is called **semantics.** We all carry a kind of mental dictionary that equates word meanings with sound structures. When you memorize the words that make up your language, when you can hear a sound sequence and assign it meaning, you are acting upon your knowledge of this subsystem of language.

So far, we have been talking about words as though they were the basic unit of meaning. Actually, the smallest unit of meaning in language is the **morpheme.** Some morphemes, called **free morphemes,** are equivalent to words. The words *boy* and *girl* are free morphemes. Other morphemes, called **bound morphemes,** must always be attached to other morphemes. The morpheme *ish,* meaning "having the quality of," is never found alone but must be combined with a noun, as in *boyish.* The plural morpheme *s* when added to *girl* creates *girls,* a new word with a new meaning. *Antidisestablishmentarianism* is one word made up of six bound morphemes attached to the free morpheme *establish* (anti-dis-*establish*-ment-ari-an-ism). A list of all the words of a language is known as a **lexicon.**

To know language is to know the rules of word formation. Young children often make errors because their morphological rules are not quite right. They learn that *s* indicates a plural form and *ed* a past form, and so they form words such as *dogs* and *barked.* But they may also construct words such as *sheeps* and *runned.* These errors show that children have inferred basic morphological rules but have not yet learned exceptions and irregularities.

TABLE 4-1

The Subsystems of Language

Phonology:
Study of the Sound System of a Language
- Phonology is the study of ways in which speech sounds form systems and patterns in human language.
- Its smallest unit is the phoneme.
- Phonological knowledge allows us to pronounce familiar words correctly, to know how unfamiliar words should sound, to know which sound variations are important in a language and which are not, to recognize foreign accents, and to make up new words that sound right.

Semantics:
Study of the Meaning System of a Language
- Semantics is the study of linguistic signs (symbols), including word formation and the internal structure of words.
- Its smallest unit is the morpheme.
- Morphological knowledge allows us to divide a stream of sound into meaningful words, to store and recall both the forms and meanings of words, to understand a word's morphemic components, to recognize how the addition or subtraction of a morpheme can change meaning, and to inflect unfamiliar words (e.g., to make plurals, to change tenses, etc.).

The Sentences of Language

If a foreign student were to memorize an English dictionary, he or she would not know English, for he or she would not know how to construct sentences. To speak English, one must know the grammatical rules that govern English sentence construction. The study of the sentence structure of a language is known as **syntactics.**

Syntactic knowledge enables us to sequence words appropriately and to determine meaning based on word order. An English speaker who wants to indicate that Elliot surprised Mary on Tuesday would not say, "It was that on Tuesday Elliot Mary surprised." This way of ordering words defies the rules of English sentence structure. Neither would the speaker say, "It was on Tuesday that Mary surprised Elliot," for that would confuse Elliot's and Mary's actions. Clearly, word order and sentence structure are important elements of communication.

What do we know about syntactic knowledge? Grammarians believe that to use language, we must have a basic sense of how the different parts of a sen-

---

Syntactics:
Study of the Structure of Phrases and Sentences
- Syntactics is the study of the rules that govern the combination of words into permissible strings.
- Its smallest unit is the sentence or utterance.
- Syntactic knowledge allows us to distinguish grammatical from ungrammatical combinations of words, to combine words in the correct order and to understand how changes in order change meaning, to produce sentences we have never heard before, and to recognize ambiguous sentences and decode their ambiguity.

Pragmatics:
Study of the Social Context of Language
- Pragmatics is the study of ways in which people use language forms to achieve goals in social contexts.
- Its basic unit is discourse.
- Pragmatic knowledge allows us to interpret another's communicative intent, to understand how context affects linguistic choices, to make language choices that communicate our intentions effectively, and to take into account information about the social world and our partner's knowledge of it.

tence (subject, verb, object, and the like) are related. To prove that we do have this knowledge, grammarians often point to ambiguous sentences; for example, "He decided on the train." This string of words can have two meanings. One meaning is "He made a decision while riding on the train." Here, "on the train" is a phrase that modifies the verb "decided." On the other hand, the sentence could mean "He decided to take the train (rather than some other form of transportation)." Here, "train" is the object of the verb "decided on." This sentence has two meanings not because the words are ambiguous but because the sentence has two different grammatical structures. If we couldn't understand this, we couldn't recognize the ambiguity.

Grammarians believe that syntactic knowledge contains information about the basic structures of sentences; the grammatical functions of words (for example, whether a word is a noun or a verb and where it fits in a sentence); rules for generating new sentences; and rules for transforming base sentences into different forms. Attempts to describe the syntactic knowledge necessary for even the simplest conversation are extraordinarily complex, and grammarians are still working on mapping syntactic structures. Luckily, we don't have to know complicated grammatical theories to use language. We can use syntactic knowledge automatically and unconsciously to generate new sentences and to recognize the sentences we hear.

The Social Context of Language

Knowing how to form grammatical sentences is a necessary, but not a sufficient, condition for good communication. To be really effective, speakers have to say the right thing at the right time in the right way. The fourth subsystem of language, the study of how we use language in social contexts, is known as **pragmatics.**

> *To be really effective, speakers have to say the right thing at the right time in the right way.*

Speech Acts

People seldom make sentences just to show off grammatical competence. We talk to accomplish goals. Pragmatic knowledge allows us to understand the intentions of others and to make our own intentions clear. The goal a speaker intends to accomplish through speech is called a **speech act.** Successful communication involves understanding the relationship between words and sentences and the speech acts they represent. To do this, we have to go beyond grammatical knowledge and draw on social knowledge.

Earlier we saw that a single utterance can have two syntactic structures. A single utterance can also have more than one pragmatic structure. Let's look at an example that has at least two interpretations and identify the speech act in each case. Consider the words "Do you have a watch?" The most likely interpretation of this sentence, if it is uttered by a stranger in the street, is that the speaker wants to know the time. Your knowledge of social behavior tells you that in our culture people often phrase a request for the time in this roundabout way. If you believe the speech act being performed is a request for the time, then the appropriate response is "Yes, it's 12:05."

Of course, the speaker might have other speech acts in mind. If he or she is carrying a clipboard and seems to be interviewing every passerby, the question might be part of a marketing survey. Then the proper response is yes or no or, perhaps, "I'm not interested in being in a survey." If the speaker is your teacher and you have just walked into class ten minutes late, the speech act is probably a criticism rather than a request for information, and the expected response is an excuse or an apology. Finally, if the speaker is a six-year-old who has been asking you a series of silly questions, the question may be part of a game, and you may decide to respond by asking silly questions of your own. To understand what is really meant by a speech act, you have to make inferences about the speaker's intentions.

In most cases, we talk to elicit a response from another person. Philosopher John Searle has outlined five kinds of speech acts that have this purpose: commissives, directives, assertives, expressives, and declarations.[12] **Commissives,** such as promises, vows, or guarantees, are speech acts that commit the speaker to a future action. **Directives** (e.g., commands, requests, and invitations) attempt to get the listener to act in a certain way. **Assertives** (e.g., statements, conclusions, and descriptions) tell receivers what the speaker believes to be true. **Expressives** (e.g., compliments, apologies, and thanks) communicate the speaker's feelings toward the receiver. Finally, **declarations** (e.g., resignations and dismissals) are statements that, simply by being uttered, bring about a certain state of affairs. The words "You're fired" accomplish the act of firing. As we learn language, we learn how to recognize and perform these kinds of linguistic acts. We learn subtle distinctions between promises, threats, and bribes; we learn how to apologize, how to congratulate, and how to command. Without this kind of social knowledge, we could not use language to do what it was meant to do: communicate.

Communication and Context

To make correct pragmatic choices, speakers must be sensitive to context, for context offers us the social information we need to understand speech acts. Context tells us who our communicative partners are and gives us clues about their assumptions and their expectations of us.

Table 4-2 shows some of the contextual information that we use to make pragmatic interpretations. This material is drawn from a larger theory of com-

TABLE 4-2

**Levels of
Context: The
CMM Hierarchy**

Cultural Patterns

General agreements shared by members of a particular cultural group about how to act in and respond to the world. Cultural patterns legitimize all lower contextual levels.

Examples: identity based on class, national, religious, or ethnic membership.

Life Script

A person's ideas about the kind of communication that matches his or her personal identity. Life script is the individual's sense of self.

Examples: aggressive executive, creative artist, loving parent, gifted orator, sensitive friend.

Relationship

All of the episodes that can reasonably be expected to occur between self and other, given reciprocal roles. Relationship identifies who communicators are to one another.

Examples: friends, lovers, strangers, business associates.

Episode

A sequence of communicative behaviors that exists as a unit and has a beginning, a middle, and an end. Episodes identify the purpose of an interaction.

Examples: a friendly chat, playing a game, solving a problem.

Speech Act

An act done by the speaker to the hearer. Speech acts identify the speaker's intention.

Examples: to persuade, to flatter, to inform, to comfort, to gather information.

munication called the Coordinated Management of Meaning theory, or CMM.[13] **CMM theory** provides a framework for understanding how individuals use context to assign pragmatic meaning. CMM theorists believe that to communicate successfully, we must take into account four levels of context: episode, relationship, life script, and cultural pattern.

An **episode** simply means the situation we find ourselves in during a given interaction. **Relationship** refers to the role obligations that we feel toward one another. **Life script** is our professional or personal identity, and **cultural pattern** consists of the cultural norms we share with others. Communicators who understand these factors interpret messages correctly and communicate clearly. Communicators who can't read these contextual cues are at a disadvantage.

Language must always match context. Thus, if a speaker's professional identity is that of an aggressive defense attorney (life script) engaged in cross-examining (episode) a hostile witness (relationship) in a U.S. court of law (cultural pattern), he or she must communicate accordingly. When the speaker leaves the courtroom to have dinner with his or her spouse, however, the speaker's language style must change. A spouse can't be treated like a witness if a marriage is to survive. What is admirable in the courtroom may be unforgivable in the dining room.

Pragmatic knowledge is essential for good communication. In linguist Robin Lakoff's words,

> *Pragmatics connects words to their speakers and the context in which they are speaking: what they hope to achieve by talking, the relation between the form they choose and the effect they want it to have (and the effect it does have), the assumptions speakers make about what their hearers already know or need to know.*[14]

Pragmatic knowledge also includes knowledge about the type of discourse employed in any situation.

Pragmatic Styles and Structures

As we move from one situation to another, we use what linguists refer to as different discourse styles. Just as the basic unit of syntax is the sentence, so the basic unit of pragmatics is discourse. **Discourse** is a unit of language larger than a single sentence; it consists of connected sentences that form an identifiable structure to fulfill a communicative function. In a typical day, you may read a newspaper article, study a college textbook, listen to a professor's lecture, take part in a group discussion, write a personal essay, give a public speech, or hold a casual conversation. All these activities are forms of discourse, and each has its own structure and rules. As we shall see in part 3 of this text, different communication contexts call for different kinds of discourse. One aspect of being a good communicator is understanding and following the rules that govern common forms of discourse.

Forms of Discourse: Classifying Kinds of Talk

In this section we'll compare two forms of discourse, one relatively private and the other slightly more public. These two forms of discourse, conversation and classroom interaction, are so familiar to us that we can engage in them automatically and effortlessly. Yet when we go from one to the other—when we move from friendly talk with friends to interaction with classmates and teachers—our pragmatic rules change quite dramatically. As you will see, the structure and function of these forms of discourse are quite different.

Understanding Conversation

The most common mode of spoken communication is the conversation. Through conversations we create and maintain relationships, explore and develop personal identities, and accomplish daily tasks. Because this form of discourse is essential for social survival, conversation has been one of the most studied of all the discourse modes.

> *Through conversations we create and maintain relationships, explore and develop personal identities, and accomplish daily tasks.*

Conversation analyst Margaret McLaughlin defines a **conversation** as "a relatively informal social interaction in which the roles of speaker and hearer are exchanged in a nonautomatic fashion under the collaborative management of all parties."[15] As the most private and most personal mode of communication, conversation differs from other forms of discourse.[16] Chiefly, it is fully interactive. That is, conversation is the most *reciprocal* and *egalitarian* of all discourse forms. Because communicative power is equally distributed in conversation, participants are permitted identical speech acts. All of the parties can tell stories, self-disclose, joke, ask questions, and so on. Of course, even in informal interpersonal relationships dominance patterns can occur, but these patterns belong more to the relationship than to the discourse itself. Generally speaking, conversation allows partners a degree of freedom not present in any other kind of communication.

Conversational style usually mirrors the participants' relationship. This means that, in most cases, *informal* language forms are chosen and *personal* information is shared. Conversations are also *spontaneous,* or locally managed. Participants make up a conversation as they go along, taking their cues from one another. Thus, conversations are characterized by hesitations, restatements, repairs, and fillers, devices that signal the absence of strategy and build trust.

Some forms of discourse are publicly accessible; they are open to a large audience and are "on the record." Conversations, on the other hand, are *pri-*

vate; they are owned by the immediate participants, and, in many cases, it is a violation of trust to repeat what is said. Even when conversations are recorded (for example, by conversation analysts), outsiders have difficulty making sense of them, because individuals use *implicit,* private codes and personal "shorthands." Through these means, they reinforce the uniqueness of their bond. This is important because the overall orientation of conversation is often *relational.* Although people may accomplish tasks through conversation, they may converse simply to pass the time and to get to know one another. More formal kinds of talk seldom focus on purely relational matters.

> *Conversations are private; they are owned by the immediate participants, and, in many cases, it is a violation of trust to repeat what is said.*

Describing Classroom Interaction

Nonprivate forms of discourse are quite different in both style and substance from private forms of talk. To understand some of these differences, let's consider the characteristics of a familiar form of communication: classroom discourse. Whether or not we admit it, the defining characteristic of classroom discourse is a *nonegalitarian* distribution of power. In almost all cases, a teacher has

> *Conversation is the most private and personal form of communication. Through conversation we create and maintain relationships while exploring and developing a sense of self.*

more power than a student. The teacher chooses the text, makes the assignments, and gives the grades. As a result, interaction is *nonreciprocal*. In a typical lecture-discussion class, teachers talk more than do students and set the topics for discussion. Although both students and teachers ask questions, the functions of these questions differ. Presumably, students ask questions to acquire information, whereas teachers already know the answers to the questions they ask.

> *Whether or not we admit it, the defining characteristic of classroom discourse is a nonegalitarian distribution of power.*

Degree of language formality varies, but generally the syntax and vocabulary used in the classroom are *formal*, and topics are relatively *impersonal*. Certainly, classroom discourse contains more jargon than do private forms of talk. Teachers' talk is also *scripted*. If being too prepared in a conversation makes a speaker seem manipulative, being unprepared in the classroom destroys a teacher's credibility. Most teachers preplan their lectures, and some use the same jokes and examples from one year to the next. One of the most difficult tasks in good teaching is finding a way to make standard material fresh.

Classroom material is *publicly accessible* and generally *explicit*, and clarity is required. Finally, although teachers and students do build personal relationships, the business of the classroom is instruction, and most classes stay *task oriented*.

Dimensions of Discourse

The dimensions we have used to describe conversations and classroom discourse are summarized in Table 4-3. These dimensions define some of the important differences between private and public forms of talk and may be

TABLE 4-3

Dimensions of Private and Public Discourse

Private Discourse	Discourse Dimension	Public Discourse
reciprocal	interaction pattern	nonreciprocal
egalitarian	power distribution	nonegalitarian
personal/informal	language choice	impersonal/formal
spontaneous	amount of forethought	scripted
privately owned	information accessibility	publicly accessible
implicit	meanings	explicit
relational	orientation	task oriented

used as tools to analyze the structure and function of any discourse form. Although you may never have thought about these dimensions before, you have probably been using them. Every time you adjust the way you talk to a different social context, you show your tacit understanding of these dimensions. Being a sensitive and skilled communicator involves understanding that different kinds of discourse call for different ways of using language and knowing the kinds of changes that are called for. We will return to these differences in more detail in chapters 6 through 9, where we'll discuss the nature and goals of interpersonal, group, public, and mass communication.

Interactive Discourse: Coherence and Structure

In addition to knowing the dimensions that describe general forms of discourse, communicators must follow specific rules in order to coordinate communication. This knowledge is of particular concern when communication is highly interactive. In interactive discourse, communicators must be particularly sensitive to coherence and structure.

Coordinating Conversational Moves

Whether we are in a relatively formal interaction, such as the classroom, or a more spontaneous private conversation, we must follow some basic rules, if interaction is to be smooth and effective. Conversational content is governed by expectations. What you say, how you say it, and how much you say about it are all matters of convention. When pragmatic conventions are violated, receivers make assumptions about senders' intentions, assumptions that can completely change the meaning of an utterance.

In his discussion of the cooperative principle and conversational maxims, H. P. Grice has described the most basic and simple of the conventions that guide talk.[17] **The cooperative principle** asserts that for talk to work, communicators must be willing to cooperate with one another by speaking in socially approved ways. To cooperate, they must follow four **conversational maxims,** or rules. First, they must make sure their contributions contain enough, but not too much, information. This is the **quantity maxim.** Second, speakers must be truthful. If they say something patently absurd, they violate the **quality maxim.** Speakers must also be sure their contributions are direct and pertinent; otherwise, they refuse to follow the **relevancy maxim.** Finally, speakers should follow the **manner maxim;** they should be

> *In order for talk to work, communicators must be willing to cooperate with one another by speaking in socially approved ways.*

direct and clear. What happens when communicators don't follow these rules? If communicators violate the maxims repeatedly, conversation becomes impossible. No one can carry on a conversation with someone who has no regard for truth or relevance, whose style is unclear, and who has no concept of an appropriate amount of talk. Were we to not believe that most people try to be cooperative most of the time, communication would become meaningless.

This does not mean that maxims are never violated, however. Sometimes we violate a maxim intentionally to send an indirect message. If, for example, Harry asks Sally a personal question and she responds, "Nice weather," her violation of the relevancy maxim probably means that she finds Harry's question too personal. If he's sensitive to pragmatic rules, he understands her indirect meaning and has the good grace to change the subject. In this example, interpreting Sally's meaning involves complex social knowledge, for her meaning is not just in the words she utters but in the fact that she purposefully violates a conversational maxim. What lesson can we draw from Grice's analysis? It suggests that *to make sense, communicators must act cooperatively; when they fail to do so by violating conversational conventions, meaning is always affected.*

One defining characteristic of conversation is its sequential nature. For conversation to work, each move must follow the previous move and must fit into the overall conversation. This means that *speakers must keep track of what is going on as they talk and must build off others' contributions without losing sight of the goal of the conversation.* This is by no means easy, and conversation analysts have spent a great deal of time and effort outlining the mechanisms that make this coordination possible. Communicators must do something more as well. *Communicators must be able to take turns, and they must know when it is time to make a conversational move.* In conversation, knowing whose turn it is may be tricky. Communicators must respond when called upon but must not interrupt. In formal classroom discourse, the convention of raising your hand helps regulate turn taking. In informal conversations, communicators must rely on subtle sets of linguistic and nonverbal cues that indicate whether the present speaker wants to continue or is relinquishing a turn. Although conversational turns commonly overlap a bit, true interruptions are social blunders and are often read as attempts to dominate.

Given the complexity of conversation, it isn't surprising that people occasionally lose track of what is going on and misunderstand one another. A final skill that communicators need is conversational repair. *Conversational partners must be able to head off problems before they occur or, if these attempts fail, to repair misunderstandings.* By using disclaimers and licenses,

> *Given the complexity of conversation, it isn't surprising that people occasionally lose track of what is going on and misunderstand one another.*

communicators can ask their partners for special understanding. "I'm not sure if I have this right, but I heard . . ." or "Now, hear me out before you object . . ." keep the conversation from breaking down. If these efforts fail, communicators must be able to explain misunderstandings and realign the conversation by making what are called conversational repairs.

Conversational Closings

To know what to say when, speakers must also understand the special expectations that govern discourse structures. Each form of communication, from the nightly newscast to the everyday conversation, has its own internal structure. A speech, for example, can be divided into a beginning, a middle, and an end, each of which accomplishes a different communicative goal. In this section we'll illustrate the importance of structural conventions by taking a brief look at one aspect of structure: conversational endings. We'll see that even in this relatively spontaneous form of interaction, people have definite expectations for what should occur—expectations the competent communicator must recognize and follow.

Endings have to do quite a bit of social work. They must signal that interaction is about to wind down, establish a sense of closure, reassure participants that the interaction has been successful, and establish conditions for future interaction. Often they also contain specific directions for future behavior on the part of both speaker and listener.

Endings have to be signaled in advance. To get up and walk out when one has nothing more to say is unconscionably rude. Often participants pre-announce an ending. A statement about upcoming commitments ("I suppose I should get back to work soon") or a metacommunication about the interaction ("I'm so glad we could get together") lets participants know the conversation is drawing to an end. A good conversational ending also contains a statement of concern and goodwill ("It was great to see you," or, "Take care") as well as a brief summary of conversational themes ("Now, don't worry; things will work out," or, "Thanks for the advice").

Because it is easy to read an ending as abandonment, conversational partners must give a reason for ending a conversation. As Robin Lakoff points out, "Farewells stress the speaker's unwillingness to depart, offering it as a necessity imposed by cruel circumstances rather than the speaker's desire. We say, 'Gotta go!' not, 'Wanna go!'"[18]

The convention of treating all interactions as successful ones is so strong that it occurs even if the parties have no intention of seeing each other again. Even on a blind date that has not worked out, it is polite to say something such as, "I had a nice time. I'll call you sometime." Although both parties may realize this is a polite fiction, it is less socially damaging than admitting, "The world would have to end before I'd go out with you again."

Endings are equally important in other forms of discourse. In courtroom communication, for example, the summation is a lawyer's last chance to impress the jury; it is here that he or she will summarize arguments and make the strongest appeals. Conclusions are equally privileged in public speeches. Beginning students of public speaking often make the mistake of trailing off ineffectually, thus undermining the entire effect of their speech.

Endings are only one part of discourse structure. To be truly competent communicators, we must understand the entire structure of a given kind of discourse. (Beginnings, for example, are another part of messages that do a lot of social work.) Although some forms of discourse are structured and formulaic and others are open and subject to spontaneous definition, all must be organized properly if they are to be effective.

Guidelines for Understanding Discourse

To communicate sucessfully, we must master many types of discourse. We must know the purpose, rules, and stylistic properties of each type, and we must be aware of hidden assumptions and unintended effects. To become more aware of the way a specific form of discourse works, we should ask ourselves the four sets of questions listed below.[19]

1. *What is the purpose of this discourse?*
   What do I and my partners hope to achieve? Do we agree about the purpose of this interaction? What would mark the success of this discourse, and what would mark its failure?

2. *What rules regulate this discourse?*
   What speech acts are expected of each participant? What speech acts are precluded?

3. *What are the normal style and structure of this discourse?*
   What specialized language choices are called for? How does one begin and end interaction? How might meanings here differ from those elsewhere?

4. *What are the effects of engaging in this form of discourse?*
   What values and assumptions are presupposed in this discourse? Do I agree with these beliefs? Can this discourse be used to manipulate or dominate? How?

Language and Social Identity

Although modes of discourse dictate certain language choices, they do not completely control communication. Not every teacher or public speaker or lawyer communicates in the same way. In this section we will look at how group memberships affect language use, beginning with one of our most important group identities: gender.

Genderlects: When Men's and Women's Talk Differs

A **dialect** is a local or regional variation of a language. People from different dialect communities speak a single common language, yet at the same time each dialect community has its own unique pronunciations, vocabularies, grammar rules, and usage norms. When dialect differences are large, people who speak the same language may nevertheless be unable to understand one another.

Recently, a number of scholars have argued that men and women use language in different habitual ways. These scholars have coined the term **genderlect** to refer to linguistic variations based on gender. In *You Just Don't Understand*, linguist Deborah Tannen discusses some of the ways genderlects can lead to miscommunication.[20]

Let's begin with a few examples. On the way to visit friends in another part of the city, Juan and Denise get lost. Denise suggests they stop and ask the way, but Juan refuses. He feels uncomfortable asking for help and believes there's no guarantee that a stranger will give accurate information anyway. He'd prefer to drive around until he finds the way. This doesn't make sense to Denise, who isn't at all embarrassed about asking for information and believes that anyone who doesn't know the way should admit it.

Maria can't wait until Tom gets home from work, so that they can talk about the day. As Tom enters the house, Maria begins a barrage of questions. What did he do? How was his presentation? Where did he and his colleagues go for lunch, and what did everyone order? She is interested in every detail, and his evasive answers hurt her. Tom, on the other hand, feels overwhelmed by Maria's "third degree" about details he barely noticed.

Michael's friends ask if it's okay to come over to watch the game on Friday. Michael says, "Sure." When he tells his girlfriend, Alyssa, she's upset—not because the friends are coming, but because Michael didn't consult her first. Had the situation been reversed, she would have asked. In fact, "I have to check with Mike" would have been a way for her to let others know that she's part of a couple. For Michael, however, asking Alyssa implies he needs to get permission. As a result of these differences, Michael thinks Alyssa is unreasonable, and she sees him as insensitive.

Deborah Tannen believes that misunderstandings like these occur because men and women grow up in different cultures. Women's culture, she believes, stresses intimacy and connection, whereas men's culture values autonomy and individual achievement. These orientations affect men's and women's topics of conversation, their conversational styles, and their interpretations of one another's meanings.

The Development of Gender Differences

Social scientists tell us we are the victims of gender expectations from the moment of birth. The first question most people ask after a child is born is "Is it a boy or a girl?" And once this question is answered, our perceptions and expectations change markedly. Psychologists John and Sandra Condry asked people to interpret why a newborn was crying. Those who were told the baby was a boy were likely to interpret his first act of communication as anger. Those who were informed the baby was a girl assumed she was afraid.[21]

As boys and girls grow up, their behaviors come to match these expectations. Play is a case in point. Boys' games tend to stress freedom and competition, whereas girls' games encourage intimacy and status equality. Boys are more likely to interact in large, hierarchically structured groups, playing rule-bound games with winners and losers. Boasting, mocking insults, and teasing often accompany boys' play. Girls, on the other hand, often play in smaller groups within which everyone gets a turn. Being directive or competitive is looked upon as "bossy" in girls' play. Girls try to avoid the appearance of conflict by proposing rather than ordering. Instead of saying, "You stand over there," girls are more likely to say, "Let's get in a circle, okay?" or, "What if you stand at that corner?" Girls' play may also be less physically active and more verbal than that of boys. Later in life, men continue to bond through shared physical activity, and women through talk.[22]

As boys and girls grow older, they develop characteristic conversational styles. One example is the way each gender responds to "trouble talk." A number of studies show that a boy often responds to another boy's report of a problem by dismissing or downplaying it or by giving straightforward advice on how to solve it. A girl, on the other hand, is likely to respond with trouble talk of her own.

This characteristic holds true in storytelling as well. Males often tell stories about contests in which they acted as either protagonist or antagonist and in which they ultimately succeeded. Females often tell stories about times when they or others violated social rules and consequently looked bad. Females exorcise their social failures by talking about them. Males, on the other hand, prefer to ignore failures and to focus on achievement. Tannen comments, "If men see life in terms of contest, a struggle against nature and other men, for women life is a struggle against the danger of being cut off from their community."[23]

In adulthood these patterns persist, and a verbal division of labor takes place. Women specialize in relationally oriented talk, whereas men specialize in task-oriented talk. Tannen uses the terms **rapport talk** and **report talk** to get at these differences. Rapport talk focuses on relational meaning; it is most appropriate for interpersonal topics and feels most natural in intimate contexts. Report talk focuses on content; as a style, it is appropriate in public situations when decision making or opinion exchange is expected.

This division of labor has its drawbacks. Men may feel uncomfortable when women want to analyze relationships and discuss feelings, and women may feel reluctant to assert their opinions in public, especially when men are present. Men's comparative silence on relational matters and their reluctance to share intimate details of their daily lives may make them appear remote. Women's unwillingness to compete for the floor and their tendency to agree rather than to argue may make them seem unknowledgeable and dull. Neither impression is accurate, but differences in genderlect make each appear so.

Tannen believes the key to understanding genderlects is that men grow up in a more hierarchically structured culture than do women. Men see the world as more competitive, and they feel most comfortable when they are carving out an individual space for themselves. Women, on the other hand, grow up in a culture that stresses equality and connection. They would rather put themselves down than build themselves up, and they feel uncomfortable with conflict and competition. Understanding these differences can explain some of the behaviors we find puzzling in one another. It can explain why many men would rather drive around for hours than ask directions (and reveal their lack of control). It can explain why many women want to know every detail of a man's day the minute he walks through the door (to build intimacy through shared talk). And it can also explain why a simple statement such as "I have to check with X" can be interpreted in entirely different ways.

Adapting to Gender Differences

The differences we have discussed are only a small part of a growing literature on gender differences in communication. Additional findings are summarized in Table 4-4 on page 107. While thinking about this information, however, keep two things in mind. First, the gender differences we have been discussing are, for the most part, culturally determined. As our culture changes, we can assume that genderlects will change too. Second, gender differences do not apply to all men and all women; they are not absolute. Not all women are sensitive, nor are all men competitive.

What can be done to ensure smoother communication between men and women? One way to avoid misunderstandings is to develop more flexibility in our styles. Women who have trouble dealing with conflict can learn that controversy is not a threat to intimacy. Men who feel uncomfortable when their position in the social hierarchy is questioned can learn that interdependence does not undermine status. And both men and women can learn when to defer to others and when to compete with them. We are likely to experience the most trouble when we respond unthinkingly in a single genderlect. As Tannen tells us,

> *There is nothing inherently wrong with automatic behavior. If we did not do most things automatically, it would take massive concentration and energy to do anything. But by becoming aware of our ways of talking and how effective they are, we can override our automatic impulses and adapt our habitual styles when they are not serving us well.*[24]

Group Identity and Rhetorical Style

All our group identities, not merely gender, have some impact on linguistic style. Ernest Bormann describes the ways in which social identity shapes discourse processes. To Bormann, a **rhetorical community** is a group of people who share rules, customs, and conventions about the nature of discourse. People within a rhetorical community share a common **rhetorical style,** or way of using language. For example, therapists share a rhetorical style, for the therapeutic enterprise calls for a form of discourse that differs radically from normal conversation. It is a kind of talk that encourages patients to disclose intimate details and that espouses unconditional acceptance as the norm. It is also a nonreciprocal form of interaction: the therapist, while collaborating with the patient in constructing a shared story, does not offer personal details of his or her own life. Over time, members of a rhetorical community come to share a common **rhetorical vision** that includes a consensus on what can or cannot be said and on what is or is not good communication. The therapeutic community is just one example of a rhetorical community. Other communities may be based on professional affiliation (academics form a rhetorical community, as do physicians or scientists), political affiliation (Marxists and conservatives belong to different rhetorical communities and share different rhetorical visions), or religious beliefs and values.

Quantity of Talk: *Who Talks the Most?*
- In task-oriented cross-gender groups, men talk more than do women.
- In friendly same-gender dyads, women prefer to spend time talking; men prefer to share activities like sports or hobbies.

Topics of Talk: *What Do Men and Women Talk About?*
- Women talk more about private matters (family, relational problems, other women, men, clothing) than do men.
- Men talk more about public matters (sports, money, and news) than do women.
- Women and men both talk about work and sexual relationships.

Vocabulary: *Do Women and Men Use Different Words?*
- Women are reported to use more detailed color terms (*mauve, teal*) than do men.
- Women more often use weaker expletives (*Oh dear, Oh my*), whereas men more often use stronger expletives, including obscenities.
- Women use certain evaluative adjectives (*adorable, cute, fabulous*) that men do not use.

Grammatical Constructions: *Does Men's and Women's Syntax Differ?*
- Women use more qualifiers (*somewhat, kind of, I guess*) than do men.
- Women use more disclaimers (*I'm no expert, but . . . , Don't get mad, but . . .*) than do men.
- Women use more tag questions (*Right? You know?*) than do men.
- Women are more likely to use polite forms than are men.

Turn Taking: *Who Controls Interaction Flow?*
- In cross-gender dyads, men interrupt women more than women interrupt men.
- Women ask more questions and men make more statements during interaction.
- Men often respond to women using delayed minimal responses (*Oh* or *right,* said after a brief pause) that discourage interaction; women's minimal responses (*hmmm, I see*) occur within turns and seem to encourage talk.

Topic Control: *Who Chooses the Topics of Talk?*
- Men successfully initiate topics more often than do women.

Humor: *Do Women or Men Tell More Jokes?*
- Boys and men offer more jokes and witticisms than do girls or women.
- Girls and women laugh more than do boys or men.

Self-Disclosure: *Are Men or Women More Open?*
- Women tend both to disclose more and to receive more disclosures from others than do men.

Note. Current research supports these conclusions; however, not every study concurs, and some contradictory findings exist.

Adapted from research reviewed by Laurie P. Arliss in *Gender Communication,* 1991, Englewood Cliffs, NJ: Prentice-Hall.

Today's hip-hop culture provides another interesting example of a rhetorical community. In his book, *Fresh Fly Flavor,* MTV personality Fab 5 Freddy describes the words and phrases that make up the rhetorical style of the hip-hop generation. In the introduction, James Bernard traces the language of today's rap fans to jazz musicians of the twenties and explains the personal and cultural importance of this new way of talking:

> *Twisting and churning the Queen's English, these jazz greats made language work for them. In their hands, it became a tool for liberation that they flaunted as defiantly as they flaunted social conventions, creating their own smoky, hep-cat world in those late night clubs where they could roam freely. . . . Rappers took this linguistic inventiveness one step further: they created an entire subculture based on hijacking the English language.*[25]

Language Choices and Pragmatic Effects

One of the themes of this chapter is that language gives us power. Our linguistic choices count: they make a difference in our lives and in those of others. If we use language wisely, we can control communication; if we do not, communication can have unintended effects. In this section we look at some of the effects of using four kinds of language. We'll discuss ambiguity, immediacy, abstraction, and figurative language.

Ambiguity: When Not Making Sense Makes Sense

You've been told that language should be concrete, simple, direct, and straightforward. You've been warned that ambiguity diminishes communication. Often this is true. In many situations clarity is the measure of the success of a message. Legal documents or technical instructions, for example, must be precise. But clarity is not always advantageous, and ambiguity can sometimes help, rather than hinder, communication.

Eric Eisenberg, an expert in organizational communication, discusses positive effects of using **ambiguous language,** language that can be interpreted in more than one way.[26] First, ambiguous language can give an organization the flexibility to adapt to future contingencies. When a university issues the statement "The University shall be responsive to its surroundings," the university is being deliberately ambiguous. It is assuring members of the surrounding community of its intention to act in good faith while leaving itself room to develop policy. On an interpersonal level, ambiguity allows members of organizations to perceive themselves as similar rather than different. Because similarity is a basic factor in attraction, ambiguity can increase group solidarity. We often employ strategic ambiguity unconsciously. For example, the first stages of group formation involve a great deal of ambiguity. Here, ambiguity allows members to avoid disagreements until the group is cohesive enough to deal with stress.

Eisenberg points out that people with high credibility often benefit most from ambiguity. If one's credibility is already high, clarity is more likely to decrease than to increase it. Strategic ambiguity also allows one to deny a stand if it should become unpopular. "That's not what I meant at all" gives a person a way to back down gracefully.

Janet Beaven Bavelas and her colleagues suggest that **equivocal communication,** another term used to describe ambiguous communication, is most often used when a communicator feels trapped between two unpleasant alternatives. When speaking the truth and lying are both problematic, people often equivocate. Ask yourself which response you would choose in each of the following situations:[27]

A fellow student has just given a class presentation. It was very badly done. After class he asks you, "How did I do?" Which response is best?
   a. You did very well. I really liked it.
   b. You were terrible; bad job.
   c. Not well, but don't feel bad about it.
   d. You were braver than I would be!

You have received a gift from someone you really like a lot, but the gift is awful. How would you respond?
   a. The gift is perfect; I really love it.
   b. I don't like the gift and am going to exchange it.
   c. I like you, but I don't like the gift.
   d. I appreciate your thoughtfulness.

You are torn between loyalties to two people you know and like equally well. Ann worked for you at one time. Bob is thinking of hiring Ann. Unfortunately, Ann is nice but incompetent. You must write a letter of reference. What would you say?
   a. Ann was an excellent employee; I recommend her.
   b. Don't hire Ann; she was not a good employee.
   c. Ann is a nice person but not a good employee.
   d. It's been years since I employed Ann, so I can't answer specifically.

In each case, *d* is the equivocal response. If you are like most people, you were probably tempted to use ambiguity in at least one of these cases, for it is a way of reponding to an uncomfortable situation without lying or hurting someone's feelings. Communication specialists differ in their evaluation of this form

Despite gender differences, men and women can communicate as equals if we are willing to develop more flexibility in our language style.

of communication. Some decry it as deceptive and misleading and tell us we should always be honest. Others, like Bavelas, defend it:

> *Equivocation is not the deliberately deceitful "dirty old man" of communication. It is subtle, often commendable, and entirely understandable, if only the observer will expand his or her analysis to include the communicative situation. . . . In our experience, real living messages do not fit prescriptive and judgmental models; they are more subtle, more skillful, and more interesting.*[28]

Immediacy: Up Close and Personal

Language can be inclusive or exclusive. It can place the listener at a distance or forge a close and personal bond.[29] **Immediate language** is personalized language, and it can be very effective in persuasive situations. Consider the following excerpt from a televised speech:

> *This historic room and the presidency belong to you. It is your right and responsibility every four years to give temporary custody of this office and of the institution of the presidency. You so honored me, and I am grateful–grateful and proud of what together we have accomplished.*

The speaker was President Ronald Reagan, and the occasion was the 1984 announcement of his decision to run for a second term.[30] This speech illustrates an effective use of immediacy. Reagan involves us directly and personally. We feel we are a part of his presidency, although what exactly "we" did together is not specified. Critics might say that this use of immediacy is misleading, yet it is certainly effective.

Empirical studies show that the use of verbal immediacy in public situations has positive effects, increasing ratings of a speaker's competence, character, similarity to audience members, and degree of relaxation, especially when the speaker agrees with audience members.[31] Immediacy is also effective in interpersonal contexts. If, however, it is blatantly used to create a bond where none exists, it can backfire. A low-status speaker might offend someone of higher status by being too familiar. Sometimes norms for considerateness preclude being too immediate. As communicators, we must find a balance between familiarity and polite deference.[32]

Abstraction: Creating General Categories

I remember in complete detail my grandmother's house. If I close my eyes, I can picture the garden in back and the broad veranda where I played as a child. When I speak of this place, I use the word *house*. Yet no single thing called "house" exists, only particular houses, such as the ones you and I grew up in. A house has no particular color, shape, or size. It is simply a structure used for human habitation. "House" is an **abstraction,** a synthesis of what many houses have in common. All words are abstractions, although some are more general than others. To call my grandmother's house a "dwelling unit" or an "abode" is to abstract it even further, and to abstract something is to make it less real.

Of course, abstraction is necessary. Abstract concepts allow us to talk about the future, to make predictions, and to think logically and mathematically. In Robin Lakoff's terms, it is "the basis of science, crucial to human understanding and the growth of our intellect and to our power as a species over the physical universe. It has made us what we are."[33]

Abstract language can also be false and dangerous. It is the basis of stereotyping. When my grandmother's house becomes merely a "house," it loses its individuality; it is reduced to a series of general qualities. Similarly, when my neighbor becomes a "New Yorker" or a "teacher" or an "American," she loses her uniqueness. Your idea of what she is like is shaped by these abstractions. Finally, when some people become "we" and others "they," the way is paved for misunderstanding and abuse.

Metaphors We Live By

We usually think of metaphors as devices that poets use, not as a feature of everyday talk. Metaphors, however, are found in every kind of discourse, and their presence affects us in interesting and important ways. A **metaphor** is a linguistic usage that allows us to understand and experience one thing in terms of another. Metaphors guide our thoughts and actions.

George Lakoff and Mark Johnson illustrate the pervasiveness of metaphor by looking at the common ways we talk about argument.[34] What underlying comparison is common to the following statements?

He *attacked every weak point* in my argument.
His criticisms were *right on target*.
I *demolished* his argument.
He *shot down* all my arguments.

The metaphor is that argument is a war—a common way of viewing argument in our culture. Lakoff and Johnson ask us to imagine instead another kind of culture,

[where] argument is viewed as a dance, the participants are seen as performers, and the goal is to perform in a balanced and aesthetically pleasing way. In such a culture, people would view arguments differently, carry them out differently, and talk about them differently.[35]

Metaphors allow us to grasp abstract or difficult concepts in terms of more understandable ideas. In doing so, however, they highlight some aspects of the concept and downplay others. Let's look at some common metaphors used to describe love. Love can be thought of as a physical force ("There's electricity between us," "When we're together, sparks fly"); as mystic power ("She's bewitching," "The magic is gone"); as madness ("I'm crazy about him"); or as war ("She conquered my heart," "He's besieged by women"). Each of these metaphors calls our attention to a different kind of experience and legitimizes a different kind of behavior. If love is a physical force or mystic power, it is beyond our control; there's nothing we can do but let it wash over us. If love is madness, then irrational behavior is defensible. What if, however, we were to think of love in a new way, as a collaborative work of art? Following from this metaphor, love would be something to be worked on, something that takes shape over time, and something that is beautiful and precious. Our reactions to and experience of love would be significantly different.

Lakoff and Johnson believe that the metaphors we live by have a political dimension. Metaphors are often imposed on us by people in power: politicians, religious leaders, economists, and advertisers control us by creating metaphorical values. Once we come to believe in a given metaphor, say, "Bigger is better" or "More is good," then it becomes difficult to see the world in any other way. Accumulation is valorized, and behaviors such as conservation are devalued. When, in *1984*, the architects of Newspeak force the masses to believe that war is peace, freedom is slavery, and ignorance is strength, they create ideological metaphors. Although metaphors can illuminate the way we see the world, they can also blind us. Metaphors, like other language choices, can shape our actions and experiences. They can give us power, or they can control us.

Improving Language Choices

Language is a powerful tool. It allows us to abstract and store experiences and to share them with others. It allows us to make contact with and to influence, regulate, persuade, and dominate one another. It makes us the humans we are. And yet, despite the great power it gives us, language also exerts power over us. Our thoughts and perceptions are filtered through language and can be distorted by it. In the words of Aldous Huxley, "Possessing language, we are . . . capable of intellectual achievements beyond the scope of any animal, but at the same time capable of systematic silliness and stupidity such as no dumb beast could ever dream of."[36] It is important, then, that we use language with care and sensitivity, realizing that it can lead us astray as often as it can lead us to the truth.

Throughout this chapter we've explored the social nature of language. We've seen that words are social agreements, agreements to express ideas in similar ways. We get into trouble if we start believing that words are complete and accurate reflections of reality. We should *always remember that talking about something doesn't necessarily mean it is real*. Language has a peculiar tendency to **reify** concepts, to make us believe that they are tangible and real rather than fallible human constructions. Two old sayings remind us not to confuse reality with talk: "The map is not the territory" and "The word is not the thing."

Another important principle to keep in mind is that meanings are in people, not in words. Although we share a language with others, we each shade its words and phrases with our own experiences. Meanings are by no means objective, and, as our discussion of speech acts points out, we often mean more than we say and say less than we mean. *Uncovering meaning involves making inferences about the communicative intentions of others*. Only a madman would take as literal everything others say. A sane and competent communicator recognizes that language involves a great deal of social inference. One should always be careful to *take context into account both when interpreting others' messages and when creating one's own*.

> *Meanings are by no means objective, and we often mean more than we say and say less than we mean.*

When we encode messages through spoken language, we have to make choices. *There is no single right way to use language; language choices must depend on our purposes, our audience, and the conventions of the discourse form we use*. We use a specific kind of language to sell a used car, host a TV talk show, tell a joke, deliver a public speech, or talk to a stranger at a party. Each form of communication has its own linguistic conventions. Although most of the time language that is direct, clear, concrete, and straightforward is preferred, there are also appropriate times for ambiguity, abstraction, and figurative language. Making language choices is no simple matter. It requires sensitivity to others, a clear sense of one's own communicative intent, a great deal of social knowledge, and an overall understanding of the communication process.

Summary

Although we use many encoding systems, the one most natural to us is spoken language. Spoken language has four important characteristics: it is symbolic, it is a kind of knowledge, it is rule-governed and productive, and it affects the way we experience the world. The first step in understanding language is to grasp the concepts of symbol and sign. A sign is any mode of expression that connects an idea (the signified) to a form (the signifier). When the signifier is an arbitrary and conventional creation of the human imagination, it is a special kind of sign known as a symbol.

Language learning is not a matter of rote repetition. When we learn language, we learn implicit rules that allow us to generate and understand novel utterances. These rules are complex and interrelated, allowing us to make the sounds in our language and to combine these sounds into words and sentences. Ultimately, language practices affect the way we see the world, as the Sapir-Whorf hypothesis shows.

Language can be divided into several subsystems. The first is the sound system. Each language recognizes certain sounds as significant and ignores others. The significant sound distinctions in a given language are called phonemes. Phonemes are combined into units of meaning called morphemes. Morphemes are roughly equivalent to words, although a single word may consist of several morphemes. In practice, human utterances are made up of strings of words. The rules that govern the way words can be combined make up the syntax of language. Although knowing how to form words and make sentences is important for communication, an understanding of pragmatic rules, or rules governing language use, is also important.

When we talk, we do so for specific reasons. The goal we want to accomplish when we talk is called a speech act. According to CMM theory, speech acts are affected by four levels of context: episode, relationship, life script, and cultural pattern. The kind of communication appropriate to a given social context is called discourse. Each form of discourse has its own style and structure. Perhaps the most common form of discourse is everyday conversation. To be successful at conversation, individuals must work together cooperatively. Their talk must follow the conversational maxims of quantity, quality, relevancy, and manner. Communicators must keep track of the conversation as it unfolds, making sure their contributions fit into what has been said previously. They must also coordinate turn taking and be able to repair problems when they occur.

All forms of discourse, whether formal or spontaneous, have a certain shape or structure. One example of structure is the conversational closing. Closings must be carried out in specific ways. They must be signaled in advance and must include an explanation of why the conversation is ending.

Often they include statements of concern as well as summaries of what has happened. A communicator who does not understand discourse conventions such as the conversational closing will be at a social disadvantage.

People from different social groups use language differently, and this difference is often a source of social identity. One important group difference associated with language is gender. Some social scientists argue that men and women speak different genderlects. Studies suggest that men tend to prefer task-oriented or report talk, while women tend to specialize in relational or rapport talk. Gender, of course, is not the only group membership that affects language use.

Although social memberships affect language usage, we are free to make our own language choices, and the way we make these choices affects communicative success. The chapter closes with a discussion of the advantages and disadvantages of four choices: the choice between ambiguity and clarity, immediacy and distance, abstraction and concreteness, and figurative and nonfigurative language.

Key Terms

Listed below are the key terms used in this chapter, along with the number of the page where each is explained.

Review Questions

1. What is Newspeak? What does Newspeak illustrate about the relationship between language, thought, and power?

2. What is language? What four characteristics define it?

3. What is a sign? What are its two parts? What form does the signifier take in natural languages? in artificial languages? What is a symbol? What does it mean to say that symbols are arbitrary and conventional?

4. What is linguistic productivity? How does linguistic productivity prove that learning is more than a matter of trial and error?

5. What did the Carmichael experiments show? What does the Sapir-Whorf hypothesis state? What are its two corollaries? Give an example that illustrates the Sapir-Whorf hypothesis.

6. What are euphemisms and jargon? Why do people use them? What are their effects?

7. What is phonology? What are phonemes? What is semantics? What is a free morpheme? a bound morpheme? What is syntax? pragmatics?

8. What is a speech act? Why do we need to understand speech acts in order to communicate? What five classes of speech acts have been identified?

9. Why is context important for pragmatic knowledge? According to CMM theory, what four levels of context must we take into account during communication? Think of an example of each level. How would each example affect communication?

10. What is discourse? What is conversation? How does conversation differ from other forms of interaction? What would happen to a conversation if any of its characteristics were to change? What are the typical characteristics of classroom discourse?

11. Conversational closings must do a certain amount of social work. What are the elements of a conversational closing? What happens if these elements are left out?

12. What four types of questions should you ask yourself to determine the rules of any form of discourse?

13. How do men's and women's genderlects differ? What is report talk? rapport talk? What is "trouble talk"? How do genderlect differences develop? What can be done to adapt to gender differences in communication?

14. What is a rhetorical community? Think of a specific rhetorical community, and identify its rhetorical style and rhetorical vision.

15. What are the advantages and disadvantages of ambiguous or equivocal language? What is immediate language, and when should it be used? How is it related to considerateness? What is abstraction? When can abstraction be useful and when dangerous? What are metaphors, and what political dimension may they have?

16. In general, how can language choices be improved?

Suggested Readings

Fab 5 Freddy. (1992). *Fresh fly flavor: Words and phrases of the hip-hop generation*. Stamford, CT: Longmeadow.

> Described as "a guide for the uninitiated and a checkpoint for hip-hop vets," this dictionary explains the latest words and phrases of the rap generation. If you're not sure what it means to be def, dope, or very fly, this source can tell you. Bus it.

Lutz, William. (1989). *Double-speak*. New York: Harper and Row.

> This book's subtitle tells it all: "From 'Revenue Enhancement' to 'Terminal Living,' How Government, Business, Advertisers, and Others Use Language to Deceive You." If you need some good examples of the more outrageous and deceptive uses of language, this popular book can provide them.

Nofsinger, Robert F. (1991). *Everyday conversation*. Newbury Park, CA: Sage.

> Nofsinger gives an excellent summary of the field of conversation analysis. If you want to understand more about the way conversations are structured and about the complex linguistic mechanisms that communicators use as they talk, this text provides a scholarly yet understandable introduction.

Tannen, Deborah. (1990). *You just don't understand: Women and men in conversation*. New York: Ballantine.

> Tannen has done a great deal to popularize the study of language and to apply linguistics to real-life problems. In this readable book, she explains why men and women don't always see eye to eye. Tannen contends that women and men grow up in separate cultures and learn different forms of speaking. Not everyone may agree, but Tannen makes her case well.

Lakoff, Robin Tolmach. (1992). *Talking power: The politics of language in our lives*. New York: Basic.

> Linguist Robin Lakoff discusses the political implications of language: how the way we talk is connected to power and status. Clear, readable, and fascinating, this book shows how we can be used by language.

Pinker, Steven. (1994). *The language instinct: How the mind creates language*. New York: William Morrow.

> Pinker explores the instinct that allows us to learn and use language. With humor and wit, he introduces us to the complex field of psycholinguistics.

Notes

1. Orwell, George. (1949). *Nineteen eighty-four*. New York: Harcourt, Brace & World, 311. See also the appendix on Newspeak.

2. Lutz, William. (1989). *Double-speak*. New York: Harper & Row, 9.

3. Fromkin, Victoria, & Rodman, Robert. (1988). *An introduction to language* (4th ed.). New York: Holt, Rinehart and Winston, 4.

4. Saussure, Ferdinand de. (1966). *Course in general linguistics*. London: McGraw-Hill.

5. Aristotle. (1963). *De interpretatione* (J. L. Ackrill, Trans.). Clarendon Aristotle Series. Oxford: Oxford University Press, 43; Arnauld, A., & Lancelot, C. (1968). *Grammaire de Port-Royal* (R. Alston, Ed. and Trans.). Menston, Eng.: Scolar, 22; cited and discussed in Sperber, Dan, & Wilson, Deirdre. (1986). *Relevance: Communication and cognition*. Cambridge: Harvard University Press, 5–6.

6. Carmichael, L., Hogan, H. P., & Walter, A. A. (1932). An experimental study of the effect of language on the representation of visually perceived form. *Journal of Experimental Psychology, 15,* 73–86; Slobin, Dan. (1971). *Psycholinguistics*. Glenview, IL: Scott, Foresman, 103.

7. Mandelbaum, D. B. (Ed). (1958). *Selected writings of Edward Sapir in language, culture and personality*. Berkeley: University of California Press, 162.

8. Slobin, 129.

9. Cohn, Carol. (1987). Sex and death in the rational world of defense intellectuals. *Signs: Journal of Women in Culture and Society, 12* (4), 690.

10. The latter example is taken from Lutz, 176. For additional examples, see 175–177.

11. Cohn, 713.

12. Searle, John. (1969). *Speech acts: An essay in the philosophy of language.* Cambridge, Eng.: Cambridge University Press. A good explication is found in Nofsinger, Robert E. (1991). *Everyday conversation.* Newbury Park, CA: Sage.

13. The originators of CMM theory are Vernon Cronen and Barnett Pearce. One of the many sources on CMM is Cronen, Vernon, Pearce, W. Barnett, & Harris, Linda. (1982). The coordinated management of meaning. In Frank E. X. Dance (Ed.), *Comparative human communication theory.* New York: Harper & Row.

14. Lakoff, Robin Tolmach. (1992). *Talking power: The politics of language in our lives.* New York: Basic, 28.

15. McLaughlin, Margaret L. (1984). *Conversation: How talk is organized.* Beverly Hills: Sage, 271.

16. My discussion of the differences between public and private forms of talk is based in part on Lakoff's discussion, but her ideas have been modified. For a discussion of this distinction as applied to relationships, see Trenholm, Sarah, & Arthur Jensen. (1992). *Interpersonal communication* (2nd ed.). Belmont, CA: Wadsworth, chapter 2.

17. Grice, H. P. (1975). Logic and conversation. In P. Cole & J. Morgan (Eds.), *Syntax and semantics* (Vol. 3). New York: Academic, 41–58.

18. Lakoff, 45.

19. The four sets of questions were suggested by, but are not identical to, those used by Lakoff, 140.

20. Tannen, Deborah. (1990). *You just don't understand: Women and men in conversation.* New York: Ballantine.

21. Condry, John, & Condry, Sandra. (1976). Sex differences: A study of the eye of the beholder. *Child Development, 47,* 812–819; cited in Tannen, 1990, 228.

22. Tannen, 1990, 44; Maltz, Daniel N., & Borker, Ruth A. (1982). A cultural approach to male-female miscommunication. In John J. Gumperz (Ed.), *Language and social identity.* Cambridge: Cambridge University Press.

23. Tannen, 1990, 177–78.

24. Ibid., 95.

25. Bernard, James. (1992). Introduction. In Fab 5 Freddy, *Fresh fly flavor: Words and phrases of the hip-hop generation.* Stamford, CT: Longmeadow, 3.

26. Eisenberg, Eric M. (1984, September). Ambiguity as strategy in organizational communication. *Communication Monographs, 51,* 227–241.

27. Bavelas, Janet Beavin, Black, Alex, Chovil, Nicole, & Mullett, Jennifer. (1990). *Equivocal communication.* Newbury Park, CA: Sage. Situations are modified from those used by Bavelas (68, 69); response alternatives are verbatim.

28. Ibid., 260.

29. Mehrabian, Albert. (1967). Attitudes inferred from nonimmediacy of verbal communications. *Journal of Verbal Learning and Verbal Behavior, 6,* 294–95.

30. *San Francisco Chronicle,* 30 January, 1984.

31. Berger, Charles R., & Bradac, James J. (1982). *Language and social knowledge: Uncertainty in interpersonal relations.* London: Edward Arnold, 203–204.

32. Tannen, Deborah. (1984). *Conversational style.* Norwood, NJ: Ablex.

33. Lakoff, 180.

34. Lakoff, George, & Johnson, Mark. (1980). *Metaphors we live by.* Chicago: The University of Chicago Press, 4.

35. Ibid., 5.

36. Huxley, Aldous. (1962). Words and their meanings. In Max Black (Ed.), *The importance of language.* Englewood Cliffs, NJ: Prentice-Hall, 4–5.

5

Encoding Messages: Nonverbal Communication

Even when we are silent,

invisible messages

crowd around us:

colors excite us, sounds

calm us, the smell or look

or feel of another human

attracts or repels us.

We live not only in a world of words but in a world of silent messages. Every day we accompany our talk with the languages of gesture and posture, space and time. Even when we are silent, invisible messages crowd around us: colors excite us, sounds calm us, the smell or look or feel of another human attracts or repels us. To communicate fully, we must learn to speak these unspoken languages.

This chapter is about **nonverbal communication,** the study of communication systems that do not involve words. As we will see, many human behaviors convey messages—messages that can be understood as clearly as words. Picture, for example, the following scene, familiar from countless movies and TV shows. Two men, standing several yards apart, face one another in a dusty street. The street is otherwise deserted, although it is high noon. One man, clean-shaven, dressed in a light-colored western-style hat and wearing a tin star on his vest, stands straight and tall, his face betraying no emotion, his eyes steady and intent. The other, dressed all in black, a sneer on his face and a glint of hatred in his eye, stands opposite, his body tensed, his hands near the holsters he wears at his side. Though not a word has been spoken, we know that we are on the main street of a small town in the Old West, and we are about to witness a gunfight. We also know something about the character and motivation of the two men. By reading their posture and gesture, their facial expressions and the symbols in their dress, we know which is the "good guy" and which is the "bad guy." All this has been coded nonverbally in a familiar language of sight and sound.

In this chapter we examine the unspoken language that allows us to find meaning not only in this scene but also in the more typical scenes we encounter every day. We begin by defining nonverbal communication, looking at its nature and purpose. We then examine each of the codes that make up the nonverbal system: body movement and gesture; facial display and eye contact; vocal characteristics; time, space, and touch; and physical appearance and the use of artifacts. Once we have considered each code in turn, we will list some skills that can increase nonverbal effectiveness.

What Is Nonverbal Communication?

One of the problems of defining nonverbal communication is deciding what counts as a nonverbal message and what does not. Because all human behavior has the potential to create meaning, is all behavior communication? This question is more than academic; it has real-life implications. Consider an example. As Lorene sits waiting for her boyfriend, Jack, she swings her foot back and forth and repeatedly taps her keys on the edge of a chair. Is Lorene's behavior nonverbal communication? If we also know that Lorene is completely alone and is totally unaware of her behavior, most of us would answer no. Lorene is behaving, but she is not communicating. But what if the situation is slightly different? What if Lorene is angry with Jack and wants him to observe her anger? What if her impatient behaviors are meant to let Jack know he should be more punctual in the future? Is Lorene's behavior nonverbal communication in this case? Most of us would answer yes. Lorene is communicating, because she is intentionally creating a message for Jack's consumption.

Nonverbal communication is spontaneous, immediate, and natural. Body movement and gestures convey messages—messages that can be understood as clearly as words.

So far, it's been easy to see the difference between behavior and communication in our examples. Unfortunately, however, it's not always this simple. Assume now that Lorene is simply bored. She is not trying to send a message to Jack; she is totally unaware of her behavior. An observer, however, watches her and thinks, "That young woman looks tense and troubled. I wonder what's wrong." The observer received a message that Lorene did not intend to send, one that she would very likely deny sending if asked. This kind of unintended message is harder to classify. Some people would argue that Lorene's behavior is not communication, because Lorene is not aware of her observer. Others would counter that, whether or not she is aware of it, Lorene is sending a message and therefore is involved in communication.

Because unintended messages occur frequently and powerfully (and because it is often difficult to determine whether or not a message is intended), we will take the second view, including as nonverbal communication any instance in which a stimulus other than words creates meaning in either a sender's or a receiver's mind. According to this view, the first scenario cannot be called nonverbal communication, because no meaning was created. Both the second and third scenarios, however, can be called nonverbal communication from this viewpoint.

How Can We Know What Nonverbals Mean?

If we include unintentional behavior as nonverbal communication, how can we be certain that our perceptions are accurate? The answer is that we can't ever be completely sure, but we can take steps to increase our chances of making correct interpretations. Consider the following scene. Kelly shudders, crosses her arms, and moves away from Cliff. Should Cliff take this to mean he has offended Kelly? Perhaps. But what if Kelly is just cold? Cliff can't be sure unless he gets additional information. He can increase his probability of being correct in three ways. First, he can *check the context.* If a breeze is blowing through an open window and Kelly is covered with goose bumps, Cliff probably shouldn't lose sleep over her behavior; she is probably physically cold rather than irritated with him. A second way for Cliff to increase his accuracy is to *compare current behavior to baseline behavior.* If Kelly usually stands quite far from people, if her body posture is generally closed, and if she habitually crosses her arms, Cliff may conclude that she is simply the kind of person who needs a lot of personal space. If, however, Kelly is normally quite open, she is more likely responding to something Cliff has done. Cliff can use one final method to check his understanding. He can *ask for verbal feedback.* He can ask Kelly what her behavior means. Like Cliff, we should be aware that every nonverbal act has several different interpretations, and we should be careful not to settle on one too soon.

Characteristics of Nonverbal Communication

Nonverbal communication has a number of characteristics that distinguish it from other communication systems. We'll look at four.

Nonverbal Communication May Be Unintentional

This characteristic has important implications for our behavior as both senders and receivers. As receivers, we should not assume that every nonverbal act is an intentional message. We should always check for alternate interpretations, and we should realize that reading nonverbals is a risky business. As senders, we should be aware that unintended nonverbal messages can easily undermine and contradict what we really want to convey. We should expend extra effort to make our verbal and nonverbal messages congruent and clear.

Nonverbal Communication Consists of Multiple Codes

The nonverbal system is made up of a number of separate codes. To be successful communicators, we must become aware of how each of these codes works. We must also learn to coordinate codes. When nonverbal codes work together to send the same message, their impact is intensified. When they work at cross-purposes, confusion results. In an interview, for example, a confident smile can be undermined by nervous foot tapping, and a firm handshake can be off-set by a too-rigid stance. The competent communicator is able to use the full range of nonverbal codes in ways that enhance messages. Later in this chapter, we will look in detail at how these codes work. For now, Table 5-1 presents an overview.

> *When nonverbal codes work together to send the same message, their impact is intensified. When they work at cross-purposes, confusion results.*

Nonverbal Communication Is Immediate, Continuous, and Natural

Because nonverbals are physical extensions of our bodies, they are immediate. We can weigh our words, carefully compose our verbal messages, and wait for the right time and place before we speak. But we can't delay most nonverbal messages. They occur whenever we are face-to-face with one another. In this regard, we cannot not communicate.

TABLE 5-1

Some Basic Nonverbal Codes

Body Movement and Gesture (Kinesics)
- Emblems
- Illustrators
- Regulators
- Affect Displays
- Adaptors

Facial Expression and Eye Behavior
- Cultural display rules
- Professional display rules
- Personal display rules

Vocal Characteristics (Paralanguage)
- Vocal qualities
- Vocalizations
- Vocal segregates

Time (Chronemics)
- Psychological time orientation
- Biological time orientation
- Cultural time orientation

Space (Proxemics)
- Territoriality
- Spatial arrangement
- Personal space
- Touch (haptics)

Physical Appearance and Object Language
- Body type
- Dress
- Object language

Nonverbal messages are also more continuous than verbal messages. Nonverbal displays flow into one another without the discrete beginnings and endings that characterize words. If we try to isolate and separate nonverbal gestures, they lose meaning. Whether a raised arm is a greeting or a sign of impending attack can only be decided by its context.

> *If we try to isolate and separate nonverbal gestures, they lose meaning. Whether a raised arm is a greeting or a sign of impending attack can only be decided by its context.*

Finally, nonverbal messages are more natural and less arbitrary than their verbal counterparts. In most, form and meaning are connected. When we gesture to someone to come nearer, the gesture traces the path we want the person to take. When we show our concern by hugging someone, the hug is part of the natural act of comforting.

Nonverbal Communication Is Universal

Although not completely free of cultural convention, many nonverbals are understandable the world over. Paul Ekman and Wallace Friesen have shown, for example, that happiness, anger, disgust, fear, surprise, and sadness are conveyed in much the same way in many different cultures. Some hand gestures, such as pointing, also transcend culture. At a very basic level, therefore, we can communicate nonverbally with people whose verbal language we do not know.[1]

Not all nonverbal behaviors, however, have universal meaning. Even emotional displays are modified by cultural rules. Although a smile conveys happiness in most cultures, in some cultures it conveys other emotions, such as embarrassment or submission. In addition, the rules for how often and when to smile vary in different cultures. And when it comes to other kinds of nonverbal meanings, such as the use of time and space, quite dramatic cultural differences occur. The implication is clear: do not assume that everyone shares your own nonverbal rules.

What Meanings Are Best Conveyed Nonverbally?

Verbal and nonverbal codes do not operate in quite the same way. What may be expressed easily in one may often be quite difficult to express in the other. We therefore tend to rely on each of these codes in slightly different situations. As we shall see, nonverbal codes are especially useful for giving us information about personal and relational topics we would be embarrassed to talk about. They allow us to express certain emotional

> *Nonverbal codes are especially useful for giving us information about personal and relational topics we would be embarrassed to talk about.*

themes that are hard to describe verbally. Nonverbal codes also allow us to refine and expand upon verbal meanings. When something can't be put into words, we turn to nonverbal channels.

Making Initial Judgments

Nonverbal cues are often used to size up other people. It is important, sometimes even vital, to know the characteristics, attitudes, and intentions of others. In the early stages of an acquaintance, we seldom volunteer much verbal information about ourselves, nor do we feel comfortable asking others personal questions. This does not mean we ignore personal information; it simply means that we turn to nonverbal channels. Simply by looking, we can tell a lot about others. In addition to information about gender, race, and cultural identity, we can pick up cues about personality, attitude, and individual style. Nonverbal behaviors tell us whether others are friendly or hostile, shy or confident, gullible or worldly-wise. They help us determine the credibility and approachability of those around us.

> *Nonverbal behaviors tell us whether others are friendly or hostile, shy or confident, gullible or worldly-wise. They help us determine the credibility and approachability of those around us.*

Relational Information

Once we have sized up others and have decided to interact with them, nonverbal cues convey relational information, helping us keep track of how an interaction is going and what others think of us. According to Albert Mehrabian, three kinds of relational messages are exchanged nonverbally during every interaction: liking, status, and responsiveness.[2]

Liking is indicated through facial expression, eye contact, proximity, and the like. If a conversational partner smiles frequently and makes eye contact, we can be relatively sure he or she likes us. If, however, the partner avoids touch and stands at some distance, there's a good chance he or she does not like us very well. **Status** is often conveyed through posture and gesture, touch and proximity, as well as by the objects we display. Of two individuals, the one who controls the most space, initiates the most touch, and seems the most relaxed is probably the one of higher status. A person's display of expensive or rare objects is also a good indication of high status.

Responsiveness, the degree to which we are psychologically involved in an interaction, is shown by such cues as rate and volume of speech, amount of gesture, and variability of facial display. Someone who responds to us in a monotone, staring straight ahead with a dull, expressionless look, is indicating low involvement and low responsiveness. All of these messages tell us how we are faring in an interaction and give us cues about how to communicate.

Although we can ask people whether they like us, whether their status is higher than ours, and how involved they are in an interaction, this approach is rather awkward. Luckily, asking is usually unnecessary. Nonverbal communication gives us a clear picture of where we stand.

Emotional Expression

Another area in which nonverbal is more effective than verbal communication is emotional expression. When a child is frightened or unhappy, a comforting hug is worth more than a verbal explanation of why it doesn't help to cry. When we care about someone, we want to reach out and touch him or her. Talk is not an entirely adequate substitute for human contact, despite what telephone company slogans would have us believe. When people have something emotionally important to say, they need the full range of nonverbal channels. Of course, when they want to break off a relationship but also want to avoid an emotional scene, they may take the coward's way out and use a purely verbal channel, sending a "Dear John" or "Dean Joan" letter rather than announcing the breakup face-to-face.

Nonverbal Codes and Verbal Messages

Finally, nonverbal cues expand upon and clarify verbal messages. Nonverbal experts such as Paul Ekman and Mark Knapp have cataloged some of the ways nonverbal messages are used in conjunction with verbal messages.[3] Table 5-2 summarizes the six ways in which nonverbal messages modify verbal messages.

Sometimes we use nonverbal cues to **repeat** what we say verbally. If I'm giving you directions, I may say, "To get to my office, go down the stairs," and, to make sure you understand where I want you to go, I may point toward the stairs. This kind of redundancy helps ensure that verbal messages are accurately received. Nonverbal cues are also used to **contradict** verbal messages. Jason may turn to his wife, Isabel, and say, "I don't know why I ever married you. For two cents I'd get a divorce." His smile and friendly tone, however, contradict the harshness of his words and let her know he is just joking. Sarcastic comments are another example of contradiction. The words may be friendly, but the tone of voice gives the real message.

Why do people use sarcasm? Why don't they just come right out and say what they think? People sometimes use sarcasm to hide their hostility. If challenged, they can deny they meant anything negative. Joking and sarcasm are culturally recognized patterns; most people understand what their meaning really is. But other forms of contradiction are not easily deciphered, for example, when a close friend says to you, "I'm fine," but grimaces with pain, or when someone says, "I love you," in a cold, distant way. Communications like

TABLE 5-2

**Some Ways
Nonverbal
and Verbal
Messages
Interact**

Repeating	The nonverbal message repeats the verbal message; resulting redundancy can increase accuracy.
	Example: "I'll give you three minutes," said while holding up three fingers.
Contradicting	The nonverbal message undermines the verbal message, often causing confusion and uncertainty.
	Example: "I'm glad to see you," said with a sneer.
Substituting	A nonverbal message is used instead of a verbal message.
	Example: In answer to "How was your day?" the communicator just sighs and shakes his or her head.
Complementing	The nonverbal message modifies the verbal message, letting the receiver know how to take it.
	Example: "I love your gift," said with a huge smile.
Accenting	Nonverbal cues emphasize part of the verbal message.
	Example: "And the most important thing is . . .," said with vocal emphasis on the most important words.
Regulating	The nonverbal message manages and controls verbal behavior.
	Example: Looking at one's watch to let the speaker know it is time to go.

these send two opposing messages at the same time. They are potentially harmful to relationships and should be avoided.

Sometimes nonverbal messages can **substitute** for verbal ones. At the end of a difficult and boring meeting, two people can just sigh and roll their eyes. They don't need to put their frustration into words. We also use substitution when verbal channels are unavailable. While scuba diving or during the filming of a TV show, we can't yell out a message, so we resort to sign language.

Nonverbal messages can also **complement,** that is, modify or elaborate on, a verbal message. When Don says to his roommate, "I had a terrible day today," the slope of his shoulders and the weariness in his voice indicate just how bad the day really was. These behaviors add to Don's message, telling us the extent of his feeling. Without the proper accompanying nonverbals, people do not believe others' verbal messages. If a winning contestant on a game show reacts by saying, "I'm glad I won," but fails to scream and clap and jump up and down, the audience doesn't believe that the message is sincere or that the contestant deserved to win.

Sometimes nonverbal behaviors **accent** the important parts of a verbal message. A teacher may emphasize the main points in a lecture by nonverbally stressing certain words. A parent may make eye contact with a child to make sure the child hears an important bit of advice. The eye contact says, "Now listen carefully. I expect you to remember this and to follow through."

Finally, nonverbal cues **regulate,** or control, social interaction. When we converse, we must carefully coordinate our contributions, finding a way to take the field when it is our turn to speak and a way to relinquish it when we are finished. Because we must do this instantly, without awkward pauses or interruptions that disrupt the flow of speech, we turn to nonverbal channels. Through changes in speech tempo, eye contact, head nodding, and the like, we manage conversations. To claim our turn to talk, we raise our index finger or lean slightly forward, taking a breath as though we are about to speak and nodding our heads to hurry up the other speaker. If the other speaker responds with decreased eye contact and begins to talk faster and louder, we know that our bid to talk has been turned down.[4] Knowing the meaning of and abiding by these nonverbals are aspects of the important interpersonal skill called **interaction management.** People who are skilled in interaction management are considered highly competent communicators.[5]

The Nonverbal Codes

So far our discussion of nonverbal communication has been general. Now we'll look at the specific channels that make up the nonverbal system. We'll start with body movement and gesture, move on to facial expression and eye behavior, and then consider the way vocal quality is related to verbal expression. We'll also discuss the messages conveyed by time, space, and touch, and we'll end by looking at the effects of personal appearance and object language.

The Kinesic Code I: Body Movement and Gesture

Our bodies are an important source of nonverbal meaning. Whether we lean in toward someone or move away, whether our stance is wide and strong or narrow and weak, whether we talk with our hands or remain completely still—we tell others a lot about us. Even the way we walk can give off signals. When prison

Although we may try to inhibit our emotions, facial displays often give us away. Feelings of affection and delight are often written all over our faces.

inmates arrested for assault were asked to look at tapes of people walking along a city street, they had little trouble agreeing on which were "muggable" and which were not. People classed as "easy rip-offs" moved awkwardly, taking either very long or very short strides, and their arm movements followed their leg movements rather than alternating with them. They appeared to walk around in a daze. Their walk signaled to potential muggers that they would put up little resistance.[6]

Whether we lean in toward someone or move away, whether our stance is wide and strong or narrow and weak, whether we talk with our hands or remain completely still—we tell others a lot about us.

The study of body movement (including movement of the face and eyes) is called **kinesics.** People who study kinesics often classify body movement into five categories: emblems, illustrators, regulators, affect displays, and adaptors.[7]

Emblems

Emblems are kinesic behaviors whose direct verbal translations are known to all of the members of a social group. Emblems are much like words, except that they are silent. If you are at a noisy party and want to send a message to a friend across the room, you can use nonverbal emblems. You can "say" to your friend, "Shame on you" (by rubbing your right index finger across your left), "All right! Excellent!" (by turning your clenched fist inward at about head height, then drawing it rapidly down and back), "What time is it?" (by pointing at your wrist), or "I'm leaving now" (by pointing to yourself and then to the door). In fact, you can have a fairly lengthy (if not intellectually stimulating) conversation using emblems. In the United States we have emblems that allow us to tell others what to do ("Wait a minute"; "I can't hear you"; "Come over here"; "Sit down next to me"; "Calm down"), that convey our physical state ("I'm hot"; "I'm cold"; "I'm sleepy"; "I don't know"; "I'm confused"), that act as replies ("Yes"; "No"; "Maybe"; "I promise"), that evaluate others ("He's crazy"; "That stinks"; "He [or she] has a great figure"), or that serve as insults, including obscenities.[8]

One of the defining characteristics of emblems is that they are culturally defined. We must be very careful when using them with members of different cultural groups. The sign that we in the United States recognize as the A-OK sign (thumb and index finger touching in a circle, the rest of the fingers outstretched) can in other countries stand for money, can indicate that something is worthless, or can obscenely signify female genitalia. Judee Burgoon comments on the way emblems vary in different cultures:

> *For example, the head throw for "no" displayed by Greeks, Southern Italians, Bulgarians, and Turks could be mistaken for "yes" in cultures where nodding signifies affirmation. The Bulgarian turn of the head for "yes" is likely to appear to be shaking the head, a sign of negation in many cultures. Beckoning gestures are also a source of misunderstandings. The palm-down fluttering fingers beckoning gesture observed in Asian and Latin American cultures may be interpreted as "go away" by North Americans. In sum, although emblematic differences allow us to identify cultural group membership, they can also create cross-cultural misunderstandings and unfavorable attributions.[9]*

Illustrators

Sometimes the best way to describe an object is to use gestures that indicate its size or shape or movement. If someone doesn't know what a scalloped edge looks like or isn't familiar with the term *zigzag,* you will convey these concepts best by using hand movements to illustrate what you mean. Gestures like these accompany speech and add to the meaning of utterances; they are called **illustrators.** Illustrators need not describe physical characteristics; they can also be used to indicate the structure of utterances. A public speaker may gesture each time a new point is raised. The gesture illustrates the central structure of the argument. People differ in the number of gestures they use. If certain people were to have their hands tied behind their backs, they would find it almost impossible to speak, because they are so used to talking with their hands.

Regulators

Regulators are nonverbal behaviors that act as "traffic signals" during interaction. They consist of the head nods and eye and hand movements that allow us to maintain, request, or deny others a turn to talk. As their name implies, they fulfill a nonverbal regulating function. Regulators usually occur so rapidly and automatically that we are not consciously aware we are using them. At a subconscious level, however, we are certainly aware of them, for without them conversations grind to a halt.

Affect Displays

Body movements that convey emotional states are called **affect displays.** When we want to know what someone is feeling, our first instinct is to look at that person's face. The rest of the body, however, is equally expressive. In fact, experts on deception tell us that to determine whether someone is lying, we should not necessarily look at the face but at the body. When people lie, they generally experience heightened emotional arousal. If this arousal is not suppressed, it will act as a **leakage cue,** letting the observer sense guilt, anxiety, and excitement. Facial cues are least likely to leak this information, because liars pay close attention to and control their facial expressions. Body movements are less controlled and are therefore a better source of information. The voice is also a good source of leakage cues.[10]

Experts on deception tell us that to determine whether someone is lying, we should not necessarily look at the face but at the body.

In addition to leakage, liars may also give themselves away through their use of **strategic cues.**[11] Strategic cues are behaviors that liars use to disassociate themselves from their messages and to reduce their responsibility for what they've said. Liars sometimes seem uncertain or vague, less immediate, and more reticent than nonliars as they try to "back away" nonverbally from their lies. These cues, shown by body movement and spatial behavior, may be detected if one knows where to look. Unfortunately, the average receiver is not very good at detecting deception, perhaps because liars control those very types of behaviors that most of us associate with lying: facial and eye behaviors. If you want to detect deception, attend instead to a sender's body and vocal channels, and compare any suspicious behavior to the sender's baseline behavior.

Of course, not all emotional displays are attempted deceptions. Most affect displays are honest depictions of internal states and are easily detected. In attempting to read emotions, remember to look at the behaviors of the other person's whole body, including those behaviors that fall into our next category, adaptors.

Adaptors

Have you ever noticed how often people engage in odd, repetitive, nervous mannerisms? The next time you're in public, say, in a classroom, watch your fellow students tap their pens, kick their feet, twirl their hair, play with their jewelry, groom themselves, and so on. As often as these behaviors happen in public, they are even more frequent in private. Called **adaptors,** they are behaviors that people use to adapt to stresses and to satisfy personal needs. Some (such as scratching) are behaviors that satisfy immediate needs, whereas others (such as pen tapping) may be residual displays of behaviors that were once functional. Fist clenching or foot kicking, for example, may be residual hitting or running motions. Rocking back and forth may be a way of recreating early childhood experiences. And playing with jewelry may be the next best thing to carrying around a security blanket. Regardless of where they originate, most adaptors are used to manage stress.

People are often completely unaware that they are using adaptors, and for this reason adaptors are a good source of information about emotions. When people touch their own bodies (for example, by rubbing their necks or playing with their hair), they are using **self-adaptors.** When they touch objects (for example, by playing with cigarettes or shredding styrofoam cups), they are using **object adaptors.** By observing these behaviors, you may uncover hidden information about people's emotional states.

The Kinesic Code II: Facial Expression and Eye Behavior

The face is the arena most people turn to for information about others. We believe that "the eyes are mirrors of the soul" and that people's character can be "written all over their faces." We like people with open, friendly faces, and we avoid "two-faced" people with shifty eyes or thin, mean lips. And when we want to look particularly honest or friendly, we smile and widen our eyes. All these behaviors indicate our faith in the face and eyes as sources of nonverbal communication.

Facial Displays

Where do **facial displays** come from? Experts believe that they are partly innate and partly learned. That is, the form that emotional expressions take is "prewired" into the human brain, but the way these expressions are exhibited is governed by culture-specific rules. Evidence for the basic innateness of facial expression comes from several sources. Studies show, for example, that blind and sighted children have very similar facial expressions, and cross-cultural studies show that basic expressions are shared across many different cultures.[12] These studies suggest that the reason we smile when happy and cry when sad is that smiling and crying are part of our biological inheritance.

The reason we smile when happy and cry when sad is that smiling and crying are part of our biological inheritance. When and where and how much we smile or cry, however, depends on learning and imitation.

When and where and how much we smile or cry, however, depends on learning and imitation. Within each culture, certain expressions are encouraged and reinforced, whereas others are discouraged.[13] People in every culture learn to modify their facial displays, **intensifying** certain emotions and **deintensifying** others. For example, most Americans feel it is impolite to show disappointment over a gift or to gloat at our own fortune. We may therefore pretend to like a birthday present more than we actually do, or we may downplay pleasure at our own success if a friend has failed. We also learn to **neutralize** other emotions, swallowing our disappointment by pretending not to care. Finally, we may **mask** one emotion with another. When the first runner-up hears she is not being crowned Miss America, not only does she not show her disappointment and jealousy, she looks positively joyful as she rushes up to hug the winner. Becoming a good communicator includes learning how to modify facial displays. The rules that govern these modifications occur at three levels: the cultural, the professional, and the personal.

By following what are called **cultural display rules,** people in some cultures learn to be "stone-faced" and stoic, whereas those in other cultures learn to be highly expressive. In American culture, for example, men follow a cultural display rule that tells them not to show fear in public. Women, on the other hand, are free to show fear but must keep anger in check.

We learn to modify our facial displays not only to meet cultural expectations but also to succeed in our careers. Service personnel, such as flight attendants, are taught to inhibit any irritation they feel and to smile no matter what. Nurses learn to be cheerful, calm, and caring, whereas lawyers learn when to put on a "poker face" and when to show justified outrage. Rules for facial expression based on career considerations are called **professional display rules.**

Finally, people also follow **personal display rules.** These rules are learned through individual experience and are often, but not always, shared with family members. Researchers have made a number of attempts to identify personal styles in emotional expression. Ross Buck argues that people are either externalizers or internalizers.[14] **Externalizers** are good at portraying emotion, whereas **internalizers** are less adept at showing emotions.

Ekman and Friesen have identified eight facial display styles.[15] **Withholders** know how to hide their emotions; they are aware that they show very little expression on their faces. **Blanked expressors** are equally expressionless but unaware of that fact; they believe they are expressing emotions when they are not. **Revealers** are the opposite of withholders; revealers show exactly how they feel no matter how hard they try to remain expressionless. And whereas revealers know they are easy to read, **unwitting expressors** are just as expressive but do not realize they are sending emotional messages. The **substitute expressor** consistently shows one emotional reaction (such as surprise or happiness) no matter what the situation. The **frozen-affect expressor** retains traces of a single facial expression even while portraying another emotion. An **ever-ready expressor** has a single initial reaction to all situations but shows other expressions later. Finally, the **flooded-affect expressor** has one or two expressions that continually flood the face.

Although some of Ekman and Friesen's distinctions seem quite fine, their point is valid: individual differences exist and are important. If a person unwittingly smiles when he or she is unhappy, people may think that that person is cold and unfeeling. If another person's face always looks hostile, his or her chances of making a good initial impression are severely affected. Look over the list above, and try to determine what kind of expressor you are. Better yet, ask someone else to give you feedback. The results could surprise you.

Eye Behavior

For centuries the eyes have been associated with mystic power. The Greek philosopher Empedocles explained vision as a flow of fiery corpuscles that pass from the eye to an object of vision and back again. This image of the glance as a fiery stream persisted; it can also be found in Renaissance love poetry, in which eyes were thought to "shoot arrows, daggers or swords [and] project fiery beams which burn the soul and kindle love's flame."[16] In addition to possessing the ability to engender love, the eyes have also been

For centuries the eyes have been associated with mystic power. The Greek philosopher Empedocles explained vision as a flow of fiery corpuscles that pass from the eye to an object of vision and back again.

Eye contact is an invitation, a way of making contact. By refusing to return a gaze we say quite clearly, "I reject your invitation; I will not enter into a relationship with you."

associated with suffering and death, perhaps because of our instinctive fear of the predatory gaze. Whatever the reason, primitive people in all ages have guarded themselves from the evil eye, a hostile glance reputed to kill instantly. Gerald Grumet reports that a certain mental disorder reverses the evil-eye superstition: the afflicted person avoids others in fear that his or her glance will injure them.[17]

Although modern Americans do not believe in primitive superstitions, we do recognize that eye behavior serves a number of important functions. Grumet tells us that dominant animals place themselves where they can watch their subordinates and where they themselves can be watched. Similarly, human leaders tend to situate themselves where they will command the center of visual attention, such as at the head of a table or the front of a conference room. Thus, *eye behavior serves to maintain social position.*

Eye behavior is also a good indication of both positive and negative emotions. We stare at sights we find agreeable and avert our eyes when a sight disgusts or horrifies us. Studies also show that when our interest and attention are high, our pupil size enlarges. Furthermore, research shows that people with enlarged pupils are judged more physically attractive than those with constricted pupils, a fact known as early as Cleopatra's time, when women used eyedrops made of belladonna to darken and enlarge their eyes.[18]

The eyes also signal our willingness to relate to one another. Mutual gaze is the first step in most relationships, for it signals both parties' awareness of one another.[19] During conversation, eyes act as nonverbal regulators, displaying typical patterns for listening and speaking. Listeners gaze more than do speakers, perhaps to pick up turn-taking cues. Speakers look away while formulating their thoughts, perhaps to cut down on visual stimuli that might interfere with concentration.

> *As any student who does not want to be called on in class knows, avoiding eye contact closes communication channels, whereas inadvertently looking up virtually guarantees being called on.*

As any student who does not want to be called on in class knows, avoiding eye contact closes communication channels, whereas inadvertently looking up virtually guarantees being called on.

Finally, like other nonverbal cues, *eye behavior is associated with specific character traits.* People who make eye contact are judged more friendly, natural, and sincere than those who avoid direct gaze. People who shift their gaze, on the other hand, are judged as cold, defensive, evasive, submissive, or inattentive.[20]

Paralinguistics: Vocal Behavior

A lot of the meaning in everyday talk lies not in our words but in how we say those words. If we were to read transcripts of conversations, we would have to mentally supply what is left out: the speakers' intonations, tones of voice, volume, pitch, timing, and the like. Characteristics that define how something is said, rather than what is said, are part of **paralinguistics,** the study of the sounds that accompany words. The importance of paralanguage was clearly demonstrated in 1974, when former president Richard Nixon, under investigation by the House Judiciary Committee, refused to supply audiotapes of his conversations and instead sent transcripts. Committee members, who needed to determine the truth-value and meaning of the tapes, argued that the tapes were incomplete, because vocal qualities and characterizers were missing.[21] The committee recognized how important vocal modifications are.

Paralanguage includes **vocal qualities** (characteristics of the voice, such as pitch, tone, and intonation patterns), **vocalizations** (special sounds that convey meaning, such as groans, cries, moans, giggles, and yawns), and **vocal segregates** (pauses and fillers, such as "um" and "uh"). All of these kinds of sounds affect the meaning of our spoken communications. They can be eloquent testimonies to emotional states, but they can also be cues used to make stereotypic judgments of personality characteristics.

It is a matter of interest that although the judgments we make based on vocal qualities are not necessarily accurate, we think they are. People generally agree about the connotations of different kinds of voices. A light, breathy voice connotes seductiveness and a lack of intelligence. A nasal voice may lead others to perceive the speaker as dull, lazy, and whiny. And the big, full, orotund voice associated with preachers and politicians can signify authority and pomposity.[22]

> *It is a matter of interest that although the judgments we make based on vocal qualities are not necessarily accurate, we think they are.*

Judgments of social status are also associated with the way we speak. Most cultures define certain accents and ways of speaking as "prestige speech." People whose grammar, word choice, or accent deviates from these standards are likely to be judged less credible and less intelligent than people who meet paralinguistic norms. On the other hand, speaking a regional or subcultural dialect may lead to higher ratings of benevolence and attractiveness. That is, the person who speaks in perfect, pear-shaped tones may appear distant and "snobby," whereas someone whose language patterns are more regional may seem like a "regular guy." Certainly, to people within a social group, accent similarity can enhance group solidarity.[23]

An often overlooked aspect of paralanguage is silence. Just as sound creates meaning, so too does the absence of sound. One use of silence is to create interpersonal distance. By not talking to someone, we can send the message "I refuse to admit your presence." The Amish use a form of silence called "shunning" to punish those who have violated important social norms.

> *An often overlooked aspect of paralanguage is silence. Just as sound creates meaning, so too does the absence of sound.*

A sudden silence can also indicate that a specific remark or behavior is inappropriate. If after telling an off-color joke at a dinner party you are greeted with stunned silence, you have likely committed a major social faux pas.

Of course, silence need not be negative. If filled by other nonverbal cues (a tender gaze, a touch), silence can signal intimacy and comfort. When we are with people, it is considered polite to make conversation. When we are nervous, we often mask our awkwardness with a steady stream of words. Only with a few people are we comfortable enough to remain silent.

Silence is also a mark of respect or reverence. We often fall silent upon entering places of worship, both to show our respect and to concentrate on inner, spiritual concerns. We also become silent when someone of high status appears, indicating that his or her words are more important than our own.[24]

Chronemics and Proxemics: Time, Territory, and Space

So far we have looked at ways we use our bodies to communicate. In this section we will look at how the dimensions of space and time can serve as nonverbal messages. We will begin by looking at **chronemics,** the study of time as it affects human behavior. We will then move on to a discussion of **proxemics,** the study of how we use space and what space means to us.

Time Orientations

Are you the kind of person who enjoys dwelling in the past? Do you retell old stories, pore over scrapbooks, and spend your time remembering past events? Or do you like making plans and imagining what the future will hold? Do you place high or low value on being punctual? Do your friends always end up waiting for you, or are you the one who's always early? The answers to these questions can tell you something about your **psychological time orientation,** the way you habitually think about and experience time. Andre, for example, takes a present-oriented ("What, me worry?") view of life, whereas his future-oriented roommate, Brook, is preoccupied with deadlines and schedules. Occasionally, these differences result in mutual frustration and irritation. Most of us have difficulty understanding someone whose use of time is very different from our own.

Alexander Gonzalez and Philip Zimbardo devised a scale called the Stanford Time Perspective Inventory to measure individual differences in time orientation. Using a variation of this scale, they surveyed more than eleven thousand readers of *Psychology Today* and found seven different time perspectives: two related to the present, four focused on the future, and one concerned with the effects of time pressures.[25] Interestingly, past-orientations were so infrequent that they were eliminated from analysis. The overwhelming emphasis on the future makes sense, given the values our culture attaches to progress. As we shall see, members of other cultures have a much different sense of time.

Two of the perspectives that Gonzalez and Zimbardo describe focus on the present. The **present, hedonism orientation** involves living for the moment. People who fall into this category are impulsive sensation seekers who like to spend their time playing and going to parties. In contrast, respondents scoring high on **present, fatalism orientation** focus on the present not because they are pleasure seekers but because they feel they have no control over fate. These people believe it doesn't make sense to plan, because events will occur unalterably no matter what one does.

Four time orientations focus on the future. The first is labeled the **future, work-motivation orientation.** People holding this orientation believe in the

Protestant work ethic, recognizing the importance of meeting obligations and completing projects no matter how difficult or uninteresting. People who take this view believe it is their duty to work hard. **Future, goal-seeking** respondents are more positive about the future. They enjoy thinking about what will happen to them and spend their time imagining the success they will achieve when their goals are met. People falling into the **future, pragmatic-action** category view the future in practical, down-to-earth ways. For them, the future is something to be prepared for in the present. They value behaviors that make the future secure, such as saving money and buying insurance. **Future, daily planning** respondents are obsessed with controlling the details of day-to-day events. They are the list makers and daily planners who map out their lives in specific detail. The final orientation is slightly different from the others. Labeled the **time sensitivity orientation,** it describes people who feel anxious and pressured by time obligations and who are somewhat compulsive about both their own and others' punctuality.

Gonzales and Zimbardo believe that time orientation may be related to the kinds of employment we seek. Thus, semiskilled or unskilled occupations may be attractive to and appropriate for people with present orientations, whereas managerial and professional occupations call for future-oriented individuals. The authors also suggest that we can all benefit from developing more flexibility in our relationship to time. Although punctuality is important for success, we should not let it become an obsession. The world will not come to an end if we are occasionally late. On the other hand, although taking a present orientation may be a fine way to approach one's social life, it can be a disaster in the world of work. A professional who is consistently a half hour late to meetings will soon be asked to look for other employment. Think about your own time perspective. When does your orientation work for you, and when does it get you into trouble? Are your relationships with others hurt or helped by the way you think of time?

In addition to being influenced by our psychological orientation to time, we are also controlled by our **biological time orientation.** Humans, like other animals, seem to have built-in **biological clocks** that govern our daily rhythms. Metabolic processes, as well as neurochemical activities in the brain, are tied to biological rhythms. When these processes are upset by changes in clock time (for example, by flying into a different time zone or by changing work shifts), we may feel irritated, tired, and even physically sick until we find a way to reset our internal clocks. Some people are extremely sensitive to seasonal changes in the amount of available light. In the short, dark days of winter, they can fall into a depression called **seasonal affective disorder,** which can sometimes be treated by using artificial light. We are beginning to find out that our mental alertness, as well as our emotional stability, is affected by biological time.

A third way time affects us is through our **cultural time orientation.** People from different cultures think differently about the value and uses of time. Judee Burgoon tells us that the Sioux have no words for "late" or "waiting," that the Pueblo people start ceremonies whenever "the time is right," and that the traditional Navajo are extremely present-oriented.[26] And Gonzalez and Zimbardo point out that clashes between different cultural time orientations account for cross-cultural misunderstandings between North Americans and people from Latin American and Mediterranean countries:

> *From their strong present and past perspectives, they see us as obsessed with working, efficiency, rationality, delaying gratification and planning for what will be. To us, they are inefficient, lazy, imprudent, backward and immature in their obsession with making the most of the moment.*[27]

The silent language of time is an extremely important part of nonverbal communication.

Territory and the Use of Space

Managing territory and distance is another important aspect of nonverbal behavior. Like birds and mammals, humans need to maintain uniform distances from one another and to occupy and defend territories. Proxemics commonly consists of three areas: territory, spatial arrangement, and personal space.

Territoriality is a basic human need. We need to have a place to call our own, a place where we are safe from attack and, even more important, where we are free to do what we want without being observed and judged.

The need to create boundaries, to control areas of space and make them ours, is called **territoriality.** Territoriality is a basic human need. We need to have a place to call our own, a place where we are safe from attack and, even more important, where we are free to do what we want without being observed and judged. People often feel most truly themselves when they are in familiar territory.

People occupy several kinds of territories. Stanford Lyman and Marvin Scott describe four: public, home, interaction, and body territories.[28] **Public territories** are territories that we share with others. City parks and shopping malls, for example, are open to everyone in the community, although what people are allowed to do there is often restricted. To avoid the potential disorder that can occur when strangers interact, public territories are usually patrolled by police, and anyone thought to be threatening community standards may be asked to leave. When we occupy public territories, we are expected to follow the rules. At the beach, for example, we are free to play Frisbee but not to sunbathe nude.

Home territories are areas owned and controlled by individuals. In these spaces we have much greater freedom to do whatever we want. A child's clubhouse with its sign warning Keep Out, This Means You! is a home territory, as is her parents' bedroom. The need to control space is so great that people may even try to make home territories out of public territories. We may, for example, consider a favorite table in a local restaurant "our" table and be irritated or outraged when it is occupied by someone else. In cities, gangs may lay claim to certain streets, marking nearby buildings with graffiti to indicate "their" turf. You may even consider your seat in your communication classroom as an extension of your home territory.

Whereas public and home territories may be bounded by physical barriers, such as walls, gates, or fences, **interaction territories** are socially marked. Groupings of people at a party or lovers in private conversation occupy interactional territories. Like other territories, these arenas may be made off limits to outsiders. By the way they position their bodies, make or avoid eye contact, or focus their attention, those who are inside the interaction separate themselves from those who are outside and indicate how permeable their invisible boundaries may be.

Body territories are the most private of all our territories. Our rights to touch and view one another's bodies are strongly restricted. From the time we are children, we are shown which parts of our own (and others') bodies can and cannot be touched. We are told how much clothing to wear, and we are expected to decorate our bodies in acceptable ways. In some cultures, practices such as tattooing or nose piercing are encouraged; in others, they are thought to be disgusting.

Lyman and Scott believe that our territories may be encroached in three ways: through contamination, violation, or invasion. In **contamination** a territory is polluted or made unacceptable. After contamination the territory must be cleansed before it can be used again. In caste societies the presence of a low-caste person is thought to pollute sacred spaces. Vandalism can encroach on home territories, and dirty jokes can contaminate an interaction. Soiling one's clothes or spattering someone else with mud are examples of body contamination.

A second form of encroachment is **violation,** any unwarranted entry into or use of a space. Homeless people sleeping in a park, a dog digging in a neighbor's flower bed, an outsider stumbling into a private conversation, or a stranger brushing against someone in a crowded subway are examples of violations.

Invasion is perhaps the most serious form of encroachment. It occurs whenever people not entitled to use a space enter and take control of that space. When a motorcycle gang takes over a public park, when a visiting relative won't leave after two weeks, or when an insensitive boor dominates a conversation, public, home, and interaction territories are being invaded. Rape and assault, of course, are invasions of body territories; most cultures consider these acts to be so serious that they are punishable by imprisonment or even death.

Territories are important to us. We build barriers against the approach of others, and we are often willing to defend these barriers to the death. Some barriers are easy to identify. Barbed-wire fences and border guards let us know when we are crossing national boundaries. Picket fences or hedges tell us where one yard ends and another begins. But other barriers are not as easy to identify. We do not always know when we are not wanted or when our behavior has violated a social norm. The ability to recognize the nonverbal signs that indicate we are encroaching on another's territory is an important communication skill.

Spatial Arrangement

The ways we arrange home and public territories affect our lives. Architects and interior designers know how important **spatial arrangement** can be. The way walls and furniture are arranged within structures affects the amount, flow, and kind of interaction in them. Seating choice in classrooms, for example, often predicts which students are likely to talk and which are not. In a seminar-style classroom, students who sit directly next to the teacher are less likely to be called on than those who sit farther down the seminar table. In a regular classroom, most participation comes from the so-called **action zone,** a roughly triangular area beginning with the seats immediately in front of the teacher and diminishing as it approaches the back of the room.[29]

The way walls and furniture are arranged within structures affects the amount, flow, and kind of interaction in them. Seating choice in classrooms, for example, often predicts which students are likely to talk and which are not.

Furniture arrangement in offices also delivers a number of messages. To observe this phenomenon yourself, visit several of your professors' offices, and note factors such as the overall amount of space and the presence or absence of barriers between instructor and student, as well as the relative amount of space "owned" by each. Ask yourself how these arrangements affect your comfort level and how they define the role of student. Figure 5-1 shows several examples of seating arrangements and furniture placement and summarizes their effects on communication.

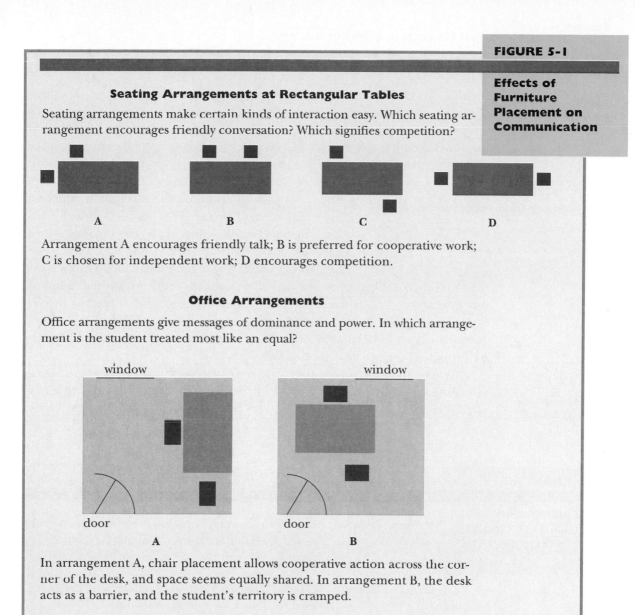

FIGURE 5-1

Effects of
Furniture
Placement on
Communication

Seating Arrangements at Rectangular Tables

Seating arrangements make certain kinds of interaction easy. Which seating arrangement encourages friendly conversation? Which signifies competition?

A   B   C   D

Arrangement A encourages friendly talk; B is preferred for cooperative work; C is chosen for independent work; D encourages competition.

Office Arrangements

Office arrangements give messages of dominance and power. In which arrangement is the student treated most like an equal?

window   window

door   door
A   B

In arrangement A, chair placement allows cooperative action across the corner of the desk, and space seems equally shared. In arrangement B, the desk acts as a barrier, and the student's territory is cramped.

Personal Space

Each one of us varies in how close we prefer to be to other people. This preference, called **personal space,** acts as a kind of portable territory that we carry with us wherever we go. If others come too close, we move away until we feel comfortable. Similarly, if people stand too far away, we move in to establish more intimacy. People with the same personal space norms have little trouble interacting. Those who vary greatly, however, find it difficult to coordinate

143

their needs. They can be observed engaging in a complex dance; as one moves closer, the other counters by backing away.

Factors that affect personal closeness include liking, status, gender, and the way we define the interaction. People who like one another usually stand closer together than do strangers; in fact, closeness is often used as a measure of attraction. The amount of personal space one controls can also indicate status, with people of higher rank being given more personal space than those with low rank. In our culture, gender too makes a difference in the way we use personal space: males generally take up more space than do females. Of course, our personal space also depends on the nature of our interaction. We expect to be at a greater distance from a teacher delivering a lecture than from a friend talking to us. Edward T. Hall investigated American cultural norms for personal space and found four kinds of interaction zones. These are described in Table 5-3.

When one's personal space needs are violated, he or she experiences **crowding.** Crowding has been shown to lead to heightened arousal and anxiety, decreased cognitive functioning, and increased verbal and physical aggres-

> *People who like one another usually stand closer together than do strangers; in fact, closeness is often used as a measure of attraction.*

TABLE 5-3

Interaction Zones for Most Americans

Intimate Distance	Extends from contact to about eighteen inches. It is reserved for intimate interaction and very private conversations.
Personal Distance	Extends from eighteen inches to about four feet. It is used for casual, friendly interactions.
Social Distance	Extends from four to twelve feet. It is used for impersonal business relationships.
Public Distance	Extends from twelve feet to the limits of visibility or hearing. It is used for public performances, lectures, and the like.

For a more extensive discussion, see Edward T. Hall (1966). *The hidden dimensions.* New York: Doubleday.

sion. To relieve discomfort, crowded individuals often avoid gaze or verbal interaction, use body blocking to decrease their sense of contact, or use objects to build barriers between themselves and others. People whose occupations cause them to violate the personal space of others (such as servers, hairdressers, or massagers) are often given the status of **nonpersons** and are thus absolved of responsibility for the violation.

Touch

The extreme of personal closeness is touch. To touch and be touched is a basic need. People deprived of touch may develop physical, mental, and social disorders. In fact, studies have linked touch depriva-tion to depression, alienation, and violence.[30] Touch is an important form of nonverbal com-munication, and its study is sometimes called **haptics.**

People deprived of touch may develop physical, mental, and social disorders. In fact, studies have linked touch deprivation to depression, alienation, and violence.

All cultures regulate how and how often their members touch. Judee Burgoon and Thomas Saine feel that, compared to other societies, our culture is "restrictive, punitive, and ritualized" in regard to touch.[31] Affectionate contact between people outside the family is discouraged, and strict norms regulate touch with-in the family. Mothers, for example, are encouraged to touch male children, but fathers are not. Fathers must also heed strict taboos about touching post-adolescent female children. In general, touch declines from early infancy on, with senior citizens suffering the most deprivation and isolation.[32] Strong anti-touch norms also affect heterosexual male-male touch. As Loretta Milandro and Larry Barker tell us, "Physical contact by a man with another man remains so potentially dangerous and unspeakable for many American males that other than a constrained handshake, no one but the dentist and doctor are permit-ted to touch the skin surface."[33]

Touch conveys a number of messages. First, the type of touch (a pat on the back versus a lingering caress) indicates how we feel about others and defines a given relationship as playful, loving, friendly, sexual, or even aggres-sive. In most cultures, negative feelings such as derision are shown by touch avoidance. Touch also communicates status, with the person who initiates touch being of higher status. It is a social error, for example, for a manage-ment trainee to casually pat his or her manager on the shoulder. Touch initia-tion is generally considered a dominant behavior; in fact, we often use touch to control or direct the action of others. For this reason, touch initiation is gov-erned by the rules that control other forms of dominance.

Touch also satisfies our own emotional needs. When we feel stressed or lonely, we may curl up our bodies and hug our knees, wring our hands, or stroke our hair. The use of these kinds of self-adaptors shows a need for body contact. When we feel the need for touch, we may also gain comfort from touching animals. Some nursing homes have recently introduced house pets. Being able to stroke a cat or dog and feel its warmth helps residents overcome isolation and loneliness.

Physical Appearance and Object Language

Professional designers—whether they design clothing, graphics, or interiors—are trained in the selection and arrangement of elements to create an overall effect. In a certain way we are all designers. When we go out to face the world each morning, we take with us a material self created by the way we look and dress and by the objects we display. Whether or not we realize it, our design efforts matter. Personal appearance affects the way others act toward us, as well as how we feel about ourselves. As Mark Knapp has pointed out,

> *In a certain way we are all designers. When we go out to face the world each morning, we take with us a material self created by the way we look and dress and by the objects we display.*

> *Physical attractiveness may be influential in determining whether you are sought out; it may have a bearing on whether you are able to persuade or manipulate others; it is often an important factor in the selection of dates and marriage partners; . . . it may be a major factor contributing to how others judge your personality, your sexuality, your popularity, your success, and often your happiness.*[34]

Body Type

People have strong reactions to body shape and appearance. All cultures favor certain **body types,** subjecting to ridicule people who don't fit the ideal. Cultures also form stereotypes about the characteristics thought to go along with various body types. Whether there is any truth to these stereotypes is less important than that we believe and act upon them.

Researchers who study body types classify people according to how closely they approximate three extremes. The **endomorph** is short, round, and fat; the **mesomorph** is of average height and is muscular and athletic; the **ectomorph** is tall, thin, and frail. A person's **somatype** is a composite score, using a seven-point scale, of each of these extremes. The somatype of an extremely fat person, for example, is a 7/1/1, that of a trained athlete, a 1/7/1, and that of a very tall, skinny person, a 1/1/7. Mark Knapp reports that the late comedian Jackie Gleason scored roughly a 6/4/1, that former heavyweight boxing champion Muhammad Ali rated a 2/7/1 at the peak of his career, and that Abraham Lincoln is considered to have been a 1/5/6.

Certain personality characteristics are generally associated with each of the three body types that make up the somatype. Descriptors such as placid, contented, affable, generous, and affectionate are used to characterize endomorphs. Mesomorphs are seen as energetic, enthusiastic, competitive, reckless, and optimistic, whereas ectomorphs seem more self-conscious, precise, shy, awkward, serious, and sensitive.[35]

One's height and body type can put one at an advantage or a disadvantage when it comes to love and career. In America, height is an advantage, especially for men. A number of studies show that—all else being equal—tall men are hired more frequently than are short men.[36] Tall men are also more successful in romance. Few women seek out a man who is "short, dark, and handsome."

Generally, North American cultural norms value men who are muscular and women who are slender, even though most Americans are overweight. Obesity is especially disliked, and fat people are often ridiculed and avoided. To escape being perceived as endomorphic, Americans will go to great lengths of exercise and diet. Victims of anorexia nervosa are quite literally willing to starve themselves to death to achieve what they consider a desirable body type.

Dress

According to Desmond Morris, clothing, or **dress,** serves three major functions. First, it provides **comfort-protection,** shielding us from extremes of heat and cold. Second, it preserves our **modesty** by covering areas of the body considered taboo. Most important, it serves as a **cultural display,** telling others about our place in a variety of culturally defined hierarchies. In earlier times, laws dictated the clothing appropriate for each profession and social class. People who dressed above their station in life could be arrested. Rank could be read in the shape of a coat or the color of a ribbon. In modern, more democratic times, we are more free to dress as we wish. Yet we are still constrained by unwritten laws, and we may still read information about socioeconomic class in others' clothing choices.

Like other nonverbal signs, clothes are often read as a sign of character and are especially important in creating first impressions. The courtroom is one place where the messages of clothes are carefully scrutinized. Heiress Patty Hearst did not appear at her trial for bank robbery wearing the beret, dark glasses, and fatigues she had assumed as a member of the "urban guerilla" band the Symbionese Liberation Army. Instead she wore a modest skirt and blouse several sizes too large for her. Her clothing was chosen to ensure that she looked frail and worn, the victim rather than the victimizer.[37]

Clothing choice is important not only for defendants but for witnesses and lawyers as well. If you were going to appear in court, say, as a character witness on behalf of a friend, how would you dress? Take a moment to imagine what you would wear. Then compare your choices to the following descriptions of clothing that, according to Lawrence Smith and Loretta Malandro, increases perceptions of credibility and likeability in a courtroom setting.[38]

To increase their credibility, men are advised to wear classic, conservative two-piece suits made of wools and wool blends. Trendy styles, unusual fabrics, and large patterns are to be avoided. Acceptable suit colors are gray and navy, but the only acceptable color for the shirt is white. Jewelry should be limited to one conservative ring, a watch, and a tie bar or tiepin. Conservative tortoise-shell eyeglasses can enhance the image. Hair should be short and conservatively styled.

Advice for women is similar. A traditional two-piece suit consisting of matching jacket and skirt in a solid color should be worn with a cotton or silk (not polyester) blouse with a simple collar. The skirt length should range from just below the knee to two inches below the knee. Shoes should have closed toes and heels approximately 2 1/2 inches high. Acceptable suit colors include gray, white, off-white, beige, and navy, with a white or light blue blouse. Jewelry should be limited to five points; for example, nondangling earrings, a simple ring, a single strand of pearls, a watch, and a pin on the jacket. As with men, eyeglasses increase women's credibility. Makeup should be moderate.

Men and women who wish to emphasize their approachability and likeability may modify their dress by wearing jackets that contrast with the rest of the suit. Men are advised to wear tans, beiges, or browns, while women may wear colors in the brown, gray, and blue families, as well as pinks and roses. Eyeglasses should be removed occasionally to increase the perception of approachability.

Although it seems patently obvious that dressing conservatively will not make one any more intelligent or more expert, violating dress norms can have serious effects. Whether or not clothes should be taken seriously, they are. Most businesses and schools have written or unwritten dress codes, and violations of dress norms are still a potent outlet for social rebellion.

> *Whether or not clothes should be taken seriously, they are. Most businesses and schools have written or unwritten dress codes, and violations of dress norms are still a potent outlet for social rebellion.*

Object Language

The objects or artifacts we own and display can also be an important mode of communication. **Object language** can be defined as "all intentional and nonintentional displays of material things, such as implements, machines, art objects, architectural structures, [as well as] the human body, and whatever clothes or covers it."[39] As we have already discussed body and dress, we will concentrate on material possessions, giving special attention to environmental design.

In the 1890s, philosopher William James talked about three aspects of the self: the social self, the spiritual self, and the material self. James believed that a person's possessions are a fair measure of his or her sense of self. As Franklin Becker notes, James defined a man's material self as:

> *the sum total of all that he can call his, not only his body and his psychic processes, but his clothes and his house, his wife and children, his ancestors and his friends, his reputation and works, his lambs and horses, his yacht and bank account. All things give him the same emotions. If they wax and prosper, he feels "triumphant"; if they dwindle and die away, he feels cast down—not necessarily in the same degree for each thing but in much the same way for all.*[40]

Even today our possessions act as public symbols of our values, status, and financial success, informing others of our identity and reinforcing our own sense of self.[41]

Nowhere is our status so clearly displayed as in the buildings we construct. From the outside, the look of a building tells people what to wear, how to act, who is allowed in, and what services they can expect. Once inside, interior design elements give off additional messages. Burgoon and Saine list a number of factors that affect communication in **built environments.** In addition to furniture arrangement (which we have already discussed), Burgoon and Saine cite size, shape and texture of materials, linear perspective, lighting, color, temperature, noise, and sensory stimulation as important communicative factors.[42]

In terms of **size,** massive spaces create a sense of awe, whereas smaller spaces are more cozy and more comfortable. Of course, if spaces are too small, we can feel cornered. The size of furnishings within spaces also sends messages. Large furniture (for example, a massive desk with a high-back swivel chair) often indicates power. The boss's and the secretary's desks are usually not the same size. The **materials** used to decorate a room can affect mood and comfort level. Rough surfaces give an effect different from smooth ones; softness invites us to relax, whereas hardness makes us more tense. A hard-edged modern office with highly polished metal furniture creates an atmosphere very different from a more traditional, wood-paneled room with leather-upholstered furniture.

Linear perspective refers to the ways in which lines created by walls or furnishings relate to one another. Figure 5-2 illustrates the meanings that can be created by different linear perspectives.

Lighting can vary our perception of the size of a room, as well as make us want to linger or to escape. A restaurant that wants to encourage leisurely dining usually uses muted lighting, whereas a restaurant designed for high volume and quick turnover uses harsher, brighter light. **Color** also affects moods; cool colors (such as blues and greens) are relaxing, whereas warm colors (reds, oranges, and yellows) are more stimulating. Colors also carry symbolic value. Most men would think twice before painting their dens pink, because pink is considered a feminine color.

Temperature and **noise** can either increase or decrease tension and irritability, as can the overall level of **sensory stimulation.** Environments must strike a balance between satisfying the needs for novelty and excitement and the need for consistency and stability.

FIGURE 5-2

Linear Perspective and Meaning

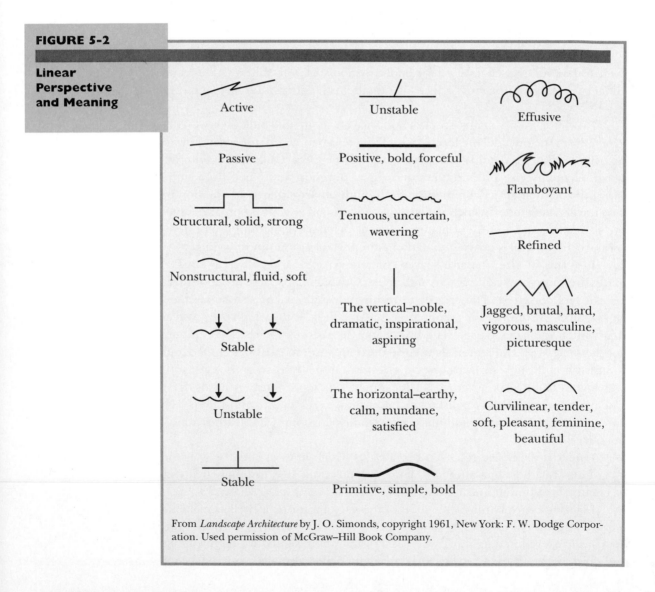

From *Landscape Architecture* by J. O. Simonds, copyright 1961, New York: F. W. Dodge Corporation. Used permission of McGraw–Hill Book Company.

Increasing Nonverbal Skills

This chapter has emphasized the importance of being aware of and making effective use of the unspoken languages available to us. In this last section we'll look at a few ways to improve nonverbal skills.

The first lesson we should learn is to *be cautious in interpreting nonverbal messages.* Most of us share the folk belief that it is possible to read another person like a book if we are sensitive to that person's nonverbal behavior. Most of us have our own theories about what to look for to judge another's character, and we use these theories as a kind of early warning device to avoid unpleasant interactions. That we never stop to test these stereotypes seldom bothers us. Yet many of our most cherished nonverbal stereotypes are false. It's important to remember that nonverbal behaviors can have many different meanings. When Anne crosses her arms over her chest, she may be inadvertently indicating a need to protect herself from contact, or she may simply find that posture comfortable. When Larry's eyes shift during a conversation, he may be lying, he may be nervous, or he may have been distracted by some extraneous stimulus.

It is not a good idea to read deep meaning into every gesture, yet it is important to *give proper attention to nonverbal cues.* Just as some people seem too sensitive to nonverbal cues, others seem completely insensitive. People will sometimes tell us nonverbally what they will not tell us with words, and we should not ignore those silent messages. Jim, for example, never seemed to notice other people's leave-taking cues. As a consequence, his employees didn't know how to get out of a conversation with him. The usual nonverbal cues—glancing toward the door, looking at one's watch, making small movements of escape—were always ignored, while more overt methods (such as saying, "Jim, stop talking. I'm leaving now") seemed too rude. The problem was so bad that people scheduled to have a meeting with Jim would often ask a friend to phone Jim a half hour into the meeting. When Jim would stop to pick up the phone, the employee would sneak out the door. Although this fact-based example may be extreme, it nevertheless illustrates that some people aren't very sensitive to nonverbals. If you're the kind of person who needs to have things spelled out, if you're often the last person to figure out what everyone else seems to know, then you may not be paying enough attention to nonverbal communication.

In addition to becoming more aware of others' messages, you should also *become aware of the messages you may be inadvertently sending.* As we've seen, people jump to conclusions about nonverbal behavior. And if they form judgments about other people in this way, you can bet that they also form judgments about you. Remember that what you do is as important as—and sometimes more important than—what you say. We're used to considering our words but much less used to monitoring our nonverbals. Think about the ways you habitually use all of the nonverbal codes. Some of these ways will be obvious to you, but others will not. Most people check out their clothes in a mirror, but fewer are aware of vocal habits, and still fewer stop to think about their use of space and time. If you're not sure what messages you're sending, ask someone you trust to give you feedback.

It's also wise to *remember that nonverbals you consider to be perfectly innocent can be invasive and even threatening to others.* When we stare at people, enter their personal space, use objects that belong to them, or make them wait for us, we may be offending them in ways we scarcely realize. That these things don't bother us doesn't mean that they don't bother others. And the potential for inadvertently committing offense is compounded whenever cultural differences exist. Take the time to find out the nonverbal meanings of others, and try to respect those meanings.

The silent messages that make up the nonverbal codes are subtle and are easily misinterpreted. Yet they are powerful modes of communication, and complete communicators are as aware of their own nonverbal messages as they are of their spoken words. If we overlook nonverbal communication, we overlook a world of meaning.

> *If we overlook nonverbal communication, we overlook a world of meaning.*

Summary

Although language is an important source of human messages, words are not our only means of communication. Messages can be encoded nonverbally. In this chapter we have looked at the nature and purpose of nonverbal communication and at the codes that make up the nonverbal system. Nonverbal communication occurs whenever a stimulus other than words creates meaning. This broad definition includes virtually all meaningful human behavior, whether intentional or not. Because behavior can convey a variety of meanings, we should be careful in interpreting nonverbal communication to remain aware of context, to compare current to baseline behavior, and to ask for verbal feedback to clear up misunderstandings.

Nonverbal communication is unique. It is often unintentional; it consists of multiple codes; it is immediate, continuous, and natural; and it may carry universal meaning. Nonverbal communication is particularly useful when direct verbal communication is socially inappropriate or difficult (e.g., when making initial judgments; when conveying relational messages of liking, status, and responsiveness; or when expressing emotion). Nonverbal communication can also expand upon, clarify, or even contradict verbal messages.

Body movement and gesture makes up the first of the nonverbal codes. We use a variety of kinesic cues, including emblems, illustrators, regulators, affect displays, and adaptors. All are potential sources of nonverbal meaning. Facial displays are another important nonverbal code. People in every culture learn to modify and to manage facial expressions by following cultural, professional, or personal display rules, and each of us develops our own display style. The eyes are a particularly important part of the face. They can signal positive and negative emotions and attraction, and they are often used as cues to character. The voice is a third nonverbal code. Paralanguage includes not only the quality of the voice but also the sounds we make and the pauses and fillers we add to our talk. Even silence can communicate.

The dimensions of time and space are rich sources of meaning. Chronemics includes the study of psychological time orientation (how we think about and experience the past, present, and future), biological time orientation (how biological clocks govern our lives), and cultural time orientation (social rules for managing time). Proxemics is the study of space. One important aspect of proxemics is territoriality. We humans need to own and control a variety of territories (public, home, interaction, and body). When these spaces are threatened, we feel compelled to defend them. This is especially true of personal space; every society has implicit rules regulating personal closeness and touch, for both convey emotional and power messages.

A final nonverbal code consists of physical appearance and object language. The way we look and dress and the objects we display affect not only the way others see us but also the way we see ourselves. For many, self-concept is tied to appearance and possessions.

With all of its complexity, the nonverbal system is a powerful source of information as well as a powerful source of misunderstanding. It is important to become more aware of our own and others' silent messages.

Key Terms

Listed below are the key terms used in this chapter, along with the number of the page on which each is explained.

Review Questions

1. What is the difference between behavior and communication? To what extent can we be sure that meanings created through nonverbal communication are accurate? In what three ways can we increase the probability that our interpretation of others' nonverbals is correct?

2. What are the four characteristics of nonverbal communication? What implications does each have for our behavior as senders and as receivers?

3. What is the meaning of the statement "You cannot not communicate"?

4. What kinds of meanings are expressed nonverbally? In what kinds of situations do we tend to rely on nonverbal codes? What three kinds of relational messages are exchanged in every interaction? In what six ways can nonverbal messages modify verbal messages?

5. Why do people use mixed nonverbal messages, such as sarcasm or joking, rather than speaking more directly?

6. What nonverbal behaviors are generally associated with conversational turn taking?

7. What is kinesics? Into what five categories can body movements be classified? What kinds of messages can be conveyed emblematically?

8. What are leakage cues? strategic cues? What parts of the body release the most reliable deception cues?

9. Are facial displays innate or learned? What are some ways we modify facial displays? What cultural display rules do we follow in our culture? What are professional display rules? What professions can you think of that have strict display rules? What are personal display rules? What eight facial styles are identified in the text?

10. How did Empedocles explain vision? What are some of the powers traditionally associated with the eyes? What four kinds of information are indicated by gaze?

11. What is paralinguistics? What three types of vocal behavior does paralinguistics include? What is prestige speech? What messages are communicated by silence?

12. What is chronemics? What is the difference between psychological, biological, and cultural time orientations? What are the seven psychological time orientations described by Gonzalez and Zimbardo? Which best describes your orientation? How does time orientation seem to relate to job preference?

13. What is territoriality? What kinds of territories do we occupy? How are they different from one another? Which is most private? In what three ways can territories be encroached?

14. What meanings can be conveyed by spatial arrangements? In a classroom, where is the action zone? What is personal space? What factors affect personal closeness? What are the effects of crowding? What is an example of a nonperson?

15. What messages are conveyed through haptics? What kind of touch behavior indicates dominance?

16. What three body types make up a somatype? What characteristics are associated with each body type?

17. What three functions are served by dress? What advice do experts give to men and women who will appear in court? How should men's and women's dress change to emphasize approachability?

18. What is object language? How is object language related to the material self? List some characteristics of built environments that can affect behavior and send nonverbal messages. Give some specific examples that illustrate the messages these characteristics might convey.

19. What are some general guidelines for increasing nonverbal effectiveness?

Suggested Readings

Burgoon, Judee K., Buller, David B., & Woodall, W. Gill. (1989). *Nonverbal communication: The unspoken dialogue.* New York: Harper & Row.

A well-written, complete guide to nonverbal communication. Burgoon and her colleagues cover all the nonverbal codes, providing lively and interesting examples.

DeVito, Joseph A., & Hecht, Michael L. (Eds.). (1990). *The nonverbal communication reader.* Belmont, CA: Wadsworth.

This reader is full of interesting case studies and real-life examples of the way nonverbal behavior affects communication.

Milandro, Loretta A., & Barker, Larry L. (1983). *Nonverbal communication.* Reading, MA: Addison-Wesley.

In another excellent survey of the nonverbal field, Milandro and Barker provide additional examples and further discussion of the silent messages that surround and affect us.

Notes

1. Ekman, Paul, & Friesen, Wallace. (1975). *Unmasking the face: A guide to recognizing emotions from facial expressions.* Englewood Cliffs, NJ: Prentice Hall.

2. Mehrabian, Albert. (1970). A semantic space for nonverbal behavior. *Journal of Counseling and Clinical Psychology, 35,* 248–257.

3. Ekman, Paul. (1965). Communication through nonverbal behavior: A source of information about an interpersonal relationship. In S. S. Tompkins & C. E. Izard (Eds.), *Affect, cognition, and personality.* New York: Springer; Knapp, Mark. (1980). *Essentials of nonverbal communication.* New York: Holt, Rinehart & Winston, 11–15.

4. Knapp, 14.

5. Weimann, John M. (1977). Explication and test of a model of communication competence. *Human Communication Research, 3,* 195–213. See also Spitzberg, Brian H., & Cupach, W. R. (1988). *Handbook for interpersonal competence research.* New York: Springer-Verlag; and Spitzberg, Brian H. (1990). Perspectives on nonverbal communication skills. In Joseph A. DeVito & Michael L. Hecht (Eds.), *The nonverbal communication reader.* Prospect Heights, IL: Waveland Press.

6. Rubenstein, C. (1980, August). Body language that speaks to muggers. *Psychology Today,* p. 20.

7. Ekman, Paul, & Friesen, W. V. (1969). The repertoire of nonverbal behavior: Categories, origins, usage, and coding. *Semiotica, 1,* 49–98; and Trager, G. L. (1958). Paralanguage: A first approximation. *Studies in Linguistics, 13,* 1–12.

8. Johnson, H. G., Ekman, P., & Friesen, W. V. (1975). Communicative body movements: American emblems. *Semiotica, 15,* 335–353.

9. Burgoon, Judee K., Buller, David B., & Woodall, W. Gill. (1989). *Nonverbal communication: The unspoken dialogue.* New York: Harper & Row, 28, 187–189.

10. Ekman, Paul, & Friesen, W. V. (1974). Detecting deception from the body or face. *Journal of Personality and Social Psychology, 29,* 288–298; Ekman, Paul, & Friesen, W. V. (1975); Zuckerman, Miron, DePaulo, Bella M., & Rosenthal, Robert. (1981).Verbal and nonverbal communication of deception. In Leonard Berkowitz (Ed.), *Advances in experimental social psychology* (Vol. 14). New York: Academic Press; Zuckerman, M., & Driver, R. E. (Eds.), (1985). Telling lies: Verbal and nonverbal correlates of deception. In A. W. Siegman & S. Feldstein (Eds.). *Multichannel integrations of nonverbal behavior.* Hillsdale, NJ: Lawrence Erlbaum Associates.

11. Burgoon, Buller, & Woodall, 281–287.

12. Charlesworth, W. R., & Kreutzer, M. A. (1973). Facial expressions of infants and children. In Paul Ekman (Ed.). *Darwin and facial expressions: A century of research in review.* New York: Academic Press; Eibl-Eibesfeldt, I. (1975). *Ethology: The biology of behavior.* New York: Holt, Rinehart & Winston.

13. Ekman, Paul, & Friesen, W. V. (1975).

14. Buck, Ross. (1979). Individual differences in nonverbal sending accuracy and electrodermal responding: The externalizing-internalizing dimension. In R. Rosenthal (Ed.). *Skill in nonverbal communication: Individual differences.* Cambridge, MA: Oelgeschlager, Gunn & Hain.

15. Ekman & Friesen, 1975, 155–157.

16. Donaldson-Evans, L. (1980). *Love's fatal glance: A study of eye imagery in the poets of the École Lyonnaise.* University, MS: *Romance Monographs, 8,* 21; cited in Grumet, Gerald W. (1983). Eye contact: The core of interpersonal relatedness. Psychiatry, 28, 172–180, and reprinted in DeVito & Hecht, 126–137, 129.

17. Grumet, 129.

18. Hess, E. H. (1975). *The tell-tale eye.* New York: Van Nostrand; Andersen, P. A., Todd-Mancillas, W. R., & Clementa, L. D. (1980). The effects of pupil dilation on physical, social, and task attraction. *Australian SCAN of Nonverbal Communication,* 7–8, 89–96; Milandro, Loretta A., & Barker, Larry L. (1983). *Nonverbal communication.* Reading, MA: Addison-Wesley, 170–172.

19. For an interesting discussion of the function of the stare in initiating interpersonal relationships, see Wilmot, William. (1979). *Dyadic communication* (2nd ed.). Reading, MA: Addison-Wesley, 9–10.

20. Grumet, 133.

21. Miller, Patrick W. (1988). *Nonverbal communication* (3rd ed.). Washington, DC: National Education Society, 14.

22. Heinberg, P. (1964). *Voice training for speaking and reading aloud.* New York: Ronald; Burgoon, Buller, & Woodall, 68–70, also offer a good discussion of vocal qualities.

23. Milandro & Barker, 281–283; Burgoon, Buller, & Woodall, 68.

24. Bruneau, Thomas. (1973). Communicative silences: Forms and functions. *Journal of Communication, 23,* 17–46.

25. Gonzalez, Alexander, & Zimbardo, Philip G. (1985, March). Time in perspective. *Psychology Today,* pp. 21–26.

26. Burgoon, Buller, & Woodall, 145. See also Hall, Edward T. (1959). *The silent language.* Garden City, NY: Doubleday.

27. Gonzalez and Zimbardo, 26.

28. Lyman, Stanford M., & Scott, Marvin B. (1967). Territoriality: A neglected sociological dimension. *Social Problems, 15* (2), 236–249. An abridged version is available in DeVito & Hecht.

29. Adams, R. S., & Biddle, B. (1970). *Realities of teaching: Exploration with video tape.* New York: Holt, Rinehart & Winston; Sommer, Richard. (1969). *Personal space: The behavioral basis of design.* Englewood Cliffs, NJ: Prentice Hall; Milandro and Barker, 202–203.

30. Burgoon, Buller, & Woodall, 77–79.

31. Burgoon, Judee, & Saine, Thomas (1978). *The unspoken dialogue: An introduction to nonverbal communication.* Boston: Houghton Mifflin, 70.

32. David, F. (1978, September 27). Skin hunger—An American disease. *Woman's Day,* pp. 48–50, 154–156; cited in Milandro and Barker, 253.

33. Milandro and Barker, 253.

34. Knapp, 119.

35. See, for example, Wells, W., & Siegel, B. (1961). Stereotyped somatypes, *Psychological Reports,* 8, 77–78.

36. Knapp, 107.

37. Milandro & Barker, 74–75.

38. Smith, Lawrence J., & Malandro, Loretta A. (Eds.). (1985). *Courtroom communication strategies.* New York: Kluwer.

39. Ruesch, Juergen, & Kees, W. (1956). *Nonverbal communication: Notes on the visual perception of human relations.* Berkeley: University of California Press.

40. Becker, Franklin D. (1977). *Housing messages.* Stroudsburg, PA: Dowden, Hutchinson & Ross, 4.

41. Becker, 5.

42. Burgoon & Saine, chapter 4.

6

Interpersonal Communication

Our survival

as social beings

depends in large part

on our interpersonal

communication

skills.

It is easy to underemphasize the importance of everyday communication. Whereas public speakers often deal with issues of national importance and members of decision-making groups often design important new products, members of interpersonal dyads tend to spend their time in what seem to be less significant pursuits: gossiping, joking, or simply passing the time. Viewed in this light, interpersonal communication hardly seems to be a topic worthy of serious study.

The goal of this chapter is to show you that interpersonal communication is far from insignificant. It is, in fact, the most frequently used and, arguably, the most important form of communication humans undertake. It's possible to make it through life without ever giving a public speech or joining a decision-making group. None of us, however, can avoid interpersonal communication. In fact, our survival as social beings depends in large part on our interpersonal communication skills.

To flub a public speech or to become tongue-tied in a committee meeting may be embarrassing, but we get over these blunders eventually. If interpersonal communication goes wrong, however, our friendships, our marriages, and in many cases our professional lives go wrong as well. In this chapter we look at how the everyday exchanges that make up interpersonal communication shape our lives. After defining interpersonal communication, we look at some of the problems that can affect interpersonal interactions; examine the stages in building interpersonal relationships; and review some basic skills that can enhance communication in everyday life.

What Is Interpersonal Communication?

In a sense, all communication is interpersonal, because all communication occurs between people. The term **interpersonal communication,** however, is generally reserved for two-person, face-to-face interaction and is often used interchangeably with the term **dyadic communication.** Whenever we tell a joke to a friend, ask a professor a question, succumb to a sales pitch, share news with a family member, or express our love to a romantic partner, we are engaging in interpersonal communication. Compared to other forms of communication, dyadic communication has several unique characteristics. It is direct, personal, immediate, spontaneous, and informal.

Compared to other forms of communication, dyadic communication has several unique characteristics. It is direct, personal, immediate, spontaneous, and informal.

Characteristics of Dyadic Communication

The first characteristic that distinguishes the dyadic context from other communication contexts is its directness. We can hide in the back of a classroom or make ourselves unobtrusive in a committee meeting, but when we communicate face-to-face with one other person, we cannot hide. Because we are in such direct contact, dyadic communication is also very personal. Public speakers cannot adapt to every audience member's specific needs. Dyadic communicators, on the other hand, can get to know one another more intimately. They can adapt their contributions to their partner's intellect and interests.

Dyadic interaction is more immediate than other forms of communication because the quality of feedback is high. As a member of a dyad, we can instantly sense when our partner is losing interest, can note when we are speaking too rapidly or too slowly, and can correct ourselves on the spot if our partner looks confused or puzzled. In other communication contexts, feedback is less immediate.

The most immediate and spontaneous of interaction forms, dyadic communication reflects the personalities and enthusiasms of each partner.

Compared to other kinds of communication, dyadic communication is the most spontaneous. Members of dyads rarely, if ever, outline and rehearse what they will say to each other; public speakers almost always do. Finally, whereas communication in other contexts is often characterized by formal role relations that signal a communicative division of labor, in dyads the roles of speaker and listener are freely exchanged. In a dyad, whatever one partner can do, the other is free to do as well.

Are All Dyads Interpersonal?

For many scholars, the defining characteristic of interpersonal communication is that it occurs between two people. This view suggests that all dyads are equally interpersonal. But are they? Is the communication between a clerk and a customer in a busy store interpersonal in the same way as the communication between a parent and a child or between two best friends? Does the quality of communication stay the same as partners get to know one another? A number of scholars answer these questions with a resounding no. They believe that dyadic communication and interpersonal communication are not the same thing. According to those who take a **developmental approach** to interpersonal communication, something special must occur to turn ordinary, impersonal, dyadic interaction into interpersonal communication. When the rules governing the relationship, the amount of data communicators have about one another, and the communicators' level of knowledge change, dyadic communication becomes interpersonal.

Gerald Miller and Mark Steinberg argue that communication is governed by rules.[1] These rules, which tell us how to communicate with one another, vary in generality. **Cultural level rules** are the most general; they apply to all of the members of a particular culture. We use cultural level rules with people we do not know well. When we greet strangers, for example, we follow rules that tell us to use polite, fairly formal forms of address. We usually nod, shake hands, and say something such as, "Hello, how are you?" Our choice of topics is very general. With strangers we talk about the weather, sports, or current events, not about personal concerns and fears.

When we interact with people who belong to specific groups within our culture, we use **sociological level rules,** rules that are tied to group membership. When college students greet each other, they seldom use the formal, stiff greetings of the cultural level. Informal modes of address, such as "What's up?" are preferred. The topics that group members talk about also differ from those that strangers discuss. In addition to more general topics, students talk about classes, upcoming social activities, and campus events. Each of the many groups we belong to employs a slightly different set of communication rules.

Finally, when we interact with people we know quite well, we abandon the sociological rules and move to the use of **psychological level rules.** Here partners in an interaction make up the rules themselves. Part of the joy of being in a close relationship is the knowledge that we are free to break everyday rules. Friends, for example, may greet each other with hugs, screams of delight, or mock blows. They may be serious, or they may joke around or even insult one another. They use behaviors that would never do with strangers, because in the course of their relationship they have made these behaviors their own. The range of topics that couples talk about is quite broad. With our close friends we can talk about very personal and emotional matters, topics we would hesitate to mention to people we don't know well.

Part of the joy of being in a close relationship is the knowledge that we are free to break everyday rules.

As we get to know one another, our sources of information also deepen. When we interact at the cultural level, we have very little data to go on. As we become more familiar, however, we can understand our partners better because we know about their backgrounds and about their attitudes and values. We begin to understand their nonverbals and can recognize when they are happy or upset or are hiding their feelings. We pick up on cues that would not be obvious to outsiders. As a result, our level of knowledge deepens. Now, not only can we describe our partners' behaviors, but we can predict and explain them as well.

Miller and Steinberg argue that interpersonal communication is "a special kind of dyadic communication, characterized by the development of personally negotiated rules, increased information exchange, and progressively deeper levels of knowledge."[2] Interpersonal communication occurs over time, as partners put effort and energy into building a personal relationship. For Miller and Steinberg, dyads start off as impersonal; only a few undergo the changes that make them interpersonal.

Why Do We Build Dyads?

In the movie *Annie Hall,* the narrator, Alvie Singer, tells a joke about a man whose uncle had convinced himself he was a chicken. When asked why he didn't send his uncle to a psychiatrist, the man replies, "We would have, but we needed the eggs." Singer goes on to explain that that's how he feels about relationships. No matter how "totally irrational and crazy and absurd" they are, we keep going through them "because most of us need the eggs."[3] Singer understands that relationships can be difficult, but he also understands that they serve us well. Among the many other things they do, dyads give us security in an often insecure world, tell us who we are, and allow us to maintain our self-esteem.

The first reason we enter dyads is that *dyads provide us with comfort and support.* Knowing that we have someone to turn to when things get bad provides a feeling of security in a rather insecure world. Having someone who will listen when we need to talk and will accept us no matter what we have done is a real source of comfort. To cope with our everyday lives, we need to make connections with others.

Second, *dyads help us develop a sense of self.* We become involved in dyads because friends and lovers not only provide security but also show us ways to live our lives and teach us who to be. Sometimes relationships can be a kind of wish fulfillment; we're attracted to others who complement our personalities, who are the people we'd secretly like to be, and who can show us how to do the things we wouldn't be able to do on our own.

> *Sometimes relationships can be a kind of wish fulfillment; we're attracted to others who complement our personalities, who are the people we'd secretly like to be, and who can show us how to do the things we wouldn't be able to do on our own.*

It is hard to overestimate the importance of other people in the development of the self-concept. Our sense of self is a product of the approval and disapproval of those with whom we come in contact. To use Charles Horton Cooley's metaphor, the appraisals of others act as a kind of mirror, reflecting back to us our **looking-glass self.**[4] William Wilmot discusses the way this cyclical process works.[5] Someone we care about responds to us. Our perception of this response affects our sense of who we are, and we behave in ways consistent with that self. This behavior then draws forth additional responses, and the cycle repeats itself.

A parent's anxiety about a child's health, for example, may be picked up by the child, who begins to think of himself or herself as weak and sickly. The child becomes fussy and gives in to every ache and pain, only increasing the parent's anxiety. The classic example (perhaps apocryphal, although several sources swear it is true) of the class who played Pygmalion to a fellow student is also illuminating. In one version of the story, five men in a graduate class chose a woman whom they saw as extremely plain. In the interests of science, each man decided to take her out and to treat her as though she were the most popular and most beautiful girl on campus. In a matter of weeks, she began to change, becoming more and more attractive and self-confident. By the time the last man asked her for a date, she was so popular that she turned him down.[6] Although the behavior of the graduate students seems chauvinistic by today's standards, it nonetheless illustrates that our self-concept is related to the ways we think others perceive us.

In addition to helping us create our identities, *dyads allow us to maintain stable views of ourselves over time.* This is the final reason we form relationships: to validate our perceptions of ourselves and our social worlds. A long time ago, psychologist Leon Festinger suggested that the reason we form connections with others is that these connections provide us with information.[7] He believed that we all have a need to know how well we are doing and whether our perceptions are correct. The only way to get this kind of information is through **social comparison,** that is, by turning to others. We do not turn to just anyone for information, however. We form close relationships with people who affirm our identities and abilities, who see the world as we do. We choose our friends in part because they allow us to be who we want to be. In this sense, "friendship is the purest illustration of picking one's propaganda."[8]

> *We form close relationships with people who affirm our identities and abilities, who see the world as we do. We choose our friends in part because they allow us to be who we want to be.*

Managing Interpersonal Communication

Although close relationships bring enormous benefits, they also involve costs. In joining a relationship, individuals take on duties and responsibilities that can leave them feeling stressed. In this section we look at some of the inevitable tensions of relational life. We begin by reviewing three dialectical forces that must be balanced if relationships are to be successful. We then discuss how members negotiate the shape their relationship will take. Finally, we look at some of the dysfunctional patterns that can beset dyads. As we shall see, all of these problems arise through, and are resolved by, interpersonal communication.

Balancing Interpersonal Tensions

A number of authors, including Leslie Baxter and William Rawlins, have written about the tensions that beset individuals as they try to balance the demands of a relationship and their own personal needs.[9] Individuals must face three sets of tensions as they decide how much of themselves to invest in relationships. These are called the expressive-protective, the autonomy-togetherness, and the novelty-predictability dialectics.

The **expressive-protective dialectic** involves finding a balance between the need to share personal information and the need to maintain privacy. When we become close to someone, we have a natural desire to share our thoughts and feelings with that person. It is a relief to find someone with whom we can be completely open, and it is gratifying to be entrusted with another's disclosures. Close relationships are built on shared information, and we usually expect a high level of **self-disclosure** (the voluntary revealing of information that would normally be unobtainable) in interpersonal relationships.

On the other hand, we can feel very uncomfortable when others ask for information that is too personal. Disclosure is a risk. When we open up to others, we make ourselves vulnerable. Just as we have a need to be open, we have a need to keep some of our thoughts and feelings to ourselves. The problem of how much information to reveal and how much to keep private must be negotiated by every couple. Failure to resolve this communication problem can lead to arguments and hurt feelings. Partners need to find a comfortable balance point that

> *When we open up to others, we make ourselves vulnerable. Just as we have a need to be open, we have a need to keep some of our thoughts and feelings to ourselves.*

will allow them to encourage disclosure without demanding it. Managing self-disclosure is a basic interpersonal skill, one we will return to at the end of the chapter when we discuss ways of increasing relational competence.

A second dialectic is the **autonomy-togetherness dialectic.** Here friends and couples decide how interdependent they want to be. This problem is often experienced by first-semester college roommates. Some people come to school expecting to spend all their time with their roommate. Others expect to spend time by themselves and feel overwhelmed by too much closeness. The person who expects high involvement can be hurt by a roommate who wants privacy, whereas the person who is more autonomous can feel pressured and annoyed by too much togetherness. Of course, roommates are not the only people to feel this tension. Dating and married couples must also decide on the proper level of autonomy and togetherness. Wilmot points out that

> some of the "craziness" and unpredictability in close, intimate relations comes from the oscillations between autonomy and interdependence. As we get farther away, we miss the other, and when we feel at "one" with the other, we sense a loss of the self.[10]

The only way to resolve this tension is to realize that others' needs may differ from our own and to talk about our feelings openly as soon as they become a problem. In the final section of this chapter, we will look at ways of expressing one's feelings without offending one's partner.

Finally, partners must resolve the **novelty-predictability dialectic.** As individuals interact, they fall into patterns. They develop ways of behaving that, for the most part, satisfy their needs. After a time these behaviors become predictable, and the couple spends much of its time repeating old routines. Obviously, a certain amount of predictability is necessary for coordinated activity. A long-term relationship couldn't sustain itself at the level of uncertainty found in a developing relationship. By repeating familiar patterns, partners bring stability to the dyad.

On the other hand, when behavior gets too patterned, partners can feel bored, and everyday interaction can become flat and stale. If no new ideas are generated, conversations lose their interest. The couple cease to explore and to change. After all, relationships do not occur in a vacuum, they occur in a constantly changing world. Relationships that aren't open to change may become obsolete. Therefore, every couple must spend some time adapting to changing conditions and finding new ways to interact. The novelty-predictability dialectic is a matter of finding ways to balance the familiar and the new.

Wilmot discusses three ways couples can resolve dialectical tensions.[11] In the first, called **dialectical emphasis,** couples simply ignore one of the opposing poles of a given dialectic. A couple may, for example, opt for complete freedom in their relationship, ignoring the need for togetherness. The problem here, however, is that the opposite pole does not go away. Later on, the couple may regret their decision when they realize that nothing binds them together. The second way to deal with dialectical tensions is called **pseudo-synthesis.** Here the couple decide that they can satisfy both dialectical forces at once. They vow to be both autonomous and interdependent at the same time. This choice is usually unrealistic, as it dismisses the power of opposing needs.

A third, and more realistic, way to deal with dialectical tensions is through **reaffirmation.** Here, a couple accept the fact that relationships move back and forth between opposing poles. When their relationship stays at one pole too long, they work to bring it back toward the other. During periods when their work loads are heavy, for example, a couple may give each other permission to spend time working. Yet they make sure this doesn't go on for too long, and they plan breaks when they can do things together once again. Through reaffirmation they learn to accept the contradictory nature of human relationships.

Adapting to Changing Relational Profiles

In the process of finding a balance between opposing needs, partners create **relational profiles.** Sarah Trenholm and Arthur Jensen have described this process in their relational continuum model.[12] They believe that most relationships fall somewhere between two extremes. At one extreme are relatively distant and formal public relationships; at the other are closer and more personal private relationships. Generally speaking, interactions with strangers, casual acquaintances, and colleagues occur at the public end of the continuum, whereas interactions with close friends, family members, romantic partners, and spouses are closer to the private end. Of course, there are exceptions. In a marriage of convenience, for example, the relationship is essentially public. Similarly, in a relationship between longtime coworkers, the bond may be quite private. Whether a relationship tends toward the public or private end of the continuum depends on the way individuals resolve a series of bipolar issues, including those that Baxter and Rawlins identified. Table 6-1 describes some of the issues that Trenholm and Jensen believe define public and private relationships. It also illustrates two hypothetical relational profiles.

In the table, the relationship marked with *Y*s is John's relationship with his boss, Phil. Their relationship profile is relatively public. John regards Phil as somewhat *substitutable;* that is, John would not be terribly upset if Phil were replaced by another boss, although the change would take a little adjustment. John and Phil are relatively, but not completely, *autonomous.* They are interdependent to the extent that Phil controls John's work life, but outside of work hours they are completely free to go their own ways. Further, the data they have about one another are *universal.* They have very little knowledge of each other's private lives. John is perhaps a bit more knowledgeable about Phil than vice versa, simply because John has learned over the years to gauge Phil's moods. The rules that govern their interaction are *normative;* in Miller and Steinberg's terms, John and Phil operate chiefly at the cultural and sociological levels. Regarding their feelings about one another, the tone is strictly *practical;*

they have no stong feelings about the relationship. Finally, the rewards they get from their association are *extrinsic,* that is, they lie outside the relationship. John and Phil maintain their relationship for purely economic motives.

John's relationship with his teenage son Jerry, however, is much more private. This is the relationship marked with Xs in Table 6-1. Jerry is *irreplaceable* to John. John and Jerry are *interdependent* to the extent that what affects John affects Jerry, but, because John has been trying to give Jerry a little freedom, they are not completely interdependent. Because they have lived together, John has very *particular* data about Jerry. John can predict Jerry's reactions, and he understands why Jerry acts as he does. John and Jerry's rules are relatively *individualistic,* but because John is a bit conservative the two of them follow some of the traditional father-son norms. Because they care a great deal for one another, the tone of their relationship is *sentimental.* Finally, their rewards are *intrinsic* to the relationship. Both enjoy being together, and each

TABLE 6-1

Trenholm and Jensen's Relational Continuum Model

Public Bonds		*Private Bonds*
Members are **substitutable**	Y ———————— X	Members are **irreplaceable**
Members are **autonomous**	Y ———— X	Members are **interdependent**
Data are **universal**	Y ———————— X	Data are **particular**
Rules are **normative**	Y ——————— X	Rules are **individualistic**
Tone is **practical**	Y ———————— X	Tone is **sentimental**
Rewards are **extrinsic**	Y ——————————— X	Rewards are **intrinsic**

Adapted from *Interpersonal Communication,* 2nd ed. (p.42) by Sarah Trenholm and Arthur Jensen, 1992, Belmont, CA: Wadsworth.

would sacrifice a great deal to stay with the other. As we can see, the relational profiles John develops with Phil and with Jerry are quite different from one another.

All couples work out their own relational profile by negotiating their position on each of the issues making up the continuum. Whether partners do this by discussing their needs and reaching an overt agreement or simply by falling into an uneasy truce, they must confront these issues if they are to create a stable relationship. And they must continue confronting these issues throughout their relationship.

As time goes by, profiles change. A small child is dependent on his or her parents. As the child matures, he or she becomes more autonomous. Both child and parents must adapt to the changing shape of their relationship and must learn to communicate in new ways. Competent communicators are willing to change their communication styles as relational profiles change.

Avoiding Dysfunctional Patterns

In the process of working out the general shape of their relationship, individuals create specific patterns of interaction. Unfortunately, these patterns often go unnoticed. When relationships run into trouble, partners rarely analyze their behavior patterns. Instead, they each place the blame on the other's character or personality. This is unfortunate because although patterns can be changed, people usually can't.

Dysfunctional patterns—especially our own—are often difficult to describe. We are so used to them that they become invisible to us. Yet with a little effort and a willingness to be objective, we can begin to identify and correct problematic behaviors. In the next section we look at some common dysfunctional communication patterns. In particular, we look at what happens when partners fall into rigid role relationships, disconfirm one another, become the victims of paradoxes, and get swept away by spirals.

Rigid Role Relations

Over time, one of the major relational themes that partners address is **dominance.**[13] Partners must distribute power within the relationship. Each must decide whether he or she feels more comfortable playing a dominant part, or **one-up role,** or a more submissive part, or **one-down role.** Although some couples share power equally, relationships often fall into one of two patterns: complementary or symmetrical.

In a **complementary pattern,** one partner takes the one-up position and the other, the one-down. Parents and their young children generally have a complementary relationship. The parent controls the child, making most of the decisions and exerting most of the influence. For the most part, the child complies, although occasional temper tantrums show the child's dissatisfaction with the one-down role.

This division of relational labor has an advantage: decisions can be made rapidly and easily. Problems occur, however, when people become trapped by **rigid complementarity.** When the submissive partner begins to resent always giving in or when the dominant partner begins to tire of being in charge, dissatisfaction can result.

The second common pattern is the **symmetrical pattern.** In **competitive symmetry,** both members fight for the one-up position. Although there are times (for example, when two athletes train together) when competition can encourage both members to do their best, in typical relationships this pattern can be stressful and frustrating and can take its toll on the patience of the partners. In **submissive symmetry,** both parties struggle to relinquish control. If you and a friend have ever spent all night deciding where to eat ("I don't care, you decide." "No, anything's okay with me; you decide"), you have experienced the problems associated with submissive symmetry. This is an especially interesting pattern, because it is paradoxical. Although both partners ostensibly avoid control, each does his or her best to control the other by forcing the other to make the decision.

Complementary or symmetrical patterns can occasionally be satisfying, but they can also take over a relationship and limit partners' options. Partners can feel trapped by a pattern they hardly realize they have created. Learning how to share the one-up and one-down positions gives a couple the flexibility they need to adapt to changing circumstances.

Disconfirmations

Engaging in interpersonal communication is always a risk. Whenever we interact with a relational partner, we open ourselves up to rejection. Evelyn Sieburg believes that during communication we offer up a version of our self for approval. Our partner can either confirm us (by accepting us for what we are) or can disconfirm us. **Disconfirmations** are rejecting responses, responses that leave us with a diminished sense of self-respect.[14]

Sieburg has described seven ways in which we can (sometimes unknowingly) disconfirm one another. These ways are shown in Table 6-2. The first of the disconfirming responses occurs when one partner ignores the other. A parent who is too busy reading the paper to listen to a child's story is giving an **impervious response.** The child is left with the message "You are not worth noticing." A second way people disconfirm one another is by giving an **interrupting response.** An interruption is a one-up move that sends the message "You are not worth listening to." Occasionally, we encounter people who burst

TABLE 6-2

Disconfirming Responses

Response	*Example*
Impervious B fails to acknowledge, even minimally, A's message.	A: "Hi!" (B continues talking on the phone, ignoring A.)
Interrupting B cuts A's message short.	A: "So I said—" B: "Got to go. Bye!"
Irrelevant B's response is unrelated to what A said.	A: "He really hurt me." B: "Do you like my coat?"
Tangential B briefly acknowledges A, then changes topic.	A: "He really hurt me." B: "Too bad. I got dumped once. It was last year . . ."
Impersonal B conducts a monologue or uses stilted, formal, or jargon-laden language.	A: "I don't understand." B: "The dependent variable is conceptually isomorphic . . ."
Incoherent B's response is rambling and hard to follow.	A: "Do you love me?" B: "Well, gosh, I mean, sure, that is, I . . ."
Incongruous B's verbal and nonverbal messages are contradictory.	A: "Do you love me?" B: "Of course" (said in a bored, offhand way).

Adapted from *Speech Communication: Concepts and Behavior* (pp. 141–143) by Frank E. X. Dance and Carl E. Larson, 1972, New York: Holt, Rinehart and Winston.

into conversations and immediately change the subject to something that has absolutely no bearing on what was said before. This is an example of an **irrelevant response.** A variation on this pattern is the **tangential response,** wherein an individual briefly acknowledges the topic but then goes on to discuss his or her own interests. Both responses send the message "My concerns are more important than yours are."

Impersonal responses are also disconfirming. The person who uses stilted, formal, distant language is signaling "I feel uncomfortable being close to you." Another response that indicates a desire to escape from interaction is the **incoherent response.** When someone seems embarrassed and tongue-tied, he or she says, in effect, "I feel uncomfortable with you." A final way to disconfirm a partner is by sending **incongruous responses,** messages wherein the verbal and nonverbal cues don't match. These double messages imply "I don't want to deal with you directly and openly."

Most people are disconfirming from time to time. Out of carelessness or irritation, we may use one of the responses just described. An occasional lapse is not necessarily problematic. However, if disconfirmations become habitual, they can destroy others' self-esteem and can severely damage relationships.

Paradoxes

Couples sometimes fall into the habit of sending one another contradictory messages. These kinds of double messages are called **paradoxes.** We have seen two paradoxical patterns already: submissive symmetry and incongruous responses. We can be paradoxical in other ways as well; for example, we may make statements such as "I know you'll do well, but don't worry if you fail" or "I don't mind if you go camping this weekend; it doesn't matter if I'm lonely and miserable." These kinds of responses are confusing and annoying, and they place the receiver in an awkward position.

Another, and a potentially more serious, form of paradox is the **double bind.** A double bind is a particularly strong and enduring paradoxical communication wherein the receiver is simultaneously given two opposing messages but is prohibited from resolving them. When a parent says to a child, "Come give me a hug," but recoils in disgust when the child approaches, the parent is delivering a double message. The child is being told to touch and not to touch at the same time. The child has no way to do the right thing. If the child obeys the verbal injunction and approaches the parent, the latter's obvious disgust places the child in the wrong. If, on the other hand, the child decides to stay away, he or she has disobeyed the parent and is likely to be accused of being unloving. Over a long period of time, double binds can damage a partner's sense of rationality and self-esteem.

Spirals

The final dysfunctional pattern we will look at is the **spiral.** In a spiral, one partner's behavior intensifies that of the other. William Wilmot gives an amusing example of how spirals can escalate:

> *My son Jason at age three saw a sleek, shiny cat. With the reckless abandon of a child his age, he rushed at the cat to pet it. The wise cat, seeing potential death, moved out of Jason's reach. Not to be outdone, Jason tried harder. The cat moved farther away. Jason started running after the cat. The cat, no dummy, ran too. In a short ten seconds from the initial lunge at the cat, Jason and the cat were running at full tilt.*[15]

The same thing can happen to couples. In some spirals, called **progressive spirals,** the partners' behaviors lead to increasing levels of involvement and satisfaction. Claudine shows trust in Michele, who decides to earn that trust by working hard. Michele's hard work earns her more trust, and so on; over time, Claudine and Michele's relationship becomes stronger. Unfortunately, not all spirals are positive. When misunderstanding leads to more misunderstanding, eventually damaging a relationship, partners have established what is called a **regressive spiral.** Leslie begins to suspect Toby of being unfaithful. Toby becomes defensive and denies being in the wrong, but the denials only increase Leslie's suspicions. As the conflict escalates, Toby begins to avoid Leslie, exhibiting behavior that convinces Leslie she was right in the first place. Finally, figuring, "If I'm going to be blamed, I might as well get something out of it," Toby actually is unfaithful. The relationship has spiraled out of control, and, in the process, Leslie and Toby have created an **interpersonal self-fulfilling prophecy.** Leslie's original prophecy (that Toby could not be trusted) has become true.

What can be done to stop spirals? In many cases, the partners need only sit down with one another and analyze the situation to determine what triggered the spiral and how it got out of control. In other cases, if the spiral has gone too far, the partners may need to turn to an objective third party who can help them describe their behaviors objectively and without defensiveness. The key to dealing with spirals is the same as that for dealing with any relational problem: partners must focus on patterns rather than on personalities.

> *The key to dealing with spirals is the same as that for dealing with any relational problem: partners must focus on patterns rather than on personalities.*

Relational Development: Stages in Intimate Dyads

As we saw in our discussion of relational profiles, relationships are in a constant state of flux. Over time, couples redefine themselves, moving toward and away from deeper involvement. In an attempt to understand more about the ways in which relationships change, several theorists have looked for global patterns of relational development. Although these theorists recognize that each couple's relational journey is slightly different, they have nonetheless attempted to chart the paths that couples take into and out of intimacy.[16] In this section we examine two aspects of this journey. We begin with one of the most widely known of the relational stage models, Mark Knapp's relational development model. We then consider some of the factors that lead couples to become attracted to one another in the first place, reviewing Steve Duck's filtering theory of attraction.

Paths to and From Intimacy

Mark Knapp provides us with a ten-step model of the way relationships grow and dissolve. These steps are summarized in Figure 6-1 and Figure 6-3 on page 178.

The Journey Toward Intimacy

The first of the **relational development stages** occurs during a couple's initial encounter as communicators and is known as the **initiating stage.** In this stage partners work to accomplish three things. They try to create a favorable initial impression; carefully observe each other for cues about personality, attitudes,

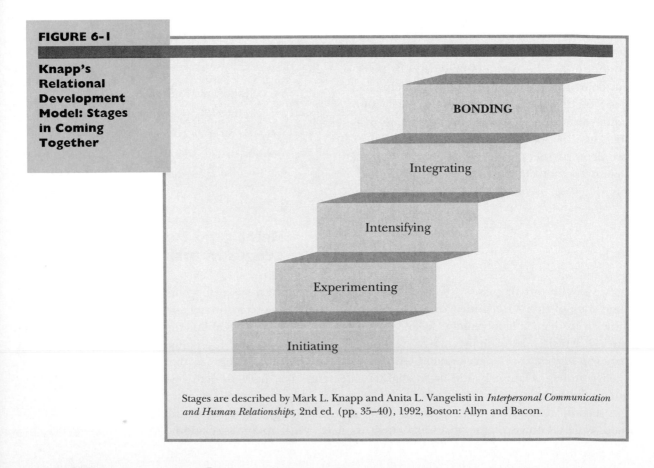

FIGURE 6-1

Knapp's Relational Development Model: Stages in Coming Together

BONDING

Integrating

Intensifying

Experimenting

Initiating

Stages are described by Mark L. Knapp and Anita L. Vangelisti in *Interpersonal Communication and Human Relationships,* 2nd ed. (pp. 35–40), 1992, Boston: Allyn and Bacon.

and willingness to engage in further interact; and look for ways to open communication channels. At this stage communication tends to be cautious, and topics are relatively shallow as individuals use tried-and-true opening lines and conventional formulas to initiate conversation.

If all goes well and initial evaluations are positive, a couple moves on to the **experimenting stage.** Here partners search for common ground upon which to begin to build their relationship. Communication at this stage is **phatic communication;** that is, it consists primarily of small talk. Although the talk may be small, it is not unimportant. As Knapp points out, phatic communication uncovers topics for further conversation; gives individuals information that reduces their uncertainty about one another; and allows them to reveal their personalities. Communication at stage two is generally relaxed, uncritical, noncommittal, and somewhat ambiguous.

> *Phatic communication uncovers topics for further conversation; gives individuals information that reduces their uncertainty about one another; and allows them to reveal their personalities.*

Most relationships stop somewhere in stage two, but others move on to the **intensifying stage.** Here individuals make initial moves toward greater involvement. Self-disclosure increases, and the use of nicknames and terms of endearment becomes more common. Inclusive pronouns such as "we" and "us" begin to be used, as do tentative expressions of commitment and private symbols for shared experiences. Finally, as partners become more familiar with each other's verbal and nonverbal styles, they start to use verbal shortcuts and may even complete each other's thoughts. In this stage satisfaction and excitement are high.

In the **integrating stage,** the individuals become a couple both in their own and in others' eyes. Attitudes and interests are shared, and social circles merge. As body rhythms synchronize, partners may even begin to talk and move in similar ways. Shared experiences and artifacts become personalized, and a couple can be overheard talking about "our" restaurant or "our" song. Finally, partners may exchange **intimacy trophies.** By wearing the other's ID bracelet or athletic jacket or by displaying the other's picture, partners signal to the rest of the world their official status as a couple.

This perception of unity is often reinforced by friends or acquaintances who now think of the partners as halves of a whole rather than as individuals. When friends see one of the partners alone, their first question is often "Where's your other half?" Friends may show their approval or disapproval of the relationship. Whereas some people outside the relationship are supportive, it is not uncommon for others to resent the couple's new status and even to try to undermine the relationship.

For the couple, the loss of individual identity that comes with integrating may be welcome or upsetting. Knapp emphasizes the fact that

In the early stages of relationships communication is generally relaxed, uncritical, and somewhat tentative. Over time, partners begin to synchronize activities and attitudes until they appear to be a couple, both in their own and others' eyes.

as we participate in the integration process, we are intensifying and minimizing various aspects of our total person. As a result, we may not be fully conscious of the idea but when we commit ourselves to integrating with another, we also agree to become another individual.[17]

With commitment often comes insecurity. An individual may wonder whether his or her partner is truly involved in the relationship and may (either consciously or subconsciously) use **secret tests** to measure the other's commitment. Leslie Baxter and William Wilmot discuss four of these secret tests: indirect suggestions, separation tests, endurance tests, and triangle tests.[18]

Indirect suggestions include flirting and joking about the seriousness of the relationship. They are designed to let partners observe each other's response. If, for example, a comment on living together is greeted with laughter, this response shows that the relationship is not intensifying very quickly. If the comment is taken seriously, however, this response indicates that commitment is high. **Separation tests** let individuals see how their partners feel about being apart. It's not a good sign if one's partner doesn't even notice a week-long absence. Daily phone calls and expressions of concern, on the other hand, indicate strong commitment. **Endurance tests** involve making demands on the time or energy of one's partner; they show individuals just how far a partner is willing to go to maintain the relationship. Finally, individuals use **triangle tests**

to see whether or not their partners are prone to jealousy. Although secret tests are frequently used, they are not necessarily good for a relationship, and they can easily backfire. No one likes to be manipulated, and, if discovered, secret tests can lead to defensiveness and resentment. They may seem to be an easy way to find out about the relationship, but they are no substitute for direct, open communication.

Once all tests are passed and both parties are sure of their feelings, they move on to **bonding.** Bonding consists of a public ritual to legitimize the relationship. Romantic couples may bond through marriage. Friends may bond by becoming "blood brothers [or sisters]" or by exchanging friendship rings. Even groups can bond, as when social clubs initiate new members. In any case, bonding rituals officially legitimize the relationship and, in subtle and not-so-subtle ways, change participants' attitudes toward and feelings about one another.

Throughout the entire journey toward intimacy, partners expand the boundaries of their relationship. According to Irwin Altman and Dalmas Taylor, relationships grow in breadth and depth as time progresses.[19] Figure 6-2

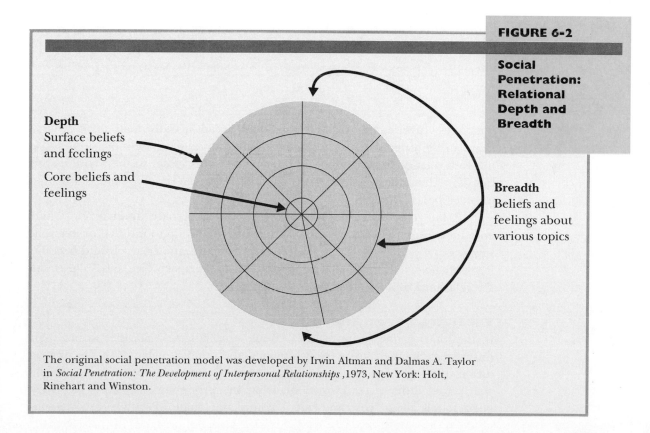

FIGURE 6-2

Social Penetration: Relational Depth and Breadth

Depth
Surface beliefs and feelings

Core beliefs and feelings

Breadth
Beliefs and feelings about various topics

The original social penetration model was developed by Irwin Altman and Dalmas A. Taylor in *Social Penetration: The Development of Interpersonal Relationships* ,1973, New York: Holt, Rinehart and Winston.

FIGURE 6-3

Knapp's
Relational
Development
Model: Stages
in Coming
Apart

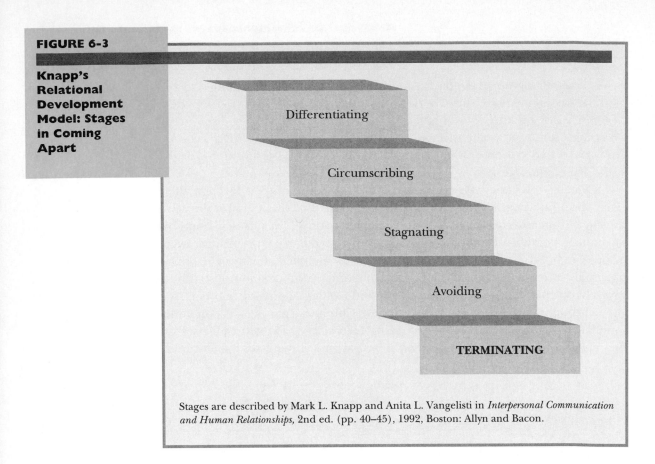

Stages are described by Mark L. Knapp and Anita L. Vangelisti in *Interpersonal Communication and Human Relationships,* 2nd ed. (pp. 40–45), 1992, Boston: Allyn and Bacon.

illustrates this idea. To expand **relational breadth,** individuals progressively share more aspects of themselves and communicate about more topics. To increase **relational depth,** they let their partners get closer to their core identities. For Altman and Taylor, the process of relational development is a matter of social penetration.

If the relationship lasts, partners continue to share intimate ideas and emotions. If, however, the relationship cannot stand up to internal or external stresses, it gradually weakens; patterns of communication narrow and become more shallow, and the relationship starts to break apart. Figure 6-3 illustrates the **relational dissolution stages.**

The Retreat From Intimacy

In the journey toward intimacy, a couple emphasizes similarities rather than differences. In the retreat from intimacy, the opposite occurs. In the first or **differentiating stage,** a couple begins to notice and comment on previously overlooked differences. Instead of using the pronouns "we" and "us," they begin to talk about "you" and "me," "yours" and "mine." Partners discover substantial areas of disagreement, which then become major topics of conversation. Arguments may be prefaced by comments such as "I don't understand how you could possibly like her" or "I can't believe you agree with him." Overt argument and conflict are hallmarks of this stage. Knapp believes that when differentiation quickly follows bonding, bonding may have taken place too rapidly, before the partners were able to negotiate a satisfactory relational culture.

In the journey toward intimacy, a couple emphasizes similarities rather than differences. In the retreat from intimacy, the opposite occurs.

Short periods of differentiation occur in all relationships; they don't always signal the beginning of the end. By reaffirming relational goals and focusing on similarities, partners may reverse their movement away from intimacy. Sometimes, however, differentiation leads to the second stage of relational breakdown, the **circumscribing stage.** In this stage members carefully restrict their communication. Certain topics are placed off limits because they are too painful. "Let's just skip it" or "I'd rather not discuss that" indicate that communication has become a mine field of potentially explosive topics. As a result, very little information is exchanged, and expressions of commitment decrease.

In a failing relationship, the next stage is the **stagnating stage.** This stage is characterized by silence and inactivity. Communication is infrequent, and when it does occur, it is stylized, rigid, and awkward, as though the partners were strangers. Talk may be overly formal and polite, with negative emotions being conveyed nonverbally. Partners don't bother to talk, because they believe it is useless. One might think that this uncomfortable stage cannot last long. Unfortunately, a couple may stagnate for months or even years, staying together because terminating seems too difficult, risky, or painful.

In the **avoiding stage,** partners separate either physically or emotionally. In a dating situation, one partner may suddenly stop answering the phone or disappear for weeks at a time. In a marriage, one spouse may spend more time at the office or visit relatives for the summer. If physical separation is impossible, couples may isolate themselves psychologically, behaving as though the other does not exist.

The final stage in relational disengagement is the **terminating stage.** If both parties are aware that their relationship is dissolving, termination may come as a relief. In other cases, it may be a heart-wrenching surprise. Either way, termination is the time when individuals come to terms with the fact that the relationship is over. Knapp believes that communication during this stage fulfills the three basic functions of other forms of leave-taking. It announces the upcoming separation, summarizes what has occurred during interaction, and determines the future of the relationship.

Variations in Relational Development

Keep in mind that Knapp's model is a general overview, not a specific prediction. It describes what often happens in relationships, not what inevitably happens. If you and a partner find yourselves in the differentiating stage, for example, you should not pack your bags and decide there is no hope for the relationship. Couples can turn relationships around by going back to and replaying earlier stages. If partners understand the problems they are facing, if they have basic interpersonal skills and sensitivities, and if they care enough, they can repair problematic relationships by exploring alternative forms of relating; taking on more functional roles; eliminating unhealthy interaction patterns; or searching for new ways to make the relationship rewarding.

In real life, couples do not always go through the stages together. One partner may think the relationship is at the casual, experimenting stage, whereas the other may believe the partners are ready to bond. Or one partner may be so busy at the office that he or she doesn't notice that the other partner is circumscribing.

Furthermore, not all couples take the same length of time to complete the steps, even when partners are in sync. Some couples are cautious and take a long time before risking commitment. Others rush through the early stages. This latter course is dangerous; if one of the early stages is skipped or rushed, later stages may be unstable, like a building constructed with a faulty foundation. For relationships to last, couples must work out agreements and develop healthy interaction patterns, processes that take time.

Duck's Relational Dissolution Model

In his **relational dissolution model,** Steve Duck looks at relational dissolution from a slightly different point of view. His model describes four kinds of work that individuals take on as they attempt to deal with a dissolving relationship. He calls these four phases the intrapsychic, dyadic, social, and grave-dressing phases. In Duck's words, the **intrapsychic phase** is founded "on a sense of grievance and distress at the partner's insensitivity or incapacity to fulfill one's needs adequately."[20] The dissatisfied individual goes over and over the relationship in his or her mind, focusing on the partner's negative behaviors and on the costs of staying in the relationship. The costs of leaving are also computed, as well as the possible rewards of entering alternative relationships. In this phase the partner who is unhappy evaluates the relationship and decides whether or not to say anything. The stress here is individual rather than dyadic, as one partner decides upon his or her best course of action.

In the **dyadic phase,** partners confront one another. They talk about their problems, deciding whether their relationship has enough positive aspects to keep them together and, if so, finding ways to repair the damage. If the partners decide to end the relationship, they deal with people outside the relationship in the **social phase,** announcing the breakup, letting friends and acquaintances know their sides of the story, and dealing with others' reactions. They also negotiate the shape any future contact will take.

Finally, in the **grave-dressing phase,** each party determines the meaning of the couple's time together, deciding what went wrong and what went right. In a sense, each looks for a way to rationalize the relationship and decides what to remember from it. This process is important because it affects future behavior and self-respect.

Duck insists that partners need a different set of communication skills to handle each phase. Although he does not specify in great detail what these skills are, it is possible to speculate about some of them. The abilities to think clearly and to interpret one's own feelings and behaviors, as well as those of one's partner, seem to be basic skills needed in the intrapsychic phase. Often relationships dissolve because partners lack empathy or because they have unrealistic expectations. Relational dissolution can be extremely stressful, and the intervention of a third party (a therapist or objective friend) can often help an individual clarify his or her feelings and perceive the situation more objectively.

In the dyadic phase the couple need good negotiation and conflict resolution skills. To work out their difficulties, they must discuss the relationship openly, without offending one another and without repressing their feelings. The ability to give straightforward feedback and to disclose personal feelings honestly is important here. In the social and grave-dressing phases, still wider skills are needed as partners communicate the news of the breakup to friends and acquaintances; reformulate their social circles; and come to understand how the relationship has affected them and how it will affect future interactions.

Interpersonal Attraction: Filtering Theory

We have seen how relationships change over time. But what causes people to enter relationships in the first place? Steve Duck feels that attraction is really a process of elimination. According to his **filtering theory,** we use a series of filters to judge how close to others we want to become.[21] At each filter, some potential partners are eliminated and some move on. The point at which someone is eliminated from further consideration determines the level of that relationship. Those who do not pass through the first filter remain strangers. Those who make it through the first but not the second become acquaintances, and so on, with those who make it to the end becoming intimates. Figure 6-4 shows how this process works.

What are the filters we use to regulate attraction? Duck identifies four filters: sociological or incidental, pre-interaction, interaction, and cognitive cues. **Sociological** or **incidental cues** are the demographic or environmental factors that determine probability of contact. They include factors such as where we work and live, how frequently we travel, and so on. Obviously, we cannot form relationships with people we have never met, and maintaining contact with someone thousands of miles away is extremely difficult. **Physical proximity** seems to be a key factor here. Numerous studies show that marriages and close friendships are most likely to occur between people who live close to one another. In fact, a classic study of friendships in a housing development showed that friendships depended on the distance between houses. Those whose houses faced inward onto a common court had more friends than those who lived in houses facing away.[22] These studies suggest that familiarity leads

FIGURE 6-4

Duck's Attraction Filters

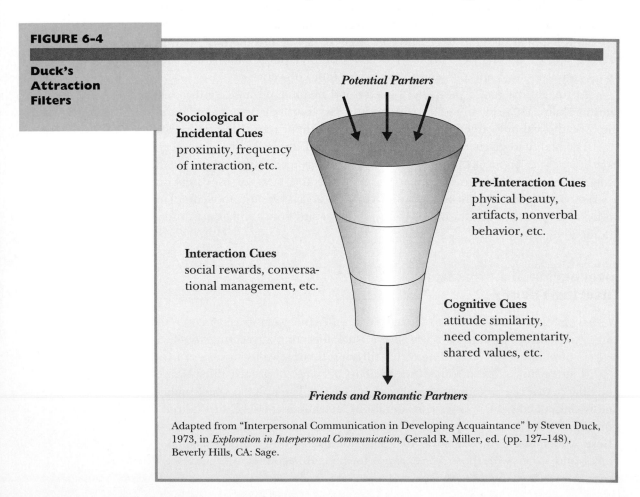

Potential Partners

Sociological or Incidental Cues
proximity, frequency of interaction, etc.

Pre-Interaction Cues
physical beauty, artifacts, nonverbal behavior, etc.

Interaction Cues
social rewards, conversational management, etc.

Cognitive Cues
attitude similarity, need complementarity, shared values, etc.

Friends and Romantic Partners

Adapted from "Interpersonal Communication in Developing Acquaintance" by Steven Duck, 1973, in *Exploration in Interpersonal Communication*, Gerald R. Miller, ed. (pp. 127–148), Beverly Hills, CA: Sage.

to attraction. To increase one's chance of forming a relationship, one must overcome isolation. *By carefully choosing where to live, work, and play, people can increase the nature and frequency of their interpersonal bonds.*

Pre-interaction cues are also important filters. People use nonverbal impressions to determine whether they wish to interact with others. We use body type, physical beauty, dress, and related artifacts to give us some idea of what others are like. We respond to some cues (hair color, height, etc.) because of personal preferences. Other cues tell us how similar or different another person may be or whether future interaction is likely to be rewarding. Whether or not they should, surface details often determine whether future interaction will occur. At least some of the time, the old expression "You never get a second chance to make a first impression" is true. Therefore, *it is important to become more aware of the ways silent nonverbal messages affect impression formation.*

Interaction cues occur once we have made initial contact. Some interactions are smooth and comfortable, whereas others are awkward and difficult. When topics flow easily, turn taking is smooth and effortless, eye contact and facial expression indicate friendliness and approval, and attraction is high. *The ability to manage conversations and to make interaction rewarding is an important factor in increasing attractiveness.* Luckily, conversational competence is learned, and, with some observation and a little practice, individuals can increase their interaction skills.

Cognitive cues constitute the last, and most important, filter. Studies show that the strongest factors in creating solid, long-lasting relationships are psychological. In the long run, the extent to which values are shared and attitudes and beliefs are similar is a more important determinant of friendship than is physical appearance. How do we get to know another person at this level? By communicating openly about our beliefs, attitudes, and values. This is why *it is important to disclose one's own beliefs and values and to elicit disclosure from others.* It is also important to be open to the possibilities in others. If we let initial filters keep us from getting to know people, we may be missing out on potentially rewarding relationships.

Increasing Relational Skills

Relationships are built through communication, and when communication goes awry, relationships fail. Thus, it is important to become aware of our own communication styles and to build relational skills. A first step in becoming better at interpersonal communication is to understand basic interpersonal processes such as those described in this chapter. By knowing how relationships develop and by realizing some of the problems that can plague relational

Relationships develop slowly. As we engage in everyday activities, we share information about who we are and what we value, information that allows us to build solid, long-lasting partnerships.

dyads, you will be better able to diagnose your own interactions. A second step is to observe your own behaviors as well as those of your partners. Because we are so involved in communication, our own communication behaviors are often hard for us to see. If you can develop the objectivity necessary to analyze your interactions, you will be well on your way to becoming a more effective communicator. A third step is to practice new behaviors. Many behaviors can increase our competence as communicators; two of the most important inter-personal skills are the ability to self-disclose appropriately and the ability to give effective feedback. These will be the last two topics of this chapter.

Toward More Effective Self-Disclosure

It is not uncommon during a period of interpersonal conflict to hear one person say to another, "But why didn't you say anything?" Neither is it uncommon to hear someone complain to a friend, "I can't believe [s]he said that. I was so embarrassed I didn't know what to do." Both of these comments indicate a problem in resolving the expressive-protective dialectic. In the first example, more openness is being called for. The speaker believes that if his or her partner had only spoken up, the conflict could have been averted. In the second example, too much openness has occurred. The speaker has been put on the spot by an inappropriate disclosure. Knowing just how open to be is an important interpersonal skill. We will now look at some guidelines for managing relational disclosure.

Self-disclosure occurs "when one person voluntarily tells another person things about himself which the other is unlikely to know or discover from other sources."[23] When we self-disclose, we share with another our past experiences, present feelings, basic values, and hopes and fears. In the process, we help our partner understand who we are, and we may even come to understand ourselves a little better.

> *When we self-disclose, we share with another our past experiences, present feelings, basic values, and hopes and fears. In the process, we help our partner understand who we are, and we may even come to understand ourselves a little better.*

Experts in interpersonal communication generally believe that although self-disclosure is good for a relationship, disclosures must be regulated. To blurt out whatever you think, whenever you think it is not a good communication practice. Remember that *not all statements about the self are true self-disclosures.* "I have to be honest and share this with you. No one around here can stand you" is not a disclosure, it's an attack. This kind of "open" communication is not going to help you build relationships, and it's not what communication experts talk about when they discuss self-disclosure.

True disclosures can be healthy for a relationship, but only if certain guidelines are followed. The first is that *self-disclosure is not appropriate in all relationships.* In deciding whether or not to reveal personal information, try to match the level of your disclosure to the level of your relationship. We usually don't tell our personal experiences to strangers (except, perhaps, for bartenders, therapists, and people sitting next to us on long-distance airline flights). We do tell our personal experiences to close friends and romantic partners. One of the reasons for not disclosing to everyone is that disclosure is a risk. Depending on what we reveal, we can lose friends, alienate family members, and ruin careers. People are not always sympathetic and understanding.

The person who discloses that he was once arrested for shoplifting or the person who confides to a friend that she is currently questioning her sexual orientation is taking a huge risk. Disclosures can come back to haunt us, for not everyone can be trusted to keep a confidence.

Another reason for not disclosing indiscriminately is that disclosures put a burden on others. Disclosures may create unwanted intimacy. The chance acquaintance who confides that he or she is in terrible trouble is asking for more than polite attention. He or she is asking for involvement. A close friend may be happy to provide the necessary counsel and comfort, a stranger usually is not. Thus, it is important to *consider the effect your disclosures will have on others.*

Even when you know that your partner will be open and receptive to disclosure, you should nonetheless be cautious about when and where to hold the discussion. It is important to *choose the right time and place for your disclosures.* Running up to your best friend in the hall and revealing a major problem ("Guess what? I think I'm pregnant. Got to run.") right before a major test is insensitive and foolish. Disclosures should not be bolts from the blue. They should take place in an environment and at a time that allows recipients to react appropriately.

Disclosures should also be related to what is happening in the "here and now." They should be connected to what is currently going on in the relationship. Any disconnected topic—particularly an unrelated disclosure—disrupts a conversation. If Elena and her roommate are discussing what to do next weekend and Elena suddenly says, "My dad lost his job when I was ten. We were so poor that I didn't get a birthday present for years," the disclosure is inappropriate. Elena doesn't seem to have a reason to bring up such a sensitive issue. The same disclosure might make perfect sense in another context. For example, if the roommate has just given Elena a small gift and Elena bursts into tears, the disclosure allows the roommate to understand Elena's behavior.

In general, *disclosure should be gradual.* It is a good idea to start out with fairly safe disclosures and then move on to more personal topics. As we have seen, relationships take time to develop and to deepen. We don't dive head-first into them, we test the waters first. The same is true for disclosures.

Finally, *disclosures should be reciprocal.* In general, we expect a disclosure by one party to be met with a disclosure by the other. If one person in a relationship does all the disclosing, the imbalance may signal opposing attitudes toward openness. Participants should learn to encourage their partners to disclose without forcing them or making them feel uncomfortable. They should also learn to modify their own disclosures and to wait until an appropriate atmosphere has been established.

Responding to Others' Disclosures

Communication is not one-sided. Disclosure is not something the sender does while the receiver sits passively by. Good communicators realize that disclosures call for helpful responses. In this section we consider some ways to respond that will help your partner with his or her problem and will bring you closer together.

Imagine this: You run into your best friend from high school. In the course of a long conversation, he turns to you and says, "I'm really depressed. I have a good job and I make an adequate salary, but I'm not happy. . . . I didn't do too well in school before, but maybe I will quit work and go back to school. I don't know what I should do." What do you say? Your response probably falls into one of the five categories identified by David Johnson. You may give advice, analyze your friend's problem, offer reassurance and support, ask questions, or help your friend clarify his thinking by paraphrasing his statement.[24] Each of these ways of responding bears a closer look.

Most people respond to this kind of statement by offering advice. They think about the problem, make a judgment about what ought to be done, and offer the individual a simple (and sometimes simplistic) solution. If your response is to encourage your friend to look for a new job, to quit immediately, or to hang on to his job and try taking a few courses in night school, you are using an **advising and evaluating response.** Sometimes people want you to offer them a plan of action, but often they don't. Note that in this example your friend said, not, "Tell me what to do," but, "I don't know what I should do." Often people jump in with an immediate plan of action, as though they were saying, "It's obvious what you should do. My judgment is superior to yours, so just follow my advice." The advice you give may be good, or it may be more appropriate for you than it is for your friend. In most cases, you won't have enough information about a problem to offer advice right away. You may eventually help your friend come up with his own plan, but it's probably best to use one of the other responses first.

If your response is to tell your friend why he feels the way he does, to analyze the causes of his dilemma, then you are using an **analyzing and interpreting response.** Telling your friend that depression is often internalized anger and suggesting that he may feel angry with himself because he dropped out of school is an example. Such a response may be insightful (if you know your friend very well), but it may be way off base (if your interpretation is based on something you heard on a daytime talk show). In either case, it is likely to cause defensiveness, for it sets you up as an expert on human behavior who knows other people's motivations better than they themselves do. As Johnson points out, "people will usually respond better when you help them think about themselves and their feelings than if you try to figure out what causes them to do the things they do."[25]

Many of you may respond to your friend's disclosure by telling him not to worry, assuring him that it will all work out, or telling him not to feel so depressed. By offering sympathy you have chosen a **reassuring and supporting response.** If your friend is so distraught that he needs to be calmed down before he can think about his problem seriously, this kind of response may be okay. It runs the danger, however, of cutting short the discussion (if everything is all right, why dwell on it?) and of making your friend feel he has no right to be unhappy.

If your immediate reaction is to gather more information, then you choose a **questioning and probing response.** This kind of response can be useful, especially if you believe that your friend can benefit from considering some aspect of the problem more fully. The response "How long have you felt depressed? How serious is your depression?" focuses attention on your friend's state of mind. "How did you do when you were in school before? Why did you drop out?" defines the problem in another way. Obviously, the questions you choose determine the direction of the conversation. Although questions can get at needed information, they can also be threatening, and they can often be veiled evaluations. "How in the world did you get yourself in such a mess?" may sound like a question, but it is really an evaluation.

Often it is a good idea to turn questions into reflective statements for the other person to respond to. Phrased as a question, "Why aren't you happy?" seems judgmental (as well as very difficult to answer). But phrased as a statement, "You're feeling very unhappy now," the response loses its judgmental tone, and the listener can more easily clarify his feelings. If your response to your friend's dilemma is something on the order of "In other words, you're depressed and puzzled because your job isn't fulfilling. Yet you're not sure your alternative, going back to school, will work out either," then you choose a **paraphrasing and understanding response.**

Many communication scholars believe that paraphrasing is the best of the alternatives, at least as a first step. Its main advantages are that it allows you to check your understanding of what is troubling your friend, it allows your friend to hear and think about what he has just said, and it shows that you are listening to him.[26] Its major disadvantage is that it may seem awkward until you get used to it.

Make sure that when you paraphrase you do not parrot back exactly what was said. Instead, offer your own understanding of what your friend was trying to say. And be careful not to get carried away in your paraphrasing. "So, what I hear you saying is that you're so depressed you don't want to live, because you're a failure at everything" puts the problem into your own words; unfortunately, it also completely misinterprets what was said. When paraphrasing, try to get at the gist of the problem without diminishing or enlarging it. This may take some practice, but the practice will pay off. By paraphrasing, you encourage your partner to explore the problem in his or her own way.

Rules for Effective Feedback

Although a paraphrase may be the most effective response in most situations, sometimes people want us to give them specific feedback. **Feedback** is information that allows individuals to control their behavior. It is information that tells people how they are doing and what they may need to change to be more effective. Competent communicators are open to feedback about their own behavior and know how to give useful feedback to others. In many cases, feedback presents no problem. "That was great!" is easy to say and is usually well received. Giving feedback about more sensitive issues, however, is not quite so simple. We will end this chapter by looking at five ways to make sure your feedback is effective.[27]

The first rule is to *own your own message*. When we have to give others unwelcome feedback, we often avoid blame by refusing to acknowledge that the message is ours. We may use phrases such as "everyone's angry" or "we're all beginning to worry," when what we really mean is "I'm angry" or "I'm worried." Although attributing the feedback to others may get you off the hook, it's basically dishonest. It's also confusing. Your partner is left with the idea that some unspecified others are upset, but he or she has no idea what you think. If others want to give your partner feedback, let them. If you want to give feedback, own up to it.

Also, *avoid apologizing for your feelings*. To avoid hurting someone else, you may place all the blame on yourself. If you are to blame, accept it. But if you aren't at fault, don't act as though you were. A statement such as, "I guess it's my fault that you borrowed my shirt and ruined it. Maybe I just didn't make it clear that I wanted it back in one piece, but, well, it did cost a lot and it was my favorite shirt" is not good feedback. This statement gives the impression that you don't really care about the shirt and that you don't expect any repayment, when in fact you do (and have every right to). The receiver of a message such as this can't be blamed if he or she doesn't understand the depth of your concern.

It is important to *make your messages specific and behavioral*. Often we avoid unpleasant topics by being vague. The object of good feedback is to give someone else useful information. Saying something such as, "Oh, I don't know, it's just your attitude" is not useful, because this statement doesn't explain what needs to be changed. "I was hurt when you didn't call me last week. It made me feel as though I don't count" is better because it relates to behavior. Your partner now knows what he or she did that caused the problem and what your feelings were. This kind of direct statement paves the way for a discussion of what each of you expects from the other and allows you to set norms for future behavior. People often hurt others simply because they are unaware that their behavior is a problem. In many cases, they would have been happy to change if only they had known. Specific behavioral information gives them this knowledge.

Verbal and nonverbal behaviors should support one another. People often have trouble expressing their emotions nonverbally. Instead, they suppress them. This is particularly true of anger. In an attempt to remain calm, an individual may smile and say (in a perfectly pleasant voice), "You know, I'm very angry right now." This double message is confusing and potentially double binding. In effective feedback, the verbal and nonverbal channels are congruent.

Finally, it is important to keep your partner from feeling defensive. This means that you should *avoid evaluating and interpreting your partner unless he or she specifically asks you to do so.* As we have seen, there are times when your partner may want to know your interpretation. In most cases, however, unsolicited judgments cause defensiveness. How helpful would it be if someone were to turn to you and say, "I think you should hear this for your own good. You are the craziest, most narcissistic, most sociopathic personality I've ever met"? Attacks like this are never helpful and can only hurt relationships.

Summary

In this chapter we begin our consideration of communication contexts with a discussion of interpersonal communication. The most frequently encountered of all communication contexts, interpersonal communication refers to two-person, face-to-face interaction. Communication of this type is direct, personal, immediate, spontaneous, and informal. If we take a developmental view, interpersonal communication is also governed by psychological level rules. In long-term dyads, we understand our partner at a very personal level and develop unique ways of interacting.

Managing communication is never easy. In every context, we must balance conflicting demands that pull us in different directions. In interpersonal relationships, we must balance the goals of expressiveness and protectiveness, autonomy and togetherness, and novelty and predictability. We must also work to create a stable and satisfying relational profile. All of this work is done through communication.

To communicate successfully, couples must avoid dysfunctional patterns such as rigid role relations, disconfirmations, paradoxical messages, and spirals. Each of these patterns limits the freedom of participants and sends ambiguous and destructive messages. One key to avoiding these potential problems is to focus as much as possible on patterns rather than on personalities.

Relationships are always changing. As individuals get to know and trust one another, they go through a series of stages: initiating, experimenting, intensifying, and integrating. As they pass through these stages, a couple often use secret tests to gather information about each others' level of commitment. Once tests are passed, the couple may decide to engage in bonding, a public legitimation of their relationship. Unfortunately, relationships don't always work out. When relationships dissolve, they pass through the stages of differentiating, circumscribing, stagnating, and avoiding until they reach termination. During each of these stages, including the last, partners do important relational work that calls for different sets of relational skills. The extent to which a couple pass through the stages of forming a relationship is often determined by their level of attraction. Interpersonal theorists have likened attraction to a sequential filtering process whereby potential relational partners are judged and eliminated.

Relationships are built and maintained through communication. How can communicators become more skillful at relational development? Because relationships are built on information, one method is to develop effective ways to exchange information. Communicators should develop the skill of self-disclosure, offering their partner access to personal information. They should know when and how much to open up to one another. Communicators should also know how to respond to disclosures by recognizing when it is appropriate to advise, interpret, support, question, or paraphrase. Finally, communicators should know how to give feedback in clear, nonevaluative ways. By practicing these skills, we can become more effective at the important, but often overlooked, form of communication: interpersonal.

Key Terms

Listed below are the key terms used in this chapter, along with the number of the page on which each is explained.

interpersonal communication   160
dyadic communication   160
developmental approach   161
cultural level rules   162
sociological level rules   162
psychological level rules   162
looking-glass self   163
social comparison   164
expressive-protective dialectic   165

self-disclosure   165
autonomy-togetherness dialectic   165
novelty-predictability dialectic   166
dialectical emphasis   166
pseudo-synthesis   166
reaffirmation   167
relational profile   167
dominance   169
one-up role   169

Review Questions

1. What is interpersonal communication? What kinds of situations are classed as interpersonal? Compared to other contexts, what are the main characteristics of communication in dyads?

2. What is the developmental approach to defining interpersonal communication? As communication becomes more personal, what changes occur? What are examples of cultural, sociological, and psychological level rules?

3. Why do we enter dyads? What do they provide us? How does interpersonal communication affect our sense of self? What is the looking-glass self? What is social comparison?

4. What three dialectical tensions do people in dyads need to balance? In what three

ways can these tensions be resolved? Which is the best way to resolve these tensions?

5. According to the text, in the process of finding a balance between opposing needs, partners create relational profiles. What issues make up a relational profile?

6. What patterns of dominance can be identified in dyads? What is the difference between complementarity and symmetry? Think of examples of one-up and one-down statements. What problems occur due to rigid complementarity, competitive symmetry, and submissive symmetry?

7. What is a disconfirmation? Why is it so damaging? In what seven ways can we disconfirm one another?

8. What is a paradox? What are the characteristics of a double bind? Why are paradoxes dysfunctional? What is a spiral? What is an interpersonal self-fulfilling prophecy? How can a couple stop a spiral once it starts?

9. What are the stages in the journey toward intimacy? What kind of communication happens at each stage? At which stage might you expect phatic communication? At which stage might people exchange intimacy trophies? What are secret tests? What do people hope to accomplish by using them? What four kinds of tests do couples often use?

10. How does the Altman-Taylor model illustrate what occurs during the journey toward intimacy? As couples move away from intimacy, how do relational breadth and depth change?

11. What are the stages in the journey away from intimacy? What occurs in each stage? Do all couples go through the stages in exactly the same way? According to the Duck relational dissolution model, what four kinds of work do individuals do as relationships dissolve? What skills do you think people need to do this work effectively?

12. What is filtering theory? What are the four filters that regulate attraction? Which filter includes physical proximity?

13. What is self-disclosure? Are all statements about the self true self-disclosures? Is self-disclosure appropriate in all relationships? If a person decides to self-disclose, what are some rules for doing so effectively?

14. When someone self-discloses to you, what responses might you use? What are the problems with using each kind of response? Which response is generally considered to be the most effective, at least as a first step?

15. What is feedback? What five rules can you follow to make sure your feedback is effective?

Suggested Readings

Johnson, David W. (1993). *Reaching out: Interpersonal effectiveness and self-actualization* (5th ed.). Boston: Allyn and Bacon.

This book gives excellent prescriptive advice about how to improve interpersonal skills. It also gives exercises and projects that can be used to practice interpersonal communication.

Knapp, Mark L., & Vangelisti, Anita L. (1992). *Interpersonal communication and human relationships* (2nd ed.). Boston: Allyn and Bacon.

This text provides a complete discussion of relational development.

Wilmot, William. (1987). *Dyadic communication* (3rd ed.). New York: Random House.

An intelligent and thorough discussion of interpersonal communication theory and research. It is especially strong on pragmatic patterns and on the relationship between self-identity and interpersonal communication.

Notes

1. Miller, Gerald R., & Steinberg, Mark. (1975). *Between people: A new analysis of interpersonal communication.* Chicago: Science Research Associates.

2. Trenholm, Sarah. (1991). *Human communication theory* (2nd ed.). Englewood Cliffs, NJ: Prentice-Hall, 161.

3. Allen, Woody. (1982). *Four films of Woody Allen.* New York: Random House, 105.

4. Cooley, Charles Horton. (1968). The social self: On the meanings of "I." In Chad Gordon & Kenneth J. Gergen (Eds.), *The self in social interactions, I: Classic and contemporary perspectives.* New York: Wiley, 87–91.

5. Wilmot, William. (1987). *Dyadic communication* (3rd ed.). New York: Random House.

6. Kinch, John W. (1972). A formalized theory of the self-concept. In Jerome Manis & Bernard N. Meltzer (Eds.), *Symbolic interaction* (2nd ed.). Boston: Allyn and Bacon, 245–252.

7. Festinger, Leon. (1954). A theory of social comparison processes. *Human Relations, 2* (2), 117–140.

8. Rosenberg, Morris. (1967). Psychological selectivity in self-esteem formation. In Carolyn W. Sherif & Muzafer Sherif (Eds.), *Attitude, ego-involvement, and change.* New York: Wiley, 26–50; cited in Wilmot, 67.

9. Rawlins, William. (1983). Openness as problematic in ongoing friendship: Two conversational dilemmas. *Communication Monographs, 50,* 1–13; Baxter, Leslie A. (1990). Dialectical contradictions in developing relationships. *Journal of Social and Personal Relationships, 7,* 69–88.

10. Wilmot, 169.

11. Ibid., 171–172.

12. Trenholm, Sarah, & Jensen, Arthur. (1992). *Interpersonal communication* (2nd ed.). Belmont, CA: Wadsworth, 41–44.

13. Burgoon, Judee K., & Hale, Jerold L. (1984). The fundamental topoi of relational communication. *Communication Monographs, 51,* 193–214.

14. Sieburg, Evelyn. (1975). *Interpersonal confirmation: A paradigm for conceptualization and measurement.* San Diego: United States International University. (ERIC Document Reproduction Service No. ED 098 634)

15. Wilmot, 148.

16. Knapp, Mark L., & Vangelisti, Anita L. (1992). *Interpersonal communication and human relationships* (2nd ed.). Boston: Allyn and Bacon; Wood, Julia T. (1982). Communication and relational culture: Bases for the study of human relationships. *Communication Quarterly, 30,* (2), 75–83.

17. Knapp & Vangelisti, 39.

18. Baxter, Leslie A., & Wilmot, William. (1984). "Secret tests": Social strategies for acquiring information about the state of the relationship. *Human Communication Research, 11,* 171–202.

19. Altman, Irwin, & Taylor, Dalmas A. (1973). *Social penetration: The development of interpersonal relationships.* New York: Holt, Rinehart and Winston.

20. Duck, Steve. (1982). A topography of relationship disengagement and dissolution. In S. W. Duck (Ed.), *Personal relationships 4: Dissolving personal relationships.* New York: Academic, 16.

21. Duck, Steven. (1973). Interpersonal communication in developing acquaintance. In Gerald R. Miller (Ed.), *Explorations in interpersonal communication.* Beverly Hills, CA: Sage, 127–148.

22. Festinger, Leon, Schachter, Stanley, & Back, K. (1950). *Social pressures in informal groups: A study of human factors in housing.* New York: Harper and Row.

23. Pearce, W. Barnett, & Sharp, Steward M. (1973). Self-disclosing communication. *Journal of Communication, 23,* 409–425, 414.

24. Johnson, David W. (1993). *Reaching out: Interpersonal effectiveness and self-actualization* (5th ed.). Boston: Allyn and Bacon, 179. Johnson gives excellent sample problems and responses, as well as good advice on how to respond helpfully.

25. Ibid., 181.

26. Ibid., 183–184.

27. Trenholm & Jensen, 327–328; see also Johnson, 112–113.

7

Group
Communication

Much as we may hate

to admit it, groups

tell us what to think

and feel and how to act.

For good or ill,

we are who we are

because of the groups we

have been a part of.

Groups affect us throughout our lives. We are born into family groups, play and learn in friendship and school groups, and spend much of our adult life in work groups. Most Americans think of the individual as the basic social unit, but others believe that the group is even more basic, that individuals are merely products of group interaction.[1] In fact, R. E. Pittinger and his colleagues argue that it is

> *not really useful to think of individuals as the units out of which groups and societies are constructed; it is more fruitful to think of an individual as the limiting case of a group when, for the moment, there is no one else around.*[2]

In many ways Pittinger is correct, for we are shaped by the groups we've belonged to, and, even after we leave them, they continue to live on in us. Much as we may hate to admit it, groups tell us what to think and feel and how to act. For good or ill, we are who we are because of the groups we have been a part of.

What Is a Group?

Not every aggregate is a group. Groups, like dyads, develop over time. A **group** is a special kind of entity. It is a collection of individuals who, as a result of interacting with one another over time, become interdependent, developing shared patterns of behavior and a collective identity.

Characteristics of Groups

One way to see how "groupness" develops is by considering the development of a team. The athletes who show up for tryouts at the beginning of a season are not yet a group. Although they hope to become a group, at this point they are merely a collection of individuals. As they begin to train together, however, they gradually take on the characteristics of a true group.

A collection of people develops into a group through interaction. It is through **interaction** that an aggregate of individual athletes becomes a functioning team. If the team is relatively small, communication is direct and participation is equal. If it is larger, specialized roles such as trainer, captain, and assistant coach develop, and messages are conveyed through specialized networks. Whichever is the case, without communication the team could not exist.

As a result of communication, *the behaviors of group members become interdependent; in a true group, any action by one affects all.* **Interdependence** is an important characteristic of groups, for it means that separate individuals have become a functioning whole. In athletics, it is not the individual but the team that wins or loses. If team members act independently, pursuing individual goals rather than team goals, the team never gels and may eventually disintegrate.

In the process of becoming interdependent, *members develop and share stable and predictable norms, values, and role structures.* Each group develops a unique culture that sets it apart from other groups, a culture that tells group members how to behave, what to value, and who to be. Once these **shared behavioral standards** develop, *members experience a sense of identity and psychological closeness.* They take pride in their shared membership, and being part of the team becomes a primary identity for them. The stronger and more cohesive their sense of membership, the stronger their **collective identity** and the more they become a true team. When all these characteristics develop—interaction, interdependence, shared behavioral standards, and a sense of membership—"groupness" has been achieved. Without these characteristics, individuals remain separate and isolated. (Table 7-1 on page 198 summarizes the characteristics of groups.)

> *Each group develops a unique culture that sets it apart from other groups, a culture that tells group members how to behave, what to value, and who to be.*

196

In true groups, members perceive themselves as interdependent parts of a whole. Their sense of identity and belonging is constructed through communication.

Group Size: How Big Is a Small Group?

In discussing the characteristics of groups, we have so far avoided one topic: group size. Exactly how big is a small group? The answer to this question is not as straightforward as it seems. Although most people agree that the lower limit of a small group is three, they disagree on a small group's upper limits. We say a group begins at three because something special happens to communication when a third person enters a relationship, something that does not occur in a dyad.

Newscaster Jane Pauley once remarked, "Somehow three children are many more than two."[3] Pauley is right. For a number of reasons, **triads,** or groups of three, are much more complex than dyads, and three-person communication is different from two-person. One reason is that the number of communication channels increases dramatically with three people. In a dyad, partners don't need to choose whom to talk to; there is only one channel, A to B. In a triad, there are suddenly six channels: A to B, A to C, B to C, A to B and C, B to A and C, and C to A and B. And as the number of people in a group increases, the number of channels rises dramatically. In a seven-person group, for example, the number of potential relationships is 966. Members in

TABLE 7-1

**Characteristics
of Groups**

Interaction	Groups are constructed through communication. As members interact with one another regularly, interaction networks develop, and repeated use of these communication channels links group members.
Interdependence	Member behaviors become interconnected. In a true group, each member affects every other member. People who are interdependent share common goals and a common fate.
Shared Behavioral Standards	Groups develop unique ways of doing things. Each member takes on a role within the group, and the group as a whole abides by shared norms. Members implicitly know and follow the kinds of behaviors that are appropriate within the group. In this way, the group develops a group structure.
Collective Identity	In true groups, members perceive themselves as part of a whole. They feel a sense of closeness to other members. In addition to having an "I" identity, they develop a "we" identity based on group membership.

large groups must work harder to include one another and to ensure equal participation. Often groups solve this problem by developing formal roles, such as leader, follower, or harmonizer, and by using specialized networks.

Triads, like larger groups, also tend to be less stable than dyads. If you have ever lived with two other people, you may have experienced the tendency of a triad to break down into a primary dyad plus one outsider.[4] Three-person groups have to work hard to maintain cohesion. If more people join a group, the tendency to divide into subunits increases markedly.

As groups increase in size, they become more unwieldy. At some point, they become too large for the members to interact directly with one another. At the point when members no longer recognize and relate to one another as

At the point when members no longer recognize and relate to one another as equal individuals, the small group ceases to exist, becoming a large group or an organization.

equal individuals, the small group ceases to exist, becoming a large group or an organization. Under extraordinary circumstances, a small group may include as many as twenty people, but most of the time the upper limit is much smaller, around ten or twelve. In reviewing a study of jury deliberations, Ernest Bormann tells us that in twelve-person groups, five to seven people often hold the discussion while the others listen silently.[5] Bormann also found that groups of more than ten or eleven tend to break into smaller cliques.

What is the ideal size for a group? Dan Rothwell tells us, "the appropriate size for a group is the smallest size capable of performing the task effectively."[6] Other experts are more specific. They feel that the optimum size for a problem-solving group is from five to seven people. A group of this size has enough members to ensure a large pool of ideas and information yet not so many members as to inhibit equal participation.

Why Communicate in Groups?

If groups are unwieldy and unstable and if one needs special skills to communicate in groups, why bother? Why not work by oneself? Because there are advantages to working in groups. Whereas some tasks are best done by individuals, other tasks benefit from the input of several people. In general, the more complex the task and the more difficult its implementation, the more it needs the multiple inputs that occur in group interaction.

The first advantage of working in a small group is that *groups provide more input than do individuals*. Often complex problems need knowledge that goes beyond that of a single individual. Having five or six heads rather than one means that more ideas can be generated and explored. Researchers who have studied small groups often speak of an effect known as **group synergy.** Put simply, group synergy is the idea that groups are often more effective than the best individuals within them. Something extraordinary happens to people when they work with others: their output surpasses what it would have been if they had worked alone.

> *Something extraordinary happens to people when they work with others: their output surpasses what it would have been if they had worked alone.*

People working in groups can pool information, share perspectives, and use one another's ideas as springboards. They can also motivate and energize one another to keep searching for a solution.

A second advantage of working with others is that *cohesive groups provide support and commitment*. Sometimes tasks are too large for a single individual, either because they require a great deal of planning or because special effort is needed to implement them. Sometimes problems are too serious to face alone. By sharing the workload and by offering encouragement and support, groups can take on difficult and complex tasks that individuals would hesitate to undertake by themselves.

A final advantage of groups is that *groups can meet members' interpersonal needs*. We often work with others because we like being with people and because we feel they can help us meet individual needs. One way to think of need satisfaction in groups is to consider the three basic **interpersonal needs** described by psychologist William Schutz: the needs for inclusion, control, and affection.[7]

The **inclusion need** is the need to establish identity by associating with others. As we saw in the previous chapter, other people give us a sense of self. Groups are especially important for enhancing identity. They tell us who we are, and, even more, they tell us that it is okay to be who we are. People with especially high needs for self-definition can find a stable sense of self in working with others. Group members can also help others establish identity by offering them inclusion.

In addition, groups satisfy control needs. The **control need** is the need to prove one's worth and competence by making effective decisions. By providing opportunities for leadership, groups can validate members' feelings of self-worth. Groups can also provide guidance and control for people who feel overwhelmed by responsibility.

Finally, groups can satisfy affection needs. The **affection need** is the need to develop close, caring relationships with others. By establishing friendships and by getting to know one another intimately, group members can satisfy their need to receive affection, as well as their need to show affection to others.

Managing Group Communication

Groups can be effective in helping individuals solve problems and complete tasks; they can also provide emotional support and personal rewards. To get the most from groups, however, members need to understand how to manage group interaction. They must be aware of potential problems that can beset inexperienced groups. In this section we turn our attention to some of these problems and look for ways to overcome them. We'll begin by discussing two group dialectics: the need for group members to balance individual and group needs and the need to resolve the tension between task and maintenance goals. We'll then look at the way poor communication can result in poor decision making and at ways groups can avoid the serious problem called groupthink.

Balancing Group and Individual Needs

In discussing interpersonal communication, we saw that couples are often beset by contradictory needs—the needs for individuality and interdependence, openness and privacy, and novelty and familiarity. Couples must work out these relational dialectics if they are to create a stable and satisfying relational culture. As we shall see, groups experience similar pressures. And unless a group balances its opposing needs, group communication can fail. The first dialectic is between the needs of the group as a whole and the needs of the individual members.

Group Socialization Processes

Richard Moreland and John Levine, two social psychologists who study group behavior, see **group socialization** as a kind of contest between the individual and the group.[8] Throughout the life of their relationship, individuals try to influence the group to meet their needs, whereas the group as a whole seeks to influence individuals to do what is best for it.

Members have their own reasons for being part of a group. They join groups, at least in part, to receive individual rewards. Throughout their membership, they repeatedly measure the extent to which they are receiving these rewards. Moreland and Levine call this process **evaluation.** As a result of evaluation, the level of member satisfaction, or **commitment,** either stays the

Transition into a group is not always easy. Groups must offer a new member acceptance and provide him or her with a place in the group. Only when the commitment of both group and individual is high will socialization be successful.

same, rises, or falls. In the first case, members determine that no change is necessary, and they simply maintain their relationship with the group. In the latter two cases, members decide that some kind of change, or **role transition,** is necessary, and they become either more or less engaged in the life of the group.

The evaluation process begins when a **prospective member** scouts out and evaluates prospective groups, committing himself or herself to the one that he or she evaluates most positively. If the group agrees to accept the person, he or she experiences the role transition from prospective member to **new member.** Often this transition is marked by an official ceremony and is followed by some kind of orientation. Over time, new members experience additional transitions. If commitment rises, they become **full members.** If commitment falls, they become either **marginal members** or **ex-members.** (Figure 7-1 shows the major role transitions that members go through as they enter, find acceptance in, diverge from, and, finally, exit group life.)

What factors cause a rise in commitment and therefore a deeper involvement in the life of the group? If a group has high status, if it can get things done, and if its social atmosphere is positive, members will feel group commitment. In addition, members become committed to groups that allow them to act in desired ways. One member may turn to a group to demonstrate leadership ability. Another member may seek friendship or security. Only if the group gives members what they want will members continue the relationship.

> *If a group has high status, if it can get things done, and if its social atmosphere is positive, members will feel group commitment.*

At the same time that members try to influence the group, the group tries to influence members. Just as prospective members shop around for the best group available, so groups try to recruit the best members, admitting only those who meet entry criteria. Think for a minute of yourself as the prospective member and the school you are now attending as the group. In deciding to admit you and to reject others, the school was attempting to maintain its standards and identity. When you decided to attend, you became a new member. In the administration's eyes, first-year students are on a kind of probation and aren't given full status until they prove themselves.

If you are at or beyond the sophomore level, you have achieved the status of a full member of your school. Of course, at any time, if your grades fall or if your conduct violates school standards, you may become a marginal member, and the school will make special efforts to resocialize you. If these efforts fail and you completely refuse to meet the school's requirements, the administration may ask you to leave.

From summer orientation to graduation, ceremonies mark your progress. Along the way, the school tries to make you into its idea of the model student, and you either go along or resist. This process happens not only in large organizations such as colleges but also in everyday small groups. Fraternities or sororities, work or friendship groups, and even families attempt to socialize members. In each case, member and group must reach agreement on what they are to receive from one another. Both must have realistic expectations, and both must be willing to meet some of the others' needs while maintaining their own standards.

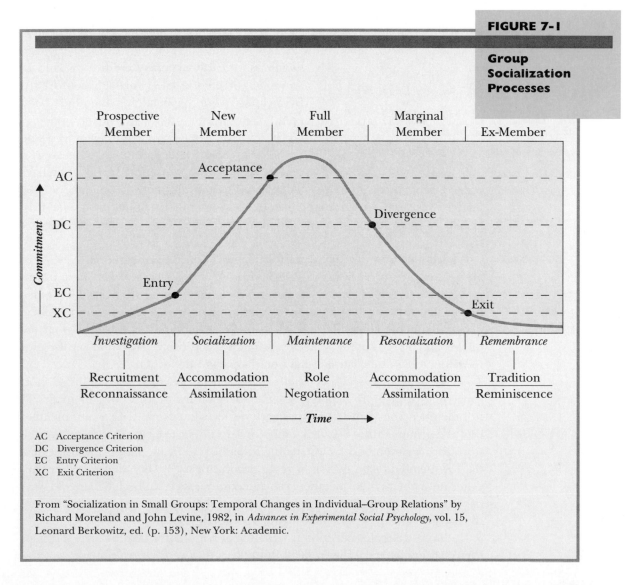

FIGURE 7-1

Group Socialization Processes

AC   Acceptance Criterion
DC   Divergence Criterion
EC   Entry Criterion
XC   Exit Criterion

From "Socialization in Small Groups: Temporal Changes in Individual–Group Relations" by Richard Moreland and John Levine, 1982, in *Advances in Experimental Social Psychology*, vol. 15, Leonard Berkowitz, ed. (p. 153), New York: Academic.

Adapting to Group Pressures

How can members adapt most easily to group socialization and find a balance between individual and group needs? One way is to *recognize that full membership comes only with time.* At different stages in one's relationship with a group, different behaviors are expected. Rookies can't make the same demands on a team that veteran players can. A first lieutenant doesn't have the same status as a general. And the brand-new, just-out-of-school management trainee doesn't sit down at the head of the table and tell the third-line manager what to do.

Before a new member can be accepted, he or she must earn the right. Using an economic metaphor, Edwin Hollander created the concept of idiosyncrasy credit to explain how groups regulate the behavior of inexperienced members.[9] An **idiosyncrasy credit** is a kind of symbolic currency earned through conformity. By meeting group expectations, members build up a "credit balance" that can later be traded in for innovative behavior. Group members who try to take over leadership too soon or who deviate from group consensus before they have earned enough credit are usually rejected by more established members. Hollander's research reinforces the idea that new members should proceed slowly, gradually increasing their participation once they have earned the group's trust.

> *Group members who try to take over leadership too soon or who deviate from group consensus before they have earned enough credit are usually rejected by more established members.*

Another way to make a successful transition into a group is to *recognize the written and unwritten norms that govern each level of membership.* These norms may be explicit rules, written down and available to all, or they may be implicit norms that can only be picked up through imitation. Whether or not members decide to follow all of the group's norms, they should be aware of what the norms are. This awareness takes careful and sensitive observation on the part of the member and clear messages on the part of the group.

Adapting to group life is usually easier with support from others. This support can come from more experienced members or from other new members. A full member who knows the ropes and who is willing to initiate a new member into the group culture is called a **mentor.** Mentors can help smooth role transitions for new members by instructing them how to fit in. Support is also essential for members who decide to resist group norms. By banding together with other newcomers, new members can sometimes successfully challenge old ways of doing things. Whereas a lone member usually cannot exert enough pressure to change a group, several new members sometimes can.

Successful role transition is a matter of negotiation and balance. Perhaps the most important thing to keep in mind is that *members have a right to expect the group to meet some of their needs, just as the group has a right to expect members to contribute to its goals.* Only by recognizing the legitimacy of both parties' goals can groups and individuals successfully work together.

Taking on Task and Maintenance Roles

Another dialectic is important in group life: the tension between task and maintenance goals. Most groups exist for a reason. Often they form to solve a problem or to reach a decision. This dimension of group behavior is called its **task dimension,** and the output of this dimension is called **productivity.** We expect groups to produce results.

At the same time, groups must also fulfill social functions. Groups must devote some of their efforts to creating a positive group climate. This dimension of a group's behavior is called its **maintenance** or **social dimension,** and its output is called **group cohesiveness.** Although productivity and cohesiveness are sometimes in conflict, they are closely related. Successful groups must achieve both. A group that works so hard on its task that it neglects member feelings eventually dissolves. Cohesiveness is the glue that holds a group together. Similarly, a group that avoids work to focus entirely on maintenance ends up losing members, for no one wants to be part of an unproductive group. One of the keys to managing group communication is to behave in ways that advance both productivity and cohesion.

> *A group that works so hard on its task that it neglects member feelings eventually dissolves. Cohesiveness is the glue that holds a group together.*

All of us find some behaviors easier than others. Often we specialize in either task or maintenance behaviors. The key to being an effective group member, however, lies in being able to take on both kinds of behaviors, depending on the needs of the group. Behaviors that help the group accomplish its task are called **task roles.** They include acting as information giver, information seeker, evaluator-critic, and so on. Behaviors that enhance the social climate of the group are called **maintenance roles.** Roles such as encourager, standard setter, or harmonizer are examples. Finally, personal goals that do not help the group reach either of its basic goals are called **negative roles.** Negative roles are generally dysfunctional and indicate that a member is having trouble balancing group and individual needs. Table 7-2 lists some of the roles necessary for group productivity and cohesiveness, and Table 7-3 on page 208 outlines negative, dysfunctional roles.

How can one person increase group effectiveness? First, it is important to *become as flexible as possible in both task and maintenance roles.* The best group member is the one who can recognize and provide whatever the group needs at a particular time. Such a member must watch the group process carefully, realizing that what the group needs may not necessarily be what the member likes to do best. Highly task-oriented members often lose patience with the group when it gets off track; they fail to understand that occasional jokes, friendly chitchat, and well-timed breaks are not a waste of time but are ways to build group cohesion. Instead of giving a steady barrage of opinions, the task-oriented group member should learn to stop and make sure other members are comfortable.

TABLE 7-2

Task Roles

Role	Description
Initiator-Contributor	Suggests new ideas to group or offers new way of regarding group problem
Information Seeker	Asks for clarification of suggestions and for information and facts pertinent to problem
Opinion Seeker	Asks for clarification of values associated with group problem or with decision suggestions
Information Giver	Offers facts or generalizations or relates experiences relevant to group problem
Opinion Giver	States beliefs or opinions pertinent to group problem or to decision suggestions
Elaborator	Thinks of examples, offers rationales, or works out details of previous suggestions
Coordinator	Pulls together ideas and suggestions and coordinates work of various subgroups
Orienter	Summarizes what has occurred or asks questions about the path the group will take
Evaluator-Critic	Develops standards for group functioning and compares group performance to standards
Energizer	Prods group to action and stimulates greater levels of group activity
Procedural Technician	Expedites group movement by taking on routine tasks
Recorder	Writes down suggestions, records decisions, and takes minutes

Similarly, the maintenance-oriented member should learn how to enhance task development. A harmonizer, for example, should realize that the line between relieving tension and being a clown is thin. Although maintenance is a good thing, there are times when the group must get down to work. One way to increase your own flexibility is to look at Tables 7-2 and 7-3 and determine the roles you play most frequently. Then practice playing different roles until you feel comfortable with a large repertoire.

Maintenance Roles

Role	Description
Encourager	Accepts and praises others' contributions
Harmonizer	Relieves tension and mediates disagreements
Compromiser	Seeks to find solution for conflict that involves own ideas
Gatekeeper-Expediter	Keeps communication channels open and facilitates others' participation
Standard Setter	Expresses maintenance standards or applies standards to group process
Group Observer	Observes group process and offers feedback about maintenance procedures
Follower	Accepts ideas of group and serves as audience

apted from "Functional Roles of Group Members," by Kenneth Benne and Paul Sheats, 1948, *Journal of ial Issues, 4,* pp. 41–49.

TABLE 7-3

Negative Roles

Role	Description
Dominator	Refuses to allow others to express their opinions and dominates discussion
Blocker	Prolongs or stops decision making by foot-dragging and nit-picking
Self-Confessor	Distracts group by disclosing personal problems and by using group for personal therapy
Help Seeker	Constantly expresses own inadequacy and asks group for sympathy and compliments
Recognition Seeker	Spends time boasting about own accomplishments in order to be center of attention
Special-Interest Pleader	Manipulates group in interests of some other group; has hidden agenda
Playboy or Playgirl	Fails to take group seriously; spends time playing around and mocks serious behavior
Joker or Clown	Uses humor and horseplay to divert group from task

In addition, it is important to *avoid disruptive individual roles.* We all bring our own hidden agendas to the groups we belong to. A **hidden agenda** is a personal goal that lies below the surface and that can get in the way of group performance. Sometimes hidden agendas are compatible with group goals (for example, when a group member channels a need for recognition into effective task leadership), and sometimes they are incompatible (as when a team member grandstands or hogs the ball instead of passing it off). Members should examine their own agendas and guard against dysfunctional behavior. At the same time, the group should be aware of member needs and try to satisfy them. If this is impossible, the group should discuss members' dysfunctional behaviors with those members, pointing out the effects of the behaviors on the group as a whole.

Combating Groupthink

We have seen that it is important for task groups to feel cohesive and confident. Sometimes, however, a group gets too confident and begins to make poor decisions. We call this state **groupthink,** and it can have very serious repercussions. A number of communication scholars have argued that the 1986 explosion of the space shuttle *Challenger* was a classic example of groupthink. They contend that poor decision making on the part of Thiokol engineers and NASA officials led these experts to underestimate risks, overestimate the likelihood of success, and ignore warnings and their own misgivings.[10] In this case, a failure of group communication may have led to death and disaster.

What exactly is groupthink? Irving Janis, who coined the term, defines it as "a mode of thinking that people engage in when they are deeply involved in a cohesive in-group, when the members' strivings for unanimity override their motivation to realistically appraise alternative courses of action."[11] In groupthink, group members believe they can do no wrong. This problem can occur when cohesion is too high, when group members are too similar (so that no new ideas challenge group consensus), or when the group is isolated from outside influences.

Groupthink has several symptoms. The first is an **illusion of invulnerability.** A group immersed in groupthink believes so strongly it is the best that it loses all sense of reality. The second symptom is **belief in the group's own morality.** Members feel that their actions and beliefs are more valuable than those of people outside the group. This symptom is closely related to a third symptom, the tendency to hold **shared stereotypes.** Members take on an "us versus them" mentality, believing that anyone who opposes the group is stupid or wrong. Problems or failures are explained away by **collective rationalizations,** which allow members to stick to an ill-advised course of action even in the face of contrary information. Individual members who begin to doubt the group feel strong pressures toward **self-censorship.** They hesitate to speak up because they know they will encounter disapproval. In fact, an **illusion of unanimity** arises, whereby a doubting member believes that everyone else agrees with the group's chosen action. Should a dissenting member speak up, he or she is severely sanctioned as other members place **pressure on dissenters.** Finally, the leader and key members of the group are protected from outside information by self-appointed **mind-guards** who "protect" them from negative information.

As a result of the groupthink atmosphere, problem solving is disrupted. Members ignore alternatives, fail to test their ideas against reality, and refuse to make contingency plans. When people believe that they are superior and invincible, they feel no need to examine their ideas carefully. Janis analyzed several historical fiascoes and showed that symptoms of groupthink occurred in all of them, including America's failure to secure Pearl Harbor, its decision to invade the Bay of Pigs, the escalation of the Vietnam War, and the Watergate cover-up. And we can add the *Challenger* disaster to this list.

Groupthink does not occur only in famous historical cases; it also characterizes everyday groups. Any speech communication teacher who has taught a course in small group communication can give examples of classroom groups that spent all their time telling themselves how great their project would be and almost no time working on the project. Talented people have a natural tendency to get lazy and overconfident unless they make special efforts to avoid groupthink.

How can groups guard against this kind of overconfidence? Groups can assign a member to take on the role of critic or devil's advocate. They can take criticisms and warnings seriously. When they hear themselves denigrating the competition or bragging about their own talents, they can become aware that they may be slipping into groupthink. And they can also make a rule that once a decision has been made, they will hold a second-chance meeting to review it and find its flaws. By carefully monitoring their behavior as they pass through the common stages of group development, groups can avoid serious errors in problem solving.

Group Development: Phases in Problem-Solving Groups

Recognizing the symptoms of groupthink can help groups make better decisions. Recognizing the stages through which groups pass can also help group members prepare for some of the stresses and strains they will normally encounter. In this section we'll look at some models of the group problem-solving process. As we saw in our discussion of interpersonal communication, couples go through recognizable stages as their relationships develop. Groups too pass through identifiable stages as members come to know one another better; several models of group development are found in the small group literature. As you look at some of these models, keep in mind that they are generalizations. Many of the groups you are a part of experience these phases, but not every group develops in exactly the same way.

Phase Models: Mapping the Life of a Group

Over the last twenty-five years or so, experts on small group communication have used classroom groups as a kind of laboratory. They have watched generations of students working together in small problem-solving groups. These

The primary tension that affects first-time groups disappears quickly if members respect one another. Nonverbal immediacy and directness are signs that group members have begun to feel comfortable together.

classroom groups are of particular interest because of several unique characteristics. First, they are made up of people with little prior history together. Second, their members are generally of equal status at the beginning of the group. Third, researchers do their best not to interfere with what happens in the group during the semester, so outside pressures are at a minimum. The groups that emerge are often called **zero-history groups** or **LGDs** (for "leaderless group discussions"). The latter label does not mean that this kind of group has no leader; it simply means that whatever happens within the group (including leader emergence) evolves naturally. By looking at these kinds of groups, researchers can examine the development of group culture from its very beginning. Of course, the characteristics that make LGDs interesting to study make them somewhat different from ongoing "real life" groups, for the latter are not as free from outside influence as are classroom groups. Nevertheless, researchers believe that we can learn a lot about group behavior in the classroom lab and that, to some extent, even formal work groups that are highly constrained by organizational cultures follow the natural phases seen in leaderless groups.

The phase models that have been developed by studying decision-making groups are remarkably similar, even though they differ in the exact number of phases they identify and in the labels they give these phases. We'll begin by looking very briefly at Bruce Tuckman's five-stage model, and we'll then move on to Aubrey Fisher's four-phase model, the best-known phase model. **Tuckman's five-stage model** gives a general overview of group development, and his labels are striking and easy to remember. **Fisher's four-phase model** concentrates more on the communication behavior of decision-making groups.

Tuckman's Five-Stage Model

In the mid-1960s, Bruce Tuckman proposed a five-stage model of group decision making. Tuckman believed that groups go through five consecutive phases: forming, storming, norming, performing, and adjourning.[12] In the first or **forming stage,** group members cautiously try to identify the nature of the task and their relationship to one another. As they become more familiar with one another, they feel freer to argue with one another and to vie for status and position within the group. This behavior constitutes the **storming stage.** Once initial disagreements are worked out, groups enter the **norming stage,** during which members settle down and find ways to work with one another. In the **performing stage,** the group focuses on the task and gets most of the work done. Finally, as the project nears completion, group members tie up loose ends and reflect on their time together. This is the final, **adjourning stage.**

Fisher's Four-Phase Model

In the 1970s, Aubrey Fisher developed a communication-based model of group development that is consistent with the findings of Tuckman and others. Fisher found that group members experience four phases of group communication as they move from being strangers to being part of an effective, interdependent system. These phases are orientation, conflict, emergence, and reinforcement.[13]

The first of Fisher's phases is the **orientation phase.** Here group members begin the complicated process of becoming interdependent. In most cases, this transition is not easy and is marked by **primary tension,** tension caused by the natural uncertainty people experience before communication norms and rules have been worked out. Primary tension is characterized by periods of silence broken by ambiguous, tentative, and occasionally awkward comments. Members tend to be polite and formal with one another and do their best to avoid controversy. By engaging in surface-level, phatic communication, members are performing a kind of social reconnaissance, giving themselves time to get a sense of one another's interests and personalities. In most cases, primary tension will dissipate naturally, but occasionally it persists. If it does persist, the group is blocked from further development and never takes on the characteristics of true "groupness."

The best way to deal with primary tension is simply to *act in an open, friendly, and positive manner and to give members time to feel comfortable with one another.* It is not a good idea to force decisions during orientation. Although highly task-oriented members may feel impatient with the vague and overly polite conversation that goes on in this phase, this communication serves an important purpose. Members who try to push the group too hard by dominating or being too original may be labeled deviants by the rest of the group. Skillful group communicators use their time during this phase to make other group members feel at ease. By responding with warmth and interest to the contributions of others, they make it possible for the group to go on to the next phase.

As groups move into the second or **conflict phase,** they experience a new kind of stress, called **secondary tension.** Secondary tension occurs as group members disagree over the best ways to accomplish the task and as they struggle to find a role within the group that will meet both group and individual needs. Secondary tension feels quite different from primary tension. Communication is less tentative and polite and may be marked by overt argument, sarcastic disagreement, and even hostile remarks. The caution that was characteristic of phase one is now gone. Members fight for their ideas, providing support for their positions and engaging in heated debate. Ambiguity is not normal at this point, as members tend to join one of the factions that polarize around decision proposals. Part of the reason for conflict at this stage is that group members are not only trying to complete their task, they are simultaneously choosing between leader contenders.

Conflict can be distressing for group members who fear argument. In fact, conflict is quite healthy, for debate and discussion mean that a variety of ideas are being aired. What is important is to learn to manage, rather than to avoid, secondary tension. Members should *learn to expect periods of conflict and find ways to benefit from the energy and ideas that are generated during these periods.* Groups that never experience conflict are not working at capacity. As Fisher explains,

> *Conflict can be distressing for group members who fear argument. In fact, conflict is quite healthy, for debate and discussion mean that a variety of ideas are being aired.*

> *a healthy group is apt to be noisy. Its members are uninhibited and probably not governed by norms of politeness. There are frequent disagreements, arguments, and constant interruptions which reflect the members' eagerness and commitment to their group–high group identification.*[14]

Secondary tension dissipates as leadership issues are resolved and as one of the competing solutions gains support. At this point, the group enters the third or **emergence phase.** Members who have opposed the leading solution begin to back down, replacing their earlier strong disagreement with noncommittal, somewhat ambiguous comments. During this phase, the eventual task outcome becomes apparent, as does the social structure of the group.

The final phase, which occurs only if the preceding phases have been successfully completed, is the **reinforcement phase.** Here members bolster their decision through the expression of favorable comments and positive reinforcement. In Fisher's words, "Pervading this final phase in group decision making is a spirit of unity . . . [Members'] interaction patterns reflect virtually no tension as members are jovial, loud, boisterous, laughing, and verbally backslap each other."[15]

Although almost all groups experience periods of primary and secondary tension, every group does not neatly file through the four phases in exactly the same way. Some groups stall, never getting over their primary tension or becoming trapped in the conflict phase, for it takes good group skills to reach reinforcement. Other groups seem to fall into cycles, running through repeated periods of primary and secondary tension at each meeting. These observations have led some researchers to criticize Fisher's and the other early phase models and to propose more complicated theories of group development.

Poole's Alternative: A Multiple-Sequence Model

The major criticism of Fisher's four-phase model is that it makes group communication seem too simple. Although it may fit many zero-history project groups, it does not apply quite as well to long-standing groups with multiple tasks to accomplish.[16] Researchers such as Marshall Scott Poole and Jonelle Roth argue that real-life groups are much "messier" and more complex than Fisher's model suggests.[17] Rather than seeing one unified progression, **Poole's multiple-sequence model** suggests that groups develop simultaneously on three different tracks: **task, topic,** and **relation tracks.** During discussion, groups work on ways to accomplish their task by analyzing problems and evaluating solutions; they move from one topic to another and back again; and they concern themselves with relational problems, dissipating tensions and conflict. If a group reaches consensus on all three tracks at once, then a unified phase such as one that Fisher discusses can occur; but work on one track often continues after work on another track has been finished. In addition, frequent delays and disruptions can serve as **break points,** momentarily disrupting the progress of the group or causing it to repeat earlier work. Thus, according to Poole, not all groups progress neatly through unitary phases.

Poole's model does not necessarily invalidate the more global phase models. As anyone who has observed group process knows, groups do experience periods of primary tension during orientation; they do experience conflicts;

decisions do eventually emerge; and successful groups do end by reinforcing one another. Members can benefit from knowing that these processes are likely to occur and from learning how to deal with them. On the other hand, the path groups take in solving problems may not be as neat and as predictable as theorists such as Tuckman and Fisher suggest.

Leader Emergence: How Not to Be Chosen Leader

As we have seen, one of the issues that a group must work out is who is to be leader. Fisher provides some interesting insights into how the leadership problem is solved in groups.[18] In Fisher's mind, leadership is not a story of one member rising through the ranks to triumph because of natural ability or clever manipulation. Rather, leadership is a matter of not making mistakes. For Fisher, the process of **leader emergence** is a process of elimination.

> *Leadership is not a story of one member rising through the ranks to triumph because of natural ability or clever manipulation. Rather, leadership is a matter of not making mistakes.*

Fisher believes that in the beginning, all members of a group are in contention for the leadership position (or positions). Every time members communicate, they are making a bid to be leader, although they may not be aware of what they are doing. Over time, most members take themselves out of contention. At first, nonparticipators and those who are ill-informed or excessively closed-minded and rigid are eliminated. Next, other members drop out of the contest by casting themselves in secondary roles. They become lieutenants for more active contenders. Often, two opposing factions emerge, each headed by a leader contender and supported by one or more lieutenants. Finally, one coalition drops out, leaving most of the influence in the hands of a single leader and his or her party.

Of course, groups do not need to have a single leader. Theoretically, there is no reason why leadership cannot be shared. **Leadership,** after all, is any behavior that moves a group toward the accomplishment of task or maintenance goals. In most groups, however, certain individuals wield more influence than others and consequently perform more leadership behaviors. Of course, groups exhibit many leadership patterns. Some groups never solve their status problem, and members are still fighting one another when they disband. Others shift between temporary leaders or appoint two leaders, one to handle task matters and the other to take charge of maintenance. And a few rare groups find a way to share leadership equally.

What kind of behaviors demonstrate that a member does not have what it takes to lead? Fisher gives eight rules for how not to emerge as leader.[19]

Although his intent is humorous, his list holds more than a little truth. If you don't want the responsibility of group leadership, try these suggestions. If, on the other hand, you want to help your group accomplish its tasks, these are behaviors to avoid.

RULE 1 *Be absent as often as possible.* And if you want to increase your chances of avoiding leadership still more, refuse to provide any excuse for your absence.

RULE 2 *Contribute as little as possible.* Here it helps to appear incompetent and disinterested as well as silent.

RULE 3 *Volunteer to be secretary or record keeper.* You run the risk of demonstrating your value to the group in this way, but, because the secretary role is generally a secondary role, you can probably avoid major leadership responsibilities.

RULE 4 *Be subservient and acquiescent,* showing a total inability to come up with useful ideas of your own.

RULE 5 *Be rude and verbally aggressive early in the discussion, and sulk and become apathetic later on* when people are sharing ideas.

RULE 6 *Become the group's joker.* In this way you get to be the center of attention, yet at the same time you warn others not to take you seriously.

RULE 7 *Come across as a know-it-all.* The use of big words and a desire to talk about every topic under the sun should do the trick.

RULE 8 *Show contempt for leadership, and attack and label others when they try to contribute.*

Strengthening Group Discussion Skills

Although avoiding all the behaviors in Fisher's list improves your chances of becoming a contributing group member, it does not assure success. For that, you need flexibility and understanding. In this section we'll look at a few ways you can prepare to be a more effective group communicator. As we have seen, groups must concern themselves with creating a positive climate as well as with working productively. We'll begin by looking at ways in which groups can increase member satisfaction. We'll then look at ways in which groups can cut down on inefficiency and increase creativity. Finally, we'll look at some of the standard formats for group discussion that are used in public settings.

Creating a Positive Climate

Some years ago, Jack Gibb described the kinds of behaviors that can lead to competitive, defensive climates and those that can lead to cooperative, supportive climates.[20] Gibb believed that in a **defensive climate,** in which group members feel threatened, the group is unproductive. To the extent that group members sense evaluation, control, strategy, neutrality, superiority, and certainty on the part of others, they close down and refuse to cooperate. By replacing these behaviors with description, problem orientation, spontaneity, empathy, equality, and provisionalism, a group can create a **supportive climate.**

Evaluation occurs when individuals are judgmental toward one another, when their comments imply that they are appraising and criticizing one another's behavior. **Description,** on the other hand, arouses little defensiveness, because it focuses on presenting feelings or opinions without assigning blame. It is better for a group member to express concern about a deadline by describing his or her feelings ("I'm concerned about getting the work done as soon as possible, because I have commitments at the end of the month") than by evaluating ("This group has got to stop wasting time and being lazy"). **Control** is another behavior that increases defensiveness. When members try to impose their will on others ("The only way to get this done is to . . .") rather than trying to collaborate ("Does anyone have ideas about how to get the job done?"), they are likely to meet resistance. The opposite of control is taking a **problem orientation.**

Strategy occurs when group members' behavior is prompted by hidden agendas. Feeling manipulated naturally leads to defensiveness. The corresponding supportive behavior is **spontaneity,** whereby the member communicates in an open and honest manner. **Neutrality,** although it sounds positive, can often signal indifference and a lack of commitment. On the other hand, **empathy** tells others that you understand their thoughts and feelings. As we saw in the last chapter, the use of the paraphrasing response can indicate concern and empathy. Compare the following two responses: "Okay, if you want to do it that way . . ." and "What you're saying is that you're really concerned about getting this done on time, and you want to do your best." The second response shows a great deal more empathy. The first might be read as indicating disinterest.

Superiority should be avoided as much as possible, for superior responses lead to jealousy and resentment. Instead, members should be careful to indicate **equality** by asking for others' opinions and weighing everyone's contributions equally. Finally, having too great a sense of **certainty** can lead to an unpleasant

By recognizing the need to be more supportive and open and by listening empathically, members can improve the social climate of their groups.

217

Controversy is a healthy group behavior that encourages creative thought. Apathy is a more difficult problem for a group leader to handle.

group climate. **Provisionalism,** in contrast, signals a willingness to listen openly to others' ideas. Group members should monitor themselves to make sure they are not inadvertently making others defensive. It is easy to come across as superior or certain even when you may not mean to; insensitivity to others' feelings can lead to neutrality or evaluation. Without realizing it, we can easily hurt one another's feelings and make groups frustrating and unpleasant. By recognizing the need to be more supportive and open and by listening empathically, members can improve the social climate of their groups.

Enhancing Problem Solving

When left to their own devices, groups are often illogical and disorderly, jumping from one idea to another. In fact, studies have shown that the average attention span of a group—the time it stays on a single topic—is approximately fifty-eight seconds.[21] One of the reasons group problem solving is so difficult is that groups have trouble staying on track.

To facilitate more orderly thinking, group members sometimes turn to the use of logical plans, or **agendas,** to guide their discussion. Agendas are often very useful when time is limited and task pressures are strong, because they focus on the task dimension. Their major disadvantage is that they may neglect maintenance issues. Following a task agenda too closely or using agendas at every meeting may increase productivity at the cost of cohesiveness. Nevertheless, there are times when agendas can be extremely useful.

The Standard Agenda

In 1910, philosopher John Dewey described a rational process for solving problems that he called **reflective thinking.** Dewey believed that reflective thinking begins with a felt difficulty. We then examine that difficulty, think of possible solutions, evaluate them, choose the best one, and then implement it. The **standard agenda** is a six-step guide to solving problems that derives directly from Dewey's theories about reflective thinking.[22] Table 7-4 summarizes the six steps.

The first step in the standard agenda is **problem identification.** Too often, groups jump into a discussion without a complete understanding of what the problem that they need to solve really is. A **problem** can be defined as a discrepancy between a present state of affairs and a desired state of affairs.[23] To define a problem, then, group members need to state explicitly what is currently bothering them and what they desire. Defining the problem can often be the most difficult step in problem solving. Let's look at an example. Most of us feel that our campuses have a parking problem. But what does that really mean? Does it mean that there are currently not enough spaces and that more are needed? (And if so, how many more?) Or does it mean that there are plenty of spaces but that they are too far from classroom buildings? Or could it be that spaces are available at some times of the day but not at others? It is important to be clear about which—if any—of these possibilities we mean, for each leads us to a different solution.

In the first case, the solution may involve setting aside new spaces or cutting down on campus traffic. In the second, it may necessitate moving spaces or classes or providing shuttle service. In the third, it may mean rescheduling some activities. Only when the definition of the problem is concrete and clear can the group move on to the next step.

Dan Rothwell gives two interesting examples of how the way a problem is framed affects the way it is ultimately solved.[24] In the first example, a service station manager found that his soda machine was out of order when customers who lost their money complained. To solve the problem, he put an Out of Order sign on the machine. Customers ignored the sign, continued to lose money, and continued to complain. He finally solved the problem by changing the sign to read $2. No one bought the soda, and no one complained. In a second example, a convenience store had a problem with teenagers loitering outside. Instead of looking for ways to confront the students, the store owners simply piped Muzak into the parking lot. The kids found the bland music so objectionable that they soon found another hangout.

Rothwell explains that in both cases, the solution became achievable as soon as it was framed in the right way. In the first example, the service station manager stopped asking himself, "How can I let the customers know the machine is out of order?" and instead asked, "How can I stop customers from putting money in the machine?" In the second example, the proprietors were successful only after they stopped thinking in terms of force and started to ask, "What will motivate the teenagers to leave on their own?"

The second step in the standard agenda is **problem analysis.** David and Frank Johnson, drawing on the work of Kurt Lewin, suggest that one of the best ways to diagnose a problem is to view the current state of affairs as a balance between two opposing forces: restraining and helping forces.[25] **Restraining forces** are forces that are negative in direction. If they prevail, the current state will get worse. **Helping forces,** on the other hand, are forces that are positive in direction. If they are strengthened, the current state will move closer to the ideal. This kind of analysis is called **force-field analysis.** By listing restraining and helping forces, group members understand the problem better. They know what they have going for them and what they must overcome. When it comes to solving the problem, they can look at solutions that either increase helping forces or remove restraining forces.

TABLE 7-4

Steps in the Standard Agenda

Step 1   *Problem Identification*
Group members clarify the problem, often by specifying the difference between a present state of affairs and a desired state of affairs. Problems should be concrete, clear, and solvable.

Step 2   *Problem Analysis*
Group members collect information about the problem, identifying factors that are causing the problem and factors that may help in solving the problem.

Step 3   *Criteria Selection*
Group members decide on the characteristics of a valid solution prior to discussing specific solutions.

Step 4   *Solution Generation*
Group members generate as many solution alternatives as possible.

Step 5   *Solution Evaluation and Selection*
Group members use previously selected criteria to evaluate each solution. The solution that best meets evaluation criteria is chosen.

Step 6   *Solution Implementation*
Group members follow through by putting the solution into effect.

Assume that a school curriculum committee has decided that a new experimental course is needed to update current offerings. Through force-field analysis, the committee finds that one of the major restraining factors is parents' resistance to the course and that this resistance is based on a misunderstanding of what the new course is all about. The committee also finds that the helping forces include the fact that current faculty members can teach the new course and that the faculty as a whole supports the idea. The group now knows that it can enlist the teachers' aid and that the solution should involve educating parents and removing their fears. Of course, to reach this conclusion, committee members had to do solid research on what was causing the problem.

The next step in the standard agenda is **criteria selection.** Before they begin to offer suggestions, group members should establish the criteria they will use in judging solutions. One group may decide, for example, that its solution must be rapid and reasonably cheap and that it must change the status quo as little as possible. Another group addressing another problem may decide that it wants a long term solution and that money is no object. The time to decide on criteria is before members' egos get too involved in specific decision proposals.

The fourth step is **solution generation.** Here group members attempt to generate as many alternative solutions as possible. To do this, they may use methods like brainstorming, a method we will look at shortly when we examine ways to enhance group creativity. The important point is to identify a number of alternatives rather than being satisfied with the first one.

In step five of the standard agenda, **solution evaluation and selection,** alternative solutions are evaluated and the best one selected. Now it is a simple matter of looking at each solution and measuring it against each criterion. The solution that meets the most criteria (without causing additional problems) is the best solution. Finally, in step six, the group follows through with **solution implementation.**

Brainstorming: Increasing Creativity

Although a standard agenda can keep a group focused and can encourage members to think critically, it doesn't tell us much about how to generate new and creative ideas. One of the major blocks to idea generation is the tendency to reject potentially good ideas by evaluating them prematurely. **Brainstorming** is a technique for overcoming this problem. In brainstorming, members are encouraged to generate as many ideas as they can, as quickly as possible. They are instructed to say whatever pops into their heads, no matter how ridiculous it may sound. The idea is to collect a large pool of ideas and then go back and criticize them. Only after all ideas have been suggested is evaluation allowed.

> *One of the major blocks to idea generation is the tendency to reject potentially good ideas by evaluating them prematurely.*

To begin brainstorming, a group selects one member to record, usually on large sheets of paper or on a flip chart, all ideas exactly as they are expressed. A single problem is presented and defined. Members are instructed to propose ideas as quickly as possible. They are encouraged to free-associate and to "hitch-hike" on others' suggestions. Once ideas have been recorded, members go back and try to clarify each idea, following up on ideas that seem feasible.

David and Frank Johnson discuss several ways to encourage idea generation, methods that can be used by themselves or in conjunction with brainstorming.[26] One is called the **part-changing method.** Here members think of new products or ideas by identifying old parts that might be altered. A group of furniture designers, for example, might decide to think of ways to change each part of a chair. They would then generate as many different colors, shapes, sizes, textures, styles, and so on, as possible without worrying whether or not the ideas were feasible.

In the **checkerboard method,** the group draws up a matrix. One set of behaviors or characteristics is written in columns across the top of the matrix, and another set is written in rows along the left-hand side. Members then examine the spaces where rows and columns intersect to see whether they can generate any creative combinations. For example, a group with the task of inventing a new sport might list equipment or materials across the top of a matrix and actions or playing surfaces along the side. Although many of the resulting combinations might seem ridiculous, some just might work.

Finally, in the **find-something-similar method,** group members are encouraged to think of analogies. A group that wants to solve a parking problem might think of how bees, squirrels, shoe stores, dry cleaners, and so on, store things. All of these methods encourage members to break away from standard ways of thinking and to become more open-minded and daring.

Nominal Group Technique

The standard agenda, brainstorming, and the Johnsons' methods for generating ideas are only some of the many techniques that have been devised to increase group problem-solving efficiency. An interesting variation combines parts of both procedures but cuts actual interaction to a minimum. This is **nominal group technique.**[27] In this technique, individuals generate solution ideas on their own and then meet to clarify these ideas. After all ideas have been listed and explained, members individually rank their five favorite ideas. The rankings are then averaged, and the idea with the highest average is chosen. By asking members to work individually, the method avoids the problem of more aggressive members overpowering quieter members. By refusing to allow members to evaluate one another's ideas, the method eliminates potential conflict. This method is also less lengthy than full-blown discussion.

More recently, Brilhart and Galanes have modified this technique to involve more discussion.[28] In their model, the group leader begins by identifying and defining the problem. Each member, working alone, generates as many solutions as possible without discussion. Once members are finished, ideas are presented in round-robin fashion, and each is posted so that everyone can see it. Members may ask for clarification, but no evaluation is allowed. Each member then individually indicates his or her top five choices, and the aggregate rankings are computed and displayed. At this point, members begin to discuss the merits of the top ideas. The discussion continues until consensus is reached or until a vote is called.

Many additional methods exist to guide group problem solving, each with its own advantages and disadvantages. A skilled group leader has a number of agendas at his or her disposal to use with different kinds of groups and different kinds of problems. A complete discussion is beyond the scope of this chapter, but if you are interested in learning more about group methods, consider taking a course in group problem solving. Being able to control a group and enhance its ability to work effectively is an important skill for anyone who is interested in working with people. The more you learn about group dynamics, the more fascinating this subject will become.

Using Special Formats for Public Discussion

The techniques we have looked at so far were designed for groups to use in private deliberations. Occasionally, group discussion takes place in public, in front of an audience. In such a case, group discussion is used to increase audience understanding of a particular issue. **Public discussion formats** designed with this goal in mind include the symposium, the forum, the panel discussion, the buzz group, and the role-playing group.[29]

The Symposium

A **symposium** is a form of public discussion in which a number of experts give brief, prepared speeches on a topic of general concern. Its purpose is to inform an audience. Although each participant speaks independently, participants often hold planning sessions in advance to decide how to divide up a problem and to determine speaking order. A typical symposium might concern a public issue such as child abuse. A sociologist might be invited to outline the extent and causes of the problem, a psychologist to discuss the symptoms and effects of abuse, a school administrator to speak on the role of teachers in discovering and reporting suspected cases, and a representative of a state agency to describe available intervention programs. The role of the chairperson of a symposium is to introduce the problem, to present each speaker, and to sum up the discussion. The symposium is a fairly formal format that involves little interaction between participants and audience. To encourage more interaction, planners often combine the symposium with another format, the forum.

The Forum

A **forum** is a much more freewheeling form of discussion than is a symposium. In a forum there are no outside experts; audience members are the discussants. They share their comments and opinions with one another and are led by a moderator whose job is to announce the topic, to provide necessary background information, to set the ground rules for participation, and generally to control the discussion. When a forum follows a symposium, it allows audience members to express their feelings and to add their comments to those of the experts. Much of the success of the discussion lies with the moderator, who must keep the audience on track and make sure everyone is heard. When talk show hosts such as Oprah Winfrey or Phil Donahue go out into the audience to solicit comments, they are using a forum format, although their forums usually follow panel discussions rather than symposia.

The Panel Discussion

In the **panel discussion,** experts interact with one another in a small group as an audience listens. Panels may be formed around a number of topics. After the Los Angeles riots of 1992, for example, many communities organized panel discussions on the topic of police-community relations. These panels included police representatives as well as leaders from minority communities, educators, and local politicians. The goals were to allow interested parties to share their feelings and to discover ways to increase cooperation between law enforcement agencies and the public.

In a well-organized panel discussion, the moderator formulates the major topics to be discussed and informs the participants of these topics ahead of time. He or she introduces participants, organizes the discussion, and summarizes panelists' contributions. The moderator may decide to follow a modified problem-solving agenda or may allow the discussion to follow its own path, but in either case, he or she controls the shape of the discussion. It is up to the moderator and participants to ensure that the discussion follows a logical plan, that participation is fair, and that enough time is allocated for each topic.

The key to moderating or participating in a panel is to be well-informed, to listen carefully to others, and to make sure that the discussion is coherent.

The key to moderating or participating in a panel is to be well-informed, to listen carefully to others, and to make sure that the discussion is coherent. The panel format is particularly interesting because it combines small group and public communication. Panelists must share ideas and reach conclusions within the group while also communicating to an audience. This is no easy task.

The Buzz Group

Some discussion formats are expressly designed to be used as supplements to formal presentations. Their goal is to increase audience response to a speech or public discussion. One such format is the **buzz group.** Once the initial presentation is finished, audience members are divided into small discussion groups and are asked to respond to the speaker's topic. For example, a conference on the topic of wellness might begin with a speech on the importance of a healthy diet. To reinforce the speaker's points, audience members might be asked to divide into groups of seven or eight people, to make a list of factors that reinforce unhealthy eating habits, and then to think of ways to resist these negative influences. After members of each group have had time to discuss their ideas, a spokesperson reports the group's conclusions to the assembly as a whole.

The buzz session increases audience involvement by placing audience members in a small, friendly group. Members who might be intimidated by speaking up in a large forum often feel comfortable in the small group context. In addition, discussion makes the speaker's points more personal and more memorable.

The Role-Playing Group

An even stronger way to involve audience members is through role-playing. In **role-playing,** people are placed in small groups, are given a scenario, and are asked to act out their responses. By experiencing a situation rather than passively discussing it, members can get in touch with their emotions and can practice new behaviors. After a role-play is over, the actors discuss what occurred and what they learned from the experience.

Role-playing is often used to help people understand one another's point of view. In a workshop designed to increase child-parent interaction, for example, children and parents might be asked to switch roles, each playing the part of the other. This role reversal may help them understand one another's concerns and motivations. Role-playing is also often used to help people practice new or difficult behaviors. A campaign against drunk driving might ask high school students to practice taking the keys away from a friend who has had too much to drink. By rehearsing this response in a supportive group context, the students learn what to do if they are ever actually confronted with the problem.

Role-playing is not for everyone. If group members are too inhibited to play their roles or do not take them seriously, this technique will not work. If the scenarios revolve around highly sensitive issues, role-plays can become highly emotional and can get out of hand. In such cases, the presence of a moderator with training and experience is a must.

Summary

We spend much of our social and work lives communicating in groups. This chapter looks at the special characteristics of group communication and offers advice for increasing group effectiveness.

A group is a collection of individuals who interact over time, becoming interdependent, developing unique patterns of behavior, and achieving a collective identity. Although it is difficult to say exactly how large a group can be before it ceases to be a group, it is safe to say that a small group must consist of at least three people. Although a triad differs from a dyad by only one person, the addition of that person dramatically changes communication. The ideal group size for effective communication is realized when the group is large enough to generate creative ideas yet small enough for equal participation.

People communicate in groups because the presence of others increases information, provides support, and helps members achieve individual needs. Like members of dyads, group members experience dialectical tensions. They must satisfy group and individual needs and must learn to balance task and maintenance roles. In groups, both the individual member and the group as a whole try to influence one another. If each meets the other's needs, commitment is high and members pass through stages that deepen their involvement. If either party fails to meet its obligations, the group becomes unstable and members drop out. Members can increase their satisfaction by recognizing that full membership comes slowly, by understanding that acceptance means following group norms, and by seeking the support of others. To function effectively, members must also fulfill task and maintenance roles, working to get the job done and to ensure that the group atmosphere is pleasant, while avoiding negative individual roles and hidden agendas. When a group becomes too confident and fails to think realistically about its task, groupthink can occur. By assigning a member to act as critic, by taking criticisms seriously, and by holding second-chance meetings, groups can avoid groupthink.

Like dyads, groups often go through phases. The best-known of the phase models consists of four phases: orientation, conflict, emergence, and reinforcement. If groups do not handle the primary and secondary tensions that arise in the first two phases, they cannot accomplish their goals. They also encounter problems if leadership conflicts are not resolved. During the life of a group, various members contend for leadership. By being absent, uncooperative, domineering, rude, or irresponsible, they eliminate themselves from contention. Only after leadership stabilizes can decisions emerge.

Members can increase group effectiveness by understanding how groups function, by becoming aware of the kinds of behaviors that lead to defensiveness, and by actively trying to be more supportive. Another way, suggested by the standard agenda, is to make sure problem definition precedes solution generation and to discuss criteria for evaluating solutions prior to making decisions. Members can also become more effective and creative by learning how to brainstorm. Finally, by understanding special public formats, such as symposia, forums, panel discussions, buzz groups, and role-playing groups, individuals increase their ability to communicate effectively in the group context.

Key Terms

Listed below are the key terms used in this chapter, along with the number of the page on which each is explained.

Review Questions

1. What is a group? What characteristics make a collection of individuals become a group? What are the upper and lower size limits of a small group? What is the ideal size for a group? How does a triad differ from a dyad?

2. What are the advantages of working in a group rather than as an individual?

3. What three interpersonal needs can be met by groups? How do groups satisfy these needs?

4. What are the stages in group socialization? How do evaluation and commitment affect movement through these stages? How do groups and individuals try to influence each other?

5. How can group members adapt to the pressures that groups put on them? How can members earn idiosyncrasy credits? How can a mentor help individuals adjust to groups?

6. What are the two dimensions of group behavior? What is the output of the task dimension? Give examples of task, maintenance, and individual roles.

7. What is groupthink? What are its symptoms? What causes groupthink?

8. What are zero-history groups? How have they been used by researchers? What are the five stages of group decision making identified by Tuckman? How can they be compared to the four phases identified by Fisher? What occurs in the forming or orientation phase? What is primary tension, and how does it dissipate? Is conflict or storming common in groups? How is secondary tension related to conflict? What occurs during emergence and reinforcement? What are Poole's criticisms of Fisher's phase model?

9. What is leadership? How does the process of leader emergence operate? In what ways can individuals avoid leadership responsibilities?

10. What is a defensive climate? a supportive climate? What behaviors lead to defensiveness? to supportiveness? Think of an example of each kind of behavior.

11. What is an agenda, and when is it most useful? What is reflective thinking, and how does it relate to the standard agenda? What are the steps in the standard agenda? Think of examples that illustrate how different ways of defining a problem can lead to different solutions. How does force-field analysis work?

12. What methods can be used to encourage idea generation in groups? Explain brainstorming and the part-changing, checkerboard, and find-something-similar methods.

13. What is nominal group technique? What are its advantages?

14. Describe the following formats: the symposium, the forum, the panel discussion, the buzz group, and the role-playing group. Think of situations appropriate for each of these formats. If you were to moderate or lead each format, what would you do?

Suggested Readings

Cathcart, Robert S., & Samovar, Larry A. (1988). *Small group communication: A reader* (5th ed.). Dubuque, IA: Brown.

Articles and essays by some of the leading group researchers make this collection of readings an excellent source on a variety of group topics.

Janis, Irving. (1972). *Victims of groupthink*. Boston: Houghton Mifflin.

This book shows what can happen when group cohesiveness clouds a group's decision-making effectiveness. If you're interested in history and politics, you should find the case studies interesting.

Johnson, David W., & Johnson, Frank P. (1991). *Joining together: Group theory and group skills* (4th ed.). Englewood Cliffs, NJ: Prentice-Hall.

This book is a practical guide to enhancing group skills. Excellent exercises are included.

Rothwell, J. Dan. (1992). *In mixed company: Small group communication*. New York: Harcourt Brace Jovanovich.

A good introduction to the basic concepts in group communication. Rothwell provides excellent examples and clear explanations.

Notes

1. Jensen, Arthur D., & Chilberg, Joseph C. (1991). *Small group communication*. Belmont, CA: Wadsworth, 5.

2. Pittinger, R. E., Hockett, C. F., & Danehy, J. J. (1960). *The first five minutes: A sample of microscopic interview analysis*. Ithaca, NY: Martineau, 223.

3. Cited in Rothwell, J. Dan. (1992). *In mixed company: Small group communication*. New York: Harcourt Brace Jovanovich, 39.

4. For a good discussion of the problems of triads, see Wilmot, William W. (1987). *Dyadic communication* (3rd ed.). New York: Random House, 21–32.

5. Bormann, Ernest. (1990). *Small group communication: Theory and practice*. New York: Harper & Row, 2.

6. Rothwell, 41.

7. Schutz, William. (1958). *Firo: A three-dimensional theory of interpersonal behavior*. New York: Holt, Rinehart & Winston.

8. Moreland, Richard, & Levine, John. (1982). Socialization in small groups: Temporal changes in individual-group relations. In Leonard Berkowitz (Ed.), *Advances in experimental social psychology* (Vol. 15). New York: Academic; and Moreland, Richard, & Levine, John. (1987). Group dynamics

over time: Development and socialization in small groups. In J. McGrath (Ed.), *The social psychology of time*. Beverly Hills, CA: Sage.

9. Hollander, Edwin. (1958). Conformity, status and idiosyncrasy credit. *Psychological Review, 65,* 117–127.

10. There are many analyses of the *Challenger* case. See Anatomy of a tragedy. (1987). *IEEE Spectrum, 24,* 44–51; Jaksa, James, Pritchard, Michael, & Kramer, Ronald. (1988). Ethics in organizations: The Challenger explosion. In James Jaksa & Michael Pritchard (Eds.), *Communication ethics: Methods of analysis.* Belmont, CA: Wadsworth; Kruglanski, A. (1986, August). Freeze-think and the Challenger. *Psychology Today,* 48–49; Hirokawa, Randy Y., Gouran, Dennis S., & Martz, A. E. (1988). Understanding the sources of faulty group decision making: A lesson from the Challenger disaster. *Small Group Behavior, 19,* 411–433; Renz, M. A., & Greg, J. (1988). Flaws in the decision making process: Assessment of risk in the decision to launch flight 51-L. *Central States Speech Journal, 39,* 67–75.

11. Janis, Irving. (1972). *Victims of groupthink.* Boston: Houghton Mifflin.

12. Tuckman, Bruce. (1965). Developmental sequence in small groups. *Psychological Bulletin, 63,* 384–399.

13. Fisher, B. Aubrey. (1970). Decision emergence: Phases in group decision making. *Speech Monographs, 37,* 53–66. See also Fisher, B. Aubrey. (1980). *Small group decision making* (2nd ed.). New York: McGraw-Hill.

14. Fisher, 1980, 56.

15. Fisher, 1980, 149.

16. Spiker, B., & Daniels, T. (1981). Information adequacy and communication relationships: An empirical examination of 18 organizations. *Western Journal of Speech Communication, 45,* 342–354.

17. Poole, Marshall Scott. (1981). Decision development in small groups I: A comparison of two models. *Communication Monographs, 48,* 1–24; Poole, Marshall Scott. (1983). Decision develop-

ment in small groups II: A study of multiple sequences in decision making. *Communication Monographs, 50,* 206–232; Poole, Marshall Scott. (1983). Decision development in small groups III: A multiple sequence model of group decision development. *Communication Monographs, 50,* 321–341; Poole, Marshall Scott, & Roth, Jonelle. (1989). Decision development in small groups V: Test of a contingency model. *Human Communication Research, 15,* 549–589.

18. Fisher, 1980, 207–212.

19. Ibid., 223–225.

20. Gibb, Jack R. (1961). Defensive communication. *Journal of Communication, 11,* 141–148.

21. Bormann, 243.

22. Dewey, John. (1910). *How we think.* Lexington, MA: Heath. For a complete and detailed discussion of the standard agenda, see Wood, Julia T., Phillips, Gerald M., & Pedersen, Douglas J. (1986). *Group discussion: A practical guide to participation and leadership.* New York: Harper & Row.

23. Johnson, David W., & Johnson, Frank P. (1991). *Joining together: Group theory and group skills* (4th ed.). Englewood Cliffs, NJ: Prentice-Hall, 238.

24. Rothwell, 223–224.

25. Johnson & Johnson, 239–241; Lewin, Kurt. (1944). Dynamics of group action. *Educational Leadership, 1,* 195–200.

26. Johnson & Johnson, 290–292. The Johnsons draw their discussion from David, G., & Houtman, S. (1968). *Thinking creatively: A guide to training imagination.* Madison: Wisconsin Research and Development Center for Cognitive Learning.

27. Delbecq, A. (1975). *Group techniques for program planning.* Glenview, IL: Scott Foresman.

28. Brilhart, J. K., & Galanes, G. J. (1989). *Effective group discussion.* Dubuque, IA: Brown.

29. For a good discussion of different formats, see Barker, Larry L., Wahlers, Kathy J., Cegala, Donald J., & Kibler, Robert J. (1991). *Groups in process: An introduction to small group communication* (4th ed.). Englewood Cliffs, NJ: Prentice-Hall, especially chapter 10.

8

Public Communication

If you plan to be a politician, an educator, a religious leader, a performer, or the like, then your living will depend on your ability to persuade, teach, inspire, and entertain large audiences.

While it's possible to get through life without ever giving a speech, being able to speak in public increases your chances for professional and personal success. If you plan to be a politician, an educator, a religious leader, a performer, or the like, then your living will depend on your ability to persuade, teach, inspire, and entertain large audiences. Even if you don't enter such a speaking-intensive career, you may still find yourself communicating in public. Consider the following situations:

- At your parents' twenty-fifth wedding anniversary, you are asked to give a speech of congratulation and to propose a toast.
- Your boss decides you should explain the company benefit package to new employees.
- Your child's teacher invites you to talk about your job during the school's career week.

- You are so outraged by a proposal for a new zoning law that you stand up and oppose it at a town council meeting.

These situations, and others like them, are common. The truth is, your chances of being asked to speak in front of an audience sometime in your life are quite good. And the probability of your being an audience for other people's speeches is one hundred percent. Both as a producer and as a consumer, you need to understand how public communication works.

In this chapter we look at communication in the public context. We begin by describing the character and functions of public communication. We then consider the relationship between speaker and audience and see how valid arguments are constructed. Finally, we'll examine ways to construct coherent and well-organized public speeches.

What Is Public Communication?

Public communication is a one-to-many form of communication wherein a single speaker addresses a large audience. Although audience members may ask questions afterward, their major role during the speech is to listen to and evaluate what the speaker has to say. Clear organization, careful preplanning, and formal language style are the hallmarks of public speeches, which are the most traditional form of public discourse.

Characteristics of Public Communication

Public speaking differs from the forms of communication we have already studied. In the public context, the spontaneity and informality of interpersonal communication and the give-and-take of group discussion are replaced by relatively formal, preplanned messages and more rigidly defined communication roles. Public speakers and their audiences do not run into each other by chance, nor do they sit around and discuss whatever comes into their minds. The occasion for public speaking is usually special and, in many cases, is prompted by an important event or issue. As a consequence, public messages are constructed with a great deal more care than is the average interpersonal message.

The occasion for public speaking is usually special and, in many cases, is prompted by an important event or issue.

One factor motivating that care is the size of the audience. Public speakers may address tens, hundreds, or even thousands of people. The speaker thus faces the problem of constructing a message that will make sense to a

Public audiences are made up of individuals with diverse needs and interests. The challenge facing the public speaker is to construct a message that will hold the attention of so many different people.

large, sometimes quite heterogeneous body of people. As we shall see, audience adaptation is one of the central challenges of communication in the public context. In addition, the physical situation—the number of people present, the size of the room, the time set aside for communicating, and so on—places special constraints on public discourse.

Time is a particularly important variable. Public communication does not allow the speaker the luxury of slowly developing a relationship with receivers over time or of going back to reexplain poorly expressed ideas. Most public speeches are one-time-only occasions. The speaker must therefore make an immediate impact and must be completely clear from the outset. Public speeches are also relatively lengthy. In conversations, turns are exchanged rapidly and rarely last longer than a minute or so. In public speeches, on the other hand, a single speaker may retain the floor for an hour or even longer. Audience members assume a relatively passive position; their task is to listen attentively for an extended period of time. Because this is hard work, the speaker must make the receivers' work as easy as possible. He or she must use a simple structure that is easy to follow, must employ transitions and repeated summaries, and must present material that retains attention.

The public speaker is also physically distanced from the audience. Whereas conversational partners sit within a few feet of one another, the public speaker may be twenty or more feet from an audience member. He or she must therefore choose a method of delivery that is larger than life, speaking loudly and clearly and using gestures and visual aids that can be seen at a distance.

Physical constraints are not the only characteristics that define public communication. Equally important, public communication takes place in a different sphere from interpersonal or group communication. In interpersonal communication, the focus of talk is on an individual relationship; in group communication, the interests of group members are the center of attention. In public communication, the focus is even wider. The issues and topics that make up public communication are focused outward, toward a community of individuals with shared interests. In other words, public communication occurs within the public sphere.

> *The issues and topics that make up public communication are focused outward, toward a community of individuals with shared interests.*

Communicating in the Public Sphere

When we communicate solely with our own interests in mind, we are acting in the **private sphere.** When, however, we communicate as members of a larger community and our topic is of concern to many, then we are operating in the **public sphere.** Rhetorician Martha Cooper explains:

> *the public sphere . . . is not a real place . . . in which you could sit down and have a conversation. Instead, it is an orientation that people take to parts of their lives. When something happens that seems to affect groups of people rather than single individuals, the public sphere is emerging. . . . we can recognize that we have entered the public sphere when we find ourselves motivated by the needs of others as well as ourselves, by the needs of the community, rather than our own personal needs.*[1]

What we say in the public sphere can affect the well-being of hundreds, or even thousands, of others. When sports celebrity Magic Johnson contracted the HIV virus, he went public with the news. Had he kept his illness a secret, he could have retained some measure of personal privacy—at least for a while. By announcing the news immediately, however, he became a major figure in the battle against AIDS. His decision to make a public issue of his private cir-cumstances had a dramatic impact on the attitudes of thousands of people.

For many of us, making the decision Johnson made would take a great deal of courage. Public communication involves risks and responsibilities. In fact, in contemporary society many people shy away from public involvement. In discussing the reluctance of modern Americans to enter the public realm, Cooper argues that the mobility of modern society and the technical, special-ized nature of the modern workplace weaken our ties with our communities. In addition, the diversity of contemporary society keeps many people from forming close bonds with those around them. As a result, our society empha-sizes individualism more than community; we are constantly urged to make it on our own, to be our own person, and to look out for number one.[2]

Despite these difficulties, many people realize how important it is to take part in public debate. Environmental issues, in particular, have awakened people to the necessity of public involvement. And the success of grassroots groups such as MADD (Mothers Against Drunk Driving) has demonstrated that public communication is a powerful tool not only for dealing with public issues but for creating them as well. A generation ago, for example, drunk driving was not an issue. People bragged about how well they could drive while drunk, and driving with open containers was perfectly legal. Now our attitude is very differ-ent: drunk drivers are considered criminals. This change in attitude occurred in part because one woman, Candy Lightner, entered the public sphere. After the death of her daughter at the hand of a drunk driver, Lightner formed MADD and began to take her message to the public. Today she is a nationally recognized figure who delivers hundreds of speeches a year. She illustrates that one determined person can make a difference. Today designated drivers are common, beer is sold only during restricted hours at sporting events, and many states are being pressured to raise the legal drinking age to twenty-one.[3]

Why Engage in Public Communication?

For most people, speaking in public is a frightening business. In 1984, re-searchers from the University of Tulsa and from the University of Iowa College of Medicine asked students to list their greatest fears. Seventy percent of those surveyed named giving a speech.[4] Other studies have found the same amount of apprehension among even ex-perienced speakers. If the experience of com-municating publicly is so frightening, why go through it? Why bother to master the skills it takes to become an effective public speaker?

In 1984, researchers from the University of Tulsa and from the University of Iowa College of Medicine asked students to list their greatest fears. Seventy percent of those surveyed named giving a speech.

One reason is that the stakes are high. Democracy depends on the free expression of ideas. In a form of government wherein voters make the ultimate decision, public communication determines public policy. Part of the responsibility of citizens in a free society is a willingness to take a stand on public issues. Public communication allows us to take that stand.

Another reason to master public speaking skills is that by engaging in public communication, we can clarify our views and sharpen our reasoning skills. The ancient Greeks believed that the ultimate aim of public discussion is the discovery of truth. Taking part in public debate allows us to grapple with controversial ideas; it encourages us to learn more about issues and to examine the validity of our logic. Like other forms of communication, public speaking "enables us to think more rigorously and to imagine more abundantly. Those activities free us to possibilities that are new, at least to us, and they unbind us from portions of our ignorance. . . ."[5]

Finally, on a very practical level, public speaking is a necessary skill in most professional and managerial positions. Modern businesses are held together by information. The ability to convey that information clearly and effectively is essential for professional advancement. As James van Oosting points out,

> speechmaking is integral to the business enterprise. Information must be conveyed; personnel must be motivated and directed; reports must be given; policies must be articulated and defended; meetings must be chaired; products and services must be sold. . . . Whether one gets up in front of a public gathering to introduce the company president or addresses a small sales staff the first thing each morning, one is engaged in public communication . . . public communication is [a] workaday expectation and not some extraordinary assignment reserved for special occasions.[6]

Audience Adaptation and Source Credibility

A central challenge facing the public speaker is creating a relationship with audience members. Successful communication in any context can only occur if speaker and listener form a bond. In other contexts, these bonds are created slowly as participants learn about one another and negotiate the rules of their relationship. In the public context, however, this slow process of discovery is not possible. How, then, do public speakers create a relationship with their audience, and how do they convince audience members to trust them? By adapting to their audience and establishing their own credibility, public communicators create a climate in which effective communication becomes possible.

Audience Attitudes and Change

When audience members come to hear a speech, they do not come with
completely open minds. They bring prior be-
liefs, attitudes, values, and life experiences
with them. In constructing messages, speakers
must take into account what audience members
may already be thinking. If speakers fail to do
so, their messages will be misunderstood or
rejected.

> *When audience members come to hear a speech,
> they do not come with completely open minds.
> They bring prior beliefs, attitudes, values, and
> life experiences with them.*

Psychologist Milton Rokeach believes that the human mind uses three
kinds of cognitive structures: beliefs, attitudes, and values.[7] Because these
structures organize perception and motivate action, it is essential that public
speakers understand them. Table 8-1 summarizes these structures.

Beliefs

Beliefs are the opinions that individuals hold about the world and about their
place in it. "The world is round," "I am a worthwhile person," "Police can [or
cannot] be trusted," "The capital of New York is Albany," and "Chocolate ice
cream is delicious" are all examples. Obviously, beliefs differ in their nature
and importance. According to Rokeach, some beliefs are **peripheral beliefs**—
that is, they are relatively inconsequential and easy to change. Matters of taste
(such as one's belief about the relative merits of chocolate ice cream) and simple, unemotional facts (such as where the capital of New York is) are more
peripheral than are beliefs about whether police can be trusted. Beliefs about
whether the world is round or flat and about one's self-worth are more central
or core beliefs. **Core beliefs** are basic beliefs that we have held for a long time
and that cannot be changed without disrupting our entire belief structure.
Core beliefs are more difficult to change than are peripheral beliefs. People
defend core beliefs against attack. Yet when core beliefs are changed, other
related beliefs change as well. Rokeach argues that beliefs are tied to one
another in complicated ways. For this reason, a speaker must understand not
only what an audience believes but also how that belief is connected to other
beliefs and how central it is to audience members.

Attitudes

In addition to beliefs, people also hold attitudes. **Attitudes** are evaluative mental structures that predispose us to act in certain ways. "Studying is important
and worthwhile" (or "Studying is a waste of time"), "Welfare programs help
people" (or "Welfare only encourages idleness"), and "Candidate X's policies
are nonsense" (or "X's policies are absolutely brilliant") are all attitudes. Atti-

TABLE 8-1

Beliefs

Opinions about what is or is not the case. Beliefs differ in nature and importance.

- *Core Beliefs*
  Fundamental beliefs held for a long period of time. Some are shared with others ("The sun rises in the east"), and others are highly personal ("I believe the world is an unfriendly place").

- *Peripheral Beliefs*
  Relatively inconsequential and less resistant beliefs about who is or is not an authority ("My dad will know what to do"), facts derived from authorities ("It's not good to bottle up your feelings"), or matters of personal taste ("Green is an ugly color").

Attitudes

Opinions that link an individual to a topic. Attitudes predispose a person to respond to a topic in a particular way. Attitudes have three components.

- *Affective Component*
  What an individual feels in regard to a topic ("I feel sad whenever I think about hungry children").

- *Cognitive Component*
  What an individual knows about a topic ("There are X number of hungry children in America").

- *Behavioral Component*
  What an individual intends to do in regard to a topic ("I will donate money to feed hungry children").

Values

General and enduring opinions about what should or should not be the case.

tudes are partially products of beliefs, but they are also products of emotions and desires.

Attitudes are commonly thought to have three dimensions: cognitive, affective, and behavioral. Attitudes toward homelessness and the homeless are an example. Most people have some response to this topic, although their attitude may not be very strong or salient. The **cognitive dimension** of our attitude toward homelessness consists of everything we know (or don't know) about it: its causes, its effects, and its solutions. If we are well-read or have researched the topic, we are likely to have a great deal of information about it; if not, we may have only a vague understanding of it.

An attitude's **affective dimension** consists of emotional reactions to the attitude object. Some people respond to the homeless with fear and distaste, others with pity and understanding, and still others with a mixture of emotions. How we feel about an issue is important, because it can motivate us to take action. This point leads us to the third dimension of an attitude, the **behavioral dimension.** An attitude's behavioral dimension consists of what we think should be done about the attitude object—for example, whether we intend to ignore homelessness or to take action.

Most public speeches are designed either to reinforce or to change existing attitudes. Speeches may be designed to give people information about an attitude object and thus to affect the cognitive dimension; to stir our feelings and thus to change the affective dimension; or to get audience members to make a direct response and thus to act on the behavioral dimension. Often a speaker's goal may be to affect all three dimensions at once.

Values

Values are the strongest and most personal of the three cognitive structures. **Values** are convictions about what ought to occur or about what is or is not desirable and right. "World peace ought to be our highest goal," "Honesty is the best policy," and "Cleanliness is next to godliness" are examples. Values are stronger and more personal than attitudes, but they are less numerous. An individual may have thousands of beliefs and hundreds of attitudes but only ten or twenty values. Values are deeply held and are closely tied to audience members' identities. Making reference to a cherished value can be a powerful way to touch an audience. In the 1992 presidential election, for example, "family values" became an important catchword as each presidential and vice presidential candidate tried to show that his commitment to the family was greater than was his opponent's.

Many authors have attempted to classify values. Shalom Schwartz, who has investigated universally recognized clusters of values, developed a recent classification.[8] Although people in the twenty countries he studied place different weight on these values, Schwartz argues that the meanings people attach to the values and the relationships people see between the values are universal. In all the cultures Schwartz examined, self-direction, stimulation, hedonism, achievement, power, security, conformity, tradition, benevolence, and universalism were identified as valuable. Figure 8-1 defines these value clusters and gives specific examples. Which values do you think are important in mainstream American culture? How committed are you to each value, and how would you respond to an appeal focused on that value?

FIGURE 8-1

Relations Among Value Clusters

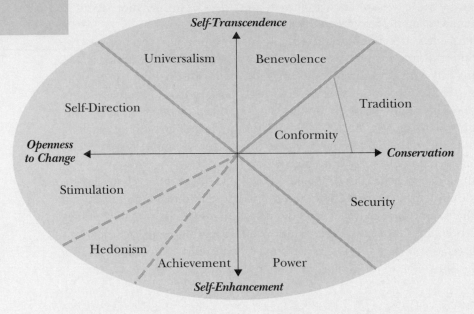

Descriptions of Value Types

1. Values associated with **universalism** focus on a concern for the welfare of all people and of nature (equality, unity with nature).

2. Values associated with **self-direction** focus on independence of thought and action (freedom, creativity, curiosity).

3. Values associated with **stimulation** focus on variety and arousal (excitement, novelty, daring).

4. Values associated with **hedonism** focus on pleasure and sensuous gratification (pleasure, enjoying life).

5. Values associated with **achievement** focus on competent performance leading to social approval (success, ambition, competence).

6. Values associated with **power** focus on attainment or preservation of a dominant social position (authority, wealth, social recognition).

7. Values associated with **security** focus on safety, harmony, and stability for self and society (health, family, national security).

8. Values associated with **conformity** focus on restraint of impulses likely to violate social norms (obedience, self-discipline).

9. Values associated with **tradition** focus on acceptance of and respect for cultural or religious customs (respect, devoutness, humility).

10. Values associated with **benevolence** focus on a concern for the welfare of those we love (helping, responsibility, loyalty).

Adapted from "Universals in Value Content and Structure" by Shalom H. Schwartz, 1992, in *Advances in Experimental Social Psychology*, vol. 25 Mark P. Zanna, ed., New York: Academic.

The Importance of Knowing Your Audience

It is important for public speakers to be aware of audience beliefs, attitudes, and values for a number of reasons. First, a speaker who violates audience members' values, dismisses their attitudes, or contradicts their cherished beliefs loses credibility. The audience will reject the rest of the message. Second, a speaker who knows what audience members are thinking can choose relevant and compelling supporting materials. He or she can use knowledge of beliefs, attitudes, and values to adapt the speech to the interests and intellectual level of audience members. Third, because beliefs, attitudes, and values motivate behaviors, a speaker can use them to form the basis of a persuasive appeal. Although we do not always behave as we intend or wish to behave, most of us try to keep faith with our ideals, and we feel anxiety and distress when we are unable to do so. By activating beliefs, attitudes, and values, a speaker can convince an audience to take action.

Adapting Messages to Audiences

We don't speak the same way to everyone, simply because every individual is different. For a kindergarten teacher to treat his or her charges as though they were enrolled in a graduate-level seminar would be ridiculous. It would be equally ridiculous to confuse the life experiences of adolescents with those of senior citizens or to assume that people reared in remote rural communities have exactly the same values as those from crowded urban environments. Factors such as educational level, age, and geography make a difference in the way people respond to messages. When

Audience adaptation doesn't mean lying to please an audience; it means making a message relevant and understandable to the audience.

we take into account what audience members currently know and think about an issue and use that information in constructing a message, we are engaging in **audience adaptation.** Audience adaptation doesn't mean lying to please an audience; it means making a message relevant and understandable to the audience.

Audience Adaptation

A good communicator uses information about the audience in constructing at least three aspects of a speech: its central idea and structure, its supporting materials, and its style. A speaker must first decide on the purpose and central idea of the speech. If the speech is intended to inform, the speaker must present new and interesting information without being too difficult or detailed. If the speech is intended to persuade, the speaker must avoid alienating an audience by advocating a proposal that is too extreme. In choosing the central idea

241

of the speech, the speaker must know what the audience currently believes, what positions it might be willing to accept, and what positions it definitely rejects.

Assume for a moment that you are planning a speech in which you will argue that there is too much sex and violence on television and that you would like to put a stop to it. If members of your audience agree with you, you might plan to advocate strong measures to combat the problem, including a boycott of products advertised on offensive programs. If your audience is less concerned about current programming, a better approach might be to show why current programming is objectionable. When an audience doesn't share your concern at all, you should identify the problem rather than offer a solution. In adjusting your proposal in this way, you are not abandoning your beliefs; rather, you are taking a realistic, incremental approach to persuasion.

The structure of the speech should also be adapted to the beliefs of audience members. With a hostile audience, for example, effective speakers begin by establishing common ground and then gradually move into their argument. In this situation it is also advisable to present both sides of an issue rather than to argue for just one. With a favorable audience, however, a direct, one-sided appeal may be most effective.

Like any communicator, the public speaker must form a personal relationship with audience members.

A speaker should also choose supporting materials with audience characteristics in mind. Assume that you support bringing a professional athletic team to your community and that meeting this goal involves raising money to build a new stadium. When speaking to a group of business leaders, you might stress the economic advantages of your proposal; when speaking to the local PTA, however, you might mention that increased spending may provide additional dollars for education and that the team will provide a new source of family entertainment. Good speakers choose appeals that are relevant to the audience.

Finally, the style of a speech should be adapted to the audience. Above all else, speeches must be understandable. It is not a good idea to try to clarify a concept by comparing it to a computer if the people in your audience are computer illiterate. If, however, you are speaking to a group of engineers, this type of clarification might be a very good idea—provided you know what you are talking about. It is also important to remember that people come to a speech with expectations. They want your speech to resemble their idea of the way a speech should sound. If you violate their expectations by using an unusual style, the speech will probably fail.

> *People come to a speech with expectations. They want your speech to resemble their idea of the way a speech should sound.*

Audience Analysis

To make the kind of adjustments just described, you must gather information about your audience. This can be done in a number of ways. **Demographic analysis** tells you about the groups to which audience members belong. Knowing the age, sex, educational level, religious affiliation, occupation, economic status, and cultural identification of audience members can help a speaker draw inferences about current beliefs and interests.

Knowing an audience's age range, for example, can help the speaker choose compelling and understandable supporting materials. A story or example that appeals to a teenage audience may mean very little to listeners in their forties, whereas personalities and issues familiar to older listeners may be over younger listeners' heads. References to the 1960s, for example, can effectively build interest or illustrate a point if the audience is full of baby boomers, but these references can mystify an audience of teens. A good speaker realizes that audience members may have very different life experiences, and he or she makes an effort to adjust for these differences.

Gender is another demographic factor that affects audience responses. Men and women are likely to have different views and concerns in some cases and identical responses in others. The trick is understanding which case is which. In decades past, adapting a speech on the basis of gender was relatively easy. In earlier times, women's place was thought to be primarily in the private sphere, and men's in the public. Women were kept ignorant of political and economic issues, whereas men knew almost nothing about domestic arrangements. Those days are, fortunately, long past, and men and women are now raised more equally. Nevertheless, even today's liberated men and women were raised in gender-specific environments and were encouraged to pursue sex-typed interests. This makes adaptation based on gender a difficult process. Stereotypic assumptions will only offend large segments of the audience, yet ignoring differences can be insensitive. As Stephen Lucas explains, "you must avoid false sex distinctions that do not exist and acknowledge true sex distinctions where they do exist."[9] To see just how difficult this is, try making your own lists of topics suitable for men and women without offending or stereotyping either group.

Lucas's rule should also be applied to other demographic categories, such as ethnicity, cultural identity, and geographic location. Speakers who address groups to which they themselves do not belong should be especially careful to check their assumptions. One way to do this is to ask for feedback from people who belong to those groups. Speakers should also remember that collecting demographic data is not an end in itself. Data are useful only to the extent that they allow a speaker to answer specific questions: What motivates the people I am preparing to speak to? Why will they attend, and how do they feel about my topic? What approach will best help me inform or convince them?

> *Speakers who address groups to which they themselves do not belong should be especially careful to check their assumptions. One way to do this is to ask for feedback from people who belong to those groups.*

A skilled speaker uses a number of sources to gather information about audiences.[10] The first source is the local media. Bert Bradley suggests that speakers listen to local news broadcasts and subscribe to a local newspaper prior to a speaking engagement. News items show the kind of information that interests members of the community, editorials indicate opinions and concerns, and classified ads can provide useful information about economic conditions. A second source is personal interviews with local individuals who are similar to audience members. By surveying local people, the speaker can get a more specific sense of how the audience will react. Finally, if invited by an organization to speak, the speaker should spend some time with people in the organization and should read the official publications of the organization. By doing this research, the speaker can build credibility, attraction, and power.

Source Characteristics and Audience Response

No matter how thorough the research and how brilliant the delivery, no speech will be successful if the audience does not respect and trust the speaker. Audience members are just as eager to gather information about the speaker as the speaker is to find out about them. In fact, audiences are often as much persuaded by who the speaker is as by what the speaker says.

> *No matter how thorough the research and how brilliant the delivery, no speech will be successful if the audience does not respect and trust the speaker.*

It is quite natural for an audience to consider the source. Most of us would find an article on vitamin therapy more believable if its source were the *New England Journal of Medicine* than if it were printed in the *National Enquirer*. In deciding on a vacation spot, most of us would respect the word of a friend who had been there more than we would an advertising brochure. And most employees would comply with a directive from a boss more readily than they would an order from a summer intern. People who are credible, attractive, and powerful have an added advantage when it comes to communicating.

This effect was noted long ago. As you recall, the Greek philosopher Aristotle believed that speakers had three tools with which to persuade an audience. **Logos** referred to logical reasoning, **pathos** to emotional appeals, and **ethos** to the impression the audience formed of the speaker's character. Aristotle advised speakers to demonstrate intelligence, character, and goodwill in order to establish ethos. Although modern investigators take a slightly different approach to classifying source characteristics, they agree with Aristotle's basic premise that the success or failure of a speech depends on how the speaker is perceived by the audience.

Herbert Kelman and William McGuire are two contemporary writers who have analyzed how source characteristics are related to audience response.[11] According to Kelman, audiences are influenced by sources in three ways: through internalization, identification, or compliance. **Internalization** occurs when audience members incorporate message content into their belief systems. When audience members think, "Yes, I agree; that argument makes sense to me and fits in with what I believe," they are experiencing internalization. What source quality leads audience members to internalize messages? According to McGuire, internalization occurs when the source possesses **credibility,** that is, when he or she is perceived to be believable and trustworthy.

In addition to internalizing a message, audience members may accept a message because they identify strongly with the source. **Identification** is based on the presence of a perceived relationship (either real or imaginary) between source and receiver. When audience members think, "By agreeing with the source, I will be more like him or her; we will have something in common," they are experiencing identification. Identification occurs when the source possesses **attractiveness,** that is, when he or she offers audience members an emotionally rewarding relationship.

Finally, audience members often respond favorably to sources who can meet audience needs or offer material incentives. This influence process is called **compliance.** Audience members experiencing compliance say to themselves, "It is in my own best interest to agree with the source." Compliance occurs whenever the source is perceived as possessing **power,** when he or she controls material resources desired by audience members. Table 8-2 summarizes these three influence processes and gives examples of ways speakers can increase ethos in each area.

Credibility

Of the three kinds of source characteristics, credibility has captured the most attention in communication research. Although different authors identify different dimensions of credibility, most agree on two: expertness and trustworthiness. Speakers who show that they are knowledgeable about a topic establish **expertness.** Speakers who indicate a concern for audience interests demonstrate **trustworthiness.** Both characteristics increase credibility and consequently enable the speaker to influence and educate audience members.

Even before a speech begins, audience members have some feelings about the speaker's credibility; that is, they have preconceived notions of how expert and how trustworthy the speaker is. These notions may be the result of direct experience, advance publicity, or information given as the speaker is introduced. Once the speech begins, this initial credibility can rise or fall. A speaker without particularly impressive titles and credentials can increase credibility by delivering a carefully prepared and well-argued speech. Conversely, the credibility of a highly respected speaker can be undermined if the speech seems to have been thrown together at the last minute or if the speaker seems insincere.

Attractiveness

All else being equal, the more attractive a speaker is, the more effective he or she will be. McGuire divides attractiveness into four dimensions: familiarity, similarity, physical attractiveness, and liking. Although unusual, new ideas are sometimes appealing, most of the time people are attracted by **familiarity.** Audiences often respond best to sources and ideas that seem "normal." Studies have also shown that the more often audiences hear an idea, the more

TABLE 8-2

Source Characteristics That Enhance Influence

The following table shows the kinds of characteristics that audiences value in public speakers. Note that the effectiveness of a given characteristic varies according to type of influence.

Influence Type	Source Characteristic	Ways of Exhibiting Characteristic
INTERNALIZATION Influence based on convincing an audience to accept an argument as part of their belief system	**Credibility** Perception that the speaker can be believed	Speakers increase credibility by emphasizing **expertness** and **trustworthiness.**
IDENTIFICATION Influence based on creating a personal and positive relationship with audience members	**Attractiveness** Perception that the speaker is likeable and is someone with whom audience members would be comfortable	Speakers increase attractiveness by emphasizing **familiarity, similarity, physical attractiveness,** and **liking.**
COMPLIANCE Influence based on persuading audience members they have something to gain by agreeing or something to lose by disagreeing	**Power** Perception that the speaker controls a resource desired by audience or has ability to affect audience members' lives directly	Speakers increase power by emphasizing their **legitimacy, control of rewards,** and **ability to act coercively,** as well as their access to scarce information and their willingness to associate with audience members.

Influence types are based on a taxonomy provided by Herbert C. Kelman in "Processes of Opinion Change," 1961, *Public Opinion Quarterly, 25,* pp. 57–78. Classification of source characteristics follows that of William McGuire in "Attitudes and Attitude Change," in *Handbook of Social Psychology,* 1985, Gardner Lindzey and Elliot Aronson, Eds. New York: Random House.

attractive the idea becomes. Many years ago, Robert Zajonc demonstrated what he called the **mere-exposure hypothesis,** the idea that "simple repeated exposure to a stimulus" results in attraction.[12] These findings suggest that speakers should ground at least some of their discussion in the familiar; they will be perceived as more attractive if their ideas resonate with ideas already accepted by audience members. The findings also suggest that it takes time for audience members to become comfortable with new ideas. The speaker who pushes new ideas too rapidly may be rejected.

Closely related to familiarity is **similarity.** Typically, people are attracted to others who share their own demographic and attitudinal characteristics. Apparently, audience members believe that these similarities imply shared interests and concerns as well, and they identify more strongly with speakers who are like them than with speakers who are very different. This same effect occurs in modeling, wherein receivers are shown someone else being rewarded or punished for a given action. The more similar the model is to the receiver, the more likely the receiver is to act like the model.[13] In general, then, people are most influenced by others who are like them in some way.

A source's **physical appearance** also affects an audience. A speaker whose physical appearance is average or above average has an advantage over one who is less physically attractive. Of course, physical attractiveness can sometimes backfire. Occasionally a speaker is too good-looking. Audiences whose primary concern is credibility may be turned off by glamor. Nevertheless, if the audience is not overly concerned with expertise, if emotional identification is at stake, then a positive physical appearance is desirable. In general, speakers should look as attractive as possible without violating audience expectations by dressing or presenting themselves in an extreme manner.

Finally, a person who offers **liking,** who provides the social rewards of warmth, humor, and respect, will be perceived as attractive. Taken to an extreme and used as a tactic, presenting oneself as likeable is known as ingratiation.[14] Although ingratiation strategies such as flattery can be overdone and obviously insincere, audiences enjoy speakers who are genuinely warm, outgoing, and friendly.

Power

The final way in which sources can influence others is through a show of power. John French and Bertram Raven believe that power is exercised whenever an individual controls a valued resource.[15] According to their analysis, sources can achieve power in five ways: by occupying an important position in society, by offering material rewards in exchange for compliance, by threatening to punish disobedience, by gaining access to scarce information, and by exhibiting personal characteristics that others admire.

The last two of these power bases—the possession of information (which French and Raven call **expert power**) and the ability to offer social rewards through personal characteristics (which French and Raven label **referent power**)—are similar to expertness and liking, which have already been discussed. The first three power bases, however, are new to our discussion. The first of these, **legitimate power,** is evident when a source acts as a representative of an important social institution. In such a case, the individual is powerful not because of personal characteristics but because of his or her position in the institution. The primary reason we obey police officers, judges, teachers, and the like, is that we consider them legitimate authorities.

The second power base, **reward power,** is used whenever an individual who has a material possession that another person values offers access to that possession in exchange for the other's compliance. An employer who can give employees bonuses, raises, and promotions has reward power. The final power base, **coercive power,** exists when an individual can harm another or can take away valued possessions. A boss who can fire or demote a worker has coercive power. Employees usually comply with the requests and suggestions of their bosses because they realize both the harm and the good their bosses can do them.

Audiences differ in the extent to which they respect power. Some people, called **high authoritarians,** are preoccupied with power and tend to identify with authority figures.[16] An audience made up of this kind of person is extremely impressed with symbols of power and will respect high-power sources. Other people are less likely to defer to the powerful. To assess their impact on an audience, sources should have a clear sense of the way audience members view power, as well as a realistic view of their own power bases.

Relationships Between Source Characteristics

As we have seen, a variety of characteristics affect audience response. Successful speakers learn to emphasize qualities that are relevant and appropriate to a given topic and speaking occasion. When the topic is serious and the goal of the speech is to inform or to persuade, audiences want speakers to be expert and trustworthy. When the topic is less serious and the speaker's goal is to entertain, attractiveness may be more important. The relationship between source characteristics is complex. Indeed, factors that increase audience acceptance in one way may inhibit it in another. Humor, for example, can increase attractiveness but may do little to enhance credibility or power. Perceived intelligence may increase credibility but may not make a speaker particularly well-liked. In predicting how an audience will perceive them, speakers must understand their own strengths and goals as well as the needs of the audience.

Overall, as a speaker you are better off sticking to your strengths and not trying to put on a front. If you're not particularly funny, avoid telling jokes in an effort to charm an audience; if you're not well-informed on a specific aspect of your subject, do not try to pass yourself off as an expert; and if you have reward power, you would be foolish to make false promises. On the other hand, you can develop characteristics an audience will value.

Establishing a positive relationship is an important part of communication in the public context, and speakers should do their best to increase their ethos.

Good research can increase expertness, and sensitivity can enhance trustworthiness and similarity. Establishing a positive relationship is an important part of communication in the public context, and speakers should do their best to increase their ethos.

Constructing Valid Arguments

Although creating ethos is extremely important, there is more to public speaking than establishing a positive relationship with audience members. Successful public speakers must also construct valid and convincing arguments. In this section we look at how to structure arguments and how to spot errors in reasoning.

The Structure of Argument: The Toulmin Model

Sometimes audience members accept a speaker's message without question; at other times, they need to be convinced. In the latter case, the speaker must provide an **argument,** an explanation of his or her reasoning.

Parts of an Argument

What constitutes a good argument? The Toulmin model provides one answer to this question. According to Stephen Toulmin, an argument is made up of six parts: claim, qualifier, data, warrant, backing, and rebuttal or reservation.[17] Although a speaker may not refer explicitly to all six parts during a speech, he or she must understand each of them to construct an argument. Figure 8-2 illustrates the Toulmin model.

The **claim** is what the speaker wishes the audience to accept. An argument succeeds to the extent that the audience accepts the claim, and it fails to the extent that the audience rejects the claim. Claims may be facts ("Smoking cigarettes is hazardous to one's health"), values ("Health is a positive value and should be safeguarded"), or policies ("Cigarette advertising should be banned").

Claims vary in strength. Some claims are absolute; others are less certain. The **qualifier** indicates the strength of the claim. Modifiers such as "always," "sometimes," "probably," "nine out of ten times," and the like are qualifiers that indicate how far the claim should be taken. Although some facts in this world are absolute, most knowledge is conditional. Unqualified claims often indicate that a speaker is overstating the case.

Intelligent audiences do not accept unsupported claims, even if the claims are qualified. Instead, audience members want some evidence that what the speaker proposes is true. Such evidence is called **data.** Although these days most people accept the claim that cigarette smoking is dangerous, when this argument was first advanced it had to be backed up by research data. In making public claims, speakers use statistics, illustrative examples, research results, expert testimony, eyewitness accounts, and the like as data.

Citing data does not guarantee an argument will be accepted. Audience members must see a relationship between data and claim; that is, they must understand the reasoning that lets the speaker move from evidence to conclusion. The connecting link between data and claim is called the **warrant.** Ulti-

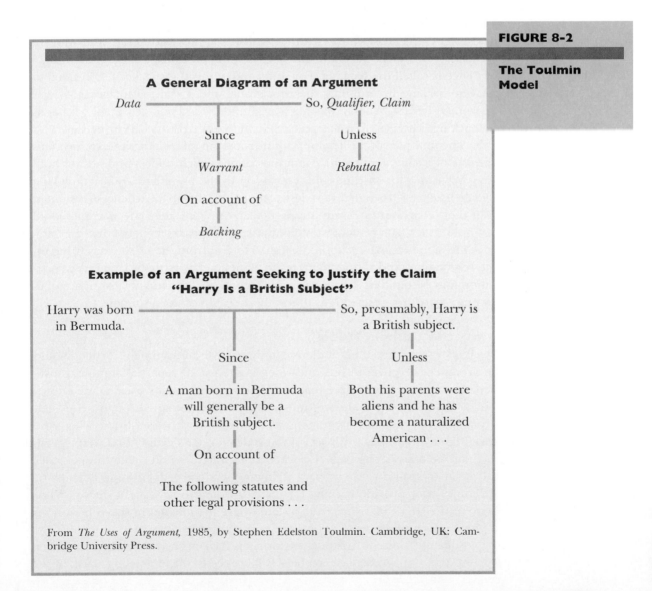

FIGURE 8-2

The Toulmin Model

A General Diagram of an Argument

Data ———————————————— So, *Qualifier, Claim*

Since   Unless

Warrant   *Rebuttal*

On account of

Backing

Example of an Argument Seeking to Justify the Claim "Harry Is a British Subject"

Harry was born ———————————————— So, presumably, Harry is
in Bermuda.   a British subject.

Since   Unless

A man born in Bermuda   Both his parents were
will generally be a   aliens and he has
British subject.   become a naturalized
                               American . . .

On account of

The following statutes and
other legal provisions . . .

From *The Uses of Argument,* 1985, by Stephen Edelston Toulmin. Cambridge, UK: Cambridge University Press.

mately, the argument lives or dies on the strength of the warrant. Warrants may or may not be spelled out explicitly during the speech, but they are always a hidden part of the argument.

Let's suppose that a speaker's claim is that the proportion of women faculty at a given school should be increased.[18] The data show that only 7% of the faculty are women and that, as a consequence, very few students have the opportunity to study with a woman teacher. What is the warrant that ties data to claim? What is the underlying reason for accepting the speaker's proposal, given the validity of the statistics? In this case the warrant is based on a value; the speaker is arguing that the presence of women faculty is worthwhile and desirable. Audiences who share the speaker's values will accept the warrant with little difficulty. Others might need additional evidence. Such additional evidence is called the **backing.** For some audiences, the speaker might need to provide backing by outlining the educational and social advantages provided by women faculty. When a warrant is well understood and acceptable, it needs no backing; when it is less acceptable, it may require detailed explanation.

The final part of the Toulmin argument is the **rebuttal** or **reservation.** This consists of a statement of the conditions under which the claim does not hold true. What might constitute the reservation in the argument about employing female teachers? If women were less competent scholars or teachers than men, or if their contributions were not particularly unique, then the warrant would not hold, and the argument would crumble. If a speaker believes that the audience has significant reservations in regard to a warrant, he or she may bring up the reservations and refute them. If the audience favors the warrant, the reservation may be omitted. In any case, it is a good idea for the creator of an argument to search for reservations to test the strength of the argument.

Using the Toulmin Model

Speakers often offer their audiences only part of an argument. When should an argument be given in full, and when is the use of a partial argument justified? Most rhetoricians agree that when the warrant and its backing are known and accepted by an audience, the speaker need not go through a detailed explanation of the entire argument. If, for example, I live in a state where the speed limit is 55 mph, I will accept the state trooper's claim "You were speeding" on the basis of the data "I clocked you going 63 mph." The trooper does not need to spell out the warrant ("Anyone who exceeds 55 mph is guilty of speeding") nor provide backing for it ("According to provisions of New York State traffic laws"). A visitor from a state where the maximum speed limit is 65 mph, however, might need to hear the entire argument.

Since the time of Aristotle, rhetoricians have argued that when a speaker is confident that audience members will correctly fill in missing parts of an argument, it is not only more efficient but also more effective to allow them to do so. That is, when people supply their own reasoning, they are more likely to be convinced than when the speaker presents the argument to them.

Of course, not every audience member fills in an argument as the speaker wishes. A line of reasoning that seems completely self-evident to a speaker may be flatly rejected by some audience members. In deciding how fully to frame an argument, the speaker must carefully consider the kinds of conclusions the audience is apt to draw and the kinds of warrants it will accept.

When we make arguments, we are often vague about them. We know the conclusion we wish the audience to reach, and we usually have some data to support it, but at times we have trouble articulating the warrant, backing, qualifier, and rebuttal. By using the Toulmin system to lay out our arguments, we can examine and clarify our thinking.

Types of Arguments

Adapting Aristotle's distinction between ethos, pathos, and logos, Wayne Brockreide and Douglas Ehninger argue that speakers have three kinds of warrants or ways of appealing to an audience.[19] Arguments can be based on authoritative, motivational, or substantive appeals.

Authoritative and Motivational Arguments

An **authoritative argument** depends entirely on the authority of a source. Some sources are automatically trusted. In matters of health, the surgeon general is a good example. Let's assume the surgeon general has stated that a particular drug is dangerous and believes that it should not be sold. A speaker can use this statement as data to support the claim that the drug ought to be removed from the market immediately. We can outline the argument, including its implied authoritative warrant.

> **Data:** *According to the surgeon general, drug X is dangerous to public health.*
>
> **Claim:** *Drug X should be removed from the market immediately.*
>
> **Warrant:** *The surgeon general is an expert and trustworthy source whose recommendations should be followed.*
>
> **Reservation:** *Unless the surgeon general is politically motivated or her data are incorrect*

When parents tell their children to do something "because I said so," they too are using an authoritative warrant.

A **motivational argument** is based on the emotional needs of the audience. When a speaker uses a highly emotional appeal or urges audience members to accept a claim because doing so will satisfy a personal desire or need, he or she is using a motivational warrant. In the following example the speaker relies on a visceral reaction of audience members. The argument is based on the speaker's belief that he and the audience share common feelings of pity and horror.

Data:	*Baby seals are being slaughtered.*
Claim:	*Laws should be enacted to protect the seals.*
Warrant:	*Brutality toward animals is emotionally repellent.*
Reservation:	*Unless animals do not have rights to humane treatment*

Whereas some motivational arguments are directed toward audience members' passions, others are directed toward members' needs. These kinds of motivational appeals assure audience members that a basic need will be fulfilled if the claim is accepted. To construct a need-focused argument, a speaker must understand the basic emotions and needs that drive an audience. Although needs are classified in several ways, the most familiar is **Maslow's need hierarchy.** According to Abraham Maslow, humans have five basic needs that are ordered in respect to one another.[20] The most urgent and basic of these needs are called **physiological needs,** the needs for food, water, air, warmth, and so on. Once these needs are satisfied, we concern ourselves with **safety needs,** our needs to be safe from external harm. Next come our needs for **love and belongingness,** and **self-esteem.** Finally, we experience the need for **self-actualization,** the need to reach our full potential. Later, Maslow came to believe that people may also be motivated by **curiosity needs,** the needs to explore and understand the environment, and by **aesthetic needs,** the needs for beauty, harmony, and balance.

Arguments can focus on any of these needs. Let's consider as an example a hypothetical advertisement for a new perfume.

Data:	(Visuals showing attractive male models being irresistibly drawn to a woman wearing Jungle Passion perfume)
Claim:	*Buy Jungle Passion today.*
Warrant:	*If you buy Jungle Passion, you too will be irresistible to men, and your needs for belongingness and love will be satisfied.*
Reservation:	*Unless men find women attractive for reasons other than their scent*

Although this is not a particularly rational argument, it may be emotionally compelling if audience members' needs are strong enough and if members identify psychologically with the models in the advertisement.

Substantive Arguments

A **substantive argument** connects data and claim through logic and reasoning. When a speaker shows audience members that the claim is the only rational conclusion, given the data, he or she is using a substantive warrant. As we shall see, certain standard patterns of argument are considered acceptable in our culture. These patterns include arguments from cause, sign, generalization, and analogy. Each takes a slightly different form and must stand up to different tests to be considered valid. Each also can be misused and can lead to faulty conclusions.[21]

Arguments from cause are common in the public context. Whenever a speaker tries to establish why a given state of affairs occurred, he or she is using a causal argument. The following example shows how a causal argument might work.

Claim: *If my opponent is reelected, the economy will grow worse.*

Data: *Since my opponent took office, inflation has risen and unemployment has grown dramatically.*

Warrant: *These economic disasters were caused by my opponent's unwise fiscal policies.*

Reservation: *Unless these economic disasters were caused by factors beyond my opponent's control*

Establishing causal connections is not always easy. A valid argument from cause must establish four things: (1) that the presumed cause (Y) preceded the presumed effect (X) in time; (2) that Y can, in fact, lead to X; (3) that there is no other, more plausible cause that might explain X; and (4) that both X and Y were not due to a third, unexplained factor. Only when all four propositions are established can we be confident that a cause really does exist.

It is not easy to prove cause. In the attempt, people often commit a **fallacy** (an error in reasoning) called the **post hoc fallacy** or doubtful cause fallacy. They assume that Y caused X simply because it preceded X. Superstitions are examples of post hoc fallacies. The driver who has an accident right after a black cat crosses the road and who assumes that the cat caused the accident is committing the post hoc fallacy.

Although the flaw in the black cat argument is fairly easy to see (unless you are unusually superstitious), post hoc fallacies can be harder to spot. Assume, for example, that right after a new coach is hired, a team has a losing season. It is tempting to blame the loss on the coach, because bad coaching can sometimes cause a team to lose. But before we recommend firing the coach, we need to rule out other possible causes. We need to be sure that nothing about this year's team (say, the players' lack of experience) makes them uncoachable. We also must assure ourselves that no third factor (say, budget cuts) has kept both team and coach from doing an effective job. Assigning cause is a common activity, but it is more difficult to do correctly than it appears.

Arguments from sign are a second kind of substantive argument. An argument from sign seeks to predict one condition (X) by pointing to another condition (Y) associated with it. Arguments from sign should not be confused with causal arguments. Smoke, for example, is a sign of fire, but it is not the cause of fire. Most people would accept the claim "This building is on fire" on the strength of the data "The hall is full of smoke." Not all arguments from sign, however, are this straightforward. Let's look at a slightly more controversial example.

Claim:	*This year's freshman class will not do as well as previous classes.*
Data:	*The class SAT scores are substantially lower than previous class scores.*
Warrant:	*SAT scores are a good indicator of academic success.*
Reservation:	*Unless SAT scores are biased or other factors intervene that contradict their validity*

For an argument from sign to be valid, four things must be established: (1) that Y is a reliable sign of X; (2) that nothing has occurred to change the relationship between X and Y; (3) that a sufficient number of signs point to X; and (4) that there are no signs that contradict X. Let's look at the argument about test scores. People who oppose using standardized scores to predict success in school often argue that although test scores may indicate some students' achievement potential, other equally reliable and less biased predictors are overlooked. When people rely on only one sign and ignore others or when they imperfectly associate the sign in question with what they think it predicts, they are using fallacious reasoning.

Arguments from generalization seek to establish a general conclusion on the basis of data taken from a small sample of cases.

Claim:	*Jones will win the election.*
Data:	*Of one thousand people surveyed, 57% said they would vote for Jones.*
Warrant:	*The rest of the public will act as did the sample.*
Reservation:	*Unless the sample was unusual in some way*

Although professional pollsters following scientific procedures can generalize with amazing accuracy, the kinds of generalizations we make every day are often flawed. Four conditions must be met for a generalization to be valid: (1) the cases examined must be representative; (2) a sufficient number of cases must be examined; (3) the data must be up-to-date; and (4) any negative cases must be negligible.

In everyday life, we often generalize on the basis of one or two instances. Unfounded stereotypes and prejudices are examples of a kind of fallacy called **hasty generalization.** Hasty generalizations are based either on too few cases or on unusual cases. If I were to draw conclusions about what students on your campus are like by surveying one student (say, the student who usually sits next to you in class), my generalization would probably be flawed. When I generalize on the basis of one case, I run the risk of choosing an atypical individual. The more cases I look at and the more careful I am to avoid selection biases, the more likely I am to reach valid conclusions. Whenever a speaker uses statistics to support a generalization, try to find out how those statistics were obtained. The more carefully the data were collected, the more valid are the results.

Arguments from analogy seek to establish that two situations, X and Y, are alike.

> **Claim:** *As president, I will be able to balance the budget.*
>
> **Data:** *As governor, I balanced the budget.*
>
> **Warrant:** *Being governor is similar enough to being president that success at the former level means success at the latter level.*
>
> **Reservation:** *Unless I have not anticipated additional difficulties*

The validity of an argument from analogy depends on two conditions: (1) that the cases being compared are alike in all important respects; and (2) that any differences between the cases are insignificant. Arguments such as "It worked for me, so it will work for you" are good examples. This argument obviously fails if the two people involved are very different from one another.

Some analogies are purely figurative. They are rhetorical devices a speaker uses to explain an idea to an audience, but they should not be taken literally. Such a **false analogy** was used by King James I. He argued that the monarch is the head of state and that just as the body dies when the head is cut off, so the nation dies without its king.[22] Although the analogy may be emotionally compelling, it is not substantive. Nations and bodies are not, in most important respects, governed by the same principles.

Guarding Against Unsound Warrants

Much as we like to believe that people are rational and logical, it simply isn't true. Much of the time we jump to conclusions, engage in wishful thinking, and believe what is easiest for us to believe. Psychologists who study the ways people reason find that most of us hold **cognitive biases** that distort our conclusions about the world. Evidence suggests, for example, that people exaggerate re-

> *Much as we like to believe that people are rational and logical, it simply isn't true. Much of the time we jump to conclusions, engage in wishful thinking, and believe what is easiest for us to believe.*

sponsibility for their successes and minimize responsibility for their failures; give themselves more credit than they deserve for collective activities; exaggerate the extent to which others agree with them; and believe they have a great deal more control over their destinies than they actually do.[23]

As audience members, we also often act as **lazy processors.**[24] We make up our minds about a speaker not by listening

TABLE 8-3

Fallacies in Argument: Usages That Mislead Audiences

Ad Hominem

The speaker attacks someone's character in areas not necessarily relevant to the issue. By accusing a political opponent of infidelity, atheism, or a flamboyant life-style, the speaker diverts attention from the issue under discussion.

Slippery Slope

The speaker predicts that taking a given line of action will inevitably lead to undesirable effects. For example, it was once seriously argued that "If women are educated, their health will be undermined, they will be unable to bear children, and the family will be destroyed." Slippery slope predictions are simplistic and often play on our fears.

False Dilemma

The speaker sets up an either-or situation, ignoring other possibilities. "America. Love it or leave it" and "You're either with me or against me" are two examples.

Straw Man

The speaker characterizes an opponent's view in simplistic terms and then easily demolishes it. Nixon's famous "Checkers speech" suggested that his only crime was in keeping a little cocker spaniel as a gift for his children. He had actually been accused of misappropriating campaign funds.

Non Sequitur

From the Latin meaning "it does not follow." The speaker, using connectives such as *therefore, so,* or *hence,* makes two unrelated ideas seem logically connected. "It's been used for years; therefore, it must be good" is a non sequitur suggesting that everything old is good.

carefully to what he or she has to say but rather by looking at surface details. A less-than-confident listener, for example, may assume a speech was good simply because everyone else liked it. An audience member with math anxiety may decide that any speaker who uses statistics must be intelligent. This kind of cognitive carelessness puts us at risk of being fooled by ignorant or unscrupulous speakers who feed us half-truths and fallacies. The only way we can guard ourselves against lazy processing is to learn to recognize some of the techniques used to fool audiences. Table 8-3 lists some ways speakers either deliberately or inadvertently create false arguments.[25]

Glittering Generality

The speaker associates self or issue with a vague virtue word. "I believe in the American dream; my opponent will create the American nightmare" sounds good, but what does it mean?

Transfer

The speaker links own ideas with popular people or issues and links opponent's ideas with unpopular people or issues. Presidential candidates may portray themselves as following in the path of Washington or Lincoln, for example.

Plain Folks

The speaker attributes an idea to a member of the audience's own group rather than to self. Politicians often read letters from "average citizens" asking for help or thanking the politicians for enacting a given law.

Bandwagon

The speaker makes it appear that anyone who does not agree will be left out or will fall behind. "Fifty thousand people have already donated" legitimizes the act of donating and makes the nondonor feel abnormal.

Ad Populum

The speaker appeals to popular prejudices. "Unless we act now, the Japanese will soon own everything of value in this country" relies more on fear and ethnic prejudice than on a realistic threat.

Preparing and Presenting the Public Speech

To someone who has never given a public speech, the challenge may seem overwhelming. Most beginning speakers don't know where to begin. They have ideas, but they don't know how to organize and structure a speech so that these ideas hang together. Luckily, some basic principles can help people communicate more effectively in public. Although understanding these principles will not turn anyone into a skilled speaker overnight—that takes practice and study—the principles are a beginning point and can be used to criticize speeches. In this section we'll look at the way simple public speeches are structured, paying particular attention to what each part of the speech accomplishes.

Introductions and Conclusions

Public speeches can be divided into separate parts, each with its own function. The first part of a public speech, known as the **introduction,** fulfills several functions. Among the most important of these are creating interest and attention in the speech topic, establishing a relationship between speaker and audience, and orienting the audience to the purpose of the speech.

Functions of the Introduction

The first function of the introduction is to create a desire in the audience to listen to the speech. As the speaker begins, audience members judge whether the speech will be interesting and lively or boring and effortful. If the speaker does not create interest at the outset, listeners are likely to tune out the rest of the speech. Audience members also judge the speaker's qualifications. Thus, the second function of the introduction is to increase audience confidence in the speaker, to convince audience members that the speaker is worthy of respect. The speaker must introduce himself or herself to the audience and establish positive ethos. Finally, the third function of the introduction is to let the audience know what the speech is about. If audience members cannot figure out what the point of the message is, they will give up on the speech. This means that at some point in the introduction, the speaker announces the **thesis,** or central purpose, of the speech. He or she may also use the introduction to foreshadow major points and themes (if the speech topic is complex) or to provide special information and definitions (if the topic is unfamiliar).

Given the necessity of accomplishing these goals, how does a speaker actually begin? Bruce Gronbeck and his colleagues provide an excellent discussion of standard ways speakers use to begin their speeches. These ways include referring to the topic or occasion, offering a personal allusion or greeting, ask-

TABLE 8-4

Ways to Open a Public Speech

Type of Opening	Example
Reference to Topic A direct statement of subject; works well with motivated audience; less effective with skeptical or apathetic receivers	"I am here tonight to speak to you about a concern we all share, the problem of . . ."
Reference to Occasion A reference to the reason for the speech; allows speaker to acknowledge special occasions	"On the 100th anniversary of the founding of this great institution, it is fitting that we gather here to celebrate."
Personal Reference or Greeting An indication of one's relation to topic or audience; builds common ground; can backfire if greeting is too familiar or intrusive	"It's a pleasure to be here today. Ten years ago, I too was a new student. Like you, I wondered what the next four years would bring."
Rhetorical Question A question the speaker wants the audience to consider; involves audience; can offend if it makes assumptions about audience or asks members to make an uncomfortable choice	"What would you do if you had no place to live and no one to turn to for help? How long would you survive on the streets?"
Startling Statement A shocking statement of fact or opinion; increases attention and interest; can offend if silly or melodramatic	"Every six seconds another child becomes a victim of . . ."
Quotation A relevant quotation from a respected source; links speaker to source; can be trite or inapplicable	"As Shakespeare said, 'All the world's a stage . . .'"
Humorous Anecdote A joke or story related to topic; shows speaker's warmth; can offend if poorly chosen	"This puts me in mind of a story. It seems there were three shipwrecked sailors . . ."
Illustration An extended example; makes topic vivid and concrete; can divert attention if point of illustration is not clear	"Let me tell you about what happened to one family whose lives were changed by our program. . . ."

ing a rhetorical question, making a startling statement, using a quotation, telling a humorous anecdote, and offering an illustration. Table 8-4 lists and illustrates these techniques and explains how they are related to the functions of the introduction.

Functions of the Conclusion

Just as the introduction is the speaker's first opportunity to make an impression on the audience, so the ending of the speech, or the **conclusion,** is the speaker's last chance to convince the audience. Both the introduction and the conclusion are extremely important, because audiences listen most closely and most critically at the beginning and at the end of a communication. Many beginning speakers fail to take advantage of this phenomenon. They trail off or simply stop without warning the audience that the speech is ending. The conclusion must be as carefully crafted as the introduction and must generally do three things: signal that the speech is ending, reiterate the significance of the topic, and summarize the main ideas of the speech. If these functions are fulfilled, the audience leaves with a feeling of closure and an understanding of what the speaker expects them to know or to do.

As with the introduction, a speech may conclude in many stock ways. These ways, summarized in Table 8-5, include issuing a challenge or appeal, summarizing main ideas, using a relevant quotation, returning to an earlier illustration, offering an inducement for action or belief, and expressing one's own intention in relation to the speech topic.

Organizing the Body of the Speech

The part of the speech that lies between the introduction and the conclusion is called the **body** of the speech. Here major ideas are developed and supported. It is important to organize these ideas so that audience members can follow the flow of the speech. Receivers exposed to written arguments can always reread a puzzling message. Receivers of spoken messages do not have that luxury; they must follow the argument as it is presented. To help them do this, speakers employ a number of devices during the speech. They **preview** the speech structure ("I'm going to give you three reasons why you should take action today"); use **transitions** to move the audience from one idea to the next ("Now let's look at the second reason"); and employ **internal summaries** ("So far we've seen that there are financial and social reasons to act"). Even more important than these stylistic devices is the use of an overall organizational scheme that arranges materials in ways that make sense to an audience. Several **stock organizational patterns** have been identified. These patterns include chronological, spatial, topical, causal, and problem-solution orders, as well as a special pattern known as the motivated sequence.

A **chronological order** arranges ideas according to a logical time sequence. If you were giving a speech on the history of the United States (putting aside for the moment the question of whether this is too broad a topic for a single speech), you might decide to talk about North America before

TABLE 8-5

Ways to Close a Public Speech

Type of Closing	Example
Challenge or Appeal A direct request for action; lets audience know what to do next; not as appropriate if change desired is attitudinal rather than behavioral	"I encourage you to join with us now . . ."
Summary A restatement of main ideas; increases audience comprehension	"There are, then, four ways we can protect ourselves. . . ."
Quotation A relevant quotation from a respected source; increases speaker credibility and inspires audience	"Let me close with the words Thomas Jefferson used when he stood in this hall exactly two hundred years ago today . . ."
Illustration An extended example; makes speech content concrete; can tie conclusion to earlier material	"So the next time you're ready to give up on yourself, remember what happened to the Jackson family. . . ."
Added Inducement A final reason for believing or acting; increases audience acceptance; can confuse if inducement is not clearly tied to proposal	"And if we work together now, not only will we be a happier and healthier community, but we will also . . ."
Personal Intention A statement of what the speaker is prepared to do; speaker leads by example and illustrates own trustworthiness	"I know I will be at the rally on Sunday, and I hope I will see you there too."

From *Principles and Types of Speech Communication* 7th ed. by Alan H. Monroe and Douglas Ehninger. Copyright © 1974, 1967, 1962, 1955, 1949, 1939, 1935 by Scott, Foresman and Company. Reprinted by permission of HarperCollins College Publishers.

Columbus, the colonies prior to the Revolution, the Revolutionary period, the early Republic, and so on up to the present. Rather than skipping from era to era in random order, it would make more sense to follow a past-to-present chronology. If you were given the job of orienting new students to your campus, one way would be to take them through a typical day, from morning to evening. In both cases, use of a time sequence would help you order your thoughts in a way audience members could easily follow.

A **spatial order** arranges ideas according to physical location. The speech on U.S. history, for example, could be arranged geographically from east to west. In the orientation speech, you could employ a spatial order by taking your audience on an imaginary tour of the campus. As you would mentally pass each building or location, you could talk about an aspect of campus life associated with that location. For example, you might start at the theater and discuss the cultural life of the campus, move on to the gym and talk about athletics, proceed to the classrooms and discuss academic life, and so on. Of course, the success of this approach would depend on whether audience members were familiar with a map of the campus. If they were unfamiliar with the way the campus is laid out, they might not understand the organization of your speech. The use of slides or other visual aids could help in this regard and could also add interest to the speech.

A **topical order** divides the speech into familiar subtopics. Yet another way of organizing the orientation speech might be to divide the college experience into separate components: academic, social, cultural, and so forth. Or, if you were explaining the kinds of majors available, you might discuss them in clusters: natural sciences, social sciences, humanities, and fine arts. Topical order works only when the subtopics seem to be sensible divisions of a field and when the subtopics are reasonably exhaustive. If a subtopic is unfamiliar to the audience, it should not be used. For example, if a student is not familiar with the term *social science,* this way of organizing the speech will be confusing.

The next two stock patterns are useful when a problem is the topic of the speech. When the speaker's goal is to discuss the causes and effects of the problem, a **causal order** may be used. Here the speech is divided into two main parts. In the first, the factors that have led to the problem are discussed; in the second, the results of these factors are explained. Imagine a speech on the depletion of the ozone layer. The speech might first explain major causes of the problem and then talk about what will result if the problem continues. For speeches in which the speaker offers a solution to a problem, **problem-solution order** is often used. As the name suggests, the two main divisions of this type of speech are the problem and the solution. Imagine a speech urging voluntary recycling. The speaker first establishes that a problem exists—that in many communities landfills are completely full and alternative forms of waste disposal are unavailable. Having convinced the audience that a serious problem exists, the speaker then offers a solution (or a partial solution)—voluntary recycling.

A final stock organizational pattern is called the **motivated sequence.** This five-part organizational plan focuses on making the topic and the claim relevant to audience needs. According to Alan Monroe, who developed this approach, the sequence follows a natural progression; that is, it mirrors the psychological reactions of receivers as they consider issues related to their needs.[26]

The five steps in the motivated sequence are attention, need, satisfaction, visualization, and action. In the attention step, which occurs in the introduction, the speaker introduces vivid and motivating materials. The goal here is to focus audience members on the message and to give them a reason for listening. Let's assume a speaker wants to convince audience members to begin to make financial investments for their old age. An audience of college age people may not find this a very compelling topic. Investments may seem to them a dull topic, and retirement may seem so far off as to be a nonexistent state. A startling statistic might serve here to gain attention. The speaker might say something such as, "In 2038, the year most of you will reach retirement, a dollar will be worth only X percent of its value today, a week's groceries will cost Y dollars, and rent on the most modest apartment will be Z dollars per month." If the numbers used are extreme, the audience will probably take note of them. Of course, the speaker's statistics should be taken from a reliable source so that they are believable as well as shocking.

The next step is the **need step.** Here the speaker shows audience members that a present state of affairs directly relevant to them is undesirable. In the investment speech example, the speaker uses the need step to establish that Social Security benefits by themselves will not be enough to allow audience members to live comfortably and that, without additional investments, audience members will have to give up many necessities. The speaker's goal is to get audience members to think, "The possibility that these things could happen to me if I don't take action is real."

Following the need step is the **satisfaction step.** Here the speaker offers a plan to meet the need. In the example we have been discussing, the speaker has used the need step to induce fear of the future. Now he or she must show the audience that there is a simple and effective way to reduce the fear. Without this step audience members may simply turn off and refuse to think about the issue. With a successful satisfaction step, however, they will see how their fear can be alleviated. At this point, then, our speaker shows how a reasonably modest amount of money invested so as to earn a modest amount of interest can, over time, create a substantial retirement fund. The investment plan should be simple and easy to understand, and the use of complicated computations should be kept to a minimum, especially if the audience is not comfortable with numbers. The important idea is to present a plan that seems simple and possible.

If the satisfaction step has worked, audience members are now thinking, "I believe I could follow the speaker's advice. The plan seems simple and effective." To cement this idea and to motivate the audience to take action on the speaker's recommendations, the speaker next uses the **visualization step.** Here the speaker describes concretely what will happen if the solution is adopted. In the investment speech, the speaker paints a picture of a retirement free from worry, a time when audience members can travel, pursue special interests and hobbies, and generally live comfortably.

Finally, in the **action step,** the speaker asks the audience to implement the proposal outlined in the satisfaction step. "So pick up one of our brochures, and open an IRA today" might constitute the action step and conclude the investment speech.

Outlining Main Points and Subpoints

Whichever pattern you choose to organize a speech, be sure to develop your ideas fully and clearly in ways an audience will find sensible. One way to check your organization is to outline your speech. An **outline** is a kind of blueprint that shows the basic ideas in your speech. When you outline, you write out each of your main ideas and, below each main idea, indicate the subpoints you wish to make. An outline allows you to see at a glance whether you are developing each point in turn or whether you are mixing up your ideas. Main points are usually indicated by roman numerals and are written next to the left-hand margin. Subpoints are indicated by capital letters and are indented below each main point. Sub-subpoints are indicated by arabic numerals and are indented below subpoints. Table 8-6 illustrates this outline form and provides a summary of our discussion of speech structure.

Your outline can also help you during delivery of the speech. During delivery the speaker must establish a communicative link with the audience. Often the best way to do this is to speak in a clear, confident, and conversational tone. If you memorize or read your speech, it may sound "canned." If you look at your outline and then explain each main point clearly in words that seem suitable at the moment, the speech will sound fresh and spontaneous. This form of delivery is called **extemporaneous delivery.** The speech is completely thought out ahead of time, but the specific wording is selected during delivery. This does not mean that extemporaneous speakers don't practice;

indeed, practice is absolutely essential. As extemporaneous speakers speak, they think about what they want to say rather than repeat exact wording from memory. Extemporaneous speakers speak from their outlines. Because the outline lists all of the ideas to be covered, an extemporaneous speaker merely glances down at the outline to see what the next idea is. Outlining is an important tool that fulfills a number of functions.

TABLE 8-6

An Example of Outline Form

How to Organize a Public Speech

I. A well-organized speech opens with an introduction.
   A. One purpose of the introduction is to get attention.
   B. A second purpose of the introduction is to establish goodwill.
   C. A third purpose of the introduction is to orient listeners to the subject.

II. Every speech should have a thesis, or central purpose statement.
   A. The thesis explains the central idea of the speech.
   B. Ideas unrelated to the thesis should be eliminated.
   C. The audience must be able to identify the thesis.

III. Main ideas are included in the body of the speech.
   A. Organizing main ideas in outline form allows the speaker to check the organization.
      1. In outlines, subpoints are subordinated to main points.
      2. If an idea is subdivided, it should include at least two subpoints.
   B. Stock organizational patterns help the speaker arrange points in a sensible order.
      1. Chronological order arranges ideas according to time.
      2. Spatial order arranges ideas according to location.
      3. Topical order arranges ideas according to subject.
      4. Causal order arranges ideas into causes and effects.
      5. Problem-solution order arranges ideas into problems and solutions.
      6. Motivated sequence arranges ideas psychologically.

IV. Speeches end with a conclusion.
   A. A conclusion should provide a sense of closure.
   B. A conclusion should sum up the argument or present a proposal for action.
   C. The conclusion is the last thing an audience hears.

Increasing Public Speaking Skills

Many people avoid giving public speeches because they think of a speech as a difficult and frightening form of communication and because they think that to speak in public, one must be a "born speaker." The truth is, of course, that no one is born able to speak in public. Even the greatest public speakers had to start somewhere. For many great speakers, that starting point was the realization that public speaking offers opportunities: an opportunity to speak up when it is important to do so, an opportunity to develop ideas in one's own way, and an opportunity to make a difference in the public sphere.

> *Public speaking offers opportunities: an opportunity to speak up when it is important to do so, an opportunity to develop ideas in one's own way, and an opportunity to make a difference in the public sphere.*

Keep in mind that although each speech you give will be different, some general principles will help you prepare to speak in public. By following these guidelines, you can improve your public messages. The first thing to keep in mind is that *you are responsible for what you say in public.* While this is, of course, true of all forms of communication, the responsibility here is of a special kind. In interpersonal discussion, people can use conversation to try out their ideas. In the public context, speakers do not usually have that luxury. If you are speaking to inform, be absolutely certain of your facts. Audiences do not want to listen to false information or half-formed ideas. If you are speaking to persuade, be sure that your proposal is a good one. Audiences do not expect to be asked to take action that may turn out to be inadvisable. This means that prior to speaking, you must *do serious research and preparation.* Researching your subject will increase your understanding of your subject area, build up your self-confidence, and, when incorporated into your speech, increase your ethos. It will also provide convincing data to back up your claims.

Once you have done sufficient research, you can start to develop your main points and arguments. First, make sure that your ideas make sense to you; then, make sure they will make sense to your audience. This means you must *make a special effort to be organized and clear.* Keep in mind that the audience has not researched and thought about the topic as you have, and conclusions that seem self-evident to you may not seem so to them. To make your ideas clear, you must develop and illustrate them. As you think about your speech, keep asking yourself, will the audience understand what I am trying to say?

Listening is a difficult, draining process, and audiences often become bored or distracted. *Incorporate vivid and interesting elements into your speech.* By using personal examples, concrete and immediate language, interesting anecdotes, and the like, you can keep your audience interested. Try also to make what you say relevant to audience members' life experiences.

This chapter stresses the importance of adapting your message to your audience. This does not mean that you should say only what audience members want to hear or that you should "water down" your presentation. It is important to *adapt to your audience but retain your individual style*. What will make you worth listening to is the unique perspective you'll bring to a problem. If you can find a balance between saying what you know the audience wants or needs to hear and expressing your own ideas, you will have gone a long way toward being a good speaker.

Summary

This chapter examines the character and structure of public communication and offers advice about how to construct public messages. Public communication is a face-to-face, one-to-many form of communication wherein a single speaker addresses a large audience. It is more formal and less spontaneous than communication in other contexts and is affected by physical constraints such as audience size, time, and space. Public communication also differs from interpersonal or group communication in that it takes place in the public sphere. It is important because it allows citizens to take a stand on public issues and to take part in public debate. It is also a valuable professional skill.

Successful public speakers must adapt their messages to audience members. By understanding the nature of audience members' beliefs, attitudes, and values, speakers can increase their perceived credibility, choose suitable supporting materials, and find a basis for persuasive appeal. In adapting to the audience, the speaker should make sure the central idea and the structure of the speech, as well as supporting materials and style, are appropriate and understandable. Demographic analysis can give the speaker useful information about audience beliefs and interests.

Because audience members do not get to know a speaker gradually, the speaker must establish trust as quickly as possible. The speaker does this by emphasizing his or her credibility, attractiveness, or power. Credibility is important when a speaker wants audience members to internalize a message; attractiveness is valuable if identification is the goal; and power is necessary for audience compliance. All three are multidimensional characteristics that can be established in a variety of ways.

Public speaking is more than a matter of image. Speakers construct arguments and make authoritative, motivational, and substantive appeals. The

Toulmin model provides one way of analyzing arguments and identifying gaps in logic. In authoritative appeals, speakers base their arguments on expert opinion. In motivational appeals, speakers focus on a variety of audience needs, including those identified by Maslow (physiological, safety, love, esteem, and self-actualization, as well as curiosity and aesthetic needs). In substantive appeals, speakers employ arguments from cause, sign, generalization, and analogy.

Public speeches, like other forms of discourse, have their own structure. Each part of a public speech is organized, and each functions in its own way. Introductions, for example, create interest, establish credibility, and orient the audience, whereas conclusions signal the end of the speech, underscore the significance of the topic, and summarize main ideas. The content of the body is also arranged in a logical order, often following one of several stock organizational patterns.

One cannot learn public speaking overnight; it takes practice and instruction. Nevertheless, some general principles can help a speaker prepare. Public speaking is a responsibility and therefore necessitates research and preparation. To ensure audience attention, comprehension, and retention, speakers should be organized and clear and should use vivid and interesting material. Finally, although speakers must adapt their speech to the needs and interests of audience members, they should never lose the unique perspective that makes a message their own.

Key Terms

Listed below are the key terms used in this chapter, along with the number of the page on which each is explained.

Review Questions

1. What is public communication? What are the characteristics of this form of discourse? How do variables such as size of audience, time, and space affect the nature of public speeches?

2. What is the public sphere? How can we recognize when we are acting in it? Why do modern Americans shy away from public involvement?

3. Who is Candy Lightner? What do her efforts illustrate about action in the public sphere?

4. Why should people learn to communicate in public?

5. How are the bonds created between audience and speaker different from those created in other contexts? What must speakers do to create these bonds?

6. What three kinds of cognitive structures exist in the human mind? What are peripheral and core beliefs? How do beliefs and attitudes differ? What are the three dimensions of attitudes? What are values? How are values related to personal identity? Why is it important for speakers to know the beliefs, attitudes, and values of audience members?

7. What is audience adaptation? Why is it important? What three aspects of a speech should a speaker adapt to an audience? What kind of analysis helps the speaker adapt a speech? What demographic factors are important for audience adaptation? What sources can a speaker use for information that will help him or her adapt the message to the audience?

8. What is source credibility? What did Aristotle have to say about it? In what three ways do speakers influence audiences? What source characteristics are necessary for internalization, identification, and compliance to take place? How can speakers establish credibility, attractiveness, and power?

9. What are the two dimensions of credibility? How can each be established in a speech?

10. What are the four dimensions of attractiveness, and how can each be established?

What are the five kinds of power? How can speakers establish power?

11. What is the Toulmin model? What are the six parts of an argument?

12. What three kinds of arguments do Brockreide and Ehninger discuss? What is an authoritative argument? a motivational argument? What are the basic motivational needs that Maslow identified? How are they ordered?

13. What four kinds of substantive arguments are discussed in the text? What conditions must be met if each is to be considered valid? Give an example of a fallacy for each type of argument.

14. What is the normal structure of a public speech? What functions should the introduction fulfill? Name some standard ways to begin a speech. What functions should the conclusion fulfill? Name some standard ways to end a speech.

15. What devices can a speaker use in the body of a speech to help the audience understand the message? Name and describe five stock organizational patterns. What are the five steps in the motivated sequence?

16. What general principles should a speaker keep in mind while preparing a public speech?

Suggested Readings

Bradley, Bert E. (1991). *Fundamentals of speech communication: The credibility of ideas* (6th ed.). Dubuque, IA: Brown.

    Bradley discusses ways in which speakers can be persuasive, focusing on the concept of credibility.

Cooper, Martha. (1989). *Analyzing public discourse.* Prospect Heights, IL: Waveland.

    An interesting analysis of what it means to engage in public communication, with especially strong discussion of criteria for judging public speeches. This text is a good source for information on logical and motivational appeals.

Lucas, Stephen E. (1986). *The art of public speaking* (2nd ed.). New York: Random House.

    This text is a popular and very readable primer for becoming a better public speaker.

Notes

1. Cooper, Martha. (1989). *Analyzing public discourse.* Prospect Heights, IL: Waveland, 5–6.

2. Ibid., 5.

3. Lucas, Stephen E. (1986). *The art of public speaking* (2nd ed.). New York: Random House, 8–9; Cooper, 16.

4. Figures are based on an unpublished study by Warren Jones and Dan Russell, which is summarized in the *New York Times,* December 18, 1984, and reported by Lucas, 10–11.

5. Delattre, Edward J. (1977, October 11). The humanities can irrigate deserts. *The Chronicle of Higher Education,* 32; cited in Bradley, Bert E. (1991). *Fundamentals of speech communication: The credibility of ideas* (6th ed.). Dubuque, IA: Brown, xxiii.

6. van Oosting, James. (1985). *The business speech: Speaker, audience, and text.* Englewood Cliffs, NJ: Prentice-Hall, 9.

7. Rokeach, Milton. (1968). *Beliefs, attitudes, and values.* San Francisco: Jossey-Bass.

8. Schwartz, Shalom H. (1992). Universals in the content and structure of values: Theoretical advances and empirical tests in 20 countries. In Mark P. Zanna (Ed.), *Advances in experimental social psychology* (Vol. 25). New York: Academic.

9. Lucas, 72.

10. Bradley, 93–95, offers an excellent discussion of sources to pursue in analyzing audiences.

11. Kelman, Herbert. (1961). Processes of opinion change. *Public Opinion Quarterly, 25,* 57–78; and McGuire, William J. (1985). Attitudes and attitude change. In Gardner Lindzey & Elliot Aronson (Eds.), *Handbook of social psychology* (3rd ed., Vol. 2). New York: Random House. For a more detailed development of these ideas, see Trenholm, Sarah. (1989). *Persuasion and social influence.* Englewood Cliffs, NJ: Prentice-Hall, chapter 9.

12. Zajonc, Robert B. (1968). The attitudinal effects of mere exposure. *Journal of Personality and Social Psychology, 9,* part 2, 1–27.

13. See Trenholm, 39; and Smith, Mary John. (1982). *Persuasion and human action.* Belmont, CA: Wadsworth, 202.

14. Jones, Edward E., & Wortman, Camille. (1973). *Ingratiation: An attributional approach.* Morristown, NJ: General Learning. For a discussion of ingratiation as a negotiation tactic, see Pruitt, Dean G., & Rubin, Jeffrey Z. (1986). *Social conflict: Escalation, stalemate, and settlement.* New York: Random House.

15. French, John, & Raven, Bertram. (1959). The basis of social power. In Dorwin Cartwright (Ed.), *Studies in social power.* Ann Arbor, MI: University of Michigan Press.

16. See Adorno, Theodor W., et al. (1950). *The authoritarian personality.* New York: Harper & Row.

17. Toulmin, Stephen Edelston. (1958). *The uses of argument.* Cambridge, Eng.: Cambridge University Press.

18. This argument is taken from Rottenberg, Annette T. (1985). *Elements of argument.* New York: St. Martin's, 118–126.

19. Brockreide, Wayne, & Ehninger, Douglas. (1960). Toulmin on argument: An interpretation and application. *Quarterly Journal of Speech, 46,* 44–53.

20. Maslow, Abraham H. (1970). *Motivation and personality* (2nd ed.). New York: Harper & Row, 35–58.

21. The distinctions between arguments from cause, sign, generalization, and analogy are standard, as are the tests of their validity. The present discussion is taken from three sources: Bradley, 226–237; Ross, Raymond S. (1985). *Understanding persuasion: Foundations and practice* (2nd ed.). Englewood Cliffs, NJ: Prentice-Hall, 165–169; and Trenholm, 232–235.

22. Fearnside, W. Ward, & Holther, William B. (1959). *Fallacy: The counterfeit of argument.* Englewood Cliffs, NJ: Prentice-Hall, 25.

23. Sears, David O., & Funk, Carolyn L. (1991). The role of self interest in social and political attitudes. In Mark P. Zanna (Ed.), *Advances in experimental social psychology* (Vol. 24). New York: Academic.

24. For research on lazy processors and heuristics, see Eagly, Alice H., & Chaiken, Shelly. (1984).

Cognitive theories of persuasion. In Leonard Berkowitz (Ed.), *Advances in experimental social psychology* (Vol. 17). New York: Academic; Langer, Ellen J. (1978). Rethinking the role of thought in social interaction. In John H. Harvey, William J. Ickes, & Robert F. Kidd (Eds.), *New directions in attribution research* (Vol. 2). Hillside, NJ: Lawrence Erlbaum Associates; and Petty, Richard E., & Cacioppo, John T. (1986). The elaboration likelihood model of persuasion. In Leonard Berkowitz (Ed.), *Advances in experimental social psychology* (Vol. 19). New York: Academic.

25. For additional information on fallacies, see Fearnside & Holther; Rottenberg; and Lee, Alfred M., & Lee, Elizabeth B. (1979). *The Fine Art of Propaganda*. San Francisco: International Institute for General Semantics.

26. For a complete discussion of the motivated sequence, see any edition of Monroe, Alan H., & Ehninger, Douglas. *Principles and types of speech communication*. Glenville, IL: Scott, Foresman.

9

Communication and the Mass Media

Like it or not,

we live in a media

culture, a culture that

affects how we experience

the world and

how we communicate

with one another.

In 1990, a woman got her hair caught in a dishwasher while trying to retrieve a fork. Instead of rushing to save her, her husband pulled out his video camera and taped the event for "America's Funniest Home Videos," occasionally tickling his wife to make the tape funnier. For many people today, appearing on national TV is the ultimate legitimating experience, well worth a little pain and inconvenience.[1]

When an earthquake hit the city of San Francisco in 1989, people in every part of the country were glued to their TV screens. The only people unable to experience the full drama of the event seemed to be those going through it. To find out what was "really happening," many San Franciscans called friends or family members outside California, people who still had TV reception. Nowadays, the only way to see the whole of an event is to see it through the eyes of a television camera.

When people go to a sporting event, they spend only part of their time watching what is going on before them. They listen to the play-by-play on portable radios and watch game highlights on giant TV screens. Without "six different camera angles, slow-motion instant replay, expert (color) analysis, and constant action," spectators feel something important is missing from the game.[2] Since the advent of television, real-life events are somehow not as satisfying as mediated events.

When in 1992 then vice president Dan Quayle criticized television for undermining moral values, he became embroiled in a debate not with a real person but with TV character Murphy Brown. In response to his accusations, the producers of "Murphy Brown" fought back, incorporating Quayle's attack into the plot and, by extension, adding Quayle to the cast. In a media culture it is sometimes hard to distinguish fictional from factual reality or politicians from sitcom characters.

Each of these situations illustrates how important the mass media have become in our daily lives. Like it or not, we live in a media culture, a culture that affects how we experience the world and how we communicate with one another. In this chapter we look at what it means to live in constant interaction with the mass media. We begin by examining the characteristics that make mass communication unique, and then we move on to consider the functions, effects, and uses of the media. Next, we turn our attention to the language and logic of newspapers, magazines, radio, and television. Finally, we take a look at technologies that will affect us in the near future.

What Is Mass Communication?

To understand how to use the media more effectively, we have to understand what mass communication is and how it differs from other kinds of communication. In this section we begin by defining mass communication and then move on to discuss media sources, receivers, and channels.

Defining Mass Communication

In modern societies, the media are important social institutions that reflect and affect the values and behaviors of large segments of the population.

Mass communication is a form of communication through which institutional sources (often referred to as "the media") address large, diverse audiences whose members are physically separated from one another. Contact is indirect; devices for the transmission, storage, and reception of information are interposed between source and receiver. Mass commu-

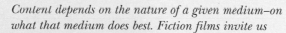

Content depends on the nature of a given medium—on what that medium does best. Fiction films invite us to enter an alternative reality that re-presents the world in concrete visual images.

nication is a powerful and pervasive mode of communication, and, in modern societies, the media are important social institutions that reflect and affect the values and behaviors of large segments of the population.

Characteristics of Media Messages

Media messages are unique in at least three ways: (1) in major mass communication contexts, the source is a complex, profit-oriented organization rather than a single individual; (2) receivers are anonymous, dispersed in time and space, and heterogeneous in their interests and background; and (3) communication occurs through indirect channels that require specialized encoding and decoding technologies.

Institutional Sources

In the communication contexts we have looked at so far, the source has been a single individual who composes and delivers his or her own message. Although the source may be influenced by friends or advisers, he or she takes primary responsibility for the message. In mass communication contexts, messages are the products of complex organizations comprised of individuals who perform specialized functions. To get a sense of how much internal specialization is involved in mediated communication, sit through the credits the next time you watch a film. You'll see that in addition to the director and actors, the film employs executive and associate producers, artistic directors, set dressers and costumers, lighting specialists, electricians, sound mixers, first- and second-unit photographers, and a host of others. Making a movie costs millions of dollars, and production companies expect to make a profit. They must therefore appeal to the largest possible audience, a fact which is inevitably reflected in their products.

Invisible Receivers

Another difference between interpersonal and mass communication lies in the relationship between source and receiver. Media sources have little, if any, direct contact with receivers. By the time audience members buy their popcorn and settle down in front of the screen, the cast and crew have packed up their equipment, have struck the set, and have moved on to other projects. In interpersonal contexts, sources and receivers are in direct contact; in mass contexts, feedback is indirect and delayed. Once a film is "in the can," the source's contribution is over. The film actor cannot modify a performance in response to the mood of the audience. The screenwriter cannot clarify an idea that's not getting across. Media communicators must anticipate audience reactions in advance of reception and must perform for invisible spectators.

Receivers are also invisible in another way: there are so many of them. Media audiences are huge. On a given night, one hundred million viewers may watch a television special. These viewers represent a variety of ages and social classes; their backgrounds and interests may be extremely varied. Even with fairly specialized media, such as technical magazines, readers may number in the tens of thousands, and, outside of the single shared interest that led them to purchase the magazine, they may have little in common. The problem of audience adaptation becomes particularly acute with such a heterogeneous public. Media messages cannot be individualized as can interpersonal messages. Anticipating the tastes and preferences of the "average viewer" or

Anticipating the tastes and preferences of the "average viewer" or "average reader" and being able to create messages that are widely acceptable are talents highly valued in the media industries.

"average reader" and being able to create messages that are widely acceptable are talents highly valued in the media industries.

A final characteristic of media receivers lies in the conditions under which reception takes place. With the exception of movie viewers, media receivers consume media messages alone or in small groups in fairly noisy environments. One source of noise is the competition of other mediated messages. It's important to remember that receivers' relationships with sources are voluntary and can be severed at any time. Audience members are free to turn off the radio if the DJ annoys them or to flip through TV channels until they find an image they like. Although all communication contexts involve some form of message competition, this competition is especially fierce in the mass media. When cable viewers have a choice of tuning into any one of twenty different stations at a given time, the producers of a single program must work especially hard to capture an adequate share of the market.

Interposed Channels

The use of interposed channels is a final characteristic of mass communication. Different media employ different technologies for the transmission and reception of messages, and these technologies make different demands on the resourcefulness of both source and receiver. Electronic media, for example, involve the use of special equipment to encode and decode messages. Not only does this equipment require a financial commitment, it may require technical expertise as well. Receivers often need manuals, special software, and workshops to learn how to use the more sophisticated types of media equipment. In designing new technologies, producers must make their products as user-friendly as possible. And to exist in a society in which new media are constantly emerging, receivers must be willing to learn how to interact with increasingly sophisticated machinery.

Different media not only call for different levels of technical sophistication, they also require different cognitive skills. Books and magazines, for example, do not require costly equipment, but they do demand that the receiver be able to read the written word, an accomplishment that takes detailed instruction. The ability to "read" a message is actually demanded by every medium. To understand a TV drama, for example, viewers must be able to decode visual messages; they must accustom themselves to

Different media not only call for different levels of technical sophistication, they also require different cognitive skills.

the language of camera angles, editing, scene composition, and so forth, just as directors must learn to tell a story in visual terms. Each medium has its own format, and successful media communicators understand their particular format.

How Audiences and Media Messages Interact

Although mediated messages have unique characteristics, mass communication is like every other form of communication in one way: sources and receivers form a relationship with one another. Since the beginning of the rise of the mass media in America, theorists have posed questions about this relationship, concerning themselves with the functions fulfilled by the media, the extent to which the media influence audiences, and the ways in which receivers process media messages. In this section we look at some of the divergent viewpoints that have emerged as scholars have tried to understand the relationship between audiences and media messages.

Functions of the Media

Sociologist Charles Wright, expanding on a model first developed by political scientist Harold Lasswell, identifies four **media functions:** surveillance, correlation, cultural transmission, and entertainment.[3] Table 9-1 summarizes these functions.

The first media function is **surveillance,** the gathering and disseminating of information. Media sources affect receivers by providing them with news, by warning them of crises or dangers, and by giving them the instrumental information they need in order to get through a day. When we speak of the media as the "watchdogs of a free society," we are referring to the surveillance function. In general, this function is fulfilled by newspapers and by radio and television news programming.

TABLE 9-1

Media Functions

Surveillance	The gathering and disseminating of information
Correlation	The analysis and evaluation of information
Cultural Transmission	The education and socialization of receivers
Entertainment	The presentation of escapist material that provides enjoyment and gratification

The second function of the media is **correlation,** the analysis and evaluation of information. In addition to reporting facts, the media affect receivers by interpreting news events and by analyzing social problems. By following up on news events, media commentators are in a position to understand the issues that lie behind a news story and to offer opinions on current social problems. The correlation function is most often found in the editorial pages of newspapers, on news analysis shows, and in magazine articles that analyze current issues.

The third function of the media is **cultural transmission,** or education and socialization. Not only do the media inform receivers about events, but they socialize receivers as well. By observing what characters do in television dramas, we internalize behavioral norms; by viewing films, we learn about our culture's history; and by reading magazines, newspapers, and books, we confront questions of values. Media personalities act as role models for us. Often our learning is **prosocial learning,** that is, it reinforces social ideals and passes on cultural understandings from one generation to the next. Sometimes, however, our learning is essentially **antisocial learning,** reinforcing socially destructive behavior. The debate about the effects of televised violence on the behavior of children indicates a very real concern—that culturally transmitted messages may inadvertently undermine cultural values.

The debate about the effects of televised violence on the behavior of children indicates a very real concern—that culturally transmitted messages may inadvertently undermine cultural values.

The final function of the media is **entertainment.** The media offer receivers an escape from the problems of everyday life. Media provide enjoyment and gratification, help us relax, allow us to experience vicarious adventure, and arouse our emotions. The entertainment function is fulfilled by almost every medium. Reading the newspaper, flipping through a magazine, and watching a TV show or a film are all ways that we give ourselves a break from the more serious aspects of our lives.

Of course, each of these functions can have negative side effects. Consider the surveillance function. News can as easily misinform as it can inform, and it can occasionally increase anxiety or cause panic. Too much information can even **narcotize,** or overwhelm and paralyze, an audience. When receivers are inundated with news reports, their knowledge of social problems may become superficial, and their social concern may be replaced by apathy.[4]

The correlation, cultural transmission, and entertainment functions all have their negative sides as well. Simplistic commentary, for example, can increase passivity and can discourage social criticism. When anchors appear after every major broadcast to summarize what we have just heard, we may stop listening carefully or lose confidence in our own conclusions. Similarly, media socialization can reduce the ability of other institutions (such as families and schools) to set standards and can foster superficial, homogenized values. Finally, mindless entertainment can encourage escapism and can lower popular taste. The functions that the media fulfill appear to be mixed blessings.

Media Effects: An Overview

Although the functional approach turns our attention to some of the outcomes of mass communication, it is ambivalent about the extent to which these outcomes control us. The functional approach does not explain whether media content responds to audience needs or whether it actually creates those needs. Given the ubiquity of the media in modern society, the question of how the media affect us is extremely important.

Do media messages brainwash a defenseless public, or are most people able to see through them? Do the media create desires, or do they simply give the public what it wants? Can the media instill values, or do they merely reflect values that already exist? The debate over these questions has resulted in two opposing schools of thought. According to the first, receivers are relatively passive; they accept media messages at face value and unconsciously allow media sources to tell them what to think. People who accept the first perspective believe in what has been called the **powerful effects model.**

According to the second point of view, far from accepting media messages as intended, audience members interpret messages according to their own preexisting beliefs and values and use these messages in unique ways. For people holding this view, audiences are active processors who are quite capable of defending themselves against media influence. Those who accept this perspective employ a **limited effects model.**

During the last fifty years, the pendulum has swung back and forth between these extremes.[5] The earliest theories of mass communication tended to portray the media as extremely influential. Metaphors used to describe the audience-media relationship emphasized audience passivity. Media influence was likened to a **magic bullet** or a **hypodermic needle** that could target unsuspecting audience members or inject them with a message. Receivers were seen as the passive victims of the all-powerful media.[6]

In the fifties and sixties, however, theorists began to take a closer look at the audience. They found that individuals were much more stubbornly resistant to media manipulation than had at first been assumed. According to the resulting **obstinate audience** theory, receivers, far from being passive victims, were viewed as creative consumers who sought out media messages according to their own needs and interpreted messages in their own ways.[7] Media effects were thought to be mediated both by the receiver's personality and by his or her group allegiances.

Despite the popularity of this view, critics were left with a nagging feeling that audiences were not so resistant. Some theorists argued that media selectivity did not necessarily mean consumers were unaffected by their choices, and others began to wonder just how much choice receivers really had. Therefore, in the seventies and eighties, a number of theorists began to reconsider the power of the media to influence audiences.

Despite attempts to negotiate a middle ground, adherents of each view still argue strongly for their own perspective. In the sections that follow, we'll take a brief look at some of the effects attributed to the media, as well as at characteristics that may make audiences at least somewhat resistant to media domination. After considering these arguments (which are summarized in Table 9-2), you be the judge.

What Media Messages Do to Receivers

Theories that argue for the power of the media generally argue one of three positions: that the media tell us what to think about, that the media tell us what not to think about, or that the media affect the way we think. We'll consider each in turn.[8]

Media Agendas

Very early on, critics identified the **agenda-setting function** of the media. According to this view, media **gatekeepers** select the issues they feel are most worthy of coverage and give those issues wide attention.[9] Receivers accept the gate-

TABLE 9-2
Media Effects and Audience Resistance

How Media Affect Audiences	*How Audiences Resist Media*
Media influence receivers by:	Receivers resist influence by:
1. Agenda setting	1. Selective processing
2. Producing hegemonic messages	2. Conducting oppositional readings
3. Affecting cognitive practices and expectations	3. Using media for individual gratification

The media often make decisions for us, alerting us today to a drug problem, tomorrow to a crisis in education, and the day after that to an erosion of family values. Why the media settle on these issues and not others seldom concerns the media consumer.

keepers' agendas without realizing that, somewhere along the line, an editor or producer is making choices about what to cover and what to ignore. As Norman Felsenthal remarks, "Neither an individual nor a society can give equal attention to everything. We are continually required to determine which problems get our immediate attention and which problems are simply endured or even ignored altogether."[10] The media often make decisions for us, alerting us today to a drug problem, tomorrow to a crisis in education, and the day after that to an erosion of family values. Why the media settle on these issues and not others seldom concerns the media consumer.

Agenda setting takes place most often in news reporting, but it can also occur in entertainment media. A movie-of-the-week about child abuse can trigger our interest in a normally overlooked problem, especially if it is followed up in other media. If, as a result of the movie, a weekly newsmagazine runs a feature about the problem and talk show hosts jump on the bandwagon, chances are that people will come to define child abuse as a serious issue. This is one way the media order our priorities and tell us not only what to think but also what to think about.

Hegemonic Messages

If media attention makes certain issues and information highly salient, it also makes some issues invisible. **Critical theorists** argue that the media reflect and reproduce only those ideas, meanings, and values that uphold the interests of the power elite and that they silence opposing views. According to these theorists, media messages are **hegemonic;** that is, media messages keep powerless groups from making their ideas known. Although the media may appear to present a variety of ideas and choices, this diversity is an illusion. Instead, the media reproduce and package a single message, or **dominant ideology.** Todd Gitlin, for example, argues that American TV encourages viewers to "experience themselves as anti-political, privately accumulating individuals." Television supports the status quo and valorizes a consumer ethic while discouraging criticism of alternate economic or political arrangements.[11]

Other critics argue that the ideological messages broadcast through the media are so powerful that opponents refuse to voice criticism or objections for fear of being socially isolated or of being scapegoated by the media.[12] And groups outside the mainstream have almost no chance to make themselves heard, because the media refuse to legitimate their ideas. In this sense, the media tell us what not to think about.

Media Logics

A final way in which the media may affect us has less to do with content and more to do with the form of media messages. According to this view, when new technologies emerge, they change the way we experience the world. They encourage certain kinds of messages and discourage others. Their very presence creates new social possibilities and changes existing power relations. For example, some critics argue that the electronic media have contributed to the emergence of an "imperial presidency." Elihu Katz sees the beginning of this trend in Franklin D. Roosevelt's "fireside chats." By broadcasting directly to the people, Roosevelt could bypass Congress.[13] Television has further increased the president's power by treating him as a media star and covering his every move. Television focuses on "personalities," and it is easier to cast a single individual as a personality than it is to cast multiple characters, such as Congress or the judiciary.[14]

The creation of an imperial presidency is only one exemplification that media formats affect both the messages that are broadcast and the surrounding social structure. When Marshall McLuhan first stated that **"the medium is the message,"** he was expressing the beliefs that the channel through which a message is transmitted is as important as the message itself and that the channel, in fact, often determines which messages will be transmitted and which will be ignored.[15] According to McLuhan's theory, each medium has its own internal logic, and each affects how we experience the world. For example, print media have **linear logic,** that is, they transmit information in an orderly sequence, word after word, idea after idea. Print media encourage rationality and individuality. Television, in contrast, has **mosaic logic,** bombarding us with changing bits of information that we must cognitively reassemble. Television encourages sensory involvement.

Because television is what McLuhan refers to as a **cool medium,** it demands that viewers fill in detail. Performers who are too hard-edged and direct are not "cool" enough to succeed on TV, although they may be perfect for a "hotter" medium, such as radio. In fact, McLuhan explains John F. Kennedy's success in the 1960 presidential debates in terms of his relative "coolness" compared to the "hotter" Richard Nixon.

Although not everyone has embraced McLuhan's cool-hot distinction, many critics accept the idea that form is as important as content in affecting audience responses. As we accustom ourselves to different media forms, our cognitive practices and expectations change. Exposure to a constant barrage of highly arousing and rapidly changing images (such as those found on TV) changes the way we think. We become impatient with nonpictorial stimuli and with nondra-

> *Many critics accept the idea that form is as important as content in affecting audience responses. As we accustom ourselves to different media forms, our cognitive practices and expectations change.*

Some media critics believe that our definition of information has been changed by the advent of television and that we all think in the language of TV.

matic messages. People raised on a steady diet of television may expect all information to be condensed, simple, short, and rapidly changing. Linear and detailed information may be rejected out of hand both by receivers and by media sources. Some media critics believe that our definition of information has been changed by the advent of television and that we all think in the language of TV.

Robert P. Snow believes that our involvement with the language of television is so strong that it is changing the language of other media. Television viewers, used to the condensing and telescoping tendencies of TV, are demanding the same features in newspapers, books, and magazines. Thus, *USA Today* is print journalism's attempt to use the language of television. Even textbooks are using "multicolored graphics, photos, boxed inserts, bold-face types, and summaries" to make reading more tolerable for the TV generation.[16]

What Receivers Do With Media Messages

Our discussion so far has portrayed viewers as fairly passive recipients of media influence. But is this a fair portrayal? Many scholars argue that it is not. These scholars view receivers as selective, rational consumers of messages who are affected as much by their own needs and group memberships as by media goals and practices. To support this viewpoint, these scholars make three basic arguments: that audience members process messages selectively, that audiences are motivated to use media by private needs and desires, and that the meanings audience members assign to media messages are social constructions.

Selective Processing

If everyone were to react to a given message in exactly the same way, the media would have very little trouble controlling receivers. Students of perception, however, know that this is not how perception works. People see the world in unique ways. As we saw in chapter three, we are capable of ignoring messages we don't like, of tuning out tedious or irrelevant details, of interpreting messages in original ways, and of forgetting inconvenient details. That is, we engage in selective exposure, attention, perception, and retention.

Selective exposure refers to people's tendency to avoid certain messages and to seek out others. Although we like to believe that we are open-minded and intellectually curious, many of us are not. Preexisting preferences guide us in the selection of media messages. Musical taste, for example, determines which radio station we listen to; a hard rock fan will not tune in to a station with an easy-listening format. Religious and political beliefs and values also affect media exposure; nonbelievers seldom watch televangelists, and liberal Democrats may refuse to read conservative columns. If we do expose ourselves to messages we usually avoid, we may do so to make fun of or to criticize those messages, not to listen with an open mind. Most of the time, however, we don't go that far; we simply refuse to expose ourselves to messages we imagine we will not like. Media can hardly affect us if we don't tune in.

Even when we choose to process a message, we may engage in **selective attention.** That is, we may only listen to parts of the message. As we saw in chapter 3, people's attention tends to wander, and messages must be vivid and novel if people are to process them. Advertisers, of course, are well aware of this fact and use music, color, sound effects, and so on, to make us pay attention.

Receivers may attend to a media message yet still come away with the "wrong" meaning. An example involves the old television program "All in the Family." Its central character was the bigoted Archie Bunker, whose intolerance was meant to make him a figure of fun. Some viewers recognized the show's social satire, but others identified with Archie and saw him as a spokesperson for their own views.

Receivers are also not immune from **selective perception,** the process of assigning meaning to messages in selective ways. Ask two different people to explain what a book or a movie or a film is about. Chances are, the explanations will be very different and will be affected as much by preconceived notions as by the intention of the media source.

Ask two different people to explain what a book or a movie or a film is about. Chances are, the explanations will be very different and will be affected as much by preconceived notions as by the intention of the media source.

Finally, receivers engage in **selective retention,** remembering only a small portion of any message. Studies have shown that "viewers of the network newscast can seldom remember more than three or four stories, or approximately 20 percent, just an hour after seeing the news." The average viewer is often ill-informed, even on issues that receive heavy coverage.[17]

Need Gratification

Why do receivers turn to the media in the first place? Many theorists argue that they do so to fulfill preexisting needs. **Uses and gratifications research** focuses on the needs that motivate media consumers. This research argues that receivers are active and goal-directed. Receivers know what they need, and they look for ways to get it. The media are only one of a number of competing sources of gratification. In Katz's terms, this approach "does not assume a direct relationship between messages and effects, but postulates instead that members of the audience put messages to use, and that such usages act as intervening variables in the process of effect."[18]

One of the earliest studies in this tradition was Herta Herzog's investigation of why women listened to radio soap operas.[19] Herzog determined that listeners used the soaps for emotional release, fantasy escape, and advice on how to deal with their own problems. Denis McQuail and his colleagues argue that the media, in general, are chosen to provide (1) diversion and emotional release; (2) substitute companionship and a shared social experience; (3) identity and value reinforcement; and (4) surveillance.[20]

Reading Media Texts

A number of theorists have focused their research efforts on describing how receivers make sense out of what they see and hear. These scholars argue that media reception does not take place in a vacuum and that receivers are not blank slates waiting to have a message inscribed on them. Instead, receivers are members of "interpretive communities" who actively construct meanings in accordance with their own social experiences. The theorists refer to the process of assigning meaning to media messages as "reading" and to the messages themselves as "texts." Scholars who take this approach argue that receivers are quite able to read media texts in ways that oppose the dominant ideology. Thus it is possible for feminists to do an oppositional reading of the ways women are portrayed in romance novels or for members of ethnic minorities to recognize ethnic biases in news reporting.

Tamar Liebes and Elihu Katz looked at how people from different cultures interpreted episodes of the TV program "Dallas." Liebes and Katz found that receivers quite often "broke frame" by standing outside the text in order to criticize it.[21] The receivers observed were not completely swept up by the content of programs but instead used media messages as a springboard for reflecting on their own lives and relationships ("J. R. is a bastard—all businessmen are—so is my uncle"). They often engaged in fantasy relationships with characters ("If I were J. R.'s mother, would I . . . ?"), analyzed ideological content ("The writers want people like us to think the rich are always unhappy"), and critiqued the rules of a genre ("Without J. R., 'Dallas' would be '*Big* House on the Prairie'"). When asked "What was that text about?" people from different cultures gave quite different answers. This seems to suggest that rather than a given text having one hegemonic message, it may have multiple meanings, a condition known as **polysemy.** In this sense, media exposure is a process of negotiating between what lies in the text itself and what lies in the social and cultural context in which the text is experienced.

The debate over how much the media affect us continues to rage. Although little doubt remains that media messages are influential, the question of just how much power they wield remains open. As media consumers, we should be aware of the potential of the media to affect our lives. One way to increase this awareness is to understand media formats, our next topic.

Media Formats and Logics

Each medium is unique not only in the conditions under which it is received but also in the way it is structured and in its internal logic. As a result, each has a distinctive capacity for influence.[22] In this section we'll look briefly at the formats employed in some of the major media. We'll focus on newspapers, magazines, radio, and television, follow with a few words about film and books, and end with a discussion of media ethics. Table 9-3 summarizes major points.

TABLE 9-3

Media Formats and Logics: Media Uses and Effects of Media Logics

Newspapers

- *used to:* pass time, find mundane information, keep in touch with events, identify self as reader
- *formats encourage:* focus on single events, avoidance of detail, interest in crises and dramatic events

Magazines

- *used to:* pass time, find detailed information, gain access to valued subgroups
- *formats encourage:* knowledge of detail, identity-related knowledge, unrealistic expectations, pressures to consume

Radio

- *used to:* pass time, find mundane information, regulate moods, ease loneliness
- *formats encourage:* conservatism, apathy, venting of emotion (through talk radio)

Television

- *used to:* pass time, provide companionship, keep in touch with events, relax, find escapist entertainment
- *formats encourage:* impatience with long or detailed material, interest in dramatic material, belief in ideal norms, dismissal of news that is not visually compelling

Newspapers

Every day more than 113 million Americans pick up a newspaper. Although the demographics describing these readers vary from paper to paper, most readers are well educated, reasonably prosperous, and neither very old nor very young.[23] Seldom spending more than half an hour with the paper, they fit their reading in during breakfast, while commuting, or during breaks. Reading is, in part, a routine way to pass time during transitional periods; because newspaper reading is seen as a useful activity, it allows us to take a break without appearing lazy. Newspaper reading is also a way to search out mundane information; people look to see what's on sale at the local department store or what's playing at the nearest movie theater. As much as sixty percent of a newspaper may be devoted to ads. Readers don't complain, because the ads provide them with needed information.

Reading the paper is also a way of keeping informed on important news of the day, a way of taking advantage of the surveillance function that the press provides. People expect the press to act as watchdogs, and readership is especially strong when the community or nation is threatened by a crisis. Finally, reading a newspaper is an act of self-definition. When a reader opens the paper on the bus or in a local coffee shop, he or she sends the message "I am the kind of person who reads a newspaper."[24] So strong is this perception that one of the major goals of adults in literacy programs is to be able to read a paper in public.

Reading a newspaper is an act of self-definition. When a reader opens the paper on the bus or in a local coffee shop, he or she sends the message "I am the kind of person who reads a newspaper."

In format, newspapers take the form of "hard copy." Information is laid out in two-dimensional space, and a variety of stories simultaneously compete for readers' attention. Readers skim the pages and select the items they find most useful or most appealing. To make readers' choices easier, headlines indicate the gist of a story, and the articles follow a standardized layout. Lead stories, for example, appear in the right-hand column, often accompanied by photos. Secondary news appears below the fold. Editorial columns and letters are grouped together on an inside page, and so on. Readers can thus easily locate the section of the paper that most interests them.

News stories are written in a special format that enables readers to fit reading into short periods of time. Called an **inverted pyramid,** this format gives the most essential information in the first few paragraphs, leaving development to final paragraphs. This structure allows editors to cut a story from the end and readers to stop reading at any point without losing the most important information. Unlike a novel, which usually positions the climax at the end, newspapers place the climax at the beginning.

Newspaper format encourages certain kinds of communication: a focus on isolated events, a tendency to omit detailed analysis, and a temptation to focus on the unusual and the dramatic. The fact that the first paragraph of a news story must sum up the entire story leads to a focus on single events, and who, when, where, and what become more important than why. Coupled with the value placed on objective reporting, news stories tend to focus on concrete details that can be easily measured and counted: the size of a crowd, the number of days hostages have been held, the cost of a new bomber. News stories are less likely to explore why the crowd assembled, what sociopolitical factors led to the hostage taking, or whether the new bomber is needed.

In addition to providing a focus on events, newspaper stories also search out the unusual and the dramatic. Although newspapers are designed to fulfill surveillance and correlation functions, they can't succeed unless they incorporate some level of entertainment as well. As any news reporter can tell you, "Dog Bites Man" is not news, but "Man Bites Dog" is. The more uncommon and sensational an event is, the more likely it will be reported. Reports of accidents and disasters are the most widely read of news stories, followed by reports of crime. As a result, "the world may seem more crime-ridden, conflict-filled, and/or absurd than it is."[25]

Kathleen Hall Jamieson and Karlyn Kohrs Campbell tell us that certain themes are considered especially newsworthy. These themes include (1) appearance versus reality (stories that uncover hypocrisy); (2) "little guys" versus "big guys" (accounts of conflict between the powerless and the powerful); (3) good versus evil (reports of crime and punishment); (4) efficiency versus inefficiency (exposures of waste and mismanagement); and (5) the unique versus the routine (the "Man Bites Dog" effect).[26]

In summary, the logic of newspaper discourse may result in events appearing isolated and separate, background information being overlooked and oversimplified, and crises and threats being exaggerated. The first two of these effects are partially offset by the analyses that appear in the editorial pages of a newspaper. It is here that the correlation function of the media is most evident. Given that TV news items are extremely short and concrete, receivers who want more thoughtful analysis of issues often turn to the print media for explanation and evaluation.

> *The logic of newspaper discourse may result in events appearing isolated and separate, background information being overlooked and oversimplified, and crises and threats being exaggerated.*

Magazines

The typical magazine is written to attract young, middle-class, reasonably well-educated readers, the people demographic analyses show are heavy purchasers. To make any further generalizations about readers is difficult, however, because magazines tend to specialize. More than do newspapers, magazines speak to and for particular segments of society. With the possible exception of magazines such as *TV Guide, Family Circle,* and *People,* which are sporadically read by large segments of the population, most modern magazines orient themselves to specific subgroups within the mass audience. The loyal readers who buy *Seventeen, Modern Photography, Field and Stream,* or *Heavy Metal,* for example, do so because these magazines understand their interests and identifications.

Readers may choose to read a magazine for a variety of reasons. Some readers simply use magazines as a means of killing time; while waiting in a doctor's office or barbershop, they may leaf through whatever happens to be available. Other readers are more involved, choosing a magazine that offers to gratify their needs. The magazines people choose to read reflect the groups to which they wish to, or actually do, belong.

The magazines people choose to read reflect the groups to which they wish to, or actually do, belong.

Magazines provide members of specific subcultures with needed information. *Vogue,* for example, appeals to a cosmopolitan, style-conscious, sophisticated female reader who wants to know the latest fashions in both clothing and pop culture. *Sports Illustrated,* on the other hand, is written primarily for male sports fans who want to know what is happening with their favorite teams. In general, the reader of *Vogue* is not the reader of *Sports Illustrated.*

Magazines often provide instructions about how to become a member of a given group. The woman who wants to improve her social standing reads *Vogue* to pick up hints on how to look and act the part. A novice tennis player purchases a tennis magazine in order to improve his or her skills. Robert Snow tells us that specialized magazines show readers how to "act like insiders, how to gain the respect of others already firmly entrenched, how to avoid being gauche, . . . and the emotional sensations that should be felt when one is achieving success."[27]

In addition to providing information, magazines reflect the norms and values of their readers. Thus *Playboy* legitimates one set of values and *Ms.* another. Each magazine offers its readers an identity and a set of priorities; each validates a different social and political philosophy.

Magazines can also serve as channels of communication to others. By publicly displaying a magazine, one can send a message about one's tastes and values. A copy of the *New York Review of Books* or the *Advocate* casually tossed on one's coffee table can let visitors know intellectual and personal interests that may become channels for conversation or identification.

Magazines are one of the least ephemeral of the mass media. Electronic messages disappear immediately after broadcast (unless they are taped for future reference). Newspapers are quickly discarded. Magazines, however, are kept for several weeks and read intermittently. In layout, they fall halfway between a newspaper and a book. Articles are generally arranged sequentially and are meant to be read all the way through, although the latter part of an article is usually separated from the first part and placed at the end of the magazine. Titles and vivid illustrations are used to catch the reader's attention and to move him or her through the text. In fact, many magazines are as much for looking at as for reading.

Unlike the terse, objective style favored by newspapers, the writing style in magazines is more narrative and personalized, often involving the use of first-person narrative. The use of a more direct form of address is in keeping with the identity function that magazines serve for readers, allowing readers entry into a valued culture. Magazine designers work hard to create a unique style for their magazines. Typestyle, photos, illustrations, and even ads reflect an overall image. The serious, functional, nonflashy format of *U.S. News & World Report* tells the conservative businessperson who reads it, "We are here not to entertain but to inform you." In contrast, *Vanity Fair* celebrates the ephemeral, using a style that is trendy and irreverent and filling its pages with glossy color photos of the rich and famous.

Magazines can offer us needed information and can provide serious analyses of important problems. They can also pander to voyeurism and can make us miserable by setting up unrealistic expectations. Some magazines are little more than gossip mills, invading the privacy of celebrities and "real people" alike to show us the sordid and the sensational. Images in magazines can also make us discontented with who and what we are. When the models in magazines set up expectations for an unrealistic level of youth or beauty or physical prowess, we may find ourselves pursuing impossible goals.

Radio

Over the years, radio use has changed. In the early days of radio, most listening occurred in the home. Families gathered together in their living rooms to listen as their favorite serials and soaps unfolded. Radio was a "communal

storyteller" as well as a source of information and musical entertainment.[28]
Now, most listening occurs outside the home. We carry our radios with us, listening as we drive, work, and play. Today radio
is a kind of "portable friend" who helps us
through the day by giving us useful information,
matching our moods, and keeping us company.
Radio is a comforting presence that we rely on
more than we imagine, as Altheide and Snow
suggest:

*Today radio is a kind of "portable friend" who
helps us through the day by giving us useful
information, matching our moods, and keeping
us company.*

> *Ask yourself if you can wash the car, clean house, study or read, or engage in a
> myriad of other activities without background radio noise? In these instances,
> radio is an integral part of the flow of the event. Indeed, without radio, some
> activity . . . would become awkward at best, and perhaps impossible.*[29]

Radio keeps people in touch with the world. In the words of a respondent interviewed in the early sixties, "To me when the radio is off, the house is
empty. There is no life without the radio being on." [30] Radio communication
has a strong interpersonal dimension. Not only does the music and talk provide a quasi-social interaction for lonely people, but also "radio binds people
together through common shared experiences and provides subjects to talk
about with others."[31] It can link people within a given subculture, validating
their group identity.

Not only is radio a companion, it is a companion who shares our identity,
understands our moods, and makes few demands on our attention. Radio stations work hard to create a personal identity that audience members will
accept and find attractive. Top 40, Album Rock, Golden Oldies, Beautiful
Music, Gospel, or Family Life—all are identities that stations form to establish a
relationship with receivers. In addition, each station programs its selections to
match audience needs and moods. Thus, wake-up music uses a lively rhythm
and a tempo designed to get the audience going, whereas late-night broadcasts
air more mellow and more romantic sounds. Even within a given time segment, programmers vary tempo from one selection to the next and, on a Top
40 station, rotate the top ten songs throughout a two- or three-hour period.
Thus, the radio listener knows with a high degree of precision what he or she
will be getting by tuning in.

Although a large part of radio content consists of musical selections, talk
radio is growing in popularity. Talk radio is an excellent example of the quasi-
interpersonal nature of radio. Talk hosts interact with audience members,
sharing ideas and opinions and allowing listeners a forum in which to express

their views. Counter to stereotypes that people who call in are pathetically lonely "crackpots," listeners are often intelligent, well-adjusted individuals who simply wish to take advantage of the forum radio provides. Altheide and Snow predict that "as urban life becomes more privatized and socially fragmented, talk radio will function both as an opportunity for vicarious and overt participation and as a source of information on issues. . . ."[32]

In many ways, radio is the most local and "demassified" of the mass media. Like magazines, radio stations tend to be specialized, catering to particular subcultures within a community. Because of this, the accusations of undue sociopolitical influence that are often leveled at the more "mass" of the mass media have not been made against radio. Perhaps the most serious charge leveled at radio is that it is conservative and uncommitted. "By creating the impression of abundance and unlimited fun, listeners may be encouraged to stand pat and go on blithely ignoring issues and controversies that are critical in the long run."[33]

Television

Television is, of course, the medium of choice for most Americans. On average, each household has 2.25 sets, which are turned on for approximately seven hours a day.[34] On a given night, tens of millions of viewers may be tuned in to a single program. This means that "in terms of audience penetration, television is the *most mass* of all the mass media."[35]

Television fulfills many functions for its viewers. Like newspapers, it provides local and national news (although the amount and type of news provided are characteristics unique to the medium). Like magazines and films, it gives viewers a glimpse into alternate worlds, and, like radio, it provides companionship. Like many other media, television teaches and socializes, although critics sometimes bemoan its content. Finally, television serves as the most popular medium for relaxation and escapist entertainment. Viewers may intentionally tune in for information, education, or entertainment, or they may simply turn on the set and watch because they think they have nothing better to do. Watching TV has become such a habit that viewers often sit through programs they don't like rather than turn off the set. When television reception is knocked out, viewers feel anxious and at loose ends, so accustomed are they to TV as background noise. In a 1992 survey reported in the October 10–16 issue of *TV Guide,* viewers were asked, "Would you take a million dollars to stop watching TV forever?" The answer for large segments of those surveyed was a resounding "No!"

We live in a culture where the separation between interpersonal and mediated communication is blurred, where people often act as walking billboards.

Because television is both auditory and visual, it (along with film) is the most perceptually compelling of all the media. Although sound is an important aspect of television, music and dialogue are often subordinated to visual information. Television is something we watch more than listen to. Television images are in constant motion, and a fundamental part of the logic of TV is a valuation of movement and change. Television has given us an appetite for highly arousing visual stimuli.

Television images are in constant motion, and a fundamental part of the logic of TV is a valuation of movement and change. Television has given us an appetite for highly arousing visual stimuli.

Television has also accustomed us to time compression. Shows that move slowly (such as annual awards shows) are generally criticized. The more rapid the tempo, the better-received a program is.[36] In both entertainment and news programming, we expect unnecessary details to be edited out, so that a story about a week in the life of a character happens in half an hour, and the gist of an hour-long speech is summarized in a ten-second "sound bite."

Another defining characteristic of television is that it is a very personal medium. The images shown on TV are intimate and personal. In comparison to film, television images are reduced in scale, and the most frequent shots are medium close-ups and close-ups. Whereas long shots provide a background and social context to a scene, close-ups personalize the audience-actor relationship.[37] This means that television encourages psychological identification. When we turn on the set, we want to identify with the characters and personalities we see. The fact that we view television in our homes rather than in more public spaces further emphasizes how personal our relationship is to this medium.

Entertainment Programming

In his discussion of the logic of television, Snow remarks on three features of television programming: speed and simplicity; a tendency to dramatize material; and a need to stay within the bounds of ideal norms. We'll look at how these work, first in entertainment programs and then in news programs.

It's important to remember that television is a business. Advertisers pay networks in an effort to gain substantial numbers of consumers. Every successful program must seize audience attention and hold it through the commercials. As viewers flip through the channels, a given show must be vivid enough to make them pause. The show must be simple enough so that viewers can understand its premise immediately (even if they tune in halfway through the program), and it must be compelling enough to get viewers to stay tuned over commercial breaks. These factors affect the language of television.

Simplicity and brevity are important aspects of television discourse. Most programs have little time for detailed character or plot development. As a result, characters are stereotyped, and plots follow a simple beginning-middle-end structure. Situation comedies, for example, are organized around a simple problem or conflict that is inevitably resolved by the end of the show. Dialogue is written to ensure that viewers know exactly what is going on. Whereas in real life a person might say, "Oh, there's Doug," on a TV soap a character says, "Look, there's Doug, Marcia's former husband who was falsely accused of the murder of old Doc Tyler and who's just been released from prison." Vocabulary must be simple and must convey plot intricacies instantly.

Extreme and dramatic situations are also a popular part of the logic of television entertainment. Characters are bigger than life, their lives more exciting or humorous or glamorous than ours. From the title to the final resolution, a show must maintain audience interest. In 1981, TV executive Ben Stein claimed that made-for-TV movie titles "must have sex, love, but especially human abuse. Human abuse works far better than sex. Sex can scare off people over 50. But roll it with abuse and you get everyone."[38] Other executives agreed that movies about love, sex, rape, or terror were surefire winners.

Now, more than ten years later, the principle remains the same. Just look through your own television listing during any sweeps week.

The tendency to sensationalize material seems, at first glance, to contradict another important aspect of television content—reference to **ideal norms.** According to Snow, ideal norms are "the tradition of hard work, honesty, modesty, fidelity, and so on, which everyone upholds in principle."[39] A program such as the "Miss America Pageant" embodies the values of youth, feminine beauty and purity, and love of God and country.

How do the sensational topics shown in TV movies fit in? The answer is that the resolution of sensational material always follows ideal norms: the rapist is punished, the drug user completes rehabilitation, the terrorist falls off a twenty-story building. The characters who commit crimes are evil and the characters who solve crimes are noble. Television producers can have it both ways: they can justify depiction of lurid and often ludicrous situations so long as these situations are placed in a moralistic frame. Television can titillate while remaining the most conservative of the major media.

> *Television producers can have it both ways: they can justify depiction of lurid and often ludicrous situations so long as these situations are placed in a moralistic frame. Television can titillate while remaining the most conservative of the major media.*

News Programming

The values that inform entertainment programming can be found in nonentertainment shows as well. A perfect illustration is television news. A successful broadcast news item is brief, visually compelling, dramatic, and moralistic.

First, news reports are kept as short as possible—seldom longer than thirty seconds, and usually about fifteen seconds long. In a fifteen-minute news broadcast, about twenty-five stories are told in about eighteen hundred words. Compare this figure to the one hundred thousand words found in an average daily newspaper and you will see that television news skims the surface of events.[40] That this brevity leaves little time for detailed analysis or carefully explained background doesn't seem to bother news producers, whose concern is to keep viewers' attention throughout the newscast. Television executives assume that the average viewer is incapable of attending to a topic for long and that he or she will tune out if not kept constantly amused by slick production values—catchy theme music, colorful sets, reporters' happy talk, and the like.

> *Television executives assume that the average viewer is incapable of attending to a topic for long and that he or she will tune out if not kept constantly amused by slick production values—catchy theme music, colorful sets, reporters' happy talk, and the like.*

Television news must also be highly visual, and a program usually leads off with the most visually interesting story. Thus, a fire may take precedence over a presidential press conference. Reporters and their subjects often go to unusual lengths to provide visuals. A reporter delivers news about the presidency while standing in the snow in front of the White House rather than sitting in the comfort of the studio, simply because location reporting is visually more interesting. A political candidate may announce a bid for a Senate seat while standing in front of Mount Rushmore, because doing so sends a visually symbolic message. During the Gulf War, not only did reports from the field present dramatic visuals, but also specially designed graphics were used to lead into coverage, giving the war the look of a slickly produced action-adventure show.

Television reporters, like newspaper reporters, seek out the most dramatic stories they can find. The more unusual, conflict-filled, or violent a story, the more likely it is to be covered. Reuven Frank, former president of NBC News, has said, "Every news story should, without any sacrifice of probity or responsibility, display the attributes of fiction, of drama. It should have structure and conflict, problem and denouement, rising action and falling action, a beginning, middle, and an end."[41]

Although it is tempting to believe that all reporting is governed by the norm of objectivity and that events can be separated from values, this is usually not true. Media gatekeepers decide what is news and what is not and, in choosing what to report, tend to follow ideal norms. Driven by the need to create stories filled with conflict, reporters inevitably build their stories about "good guys" and "bad guys." International conflicts involving the United States are particularly open to oversimplified, "us-versus-them" reporting.

The Pervasiveness of TV Logic

In both entertainment and nonentertainment formats, television provides us with important services. It entertains, educates, and informs us. It can, however, be criticized on a number of levels. Perhaps the greatest criticism is that TV makes us want our everyday experience to come in short, vivid, entertaining form. We want everyday life to be like television. According to an article in the *Los Angeles Times,* lawyers have recently changed their style of presentation to more closely resemble a television courtroom scene. Some lawyers now call their strongest witnesses first and make their points in a rapid, dramatic way.[42] Members of the television generation are impatient with slow-moving events; with serious, detailed analyses of news events; and with narratives that deal with complex issues or personalities.

Television invites us into alternate realities. Unfortunately, these realities are seldom trustworthy. Television overrepresents certain kinds of people (handsome, well-to-do, young, blond adults). It oversimplifies, glamorizes, and sensationalizes everyday life. Unfortunately, not everyone realizes that televised realities are works of fiction. Some people buy into the glamorous life-styles that they see, and they come to identify so strongly with favorite characters that they have difficulty separating fact from illusion. Soap opera actors frequently receive fan mail addressed to their on-screen personas.

Although most of us are not mesmerized by television to such a degree, we do regard media figures as role models. This is especially significant in children, who often take what they see quite literally. Joshua Meyerowitz has pointed out that one of the effects of television is to "obliterate childhood" by letting children see adult behavior that is otherwise kept from them and by showing children how to act like adults.[43] Children may also come to expect the adults in their world to act like those on TV. Today, when a young child can turn to her mother and ask, "Mommy, why can't you be more peppy like those ladies in the Pepsi commercial?" we have clear evidence that media images and values can affect everyday relationships.[44]

Another potential danger of television is the power of the visual image. Seeing an event makes us believe in that event, and seeing a person on TV legitimates that person. When we see a picture of something, we assume it is an objective representation of that thing. The fact that camera angle, shot composition, and the like might bias a perception seldom occurs to us. The possibility that people might be using the media to legitimate questionable causes is often ignored. One of the potential dangers of television is that we come to believe what we see on it.

> *One of the potential dangers of television is that we come to believe what we see on it.*

Other Media

Two media we have not yet discussed are novels and films, both of which are important sources of cultural transmission and entertainment. Each has its own logic and vocabulary and its own specialized genres. Using the written word to convey meaning, novelists describe fantasy worlds that the reader re-creates through personal, internal "mind images." Fictional films also invite us to enter an alternate reality; but here the world is shown to us in concrete visual images provided by the director and the cinematographer.[45]

Both novels and films (as well as television programs) may be classed into **genres,** categories of artistic composition each with its own content and conventions. Go to your local bookstore and you can find true crime, romance, or mystery novels; go to your neighborhood movie theater and you can see horror, Western, or detective films. Genre books or films are often appealing because the formats they use are familiar and predictable. Each genre provides a different set of uses and gratifications.

Although many books and movies do follow tried-and-true conventions, others do not. Generally free of the constraints that govern a mass medium such as television, novels and films allow their creators greater scope to create new forms and to describe human experience and explore social issues. Whereas we do not expect a half-hour television situation comedy to do much to illuminate the human condition, we often expect a great novel or film to do just that.

All media content depends in part on the nature of a given medium—on what that medium does best. Novels, for example, can explore human psychology in a way that television cannot. Because novels employ the written word, they can describe interior states, a feat much harder to achieve in film or television. Because novels are not constrained by scheduling, they can develop a subject slowly and in detail. Films, on the other hand, let us see events; directors can compose shots that stun us with their sheer visual impact. Each medium has its own way of communicating information.

The content of one medium is determined in part by the content of other media and by the role each medium plays in society.[46] At one time, for example, receivers depended on newspapers to provide family-oriented entertainment; then, in the thirties and forties, film and radio took over this function. In the fifties, television became the dominant channel for escapist entertainment, and, as a result, newspapers and radio took on different formats and functions. Media are in constant interaction both with receivers and with one another.

> *The content of one medium is determined in part by the content of other media and by the role each medium plays in society.*

Problems and Challenges for Media Communicators

In the last section of this chapter, we'll look at some of the ethical dilemmas that media communicators face. We'll also look at some emerging technologies and consider their effects on how we will live our lives and how we will interact with one another in the near future.

Ethical Issues in the Media

Because the media are in business to make money and because media communicators are human, the potential for unethical practices is great. Hiebert and his colleagues present an excellent discussion of the kinds of ethical problems media communicators face on a daily basis.[47] Although many of the examples they provide are related to news reporting, the ethical conflicts they discuss arise in all forms of media messages.

One problem media communicators face is *conflict of interest,* a situation that occurs when a media communicator's professional role conflicts with a personal interest. Does, for example, a reporter have the right to march in a public demonstration, as a *New York Times* reporter who attended an pro-choice rally did? Does this kind of activity damage a reporter's ability to report events objectively or decrease his or her credibility? And, to consider a more extreme case, does a reporter have the right to send out letters in support of an issue or a candidate? A Florida pro-choice reporter sent small wire coat hangers to 160 legislators in an attempt to dramatize the restricting of women's access to abortion. Did the reporter have the right to express her own views? What would you have done if you had been these reporters' editor? Would you feel the same way if they had taken a pro-life stand? In these cases, the reporters' right to act as private citizens clashed with their role as objective news sources. In the first case, the reporter continued to work; in the second, the reporter was fired.[48]

Media communicators also face problems concerning *truth, accuracy, and fairness issues*. The use of composite characters and reenactments are two examples of techniques that either mislead or utterly fabricate, depending on your point of view. In 1981, *Washington Post* reporter Janet Cooke was awarded a Pulitzer prize for a compelling series on an eight-year-old heroin addict. Later it was revealed that the child she described did not exist but was instead a fictionalized composite. Cooke's career as a journalist was ruined. She was fired, and she lost the Pulitzer. In another incident, ABC News came under fire for presenting a video segment showing a U.S. diplomat handing a briefcase to a Soviet agent. Ostensibly the incident was taped during the actual transfer of secret information. In reality, however, the scene was a staged reenactment. What responsibility did ABC have to make clear to viewers that what was broadcast was not a real event?

Methods of information gathering also present potential ethical problems. To gather information, most journalists promise confidentiality to their sources. What happens, however, if, off the record, a reporter finds out about a source's criminal activity? What if a reporter feels he or she is being used by an informant? Is it ever right for a reporter to reveal confidential sources? And how should a reporter treat a source? Overzealous reporters have ambushed sources during interviews, have lied about their own identity, and have bribed and threatened informants.

Reporters have even set out to break the law to demonstrate problems in law enforcement. Should a reporter be encouraged to smuggle a fake bomb onto a plane to show lax security measures or to make a drug buy to show how available drugs are? Are there limits to how far a reporter should go to get a story?

Privacy and propriety issues are also ethically gray areas. In an effort to get a compelling picture, is it right to invade a grief-stricken victim's privacy? Is every aspect of a public figure's life open for scrutiny? Is it defensible to pry into the private domestic arrangements of political candidates and to publish detailed exposés of their sex lives? What rights do crime victims have to keep their identities hidden?

Sometimes reporters know that reporting a story can lead to *physical or emotional harm* or can encourage dangerous practices. What if a story gives people ideas about how to commit a crime or how to hurt themselves? In this regard, critics have voiced concern about articles on teen suicide encouraging more suicides and about exposés on cheating serving as lessons on how to beat the system. Covering terrorist activities is probably the prime example of this kind of ethical dilemma, because terrorist acts are primarily symbolic and depend on publicity for their effectiveness.

Although our focus has been on the news, ethical decisions arise in other areas of the media. Advertising certainly provides an arena for unethical communication, as does entertainment programming. The latter has been criticized for violence and sexually explicit material and for stereotypical portrayals of members of minority groups. And there are sins of omission as well as of commission. R-rated movies, for example, often show people involved in sexual situations, yet they seldom depict any discussion of condom use. Social psychologists argue that the behavioral scripts individuals internalize as a result of this modeling encourage potentially dangerous sexual practices. In an age of AIDS, do screenwriters have a responsibility in their scripts either to model safer sex or to stop modeling unsafe sex altogether?

The ethical questions raised in regard to media practices are complex and difficult. Each communicator must resolve them in his or her own way. Clearly, however, thoughtless, irresponsible actions cannot be tolerated, and media communicators must examine their own practices and must make decisions based not on expediency but on values.

Emerging Communication Technologies

As we have seen throughout this chapter, mediated communication has a powerful effect on our lives. As each new medium comes into use, it increases our ability to communicate and at the same time changes our behavior. The telephone, for example, allows us to reach out and touch one another instantly. It shrinks space and compresses time. Before the advent of the telephone, people who were separated had to write letters, a slow, cumbersome process whose major advantage was that it resulted in a tangible and permanent record of the relationship. The speed, convenience, and intimacy of the telephone has now made letter writing almost obsolete, but, like any technological advance, it too has disadvantages. We can now be bothered by telemarketers, harassed by obscene or crank callers, interrupted by call-waiting, or put permanently on hold. The telephone has changed people's lives and has materially affected the

Although emerging technologies enhance our ability to communicate, they also place demands on us. We must be willing to interact with increasingly sophisticated machinery and accept the changes new media make in our lives.

ways we relate to one another. The same is true of all new communication technologies.

In this section we look at several technologies that are currently becoming popular, ones that most of you will use in your professional lives. The systems we will describe include on-line databases, electronic bulletin boards, videotex, teletext, cabletext, and audiotext. In discussing these systems we follow Hiebert, Ungurait, and Bohn's excellent summary in *Mass Media VI*.

On-line databases are subscription services each of which allows subscribers to retrieve information stored in that service's mainframe computer. By calling an on-line service, you can gain access to a number of specialized databases. The information requested is transmitted, usually by phone line, to your own computer. Special transmission lines and telecommunication software are necessary to use the system. Generally quite expensive, on-line systems provide businesses with general news, legal information, financial news, and the like.

Electronic bulletin boards are two-way services that allow subscribers sharing specific interests to "talk" to one another through their personal computers. Members can talk in real time, leave one another messages, and access information stored in the bulletin board's data library. Most electronic bulletin boards are operated by private individuals, although some small businesses and professional associations also use them.

Videotex services combine the features of on-line databases and electronic bulletin boards. Subscribers can retrieve information stored in a service's mainframe computer. This may include information from newspapers, newsletters, reference books, catalogs, timetables, and the like. Subscribers can also converse with one another and conduct a variety of transactions, including paying bills, shopping, and making travel reservations.

Teletext, cabletext, and **audiotext** follow the same basic process as videotex. What differs is how information is received. Teletext and cabletext are broadcast from one's local cable or broadcast stations. With teletext, information passes through a decoder and appears in an area on the bottom of one's TV screen, whereas with cabletext, information is transmitted through a cable channel. Audiotext is voice information given over the telephone. The consumer simply dials a number and listens to a computer voice relaying the latest sports scores, weather conditons, soap opera updates, and the like.

CD-ROM (compact disc read-only memory) is an optical disc containing information (say, the contents of a complete encyclopedia) that is decoded by a CD player connected to a personal computer. Because information is not on-line, it cannot be readily updated; thus, it is generally used for reference materials rather than for news. Updates are issued periodically.

Finally, **fax newspapers** provide individualized information to subscribers who ask news organizations to send them a particular kind of news at a specified time through a personal fax machine. A businessperson engaged in an international joint venture, for example, could ask for international, national, and financial news related to the country with which he or she does business. A two- or three-page digest of relevant articles might be sent at six o'clock each morning so that he or she is prepared for the business day.

In *The Media Lab*, Stewart Brand warns that "once a new technology rolls over you, if you're not part of the steamroller, you're part of the road."[49] Although he may be overstating the case a bit, it is nonetheless true that competent communicators learn how to make the best use of advances in communication technology. The emerging technologies we have just described, as well as older ones such as VCRs, provide us more personal choice. They allow us to choose what we want to know and experience.

Emerging technologies can also, theoretically, free us from face-to-face contact with one another. It is certainly possible, given the available technology, for you to attend college from your home. You could get up in the morning, listen to the news as you shower, and turn on your personal computer and have it remind you of what you need to do today. You could then check your E-mail to see whether you have any messages. You could listen to an audiotape or watch a videotape of your professor's lectures, take a quiz whenever you are ready, and either type your assignments into the computer or fax them to school. When you want a break, you could log on to your electronic bulletin board and have a real-time conversation with strangers or friends. Later, you could watch your VCR or play a video game and then get back to work, all without leaving your house. What would this do to the quality of your life? How would your communication change? What kinds of relationships could you have that you don't have now? Certainly, some things would be added to, and others missing from, your world. For we know that whenever communications media change, our world changes. Let's close this discussion of mediated communication by considering a quote from Stewart Brand:

> What we mean by the word "world" usually is the world encompassed by human communications. The world was one thing when word seeped around from tribe to tribe. It became another when traders and religious enthusiasts set forth journeying. So it progressed through centuries–mail service, print, telegraph, telephone, electronic credit. Each time the means of communication advanced, the "world" metamorphosed.[50]

We'll just have to wait to see what the next metamorphosis will be.

Summary

We live in constant interaction with the media. This chapter looks at mass communication, describing the language and logics of popular media as well as the effects of emerging technologies. Mass communication is a form of communication through which institutional sources address large, anonymous, heterogeneous audiences through interposed channels. That sources are complex organizations, that audiences are separated from sources by time and space, and that messages are conveyed through interposed channels are facts that make the relationship between media sources and their audiences unique.

Mediated mass communication serves at least four functions: surveillance, the gathering and disseminating of information; correlation, the analysis and evaluation of data; cultural transmission, the education and socialization of the audience; and entertainment, the offer of escape and gratification. Offsetting their positive impact, media can also narcotize audiences, increase passivity, teach antisocial behavior, and lower popular taste.

A lively debate is taking place between those who believe the media have powerful effects on audiences and those who believe they have limited effects. Early media theorists believed audiences were largely powerless to resist media messages, whereas later theorists viewed audiences as more obstinate and resistant. Current theorists recognize that both sides have valid arguments. The media do affect us. They can set agendas, deliver hegemonic messages, and affect the ways we think. The language employed by one medium can even change the nature of other media. At the same time, receivers are not entirely helpless. They process media selectively, choose media according to the uses and gratifications the media offer, and resist hegemonic messages with oppositional readings.

We turn to different media for different reasons, some of which relate to the format of a medium. People use newspapers to pass the time, to gain practical information, to keep in touch with public issues, and to maintain a valued self-image. Newspaper format encourages a focus on isolated events, a tendency to leave out detail, and a temptation to focus only on the dramatic.

Magazines are more specialized and more personal than newspapers. They are read to pass the time, to gain information, and to learn how to live like "insiders." Radio has a strong interpersonal dimension, acting as a "portable friend" and binding people together through shared experience. Like magazines, radio is one of the most specialized of the media.

The medium of choice for most Americans is television. It provides news, gives us a glimpse of alternate worlds, and provides companionship. It also socializes us and provides entertainment. As a highly visual medium, it values movement, brevity, and intimate images. Entertainment programming favors speed and simplicity and tends to uphold ideal values. News programming tries to be brief, visuals-oriented, dramatic, and moralistic.

Because of the effects of the media, media communicators must be concerned with such ethical issues as conflict of interest, fairness, appropriate ways of gathering information, privacy and propriety, and the risk of abetting physical and emotional harm. In addition, communication technologies that will have a great impact on our lives are currently being developed. To succeed as communicators, we must learn to use these technologies while recognizing their power to affect communication in all contexts.

Key Terms

Listed below are the key terms used in this chapter, along with the number of the page on which each is explained.

Review Questions

1. What is mass communication? What are the three characteristics of media messages? How is the media source different from the source in other contexts? In what senses are mass audiences invisible? What effects do interposed channels have on audience responses?

2. What are the four media functions? When we describe the media as "watchdogs of a free society," to which function are we referring? When newspaper editors analyze and evaluate events, which function are they fulfilling? When the media provide role models and project social values, which function are they fulfilling?

3. What are the negative side effects of surveillance, correlation, cultural transmission, and entertainment?

4. What is the difference between the powerful effects and the limited effects models? Which model is associated with the magic bullet and hypodermic needle metaphors? Which sees the audience as obstinate?

5. What is the agenda-setting function of the media? What are gatekeepers? What do critical theorists mean when they talk about hegemonic messages?

6. What is the imperial presidency? How is it related to media logic? What does it mean to say that the medium is the message? Why is television considered a cool medium?

7. What are selective exposure, selective attention, selective perception, and selective retention? On what does uses and gratifications research focus? What are interpretive communities, and how do they affect the ways we read media texts?

8. Why do people read the newspaper? How does layout affect the way newspaper messages are consumed? What is an inverted pyramid? In general, what kinds of communication do newspapers encourage? What five themes are considered especially newsworthy?

9. Why do people read magazines? What is the relationship between magazines and group identity? How is identity reflected in the design features of magazines? What are the negative effects of magazines on readers?

10. How does radio use today differ from previous radio use? In what sense is radio a portable friend? How does radio programming use tempo to match audience moods?

11. What does it mean to say that television is the most mass of all the mass media? Why does television value movement and change? How has it affected the way we experience time? How does television encourage psychological identification? What are ideal norms?

12. What are the four major characteristics of successful broadcast news items?

13. Name some common film genres. What are their conventions? What can novels and films do that television cannot?

14. What are conflicts of interest and fairness issues? What must a reporter consider when gathering information? What are privacy and propriety issues? In what ways can media communicators contribute to physical or emotional harm?

15. What communication technologies are currently emerging? What are on-line databases, electronic bulletin boards, videotex services, teletext and related media, CD-ROM discs, and fax newspapers? How might each affect the way we live our lives?

Suggested Readings

Altheide, David L., & Snow, Robert P. (1991). *Media worlds in the post-journalism era.* New York: Aldine de Gruyter.

> This book is an excellent source of information on media logics and formats. In discussing how media languages affect us, the authors show that the medium may indeed be the message.

Brand, Stewart. (1988). *The Media Lab: Inventing the future at MIT.* New York: Viking Penguin.

> A lively discussion of how communication technologies affect us and of the visionary inventors of some of today's emerging technologies. Although focused on the Media Lab At MIT, this book is also about the "worldwide media laboratory in which we are all likely to be experimenters for the rest of our lives."

Hiebert, Ray Eldon, Ungurait, Donald F., & Bohn, Thomas W. (1991). *Mass media VI: An introduction to modern communication.* New York: Longman.

> This is a good overall introduction to media issues, with especially useful sections on emerging technologies and the ethics of the media.

Jamieson, Kathleen Hall, & Campbell, Karlyn Kohrs. (1992). *The interplay of influence: News, advertising, politics, and the mass media.* Belmont, CA: Wadsworth.

> If you're interested in learning more about the rhetoric of the media and the way media messages influence us, this book is an excellent source full of interesting information on the connections between advertising and political communication.

Notes

1. This and the next example are found in Altheide, David L., & Snow, Robert P. (1991). *Media worlds in the post-journalism era.* New York: Aldine de Gruyter, 41, 43.

2. Snow, Robert P. (1983). *Creating media culture.* Beverly Hills, CA: Sage, 29.

3. Lasswell, Harold D. (1948). The structure and function of communication in society. In Lyman Bryson (Ed.), *The communication of ideas.* New York: Institute for Religious and Social Studies; Wright, Charles R. (1960). Functional analysis and mass communication. *Public Opinion Quarterly, 24,* 605–620; Wright, Charles R. (1975). *Mass communication: A sociological perspective* (2nd ed.). New York: Random House, 8–22.

4. Lazarfeld, Paul F., & Merton, Robert K. (1971). Mass communication, popular taste, and organized social action. In Wilbur Schramm & Donald F. Roberts (Eds.), *The process and effects of mass communication* (Rev. ed.). Urbana: University of Illinois Press, 565. For a good brief review, with examples, of the functions of the media, see Felsenthal, Norman. (1976). Orientations to mass communication. In Ronald L. Applbaum & Roderick P. Hart (Eds.), *Modules in speech communication.* Palo Alto, CA: SRA, 6–8.

5. For a summary of some of the major effects theories, see Littlejohn, Stephen W. (1989). *Theories of human communication* (3rd ed.). Belmont, CA: Wadsworth, chapter 13.

6. Schramm, Wilbur. (1971). The nature of communications between humans. In Schramm & Roberts, 8.

7. Bauer, Raymond. (1971). The obstinate audience: The influence process from the point of view of social communication. In Schramm & Roberts. See also Klapper, Joseph. (1960). *The effects of mass communication.* Glencoe, IL: Free Press; and Weiss, Walter. (1969). Effects of the mass media of communication. In Gardner Lindzey & Elliot Aronson (Eds.), *Handbook of social psychology.* Reading, MA: Addison-Wesley.

8. Katz, Elihu. (1987). Communications research since Lazarfeld. *Public Opinion Quarterly, 51* (4), S25–S45, suggests this typology, although his examples differ.

9. See, for example, Shaw, Donald L., & McCombs, Maxwell E. (1977). *The emergence of American political issues.* St. Paul, MN: West Publishing.

10. Felsenthal, 31.

11. Gitlin, Todd. (1979). Prime time ideology: The hegemonic process in television entertainment. *Social Problems, 26* (3), 251–266; also reprinted in Horace Newcomb (Ed.), *Television: The critical view* (4th ed.). Oxford, Eng.: Oxford University Press, 510.

12. Noelle-Neumann, Elisabeth. (1984). *The spiral of silence: Public opinion–our social skin.* Chicago: University of Chicago Press.

13. Katz.

14. Felsenthal, 33.

15. McLuhan, Marshall. (1964). *Understanding media: The extensions of man.* New York: McGraw-Hill.

16. Snow, 162–163.

17. Book, Cassandra, et al. (1980). *Human communication: Principles, contexts, and skills.* New York: St. Martin's, 206; and Booth, Alan. (1970–1971). The recall of news items. *Public Opinion Quarterly, 34,* 604–610.

18. For a brief summary and critique of uses and gratifications research, see Littlejohn. See also Katz, Elihu, Blumer, Jay, & Gurevitch, Michael. (1974). Uses of mass communication by the individual. In W. Phillips Davidson & Frederick Yu (Eds.), *Mass communication research: Major issues and future directions.* New York: Praeger, 12.

19. Herzog, Herta. (1944). What do we really know about daytime serial listeners? In Paul Lazarfeld & Frank Stanton (Eds.), *Radio research, 1942–43.* New York: Dull, Sloan & Pearce.

20. McQuail, Denis, Blumer, Jay G., & Brown, J. R. (1972). The television audience: A revised perspective. In Denis McQuail (Ed.), *Sociology of mass communications.* Middlesex, Eng.: Penguin, 155–161.

21. Liebes, Tamar. (1989). On the convergence of theories of mass communication and literature regarding the role of the "reader." In Brenda Dewin & Melvin J. Voight (Eds.), *Progress in communication sciences.* Norwood, NJ: Ablex, 123–143; Liebes, Tamar. (1988). Cultural differences in the retelling of television fiction. *Critical Studies in Mass Communication, 5* (4), 277–292.

22. Jamieson, Kathleen Hall, & Campbell, Karlyn Kohrs. (1992). *The interplay of influence: News, advertising, politics, and the mass media.* Belmont, CA: Wadsworth, 2.

23. Hiebert, Ray Eldon, Ungurait, Donald F., & Bohn, Thomas W. (1991). *Mass media VI: An introduction to modern communication.* New York: Longman, 236.

24. Snow, 53.

25. Ibid., 59.

26. Jamieson & Campbell, 24.

27. Snow, 91.

28. Hiebert, Ungurait, & Bohn, 288.

29. Altheide & Snow, 21.

30. Mendelsohn, Harold. (1964). Listening to radio. In A. Lewis Dexter & David M. White (Eds.), *People, society, and mass communication.* London: Collier-Macmillan, 91.

31. Snow, 101.

32. Altheide & Snow, 26.

33. Snow, 121.

34. Jamieson & Campbell, 2.

35. Felsenthal, 11.

36. Altheide & Snow, 31.

37. Jamieson & Campbell, 63.

38. Stein, Ben. (1981, July 25). Love, rape, highway, diary. *TV Guide,* 34–35; cited in Snow, 137.

39. Snow, 142.

40. Hiebert, Ungurait, & Bohn, 428.

41. Cited in Epstein, Edward J. (1974). *News from nowhere.* New York: Hastings, 4.

42. Ferguson, E. B. (1980, July 20). Media hype for fun and profit. *Los Angeles Times,* part VII, p. 5.

43. Meyerowitz, Joshua. (1983). Television and the obliteration of "childhood." In Sari Thomas (Ed.), *Studies in mass communication and technology.* Norwood, NJ: Ablex.

44. Snow, 157.

45. Jowett, Garth, & Linton, James. (1980). *Movies as mass communication.* Beverly Hills, CA: Sage, 104–105.

46. Felsenthal, 11.

47. Hiebert, Ungurait, & Bohn.

48. Saul, Stephanie. (1989, July/August). Judgment call: Do reporters have a right to march? *Columbia Journalism Review,* 51; Gersh, Debra. (1989, August 19). Question of conflict. *Editor and Publisher,* 11.

49. Brand, Stewart. (1988). *The Media Lab: Inventing the future at MIT.* New York: Viking Penguin, 9.

50. Ibid., xiii.

10

Intercultural Communication

Intercultural communication, however wide the differences between cultures may be, is not impossible. It is simply more or less difficult.

For communication to work, people must have something in common. If communicators know and respect one another, communication is relatively easy. They can predict one another's moods and meanings, they know what topics to avoid, and they can sometimes even complete one another's thoughts. Uncertainty and stress are at a minimum; communication is spontaneous, open, and comfortable.

Communicating with strangers is more difficult. If the strangers come from our own culture, we can at least base our messages on shared attitudes, beliefs, and life experiences; but if the strangers are from another culture, we may be at a loss. In such a case, uncertainty is maximized. The actual forms, and even the functions, of communication may be strange to us.

Cultural differences can be a barrier to communication, but that does not mean that intercultural communication is always doomed to failure. As Harry Hoijer has remarked, "No culture is wholly isolated, self-contained, and unique. There are important resemblances between all known cultures. . . . Intercultural communication, however wide the differences between cultures may be, is not impossible. It is simply more or less difficult. . . ."[1] Intercultural communication is possible because people are not "helplessly suspended in their cultures."[2] By developing an openness to new ideas and a willingness to listen and to observe, we can surmount the difficulties inherent in intercultural interaction. This chapter discusses ways in which people from different cultures can learn to communicate more effectively.

What Is Culture?

According to anthropologist Ruth Benedict, we spend our lives following the patterns and standards handed down to us by our cultures:

> *From the moment of birth the customs into which [an individual] is born shape his experience and behavior. By the time he can talk, he is a little creature of his culture, and by the time he is grown and able to take part in its activities, its habits are his habits, its beliefs his beliefs, its impossibilities his impossibilities.*[3]

As Benedict points out, we are, in an important sense, the products of our cultures.

Defining Culture

But what exactly is culture? Donald Klopf gives a simple definition. For him, **culture** is "that part of the environment made by humans."[4] According to this definition, culture includes all the material objects and possessions that a social group invents or acquires. Even more important, it includes the group's less tangible creations: the shared customs and values that bind its members together and give them a sense of commonality. Thus, culture includes a group's "collective answer to the fundamental questions . . ." Who are we? What is our place in the world? and How are we to live our lives?[5]

Culture includes a group's "collective answer to the fundamental questions . . ." Who are we? What is our place in the world? and How are we to live our lives?

Characteristics of Cultures

Cultures are "templates for living" that have certain basic characteristics. Cultures are learned, shared, multifaceted, dynamic, and overlapping.

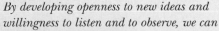

By developing openness to new ideas and willingness to listen and to observe, we can surmount the differences inherent in intercultural interaction.

Cultures Are Learned

The first point about cultures is that they are learned. Americans act like other Americans not because we are innately predisposed to do so, but because we learn to do so. Much of our early training is an attempt to make us fit cultural patterns. If we do not learn the lessons of our cultures, we pay—"through a loss of comfort, status, peace of mind, safety, or some other value. . . ."[6] We may even be imprisoned or labeled insane for acting in ways that would be perfectly acceptable in other cultures.

We are so well-programmed that we seldom stop to think that culture is learned. Our cultural norms appear to be natural and right, and we can't imagine acting differently. Yet had we been brought up in Korea by Korean parents, an entirely different set of norms would appear natural. We would be culturally Korean. We would speak Korean, follow Korean norms and customs, and see the world in typically Asian ways. Although this point seems obvious, it is one we often forget. When we see someone from another culture act in ways we consider strange, our first impulse is to attribute the action to personality. For example, we label someone "pushy" who speaks more loudly and forcefully than we do; we seldom stop to realize that had we been brought up in that person's culture, we would probably express ourselves just as loudly and forcefully.

Cultures Are Shared

Another important characteristic of culture is that it is shared. Cultures are group understandings rather than individual ones, and belonging to a culture means acting according to group norms. For most people, fitting into a cultural group is very important. Being like others provides security, perhaps because we equate being alike with being right and being different with being wrong. Regardless of the reason, we learn very early to separate the world into "us" and "them," and we work very hard to make sure that others recognize which of the two we are. Little boys are mortified if they are mistaken for little girls; they will spend a good part of the rest of their lives living up to the masculine ideal. The wealthy do not wish to be thought poor; thus, they act in ways that signal their status. Mistakes that mix "us" with "them" undermine our sense of self.

Regardless of the reason, we learn very early to separate the world into "us" and "them," and we work very hard to make sure that others recognize which of the two we are.

Because cultures are shared, we are not entirely free to act as we wish. Indeed, we spend a good deal of time proving who we are and living up to the expectations of others. This process of living out cultural rules is largely invisible and seldom problematic if we stay within a single culture. A white, middle-class, American male who associates only with others like himself seldom stops to think about the effects of national, racial, class, or gender rules on his beliefs and behaviors. Only when he steps outside his circle of friends, his neighborhood, or his country and experiences other cultures is he likely to see the extent to which culture affects him.[7]

People who frequently move between cultures are often more sensitive to the fact that culture is shared. Lawrence Wieder and Steven Pratt give an interesting example of the importance of shared cultural identity and the difficulties it presents for minority group members. In an article entitled "On Being a Recognizable Indian Among Indians," Wieder and Pratt discuss ways in which Native Americans of the Osage people let one another know that they are "real Indians" rather than "White Indians." Wieder and Pratt's research not only illustrates the universal need to demonstrate cultural identity but also shows how central communication style is to that demonstration.[8]

According to Wieder and Pratt, one of the primary differences between the communication styles of European Americans and Native Americans is the value the latter place on being silent. "When real Indians who are strangers to one another pass each other in a public place, wait in line, occupy adjoining seats, and so forth, they take it that it is proper to remain silent and to not initiate conversation."[9] Once Native Americans do engage in conversation with one another, they take on substantial obligations, among them the necessity of interacting whenever their paths cross. For students and businesspeople, this obligation may be problematic, for it takes precedence over attending class or keeping appointments.

Talking like a "real Indian" also means being modest and not showing oneself to be more knowledgeable than other Native Americans. Being asked by a European-American teacher to volunteer information in a group discussion where other Native Americans are present puts a well-informed Native-American student in a difficult bind. To avoid appearing arrogant, he or she may simply refuse to participate.

The desire to avoid seeming immodest occurs in public speaking situations as well, where speaking is reserved for tribal elders. Only certain individuals are entitled to speak, and they often speak for someone else rather than for themselves. It is customary to begin a speech with a disclaimer such as "I really don't feel that I am qualified to express [the wishes of the people I am speaking for] but I'm going to do the best I can, so please bear with me."[10] Compare this custom to the rule taught by most European-American communication teachers that a speaker should build his or her credibility at the beginning of a speech, and you will see how communication styles across cultures can conflict.

The need to use Native-American styles of communication in front of other Native Americans often means the "real Indian" is misunderstood or misjudged by European Americans. Steven Pratt, who collected the primary data for this research and who is himself a participating member of the Osage people, reported instances in which his identity as a graduate student conflicted with his identity as a Native American. He and Wieder conclude thus:

Being a real Indian is not a material thing that can be possessed and displayed. It consists of those patterns of appropriate conduct that are articulated in such a way that they are visible and recognizable to other Indians as specific Indian ways of conducting oneself. In the performance of these visible patterns, being a real Indian is realized.[11]

Although the display of cultural identity may be more problematic for the Native-American communicator living in a predominantly European-American society, each member of a culture must prove himself or herself to other members by acting in ways that are culturally approved. For another example, look ahead to the discussion of role enactment in Teamsterville in the next chapter.

Cultures Are Multifaceted

If we define culture as everything surrounding us that is not natural and biological in character, then clearly culture has many facets. At a minimum, culture affects language, religion, basic worldview, education, social organization, technology, politics, and law, and all of these factors affect one another.[12] As Edward Hall points out, if you touch a culture in one place, everything else is affected.[13]

> *At a minimum, culture affects language, religion, basic worldview, education, social organization, technology, politics, and law, and all of these factors affect one another.*

Table 10-1 gives an idea of the variety of interconnected activities that are found in virtually every culture. These activities are common to all people who live together in social groups and are thus examples of **cultural universals,** yet the enactment of these activities varies dramatically from culture to culture. In every culture, for example, people adorn their bodies, eat, educate their children, recognize family groupings, keep track of time, and so on. How

TABLE 10-1

A Partial List of Cultural Universals

Age Grading	Ethics	Language
Athletics	Etiquette	Law
Bodily Adornment	Family	Magic
Calendar	Folklore	Marriage
Cleanliness	Funeral Rites	Numbers
Cooking	Gestures	Puberty Customs
Cosmology	Greetings	Rituals
Courtship	Hairstyles	Sex Restrictions
Dancing	Hygiene	Surgery
Education	Kinship	Toolmaking

Adapted from "The Common Denominator of Cultures," p. 124 by George P. Murdock, 1945, in Ralph Linton (Ed.), *The Science of Man in the World Crisis*. New York: Harcourt, Brace & World.

people in a particular culture do these things, however, is unique. Although all people eat, what they consider edible and how they prepare food vary widely. The idea of eating dog, a food offered in many of the best hotels in South China, is considered revolting by most Americans. The idea of eating a ham and cheese sandwich, a perfectly acceptable meal for many Americans, is offensive to Arabs and Orthodox Jews. Thus, what is common practice in one culture may be taboo in another. To be functioning members of a culture, we must internalize rules governing a huge variety of activities; and to communicate with people from other cultures, we must recognize and learn to respect their customs.

Cultures Are Dynamic

Cultures are constantly changing. As economic conditions change, as new technologies are developed, and as cultural contact increases, old ways of doing things change and people must learn new behaviors. This important fact is one reason that memorizing lists of do's and don'ts is not the best way to prepare for intercultural contact. For just as soon as you've learned a rule about how to communicate with the "natives" of a culture, you'll find that the rule is obsolete. A better way to prepare for intercultural contact is to become sensitive to the kinds of differences that occur between cultures and to develop the ability to learn by observing.

> *Memorizing lists of do's and don'ts is not the best way to prepare for intercultural contact. For just as soon as you've learned a rule about how to communicate with the "natives" of a culture, you'll find that the rule is obsolete.*

Cultural Identities Are Overlapping

As our discussion of the communication patterns of some Native Americans showed, we belong to multiple overlapping cultures, some of which work together and some of which conflict. At a minimum we all belong to national, regional, class, ethnic, religious, professional, age, and gender cultures. At various times, one or more of these identities may become crucial while the rest fade into the background.

If we are lucky, our overlapping identities fit together into a coherent whole. If we are less fortunate, we experience conflicts. The woman who believes in equal rights yet belongs to a traditional culture in which women are subservient to men feels pressure from each identity. The immigrant who wishes to assimilate into his adopted country but does not wish to abandon tradition also experiences stress. The adolescent who is no longer a child and yet is not an adult has difficulty determining how to act.

Although multiple cultural memberships can cause stress, they can also be a source of strength, allowing us to be unique individuals rather than cultural clones. Seldom are any two people members of exactly the same group cultures, and none of us manage to follow all of the rules of the cultures to which we belong. As Marshall Singer points out, "that is precisely what makes each of us humans unique. And while that makes for a more rich, varied, and interesting world, it also makes generalizing about people . . . that much more hazardous and difficult."[14] The task that confronts each of us is to find a unique sense of self in the face of our own conflicting cultural identities and to recognize when we speak to others that their cultural identities are also complex and overlapping.

> *The task that confronts each of us is to find a unique sense of self in the face of our own conflicting cultural identities and to recognize when we speak to others that their cultural identities are also complex and overlapping.*

Why Communicate Cross-Culturally?

Admittedly, communication becomes more difficult when people do not share the same attitudes and values. Why, then, should we bother to communicate cross-culturally? The answer is that we cannot afford to ignore people from other cultures. There may have been a time when people could spend their entire lives communicating only with others who shared their own cultural identities. In such a time learning how to communicate across cultural boundaries was a luxury rather than a necessity. Nowadays it is impossible to remain isolated from others, and **intercultural communication,** communication wherein sender and receiver come from different cultures, cannot be avoided.

Living in the Global Village

One reason for the rise in importance of intercultural communication is that the world is shrinking daily. We live in a global village where intercultural encounters are commonplace. Advances in telecommunication and transportation technology have changed our sense of distance and of place. We can board a plane in New York and be in Hong Kong or Singapore within a day. We can walk to the corner store and find products from every part of the globe. We can go to a local movie house and see the latest film from France or Hungary. We can switch on CNN and watch a military campaign in Somalia or a civil war in Bosnia from the comfort of our living rooms. It is no longer possible to remain isolated—from events, ideas, or cultural products.

Many of you will travel internationally, either on business or for pleasure, at least once in your life (if you have not already done so). Whether you travel as a business representative, diplomat or technical adviser, member of the military, student, teacher, or tourist, you will find yourself communicating with people whose beliefs, values, and ways of existing may be vastly different from yours. The greater your understanding of intercultural communication, the richer this experience will be.

Even if you don't travel outside the United States, you may still find yourself interacting with people from other cultures, for just as Americans travel abroad more and more frequently, so foreign nationals come to America. As individuals from Vietnam, Cambodia, Cuba, Haiti, the former Soviet Union, and a host of other countries come to the United States to escape political upheaval or to flee war or famine, "contacts with cultures that previously appeared unfamiliar, alien, and at times mysterious are now a normal part of our day-to-day routine."[15]

Familiarity with the problems that arise when people communicate interculturally can ease the adaptation that both immigrants and host nationals must make. For adjusting to the global village is by no means easy. As Richard Porter and Larry Samovar express it, "The difficulty with being thrust into a global village is that we do not yet know how to live like villagers; there are too many of 'us' who do not want to live with 'them.'"[16]

Coming to Terms With Diversity

Of course, we don't have to look to newly arrived immigrants to experience intercultural communication. We are a country of many coexisting cultures. Americans from different ethnic or religious backgrounds may seem as alien as someone "just off the boat." It is becoming increasingly difficult to ignore the presence of **co-cultures** within our own country. Groups that were outside the mainstream several years ago are now demanding recognition and respect from majority cultures. Even when we speak the same language, we may find overcoming cultural differences difficult. Yet if we are to live in harmony with our neighbors, overcoming differences is a necessity.

Intercultural Communication and Personal Growth

Intercultural understandings serve not only to make contacts more comfortable but also to enrich us on a personal level. Communicating with people from other cultures allows us access to the experiences of other human beings. Intercultural contact shows us that there are other ways to act in the world than those we have been taught; it widens our field of choices and stimulates our imagination. Students of intercultural communication often talk about the development of an **intercultural identity,** a sense of belonging to an original and a new cul-

Intercultural contact shows us that there are other ways to act in the world than those we have been taught; it widens our field of choices and stimulates our imagination.

We live in a global village where intercultural encounters are common. We can walk to the corner store and find products from every part of the globe.

ture at the same time. People who achieve this identity are more open to change and are willing to transcend their own cultural premises. Young Yun Kim expresses it this way:

> Not all strangers may evolve this far in their adaptation process. Yet those who do will be able to enjoy a special kind of freedom, making deliberate choices for actions in specific situations rather than simply being bound by the culturally normative courses of action.[17]

Barriers to Intercultural Communication

Despite its importance, learning to communicate interculturally is extremely difficult. A variety of barriers keep people from different cultures from understanding one another. In this section we'll look at some of the attitudes that impede our ability to communicate clearly with one another—attitudes such as prejudice, ethnocentrism, and a refusal to acknowledge differences. But before we look at these barriers, we need to understand how culture affects communication.

How Culture Affects Communication

We have seen that culture is multifaceted, that it affects every aspect of our lives. That culture affects communication should therefore come as no surprise. Culture affects a number of aspects of communication: interpretation of reality, understanding of role relations, goal oriented behavior, sense of self, and message making.

Culture and Perception

As we saw in chapter 3, perception is not simply a matter of receiving what already exists: it is an active interpretive process. Meaning is "not extracted from Nature but projected by people on it. People's behavior can be understood only in terms of their own constructs," and many of these constructs are products of culture.[18] When we perceive events and people, we attach values to them and make attributions about them. Our values and attributions are culture-specific, as the following example, reported by Donald Klopf, shows.[19]

Nancy, a native Californian, moved with her husband, an executive with an oil company, to Iran. Because the climate was very hot and humid, Nancy often wore shorts and casual tops when she went to the local market to shop. As she walked alone to the market one day, an Iranian man grabbed her and made lewd suggestions. Upset, she shook herself free and called the police.

Nancy, working from an American point of view, saw the Iranian as a degenerate and his behavior as an attack. The Iranian, however, was astonished by her reaction. When he looked at Nancy, he saw a prostitute, for in Iran no other woman would ever appear in public in shorts or walk alone. From an Iranian point of view, Nancy was giving clear signals that she was sexually available. The way each saw the other was influenced by cultural values and beliefs.

To communicate effectively, we have to be able to size up situations and people realistically. In an intercultural context, this means being aware of cultural conventions and familiarizing oneself with basic values and customs. Not knowing the values of another country can result in momentary embarrassment, as it did with Nancy, or can lead to the loss of millions of dollars and months of work, as the following story illustrates.[20]

An American engineering company spent months negotiating a huge contract with a Saudi Arabian firm. To signal the importance of the contract, the American executives bound their final proposal in costly leather. Unfortunately, they chose pigskin, unaware that Saudis consider the pig an unclean animal. Had the Americans wanted to insult their hosts, they could have found no better way. The proposal and binder were consequently burned, and the

Saudi firm threw the American company out of the country. A cursory knowledge of religious custom could have averted this disaster. Unfortunately, however, no one had bothered to do basic research on Saudi beliefs.

Culture and Role Identities

Culture also tells us who to be and how to act. In every culture people are classified according to factors such as age, status, occupation, gender, and so on. We do not expect the young and the old, princes and peasants, or men and women to act the same way; nor do we act the same way toward each of these groups. Being a good communicator means, in part, understanding role distinctions and adapting one's communication accordingly.

> *We do not expect the young and the old, princes and peasants, or men and women to act the same way; nor do we act the same way toward each of these groups. Being a good communicator means, in part, understanding role distinctions and adapting one's communication accordingly.*

An example of the way culture affects role identity can be found in varying attitudes toward age. The Ashanti of Ghana, for example, address all older men as "my grandfather," a title of respect.[21] The Maasai of East Africa also afford great honor to their elders. Lisa Skow and Larry Samovar explain that the Maasai equate age with wisdom and believe that those who are wise must be treated with special deference. Young people, no matter how clever, cannot reach the truth until they pass through all of life's stages.[22] The Chinese hold a similar view.

By comparison, Americans value youth more than age. Rather than welcoming old age, we see it as a time of diminished capacity. In fact, American beliefs about age may induce psychological states of "oldness." Carl Carmichael argues that "it is quite possible that many older people have aged prematurely by adopting the age-related characteristics they have come to believe must exist after a certain age."[23] If so, this is a dramatic example of the costs of false cultural beliefs.

Gender roles are also culturally derived. In parts of the Arab world, women do not work or drive cars, whereas in Israel and China, women do the same jobs as men. In parts of India, women must wait to eat until after men have finished, and in traditional Vietnamese households, women must eat smaller portions of food than men.[24] In modern America these kinds of distinctions are seen as demeaning and offensive. Even the characteristics that we think are basic to the sexes may differ from culture to culture. According to Edward Hall, in Iran it is men who express their emotions freely, whereas women are considered to be coldly practical.[25]

Culture and Goals

Our cultures also affect us by telling us what goals we should pursue and how to pursue them. Americans have relatively high achievement motivation. We are generally characterized by **effort-optimism,** the belief that hard work will pay off. People in other countries may "expect to be rewarded on the basis of the social position of their family or clan" rather than on their own efforts, or, in some cases, they may not expect to be rewarded at all.[26] K. S. Sitaram and Roy T. Cogdell explain the difference between the attitude in some countries that individuals can do little to change their future and the attitude in other countries, such as the United States, that people are able to control their fate:

> *If you ask a Hindu why he got only ten bags of corn from his land while nearby farmers got much more, he would say it was the wish of God. An American farmer's answer to the same question would be, "Hell, I didn't work hard enough."*[27]

The goal-oriented nature of middle-class American culture is evident in popular slogans such as "No pain, no gain," and "Just do it." It is also evident in high stress levels and burnout. To people in many countries, Americans are overly ambitious. What we think of as a healthy work ethic, they see as needless effort or even arrogance.

Culture and Images of the Self

In addition to affecting roles and goals, culture affects basic notions of human nature, including the extent to which the individual self is valued. Beliefs about the self are important because they are central to all other values and because they affect every aspect of behavior, including communication. Despite their importance, however, they often go unexamined.

Larry Samovar, Richard Porter, and Nemi Jain argue that most Americans hold three basic beliefs about human nature: that humans are, at heart, rational; that they are perfectible; and that human nature is highly susceptible to social and cultural influence.[28] The **rationality premise**—the belief that most people are capable of discovering the truth through logical analysis—underlies many American institutions, including democracy, trial by jury, and free enterprise, all of which are based on the idea that the average person can be trusted to make good decisions. The **perfectibility premise** is

> *Most Americans hold three basic beliefs about human nature: that humans are, at heart, rational; that they are perfectible; and that human nature is highly susceptible to social and cultural influence.*

based on the old Puritan idea that humans are born in sin but are capable of achieving goodness through effort and control. Finally, the **mutability premise** assumes that human behavior is shaped by environmental factors and that the way to improve humans is to improve their physical and psychological circumstances. A belief in universal education follows from this assumption.

Another important value related to human nature and the self is **individualism,** the belief that the most important social unit is the person, who acts in his or her own interest. American individualism is evident from the fact that Americans are encouraged "to make their own decisions, develop their own opinions, solve their own problems, have their own things, and, in general, learn to view the world from the point of view of the self."[29] In fact, researcher Geert Hofstede found the United States to be the most individualistic of the forty nations he studied. The countries highest in individualism were Western or European countries, while those lowest in individualism were Asian or South American.[30]

The opposite of individualism is **collectivism.** In collectivist cultures, people believe it is right to subordinate personal goals for the good of others. For collectivists, shared identity is more important than personal identity. Harry Triandis and his colleagues argue that naming practices may reflect where a culture stands on the collectivist-individualist continuum. In Bali, they report, a person is referred to by his or her position in the family (for example, "the first son of X family" or "mother of Y"). Similarly, in China, one's family name (what we call the last name) comes first, followed by a personal name. In more individualist cultures, the personal name comes first.[31]

People in collectivist cultures are comfortable in **vertical relationships** (relationships in which some people are afforded more status than others), whereas individualists feel most comfortable in **horizontal relationships** (relationships with status equals). Members of collectivist cultures rarely compete on a personal basis, although they will fight fiercely for the good of their group. The converse is true in individualist cultures. In a collectivist culture like Japan, for example, workers feel strong loyalties to their work groups, and the qualities sought in a leader are patience and the ability to listen.[32] Leaders in individualist cultures are more likely to be prized for quick thinking and an ability to take the initiative.

According to Triandis and colleagues, the most important collectivist values are harmony, face-saving, duty to parents, modesty, moderation, thrift, equality in reward distribution, and the fulfillment of others' needs. The top values for individualists are freedom, honesty, social recognition, comfort, hedonism, and reward distribution based on individual performance. Table 10-2 outlines some other differences between collectivist and individualist cultures.

Culture and Language Style

It almost goes without saying that people from different cultures often speak different languages and that difficulties in making oneself understood are an important barrier to cross-cultural interaction. But the problem is not just that people from different cultures use different words to express their thoughts but also that the thoughts they express may be different. The world is filtered through our language habits, and it therefore stands to reason that people from different language communities may perceive the world differently.

One of the attitudes that most interferes with successful intercultural communication is the belief that everything that can be said in one language can be said in another, that meanings are directly translatable. This is simply not the case. A concept central to the language of one culture may be translated into another language only with difficulty. The Japanese concept of *amae* is an example. According to Edward Hall and Mildred Reed Hall, *amae* comes from the verb *amaeru*, "to look to others for support and affection." As Hall and Hall explain, *amae* has its roots in the psychological relationship between a child and his or her mother, but the child later transfers *amae* to teachers, bosses, and other authority figures. Although *amae* may be translated as "dependence," it is more than that: it is a willingly assumed, reciprocal relationship that blurs the distinction between the world of work and the interpersonal realm.[33]

> *One of the attitudes that most interferes with successful intercultural communication is the belief that everything that can be said in one language can be said in another, that meanings are directly translatable.*

Because English speakers have no exactly comparable term, we may have difficulty grasping the subtleties of the concept. This does not mean that we can't learn to use the word when it is explained to us (after all, Hall and Hall give us a detailed description written in English), but it does mean the concept won't seem natural to us. One of the reasons that learning a foreign language is both frustrating and exhilarating is that it opens up new ways of viewing the world.

Culture affects not only semantic content but pragmatic rules as well. It is important to keep in mind that language style is part of culture; what we do with language, how we use it, is a product of shared understanding. Speech forms such as teasing, flattery, charm, effusiveness, or directness have different values in different cultures. Even lying (which Americans tend to class as one of the worst possible sins) may be valued in a culture in which maintaining harmonious relations is more important than being certain about facts.

In general, Americans value plain, direct, efficient language use. In many other cultures, people are expected to circle around a point rather than to attack it directly. In cultures that value ambiguity, plain speaking may be shockingly rude. And whereas we distrust anyone who "lays it on too thick," members of other cultures may believe in offering one another effusive praise.

It is important for people who intend to engage in intercultural communication to recognize the essential ambiguity of both verbal and nonverbal language and to realize that a single behavior may signify different meanings in different cultures. In some cultures, for example, looking away from or momentarily turning one's back and walking away from a speaker is a mark of respect and appreciation. It should not, therefore, be taken as an insult. As we

TABLE 10-2

Rules to Increase Cooperation Between Collectivists and Individualists

Rules Collectivists Should Follow When Interacting With Individualists

1. Don't expect to be able to predict an individualist's attitudes and behavior on the basis of group affiliations. Although this works in your country, individualists have their own ideas.
2. Don't be put off when individualists take pride in personal achievement, and do not be too modest yourself.
3. Expect individualists to be less emotionally involved in group affiliations than is the norm for you. Do not interpret this as coldness or as a personality defect.
4. Do not expect persuasive arguments that emphasize cooperation and conflict avoidance to be as effective as they are in your culture. Do not be offended by arguments that emphasize personal rewards and costs.
5. Do not interpret initial friendliness as a signal of intimacy or commitment. Expect relationships to be good-natured but superficial and fleeting according to your own standards.
6. Pay attention to written contracts. They are considered binding.
7. Do not expect to be respected because of your position, age, sex, or status. Do not be surprised if individualists lack respect for authority figures.
8. Expect individualists to be upset by nepotism, bribery, and other behaviors that give in-group members an advantage over others.
9. Do not expect to receive as much help as you would in your own country. After initial orientation, you may be left to do things on your own.
10. Do not expect an individualist to work well in groups.

saw in chapter 5, shared behavior is an important hidden language that can affect the success of any interaction.

Because culture affects so many aspects of our lives, it can be a barrier to effective communication. This is especially likely if we hold negative attitudes about cultural differences. In the following section we will look at some destructive beliefs that can guarantee intercultural misunderstandings.

Attitudes That Diminish Understanding

Why are intercultural contacts so often frustrating rather than liberating? Because we often enter them with preconceived attitudes that impede the possibility of understanding. Among these attitudes are stereotypes and prejudices, assumptions of similarity, a tendency to withdraw from novelty, and a deep belief in the superiority of one's own culture.

Stereotypes and Prejudices

The tendency to prejudge and stereotype members of other groups is one of the main barriers to intercultural understanding. Many people enter cross-cultural interactions with preconceived notions that make it impossible to find any common ground and that distort accurate perception. **Stereotypes,** which are "generalized 2nd-hand beliefs that provide conceptual biases from which we 'make sense' out of what goes on around us, whether they are accurate or fit the circumstances," are one kind of preconception.[34] Although stereotypes fulfill certain functions (for example, reducing the anxiety that comes with uncertainty and making the world seem more predictable), they interfere with objective perception. Once we have decided that Germans are obsessed with order, that Japanese are workaholics, or that Central Americans lack ambition, we stop thinking about people objectively.

A **prejudice** is a special kind of stereotype, a "negative social attitude held by members of one group toward members of another group," an attitude that biases perception and provides a rationale for discrimination.[35] Prejudices are the products of in-group inter-action; very rarely are they the result of direct contact with out-group members. People learn prejudices from secondary sources and seldom make any attempt to check their validity. Having decided that members of a target group are dangerous, unintelligent, or lazy, people who hold prejudices avoid contact.

> *Prejudices are the products of in-group interaction; very rarely are they the result of direct contact with out-group members.*

The purpose of prejudices is not to enable us to understand the world accurately but to "draw a line between in-group and out-group members, a line that divides those who are 'superior' from those who are 'inferior.' In drawing this line people often use distorted data and unwarranted assumptions."[36] Table 10-3 shows some of the cognitive biases people use to keep their prejudices intact, biases that allow them to see differences where none exist or to distort differences that do exist.

Assumed Similarity

Almost as serious a stumbling block to intercultural understanding as prejudice is an unwarranted **assumption of similarity,** a refusal to see true differences where they exist. Assuming that everyone is "the same under the skin" may reduce uncomfortable feelings of strangeness, but it may also result in insensitivity. By assuming that members of a different culture see the world in the same way we do, we overlook real differences. When, for example, an American sees a foreign visitor smiling and nodding as the two interact, the American may assume the interaction is a success. It may be the case, however, "that the foreigner actually [understands] very little of the verbal and nonverbal content and [is] merely indicating polite interest or trying not to embarrass him or herself."[37]

Smiling is a good example of an assumption of similarity, for this "universal expression" takes on quite different meanings in different cultures. In some countries it is considered extremely impolite to smile at a stranger; a smile may be interpreted as a sexual invitation or as a sign of derision. Foreign travelers

TABLE 10-3

Cognitive Biases Used to Maintain Prejudices

Negative Interpretation	Interpreting everything the target group does as negative *Example:* If we see "them" relaxing, we interpret their behavior as shiftless and irresponsible; when we relax, we are simply unwinding after a hard day.
Discounting	Dismissing information that doesn't fit a negative stereotype *Example:* If one of "them" succeeds, it must be due to favoritism or luck; their success is simply the exception that proves the rule.
Fundamental Attribution Bias	Interpreting another's negative behavior as internal rather than external *Example:* If one of "them" is rude, it's because they're that way by nature; if one of "us" is rude, it's because we're under stress.
Exaggeration	Making negative aspects of out-group behavior seem more extreme *Example:* A simple argument is seen as a violent confrontation; a demonstration is reported as a riot.
Polarization	Looking for differences and ignoring similarities *Example:* An immigrant who has assimilated in almost every respect is still seen as one of "them" and as fundamentally different from "us."

Adapted from *Communicating Racism: Ethnic Prejudice in Thought and Talk* by Teun van Dijk, 1987. Newbury Park, CA: Sage.

in the United States may be insulted or taken aback by the Americans' friendly smile, as is evidenced by this Japanese student's comment:

> *On my way to and from school I have received a smile by non-acquaintance American girls several times. I have finally learned they have no interest for me; it means only a kind of greeting to a foreigner. If someone smiles at a stranger in Japan, especially a girl, she can assume he is either a sexual maniac or an impolite person.*[38]

Conversely, an American sojourner whose greetings are not returned may consider host nationals rude or standoffish. These misinterpretations are a direct result of failing to acknowledge that cultural differences in nonverbal behavior exist.

Anxiety and Withdrawal

Other potential barriers to intercultural understanding are anxiety and tension. Novel situations almost always cause stress. A small amount of tension and excitement can be energizing, but a large amount is extremely debilitating. If you have ever lived in a foreign country, you know how exhausting it is to decipher an unfamiliar language or to find your way around. When the tension rises too high, individuals experience **culture shock,** "the anxiety that results from losing all of our familiar signs and symbols of social intercourse."[39]

When culture shock is severe, individuals develop feelings of helplessness and lowered self-esteem, a desire to return home, insomnia, depression, and even physical illness. They become almost completely dysfunctional and may have to withdraw from contact with the native culture. During severe culture shock, people are likely to distort perceptions and feel hostility toward members of the host culture.

Although severe culture shock can be devastating, mild periods of stress followed by withdrawal can be productive. In her **draw-back-to-leap model,** Young Yun Kim argues that brief periods of culture shock may be "a necessary precondition for adaptive change, as individuals strive to regain their inner balance by adapting to the demands and opportunities of their new life circumstances."[40]

As sojourners experience stress, they often withdraw (the draw-back phase), engaging in tension-reducing behaviors that allow them an opportunity to reorganize their thoughts and feelings. Once they have processed cultural differences, they have the strength to continue to adapt (the leap-forward phase). According to Kim, some degree of stress is to be expected. By taking it easy when stress occurs, the individual avoids complete withdrawal.

Ethnocentrism

A final barrier to intercultural understanding is **ethnocentrism,** the belief that one's own culture is superior to all others and the tendency to judge all cultures by one's own criteria. Although it may be natural to believe that anything different is wrong, this is not a very productive attitude. Blaming people for not behaving the same way we do is irrational, especially when economic or physical factors may explain the difference. An ethnocentric American may be aghast to find out that people in another culture "waste" two hours of the middle of the day in resting. He or she may fail to consider that in that location the temperature often rises above ninety degrees and there is no air-conditioning. An ethnocentric individual may look down on the "natives" for using "primitive" farming methods without understanding they have no money to buy modern machinery. In many cases, the way "they" do things makes sense, given their circumstances.

Samovar and his colleagues argue that it is naive to believe that our culture has all the answers. They ask us to consider the following questions:

> *The Jew covers his head to pray, the Protestant does not—is one more correct than the other? In Saudi Arabia women cover their faces, in America they cover very little—is one more correct than the other? The Occidental speaks to God, the Oriental has God speak to him—is one more correct than the other? The American Indian values and accepts nature, the average American seeks to alter nature—is one more correct than the other? A listing of these questions is never-ending. We must remember, however, that it is not the questions that are important, but rather the dogmatic way in which we answer them.*[11]

Unless we can admit that differences do not always mean deficiencies and that our culture is not necessarily superior in all things, we will never be able to establish the trust and respect that are necessary counterparts of successful intercultural interaction.

Adapting to New Cultures

Despite all the difficulties we have described, people do manage to adapt to one another. In the final section of this chapter, we explore how people from different cultures accomplish this feat. We will begin by looking at factors related to successful international adaptation, and then we will look at ways to increase co-cultural understanding.

Factors That Affect Successful International Contact

All individuals who leave their home countries and immerse themselves in strange new lands experience stress. Some overcome this stress better than others, finding ways to feel at home with people who are quite different. Research has identified a number of factors associated with successful adaptation. These include the nature of the host culture, the personal attitudes and predispositions of the newcomer, and, most important, the kind of communicative bonds the newcomer makes. For just as one maintains contact with one's own culture through communication, one's ability to enter a new culture successfully is also determined by communicative behavior.

Nature of the Host Culture

Some cultures have more permeable boundaries than do others. Some make outsiders feel more at home than do others. One factor associated with successful adaptation is the host country's attitude toward foreigners. If citizens of a country consider outsiders barbarians and infidels, then adaptation will be rough going.

Generally speaking, **cultural distance,** the extent to which two cultures differ, affects ease of communication. This point is illustrated in Table 10-4, which ranks cultural exchanges in terms of their relative difficulty. At the top of the table are cultural pairings with maximal difference. Japan and the United States, for example, are quite different in a number of important dimensions; as we have already seen, one of these cultures is collectivist and the

---

TABLE 10-4

Cultural Differences: Cultural Pairings Arranged According to Sociocultural Distance

Maximum Difference

Western/Asian
Italian/Saudi Arabian
U.S. American/Greek
U.S. American/French-Canadian
White Anglo-American/Reservation Native American
White Anglo-American/African American, Asian
American, Mexican American, or Urban Native American
U.S. American/British
U.S. American/English-Canadian
Urban American/Rural American
Catholic/Baptist
Male Dominance/Female Equality
Heterosexual/Homosexual
Environmentalist/Developer

Minimum Difference

Adapted from *Intercultural Communication: A Reader,* 6th ed. (p. 12) by Larry A. Samovar and Richard E. Porter, eds., 1991. Belmont, CA: Wadsworth.

other individualist. In addition, Americans have what Hall and Hall call a **monochronic** sense of time; Americans tend to segment and sequence time and to value speed. Although on the surface the Japanese may seem monochronic, below the surface they are **polychronic,** especially when it comes to interpersonal behavior. People in polychronic cultures change plans often and easily and consider schedules as objectives to be met, not as definite commitments. Thus, in polychronic cultures it may take a lot longer to do things than in monochronic cultures.[42]

Another difference between Japan and the United States is that Japanese and English are very different languages. The distinction between them is much greater than, say, the distinction between English and French or German. Aspects of material culture (housing, transportation, and so on), as well as artistic and literary conventions, are also quite distinct. Except for the fact that in both Japan and the United States technology is quite advanced, these two countries exhibit large differences.

Germany and the United States, in contrast, may differ in some ways, but these countries share more similarities. Although their languages, educational systems, managerial styles, and problem-solving approaches exhibit some differences, people in these countries share common beliefs and impulses as well as mutually familiar material cultures.

Toward the bottom of Table 10-4 are cultural pairings of people who speak the same language and live side by side in the same country. People from the same nation show the smallest amount of difference. Unfortunately, this does not preclude volatile interactions. Although Catholics and Protestants coexist quite peacefully in the United States, this is obviously not the case in Northern Ireland. And although homosexuals and heterosexuals may share almost all aspects of national identity, the one difference that separates them may be highly salient to some—so much so that some heterosexuals may commit vandalism and acts of violence against members of homosexual cultures. In general, the more aspects of a culture that differ, the more problematic intercultural communication becomes.

Personal Predispositions

Having an open mind is clearly a prerequisite for adaptation. This brings us to a second factor related to intercultural interactions: the newcomer's personality. Included here are such factors as one's openness, resilience, and self-esteem. Some people have a low tolerance for ambiguity and find being an outsider distressing. Others lack confidence and may displace their feelings of anxiety onto those around them. Still others have great difficulty handling tension. Since adapting necessitates change and is always accompanied by stress, people with these predispositions will experience difficulty in adaptation.

In addition to personality variables, education and preentry training are also important. The more a newcomer knows about a culture ahead of time, the more prepared he or she is for contact. The traveler who reads about the host culture and makes contacts with host nationals prior to entry will be more comfortable in the new setting.

Communication Bonds

The third factor affecting successful adaptation is the way in which the newcomer interacts once he or she is in the host culture. Although openness and confidence can help, these internal predispositions must be implemented in actual communicative behaviors. In discussing the communicative aspects of adaptation, Kim argues that a newcomer's exposure to communication networks in the host culture (what Kim refers to as **host social communication**) and his or her relationships with members of the home culture (**ethnic social communication**) are two important determinants of intercultural success.[43]

Kim believes that sojourners interested in **acculturation** (i.e., becoming part of a new culture) should expose themselves as much as possible to host social communication. They should make interpersonal contacts and familiarize themselves with mass communication within the host culture. They should also avoid depending too heavily on ethnic communication networks. The newcomer who interacts only with other foreigners, who refuses to make any attempt to learn the language, and who reads only books and newspapers from home needlessly isolates himself or herself. Although others who share the same ethnic identity can form a support group and can teach a newcomer the ropes, they often inhibit real cross-cultural contact.

Developing an open communication style is a key variable in successful adaptation. This means being willing to plunge in and explore new cultures with enthusiasm.

Developing an open communication style is a key variable in successful adaptation. This means being willing to plunge in and explore new cultures with enthusiasm. It also means developing—often through trial and error—the behavioral competence to act in new ways that are more appropriate to one's new situation.

Increasing Co-Cultural Understanding

As we saw earlier, misunderstandings can occur between people who live side by side. We end this chapter by considering five ways to become more comfortable with co-cultural diversity.[44] The first way is to *open yourself up to new contacts*. Remember that prejudiced people hold distorted and erroneous

The first way to become more comfortable with diversity is to open oneself to new contacts.

beliefs and seldom have any direct experience with members of the groups they target. Although contact can reinforce negative perceptions, it can also disconfirm negative expectations. The best way to find out that "they" are not all alike is through contact. Unfortunately, we tend to associate and feel most comfortable with others who are similar. Think of your own circle of friends. How many of them are from a different racial, ethnic, or religious background? If your answer is none or few, you might consider widening your field of experience.

Another way to feel more comfortable with diversity is to *learn about the history and experiences of people from diverse cultures*. One of the major complaints of minority cultures is that their history has been rendered invisible by dominant groups. Most people know very little about other co-cultural groups, and this ignorance is a barrier to understanding. By taking a course about, or by experiencing on your own, the cultural history of another group, you can gain a deeper understanding of its members' perspectives.

Understanding can also be increased if we *test out stereotypes*. Prejudices and stereotypes are insidious. Although these barriers are all too apparent in others, we may not recognize them in ourselves. The first step in becoming more fair-minded lies in admitting the possibility that some of our judgments are unfair.

In addition, people who wish to cope with diversity should *develop the ability to role-take*. Role-taking means seeing the world from another's perspective—imaginatively taking on another's viewpoint. It means actively trying to understand how others make sense of their world and actively trying to experience what they feel. Although complete empathy is impossible, getting a better sense of what others think and feel is possible. Finally, each of us should *work on becoming more self-confident*. The better we feel about ourselves, the more likely we are to feel good about others and the more able we are to learn from them.

Summary

Now more than ever, learning to communicate across cultures is important. This chapter discusses how culture affects us and how we can become more effective cross-cultural communicators.

Culture consists of all those parts of the environment constructed by humans, including the shared customs and values that create community, as well as material objects and possessions. Cultural understandings are learned, shared, multifaceted, dynamic, and overlapping. Cultural norms are learned from and shared with others, and we spend substantial amounts of time and energy proving to others that we are "real" members of our cultures and that we are different from outsiders. Cultures control many interrelated facets of our lives. In this sense, it is true that if you touch a culture in one place, everything else is affected. Moreover, cultures constantly grow and change, and people belong to multiple overlapping cultural groups. All of these factors make learning the rules of a new culture difficult.

Understanding culture is important in today's global village. As international business becomes more common and as cultural groups within our own country demand recognition and respect, it is less and less possible to avoid intercultural interaction. By improving cross-cultural communication, we can make contacts with members of other cultures more comfortable and can enrich our own intercultural identities.

Intercultural communication is difficult for several reasons. First, people from different cultures perceive the world differently, attaching their own culture-specific values to events. Second, people from different cultures have different attitudes toward roles. Third, cultures differ in the goals their members value. Americans, for example, are characterized by effort-optimism, whereas people in other cultures may be more fatalistic. Fourth, cultures affect basic notions of self and humanity. Americans believe people are rational, perfectible, and mutable; for us, the most important social unit is the individual. Finally, language differences indicate that what can be said easily in one culture may be almost impossible to convey in another.

A number of attitudes diminish cross-cultural communication. When we stereotype, assume similarity while ignoring real differences, feel anxious about diversity, or take ethnocentric pride in the superiority of our own culture, we create blocks to understanding. Despite these barriers, intercultural communication can succeed. A number of factors are associated with successful adaptation to a foreign culture: the openness of the host culture and the degree to which it is culturally distant from one's own; the extent to which newcomers are open, resilient, and self-confident; and the willingness of newcomers to build bonds with members of host cultures.

Being comfortable with diversity is not easy. But by being as open as possible, by educating yourself on cultural issues, by challenging stereotypes, and by trying to see the world as others do, you will become a more confident and competent cultural communicator.

Key Terms

Listed below are the key terms used in this chapter, along with the number of the page on which each is explained.

culture   314
cultural universals   318
intercultural communication   320
co-cultures   321
intercultural identity   321
effort-optimism   325
rationality premise   325
perfectibility premise   325
mutability premise   325
individualism   326
collectivism   326
vertical relationship   326
horizontal relationship   326

stereotype   329
prejudice   330
assumption of similarity   330
culture shock   332
draw-back-to-leap model   332
ethnocentrism   332
cultural distance   334
monochronic time   335
polychronic time   335
host social communication   336
ethnic social communication   336
acculturation   336

Review Questions

1. What is culture? What human constructions make up culture? What are the five characteristics of culture?
2. What are some of the differences between the communication styles of European Americans and Native Americans? How can these differences lead to misunderstandings in the classroom or in business settings?
3. What are some of the common activities (cultural universals) found in all cultures? In what sense do we belong to multiple overlapping cultures? What different cultural groups do you belong to?
4. What is the global village? Why does its existence signal a need for better intercultural communication? What is a co-culture?
5. What are the advantages of developing an intercultural identity?
6. How does culture affect perception? role identity? goal setting and achievement? What is effort-optimism?
7. How does culture affect images of self and humanity? What three premises underlie American views of human behavior? Is the United States a collectivist or an individualist country? Why?
8. How does culture affect both semantic content and pragmatic language behavior?
9. What are stereotypes and prejudices? From whom are they learned, and what are their purposes? What cognitive biases do we use to keep prejudices in place?
10. If assuming "they" are different from "us" is a problem, why is assuming too much similarity also a problem?
11. What is culture shock? Explain the drawback-to-leap model.
12. What is ethnocentrism? Why is it a problem?
13. What factors affect successful assimilation and adaptation to a new culture? What is cultural distance? Name two cultures that are maximally distant and two that are quite close. What characteristics make the first two so different?
14. What personality variables are associated with successful cross-cultural adaptation? What should individuals do to speed up acculturation?
15. List five ways to increase one's comfort with diversity.

Suggested Readings

Carbaugh, Donal (Ed.). (1990). *Cultural communication and intercultural contact.* Hillsdale, NJ: Lawrence Erlbaum Associates.

    This anthology of readings includes a number of fascinating ethnographies of communication as well as comments by researchers on their work. It contains some classic studies in the field.

Hall, Edward T., & Hall, Mildred Reed. (1987). *Hidden differences: Doing business with the Japanese.* Garden City, NY: Doubleday, Anchor.

    Because of its importance as a business leader, Japan is of special interest to many American students. Even if you have no special plans to do business with the Japanese, this volume gives an interesting case study that illustrates how cross-cultural differences affect interaction.

Samovar, Larry A., & Porter, Richard E. (Eds.). (1991). *Intercultural communication: A reader* (6th ed.). Belmont, CA: Wadsworth.

This collection of readings gives an excellent overview of the field of intercultural communication and provides many examples from diverse cultures. If you want to read more about specific cultures or to increase your understanding of intercultural issues, this is an excellent source.

Samovar, Larry A., & Porter, Richard E. (1991). *Communication between cultures.* Belmont, CA: Wadsworth.

A good, solid introduction to basic concepts in intercultural communication, including a particularly strong section on the nature of culture and how it affects us.

Wood, Julia T. (1994). *Gendered lives: Communication, gender, and culture.* Belmont, CA: Wadsworth.

One of the most important cultural groups we belong to is our gender. This up-to-date book looks at how gender affects our lives.

Notes

1. Hoijer, Harry. (1954). The Sapir-Whorf hypothesis. In Harry Hoijer (Ed.), *Language in culture.* Chicago: University of Chicago Press, 94; cited in Singer, Marshall R. (1987). *Intercultural communication: A perceptual approach.* Englewood Cliffs, NJ: Prentice-Hall, 7.

2. The phrase comes from Diamond, C. T. Patrick. (1982). Understanding others: Kellyian theory, methodology and applications. *International Journal of Intercultural Relations, 6,* 403; cited in Singer, 8.

3. Benedict, Ruth. (1946). *Patterns of culture.* New York: Penguin, 2.

4. Klopf, Donald W. (1991). *Intercultural encounters: The fundamentals of intercultural communication* (2nd ed.). Englewood, CO: Morton, 31.

5. Trenholm, Sarah, & Jensen, Arthur. (1992). *Interpersonal communication.* Belmont, CA: Wadsworth, 368.

6. Klopf, 33.

7. For a discussion of cultural identity, see Singer, 46.

8. Wieder, D. Lawrence, & Pratt, Steven. (1990). On being a recognizable Indian among Indians. In Donal Carbaugh (Ed.), *Cultural communication and intercultural contact.* Hillsdale, NJ: Lawrence Erlbaum Associates, 45–64.

9. Ibid., 51.

10. Ibid., 61.

11. Ibid., 63.

12. Samovar, Larry A., & Porter, Richard E. (1991). *Communication between cultures.* Belmont, CA: Wadsworth, 15.

13. Ibid., 20.

14. Singer, 53.

15. Porter, Richard E., & Samovar, Larry A. (1991). Basic principles of intercultural communication. In Larry A. Samovar & Richard E. Porter (Eds.), *Intercultural communication: A reader.* Belmont, CA: Wadsworth, 6.

16. Ibid., 6.

17. Kim, Young Yun. (1988). *Communication and cross-cultural adaptation: An integrative theory.* Philadelphia: Multilingual Matters, 145–146.

18. George Kelly, as cited in Diamond, 396–397.

19. Klopf, 57.

20. Ibid., 20.

21. Dodd, Carley H. (1987). *Dynamics of intercultural communication* (2nd ed.). Dubuque, IA: Brown, 44.

22. Skow, Lisa, & Samovar, Larry A. (1991). Cultural patterns of the Maasai. In Samovar & Porter, *Intercultural Communication,* 90.

23. Carmichael, Carl W. (1991). Intercultural perspectives on aging. In Samovar & Porter, *Intercultural Communication,* 130.

24. For examples of these kinds of differences, see Samovar, Larry A., Porter, Richard E., & Jain, Nemi C. (1981). *Understanding intercultural communication.* Belmont, CA: Wadsworth, 119; and Dodd, 45.

25. Hall, Edward T. (1959). *The silent language.* Garden City, NY: Doubleday, 67.

26. Argyle, Michael. (1991). Intercultural communication. In Samovar & Porter, *Intercultural Communication,* 40; reprinted from Stephen Bochner (Ed.), *Cultures in contact: Studies in cross-cultural interaction.* Oxford, Eng.: Pergamon, 61–79.

27. Sitaram, K. S., & Cogdell, Roy T. (1976). *Foundations of intercultural communication.* Columbus, OH: Merrill, 51; cited in Samovar, Porter, & Jain, 94.

28. Samovar, Porter, & Jain, 73–74.

29. Ibid., 76.

30. Hofstede, Geert. (1982). *Culture's consequences.* Newbury Park, CA: Sage.

31. Triandis, Harry C., Briskin, Richard, & Hui, C. Harry. (1988). Cross-cultural training across the individualism-collectivism divide. *The International Journal of Intercultural Relations, 12;* reprinted in Samovar & Porter, *Intercultural Communication.*

32. Hall, Edward T., & Hall, Mildred Reed. (1987). *Hidden differences: Doing business with the Japanese.* Garden City, NY: Doubleday, Anchor.

33. Hall & Hall, 54–56, 157.

34. Barna, Laray M. (1991). Stumbling blocks in intercultural communication. In Samovar & Porter, *Intercultural Communication,* 348.

35. Trenholm & Jensen, 386.

36. Ibid., 388.

37. Barna, 346.

38. Ibid., 345.

39. Oberg, Kalvero. (1985). Culture shock: Adjustment to new cultural environments. *Practicing Anthropology, 7,* 170–179.

40. Kim, 56–57.

41. Samovar, Porter, & Jain, 195.

42. Hall & Hall, 18–20, 115.

43. Kim.

44. Trenholm & Jensen, 404–405.

11

Methods of Discovery

When people know how to communicate skillfully, the quality of their lives and of the lives of those around them is improved; when people lack this knowledge, their social and personal worlds can crumble.

The factor that makes communication different from many other subjects is the close link between communication theory and communication practice. Scholars are drawn to communication not only because it is a fascinating subject in its own right but also because understanding how communication works is a practical necessity. When people know how to communicate skillfully, the quality of their lives and of the lives of those around them is improved; when people lack this knowledge, their social and personal worlds can crumble. In short, discoveries about communication are important.

This chapter is about methods of discovery—methods professional scholars use to further their understanding of communication as well as methods you can use to widen your own knowledge. We begin by reviewing some of the basic research methodologies that critics and communication scientists use. Although you may not plan on becoming a professional scholar, knowing how professionals study communication can be useful. Professional methods can guide your own efforts to understand communication and can make you a more critical consumer of communication research.

We will also look at some sources you can turn to for information about communication once this class is over. First, we will look at the way the field of communication is structured and at the kinds of courses offered in communication departments at large universities. Although not all of these courses may be offered at your school, each draws upon a rich body of literature that is readily available. Second, we will look at other sources of information on communication. You don't have to take a course in a speech communication department to learn about communication; almost every course you take can provide insights into human interaction. And you can learn about communication outside of class by reading a novel, talking to a friend, or observing the world around you. Once you have learned where to look, you will find sources of discovery all around you.

How Is Communication Research Done?

Forming hypotheses about the social world and looking for evidence to test those hypotheses are not activities unique to professional scholars. We do these things whenever we try to understand the social world. Our lives are guided, to a large extent, by commonsense theories of human action. When we try to explain the success or failure of a relationship or think up a strategy for getting what we want, we are theorizing about communication. "We were so different; we never really had a chance" is a theory about relationships. "If I do a favor for her now, she'll have to repay me later" is a hypothesis about the way interpersonal influence works. The theorizing and research of professionals is set apart from commonsense ways of knowing in that professional researchers are more sys-

> *When we try to explain the success or failure of a relationship or think up a strategy for getting what we want, we are theorizing about communication.*

tematic and more suspicious; researchers challenge their own thinking, looking for biases and errors. This readiness to reexamine one's work is indicated in the word *research:*

> *To research is to search again, to take another, more careful look, to find out more. . . .What the research attitude presumes is that the first look–and every later look–may be prone to error, so that one must look again and again, differently and thoroughly each time.*[1]

Problems With Commonsense Ways of Knowing

One of the biggest differences between research and everyday thinking is that in everyday life we often accept the first reasonable explanation we come across. Seldom do we ask ourselves whether there is another, better explanation for what is happening. Commonsense knowing is often careless and biased. We tend to rely too heavily on our own experiences, to engage in wishful thinking, and to accept simple heuristics. Because of these tendencies, the conclusions we draw about the social world are often seriously flawed.

One of the biggest differences between research and everyday thinking is that in everyday life we often accept the first reasonable explanation we come across.

The first problem with commonsense knowledge is that we privilege our own experiences. Most people find it hard to accept generalizations that contradict what they have seen with their own eyes. Most project their own beliefs and motivations onto others. Thus, *our everyday models of human behavior are often models of our own behavior.*

We also let our own desires get in our way. We see what we want to see and turn a blind eye to information that makes us uncomfortable. Our prejudices make us dismiss anything that contradicts what we've decided is true. Our superstitions lead us to accept any message that gives us an illusion of control over unexplained events. Thus, *our everyday models of human behavior may also be models of what we wish were true rather than what is true.*

In everyday life we also rely on simple **heuristics,** rules of thumb that allow us to avoid careful information processing.[2] When we encounter difficult information, we look for simple cues that tell us what to think. We may rely on authorities ("I didn't understand it, but my dad said it was true") or status cues ("The argument seemed odd, but after all, the author did go to Harvard"). We may look at formal aspects, rather than content, of the message ("She used a lot of statistics and graphs, so she must know what she's talking about"). Too often *our everyday models of human behavior are based on simplistic thinking.*

Systematic Ways of Knowing

Researchers try to avoid the errors that affect everyday thinking. In many ways good researchers are like detectives or investigative reporters. They don't accept things at face value. They are suspicious. And they often set out to overturn commonsense beliefs. In this sense, researchers "are professional troublemakers: they must challenge old beliefs, create new ones, and then turn the challenge upon those new ones."[3]

> *In many ways good researchers are like detectives or investigative reporters. They don't accept things at face value. They are suspicious.*

Lawrence Frey and his colleagues offer an excellent discussion of the characteristics of scholarly research. This discussion is summarized in Table 11-1. According to these authors, research has eight basic characteristics; it is question-oriented, methodological, creative, replicable, self-critical, public, cumulative and self-correcting, and cyclical.[4]

The first characteristic of research is that it is question-oriented. Research begins when the researcher encounters a state of affairs that needs explanation. Rather than simply accepting the status quo, the researcher formulates questions about it and then tries to answer these questions. At heart, research "requires the capacity to ask the right questions as well as a sense of what form the answer should take."[5]

Research is also methodological; that is, it is systematic and ordered, with built-in guarantees that the findings will be as accurate as possible. As we shall see, researchers are guided by systematic methods and procedures during their investigations.

That research is as careful and as accurate as possible does not mean that researchers lack imagination. Scholarly research is also creative. After all, researchers must see below the surface of things; they often must make counterintuitive leaps and think their way past cultural biases. They also must devise imaginative ways of gathering information and testing hypotheses.

When Frey and his colleagues say that research must be replicable, they mean that it must be repeatable. The methods employed must be so objective that if the research were conducted again, the same results would occur and the same conclusions would be drawn. A result that occurs only once in only one study is questionable. Such a result may be due to some unusual aspect of the research (or the researcher) rather than to the underlying phenomenon the researcher is trying to explain. Scholars make an effort to test and retest their theories before they generalize about them.

Scholarly research is also self-critical. This means that researchers make special efforts to find the flaws in their arguments and to disprove their own theories. A scholar should be his or her own most exacting critic. In addition, to make sure that research is replicated and criticized, researchers make their

TABLE 11-1

- *Question-Oriented*
  "At the heart of all research is a question worth answering."

- *Methodological*
  "Objective procedures are used to ensure that researchers find and report what is accurate."

- *Creative*
  "Scholarship begins with inventive ingenuity. . . ."

- *Replicable*
  Other scholars must be able to "replicate, or reproduce, the entire inquiry process."

- *Self-Critical*
  Scholarly research "explicitly examines itself to discover and report flaws . . ."

- *Public*
  Scholarship "must be open to examination, questioning, and criticism by the public and other scholars."

- *Cumulative and Self-Correcting*
  "The accumulation of information . . . allows for knowledge to evolve and grow."

- *Cyclical*
  Research "ends up back where it started," with new questions emerging from previous answers.

Adapted from *Investigating Communication: An Introduction to Research Methods* (pp. 6–8) by Lawrence R. Frey, Carl H. Botan, Paul G. Friedman, and Gary L. Kreps, 1991, Englewood Cliffs, NJ: Prentice-Hall.

results public. They show their results to others for examination and questioning. To keep results secret violates the purpose of research, which is to further knowledge.

Another important characteristic of research is that it is cumulative and self-correcting. The first step in doing research is to review all of the previous studies on one's topic and to build on others' work. Researchers do not want to spend time and effort "reinventing the wheel" or disproving a theory that has already been disproved. Researchers belong to a community of scientists and critics, a community that works together to correct old mistakes and to discover new information.

Researchers belong to a community of scientists and critics, a community that works together to correct old mistakes and to discover new information.

Scholarship is, then, ultimately cyclical. Just as good research begins with a question, it ends with another question. In the words of Frey and his colleagues,

a researcher begins with a topic worth studying, asks questions and/or makes predictions, plans research carefully, carries out the planned research, analyzes the data to provide tentative answers, and starts all over again by posing new topics and questions worth studying.[6]

Common Research Tasks

As we shall see shortly, researchers use a wide variety of methods in communication research. Some researchers rely on historical-critical methods, whereas others devise elaborate experiments. Nevertheless, all go through the basic activities shown in Table 11-2. The first task is to *find a subject of study and formulate a research question.* As Frey and his colleagues point out, inquiry is prompted by curiosity. The question a researcher attempts to answer in a given study is called a **research question.** The question should be specific and clear, for it will act as a guide throughout the research. Some researchers begin with a very specific question, whereas others start broadly and narrow the scope of their study as they proceed. For example, a researcher may be initially interested in political persuasion. The question "How do politicians persuade the public?" is an intriguing one, but it is too broad. A researcher could spend his or her lifetime studying political persuasion and only scratch the surface. Researchers narrow their focus by reformulating a general question into more specific questions. One interesting aspect of political communication is the use of surrogates, people who speak for a candidate. "What is the communicative

TABLE 11-2

Common Tasks in Communication Inquiry

Task 1	Framing a Research Question
Task 2	Choosing a Research Methodology
Task 3	Designing a Sampling Strategy
Task 4	Gathering and Analyzing Data
Task 5	Interpreting Data and Sharing Results

role of surrogates in a political campaign?" narrows the focus, although it too must eventually be refined. Ultimately, the researcher must decide which surrogates and which campaigns to study. An even more specific research question might be "What kinds of themes characterized the speeches of the vice presidential candidates in the 1992 presidential campaign?"

An important part of framing a research question is defining key concepts and terms. The researcher who wishes to look at surrogates' roles must understand what a surrogate is and must be able to define the aspect of surrogates' communication behavior that he or she wants to investigate. The researcher who wants to study the effects of negative campaigning on a candidate's credibility and popularity must offer clear definitions of *negative campaigning, credibility,* and *popularity.*

Definitions are generally of two types: conceptual and operational. A **conceptual definition** explains the meaning of a term in a general, abstract way. *Credibility,* for example, might be conceptually defined as "the extent to which a candidate is seen by an audience as worthy of belief." An **operational definition** explains how a term will be measured in the study. An operational definition of *credibility* might be "the candidate's mean score on a ten-point rating scale of trustworthiness and expertness." An operational definition is necessary whenever the values of a variable are to be measured. Although the researcher knows conceptually what negative campaigning means, he or she also has to know how to recognize specific examples of negative campaigning. If a candidate refers to his opponent as "sleazy" and "dishonest," the characterizations are clearly negative. But what if the candidate refers to his opponent as a "liberal"? Is this a description or a slur? Before starting the study, the researcher must decide how negative a message must be to count as an instance of negative campaigning—an often quite difficult task.

In addition to formulating a research question and defining key terms, the researcher must *choose a particular research methodology.* Often these first three tasks go hand in hand. The topic area may suggest a research methodology, or the methodology may guide formulation of the research question. Researchers use a variety of methodologies. Some researchers take a historical-critical approach. They might decide to investigate surrogate behavior by analyzing a given surrogate's public rhetoric. Other researchers might choose an ethnographic approach, actually joining a campaign to make behind-the-scenes observations. Still others might rely on survey methods, sending out questionnaires to track public opinion over the course of the campaign. Researchers with an experimental bent might even test whether certain kinds of information are more acceptable when attributed to a surrogate or when attributed to a candidate.

Having chosen a research approach, the researcher must *design a sampling strategy* to decide who or what to study. The researcher who has decided to do a rhetorical analysis of surrogates' public speeches must decide which surrogates are of interest and which speeches to analyze. One researcher might decide to focus on a single individual (say, a presidential candidate's running mate), comparing speeches at the beginning, middle, and end of the campaign to see how themes and topics evolve. Another researcher might be interested in a single speech given at the nominating convention.

The researcher who decides to conduct a survey must decide what questions to ask and whom to ask. Because it is impossible to ask everyone in the country all the possible questions related to political persuasion, the researcher must choose a small subset of people and items. This process of sampling occurs in every case of research, no matter what the approach is.

Once the researcher has decided whom or what to study, he or she must *gather and analyze data*. For one study, the researcher might analyze data by poring over transcripts of public speeches, searching for themes and metaphors. For another study, data gathering might involve exposing subjects to an elaborate experimental manipulation and measuring their responses, and analysis might use statistical tests of significance. Regardless of the form of the data-gathering and -analyzing process, the final research activity is to *interpret the data and report the results*. The researcher must attempt to make sense of the data, draw conclusions about them, and share those conclusions with others.

Four Popular Research Methods

There are many research methodologies. Table 11-3 lists some of the most common. In the next four sections we will look at four of the most important methodologies: rhetorical criticism, ethnographic inquiry, survey research, and experimental research. Although each method has its own assumptions and procedures, each shares the goal of furthering our understanding of how communication works. As we discuss each methodology, we will first describe the goals and procedures researchers follow when using that methodology, and we will then look at a representative sample of research so that you can see how these methods are applied.

Rhetorical Criticism

In everyday life we frequently act as critics, analyzing and evaluating messages. Most of us enjoy expressing opinions; after attending a lecture or seeing a film, we like to discuss what we experienced. Our response may be a fairly simple description of what we liked or disliked about the communication, or it may be a more detailed analysis of the intended and unintended effects of the message

TABLE 11-3

Rhetorical Criticism

The rhetorical critic begins by choosing a rhetorical act to study. After describing the purpose of the rhetorical act, the audience to which it is directed, and the context in which it occurs, the critic examines the rhetorical strategies it employs and evaluates the effectiveness of these strategies.

Sample research questions:
- How did the "family values" issue build audience identification in the 1992 presidential campaign?
- How did the narrative structure that Spike Lee used in the film *Malcolm X* add to Malcolm's image?
- How did Mario Cuomo use metaphor to reach multiple audiences in his keynote address at the 1984 Democratic National Convention?

Content Analysis

Focusing on a text, the researcher systematically identifies and measures message content to determine how often a given unit of content occurs within the text. The units studied may be general (themes, topics, viewpoints) or specific (kinds of words, grammatical forms). Results generally involve reporting the frequency of a given kind of content. Content category frequencies may be related to variables outside the text.

Sample research questions:
- What is the average number of violent acts on prime-time television shows on each of the major networks?
- Do Republican and Democratic senatorial candidates employ different kinds of symbols in campaign speeches?
- How do children's fairy tales portray family relationships?

Conversation Analysis

To describe the content, structure, and function of everyday spoken interaction, the researcher obtains a sample of talk, transcribes and examines it, and draws inferences about it. Researchers frequently focus on the conversational moves that individuals use as they talk, examining the sequential relationship, functions, and effects of the moves in a given conversation.

Sample research questions:
- What kinds of conversational moves do teachers use to encourage classroom participation?
- How are conversational openings and closings structured?
- What kinds of actions and utterances signal dominance in male-female interactions?

Ethnography

The researcher directly observes behavior in its natural setting to describe the communication practices of a group of people. To make these observations, the researcher may actually "go undercover" and join the group as a participant. The research goal is to understand the world from the perspective of those being observed. The researcher therefore avoids imposing his or her own values and assumptions on the data. Instead of testing an existing hypothesis, he or she allows conclusions to emerge from observations.

Sample research questions:
- What are the primary functions of talk for male members of an urban, blue-collar neighborhood?
- How do middle-class mothers communicate to their children during play?
- How do established members of religious cults recruit and treat new members?

Unobtrusive Methods

To avoid the behavioral changes that can occur when people know they're being observed, researchers rely on observing traces of communicative behavior and drawing conclusions from their observations. Researchers may focus on measures of erosion (how objects are worn down by use) or on measures of accretion (physical traces or artifacts that build up over time).

Sample research questions:
- What museum exhibits are most popular (measured by wear and tear on carpets or amount of dirt on floors)?
- Is racial tension increasing at a certain high school (measured by kinds of graffiti in the school's public areas)?
- Which of a series of cover designs makes a brochure most appealing (measured by the number of each brochure removed from racks)?

Survey Research

To learn about people, researchers ask them questions. Using either written questionnaires or face-to-face interviews, the researcher questions subjects and records and codes their responses. Researchers make an effort to question representative members of a given population so that the findings will be generalizable.

Sample research questions:
- What issues were most important in influencing young people to vote in the last presidential election?
- What kind of parental advice do young adults remember as being most influential?
- What do college students report as the most significant factors in choosing a romantic partner?

(continued)

TABLE 11-3

Continued

Experimental Research

To examine causal connections, researchers systematically manipulate causal variables and measure the effects of their manipulation on subject responses. Extraneous influences are controlled or held constant in order to see the relationship between specific variables. Subject responses are normally converted to numerical form and analyzed statistically.

Sample research questions:
- Does watching violent cartoons lead children to act aggressively toward one another?
- Is a one-sided or two-sided argument more effective for persuading a hostile audience?
- Are women more likely to turn to other women or to men when they need advice about career moves?

Mixed Methods

Researchers may combine several methodologies in a single study. For example, within the framework of an experiment, samples of talk may be collected under different conditions and then content analyzed. Ethnographic observations may be followed up with surveys. The term used to describe the process of approaching a research question from multiple perspectives is **triangulation.**

on the audience. In either case, by discussing a message critically, we increase our understanding and appreciation of that message and of the communication process in general.

Rhetorical criticism is an extension and refinement of the everyday critical impulse; it is a systematic way of describing, analyzing, and evaluating a given act of communication. The kind of criticism we do in everyday life is often limited to a general description of how we personally react to a given message ("I really liked her speech. It was inspiring"). Although we may explain some of the things we liked about it ("The part where she described her childhood really hit home"), we seldom do so in much detail. Unless we are challenged, we do not spend a great deal of time making a strong case for our beliefs. We simply state our criticism and move on.

> *Rhetorical criticism is an extension and refinement of the everyday critical impulse; it is a systematic way of describing, analyzing, and evaluating a given act of communication.*

Rhetorical critics engage in a thorough examination of a given message and its effects, giving special attention to the situation that prompted the message as well as the social and personal constraints that affected the speaker. Rhetorical critics also examine the purpose, structure, and style of the message, evaluating the ways in which the speaker's rhetorical choices affected audience response, and critics are careful to articulate the critical standards they use to judge a message.

There is no one right way to criticize a message. The same message may be evaluated in a number of different ways. One critic might criticize a speech by looking at the kinds of arguments a speaker used. Another might examine the speaker's use of metaphor. A third might look at the ideological values of a speech, and a fourth might analyze its social and historical importance. Each evaluation can add to our understanding of how the speech operates.

In their book *Communication Criticism,* Karyn Rybacki and Don Rybacki discuss the process of criticism. They argue that whatever the act being investigated is, the rhetorical critic has an obligation to do three things: to describe the significant qualities of a rhetorical act, to describe those aspects of the rhetorical situation that influenced the form of the rhetorical act, and to render a judgment about the quality and consequences of the rhetorical act.[7]

Steps in Rhetorical Criticism

Rhetorical criticism seeks to explain and evaluate a rhetorical act. A **rhetorical act** is any act of communication deliberately designed to influence the belief or behavior of an audience. Rhetorical acts can take many forms. An inaugural speech, a political cartoon, a propaganda film, a protest song, a satirical television show, an advertising campaign, an act of civil disobedience—all can influence an audience and may thus be classified as rhetorical acts.

In evaluating a given rhetorical act, the critic must take a critical approach. Each approach is based on a theory that defines rhetoric and the role of a critic, and each provides a slightly different set of criteria for judging rhetorical success. Table 11-4 gives a brief overview of some of the more popular contemporary critical approaches.

Like all research, rhetorical criticism is designed to be shared. The rhetorical critic's goal is to increase understanding and appreciation of a rhetorical act. The critic does this by making critical claims and by offering supporting evidence. Not all acts of criticism are equally valid; some may be careless or misguided and may fail to convince their audiences. A rhetorical critic must make a strong case for his or her point of view by showing that he or she understands the context and the structure of the rhetorical act being judged and by provid-

> *Like all research, rhetorical criticism is designed to be shared. The rhetorical critic's goal is to increase understanding and appreciation of a rhetorical act.*

ing support for critical claims. Rhetorical criticism is a rhetorical act in its own right, an act of argumentation that succeeds only when it enables us to understand and appreciate a message more fully.

The Myth of the American Cowboy: An Example of Social Values Criticism

Throughout U.S. history, the myth of the West has fascinated Americans. In a piece of rhetorical criticism written in 1983, Janice Hocker Rushing sets out to answer two questions: what values are contained in the mythology of the West-

TABLE 11-4

Contemporary Critical Approaches

Neo-Aristotelian Criticism

Using the concepts and principles set forth by Aristotle and other classical theorists, the rhetorical critic evaluates a speaker's rhetorical choices. The critic may evaluate the modes of proof used in the speech, the structure and organization of the speaker's arguments, and the speaker's stylistic choices and delivery, all as they affect audience response.

Genre Criticism

Using evaluative criteria developed for a specific type of communication, critics discuss how the message fits its genre and describe how the message achieves its effects. Traditional genres include the apologia (an apology, or defense of character), the eulogy, the epideictic (ceremonial) speech, the political or legislative speech, the sermon, and so on. Rhetorical acts other than speeches also have their own genres, for example, the Western film or the romantic novel.

Burkean Dramatistic Analysis

Viewing symbolic acts as "drama," the critic analyzes how various aspects of a given "performance" (act, purpose, agent, agency, and scene) are symbolically represented and how they serve to evoke identification between speaker and audience.

Fantasy Theme Analysis

Working from the idea that we understand our world by telling stories about it, the critic examines the implicit narrative structure of rhetorical acts, describing the myths and fantasies that the acts convey. A fantasy theme analyst seeks to uncover fantasy themes (basic story lines and characters that dra-

ern film, and how have these values survived threats to their existence and vitality?[8] Using the social values model as the basis of her criticism, Rushing argues that the Western myth embodies a dialectical tension between two opposing values: community and individualism. She also contends that modern versions of the myth (as seen in movies such as *The Electric Horseman* and *Urban Cowboy* and in television shows such as *Dallas*) undermine this central tension and are thus "seriously subversive" of the fundamental archetype.

Rushing believes that the core tension worked out in Western films is the opposition between individuality and community. The cowboy hero must be

---

matize a situation), fantasy types (recurring tales that embody the fears or values of a culture), and rhetorical visions (shared schemata for interpreting reality) shared by members of rhetorical communities.

Social Movement Studies

Focusing on a group involved in a social cause, the critic analyzes how the cause gains adherents, how its members present their movement to the public, and what the impact of the movement is on the culture at large. A social movement critic might study the rhetorical strategies of groups such as civil rights activists, the religious Right, supporters of Jewish statehood, the right-to-life movement, and so on.

Ideological Criticism

The critic examines rhetorical acts for implicit ideological messages and evaluates how these messages uphold or subvert existing power relations. Often the critic evaluates what is deliberately left out of a message as well as what the message contains. Any political ideology may form the basis of criticism. In recent years, feminist and Marxist criteria have been used to show how a variety of cultural products encourage patriarchal and capitalist structures.

Social Values Criticism

Rhetorical critics look at the way cultural products (speeches, films, TV shows, etc.) re-present a culture's basic values. Critics are particularly interested in uncovering ways in which rhetorical acts combine potentially conflicting values. A social values critic might investigate how a given rhetorical act synthesizes oppositional values such as individualism and community or morality and materialism.

both a rugged individualist, a lone pioneer beholden to no one, and an embodiment of law and order, a protector of the community that will ultimately civilize and tame the West. Rushing believes that "this potent myth is able to express, then, the universal tendency of humans to both divide from and identify with one another, and to do so in a uniquely American way."[9]

Rushing argues that throughout history, Westerns have shifted emphasis from one side of the individuality-community dichotomy to the other. In the early B Westerns of the 1940s, the cowboy hero was clearly on the side of civilization and order. In cowboy star Gene Autry's *Ten Commandments of the Cowboy*, the cowboy was described as fair, trustworthy, honest, kind, unprejudiced, helpful, hardworking, clean, respectful, and patriotic. The screen Western of the forties valued community over individuality. However, by coming down so strongly on one side of the mythic paradox, it threatened to destabilize the basic archetype.

In the fifties, Westerns regained complexity at the hands of directors such as John Ford, Howard Hawks, Anthony Mann, Fritz Lang, and Arthur Penn. The archetypal hero of the classic Western was an outsider. Forced to take over leadership and to use violence to protect the community, he did what he had to do and then rode on, unable to settle down with the "good girl" (a symbol of civilization) and unwilling to take up with the "bad girl." One explanation for the reemergence of the hero as loner and the resulting reaffirmation of the basic dialectical tension of the Western myth is that during the fifties, workers felt their individuality threatened by increasingly powerful corporate structures.

In the sixties and seventies, the cowboy hero was not only individualistic but also hostile to the civilizing forces of society. Outlaw-as-hero and Indian-as-hero movies became the norm. That this development occurred during the social upheavals of the sixties, when many people identified with the counterculture, should come as no surprise. Once again the rhetorical function of the Western film was shifting, this time toward individualism.

Rushing argues that in the eighties, the cowboy myth was threatened by a number of forces. Feminism questioned a myth in which women played such a passive and two-dimensional role. People realized that there was no longer any frontier to conquer, and their sense of community was undermined. The old environment of the Western had become extinct. Nevertheless, cowboy themes were still popular—this time in the form of the urban cowboy, the classic example of whom was President Ronald Reagan. With his Western origins, his ranch, his penchant for Western garb, and his rugged appearance, Reagan played the role of town marshal. The reemergence of the cowboy hero in this guise did not signal a new value synthesis, however. Instead, Rushing argues that it resulted in a pseudosynthesis that only gave the appearance of reaffirming the Western myth.

In 1983, Rushing was unsure what the future would bring, whether the myth would turn to older forms, stagnate, and die or reinvent itself in another form (for example, in space Westerns such as *Star Wars*). Despite the uncertain future of the myth, Rushing believed that Americans need myths and heroes to embody their most basic values.

Ethnographic Research

If in everyday life we often act as critics, we also often act as ethnographers. Whenever curiosity about human behavior motivates us to observe others, we are engaging in our own private version of ethnography. Watching people and trying to figure out the rules that guide their actions are basic mechanisms for survival; without them, we wouldn't be able to fit into our own culture.

Whenever curiosity about human behavior motivates us to observe others, we are engaging in our own private version of ethnography.

Like the rest of us, professional **ethnographers** learn from observation. Their reasons for observing behavior, however, are scientific, not personal. Ethnographers want to understand how members of other cultures interpret their world. To do so, ethnographers immerse themselves in a culture in an effort to see it through the eyes of its members. As Howard Schwartz and Jerry Jacobs point out, the ethnographer has two goals:

> *First, he wants to learn the actor's "definition of the situation"–to see what the actor sees, know what he knows, and think as he thinks. Second, having accomplished this reconstruction of the other's reality, the researcher hopes to transcend this view, to see what the actor does* not *see–the formal features, processes, patterns, or common denominators that characterize the actor's view and situation.*[10]

To achieve these goals, the researcher must make direct contact with the individuals he or she wishes to observe. As J. Kirk and M. L. Miller explain, ethnographic research depends on "watching people in their own territory and interacting with them in their own language, on their own terms."[11]

Ethnographic research depends on "watching people in their own territory and interacting with them in their own language, on their own terms."

Steps in Ethnographic Research

If the ethnographer is to observe people in their own territory, he or she must assume a role. One approach is to observe people without their being aware of one's presence. The ethnographer who chooses to take this **covert role** goes "undercover" by becoming a member of the group being studied. To understand how cult members are socialized, for example, a researcher might join a cult under the guise of being a spiritual seeker. Or to understand the culture of a New York City cab driver, a researcher might drive a cab for several months. The problem with this approach is that it is deceptive. As the researcher forms relationships with group members, he or she may feel uncomfortable about lying to them. Another problem is in becoming so emotionally involved that one's ability to make objective observations is threatened.

Another approach is to take a more **overt role.** Here the ethnographer enters the field as a scientist, and people know full well they are being observed. The problem here is that when people know they are being watched, they may try to impress the observer. The ethnographer who takes an overt role must make special efforts to gain the trust of group members and to blend into the background as much as possible.

The key to ethnographic research is the ability to make accurate and insightful observations. Observations take the form of **field notes,** a record of critical events and behaviors accompanied by the ethnographer's self-observations, feelings, and interpretations. Field notes can run to thousands of pages in a lengthy study. Because it is hard to tell what details will be significant in the final analysis, good ethnographers note as much as possible as it occurs.

To gather data, the ethnographer may work with an **informant,** a member of the culture who is willing to show the researcher around, to answer questions, and to set up interviews with other people. Interviews are an important part of ethnographic research. By talking to as many people as possible about their communicative experiences, the researcher can check his or her own perceptions and can begin to understand how people within the culture view their own experiences.

Ethnographers must constantly be on the lookout for prejudices that may bias their ability to understand a culture. Although ethnographic research strives to be **presuppositionless research,** the researcher's own norms and values are hard to set aside.

The final step in ethnographic research is making sense of the data. Most researchers analyze their data inductively. This means that their conclusions flow directly from the data themselves rather than from a preexisting theory. Frey and his colleagues offer four criteria for good, inductively generated results. Conclusions should be

believable, *in that they should seem plausible to the reader. They should be* comprehensive *or account for all (or most) of the data. They should be* grounded *or tied clearly to the data. Finally, they should be* applicable *and lead to testable hypotheses and additional investigation.*[12]

Talking Like a Man in Teamsterville:
An Ethnography of Communication

What it means to talk like a man depends on where you're from. In some places, men are expected to be strong and silent; in others, sensitive and caring; and in still others, brash and boasting. The way people express themselves—an important aspect of their gender identity—differs significantly from culture to culture.

"Teamsterville" is a code name for a blue-collar, low-income, white neighborhood on the near south side of Chicago. Like members of other cultural groups, the inhabitants of Teamsterville share general attitudes about the functions of communication and specific views about how to talk. In the early seventies, when Gerry Philipsen conducted an ethnographic study of Teamsterville, images of manliness were particularly important and were a frequent topic of conversation. Philipsen therefore decided to focus his attention on understanding the value associated with male role-enactment in Teamsterville.

Philipsen first entered the culture for a twenty-one-month period from 1969 to 1970, during which time he was employed as a social group worker. After a year's absence, he returned for an additional nine months devoted entirely to field research. Participant observation and interviewing were his primary methods. He recorded field notes on the speech behaviors he observed and on the statements (both spontaneous and elicited) of informants. He also tape-recorded verbal interaction.

Philipsen reported his results in two articles.[13] In the first, he described the rules governing male role-enactment, focusing specifically on activities avoided by Teamsterville men because they were considered unmanly. In the second article, Philipsen described the places where Teamsterville residents could speak comfortably.

In his first study, Philipsen found that when Teamsterville men were involved in symmetrical interactions (that is, interactions with other men of the same status), talk was encouraged. In asymmetrical relationships, however (for example, relationships with wives and children), talk was less valued. And in three situations, talk was proscribed: (1) when responding to an insult; (2) when disciplining a status inferior; and (3) when interacting with status superiors.

Philipsen became aware of the first situation when he inadvertently violated normative behavior. During a trip outside the neighborhood with a group of boys, Philipsen was asked whether he would hit a man who insulted his (Philipsen's) wife. When Philipsen answered that he probably would not, the boys became visibly shaken and asked to be taken home. Although puzzled at the time, Philipsen later recognized the boys' behavior as fright. When they set out into what was, for them, foreign territory, the boys had assumed they were with an adult male who would protect them. When they found they were with a man who would choose silence or talk, rather than fighting, they felt threatened.

As Philipsen became more accustomed to Teamsterville, he was able to gather additional critical incidents that illuminated speaking norms. He realized, for example, that the appropriate way for an adult male to discipline a disobedient child was thought to be to subdue the child physically. A man who tried to reason with a status inferior cast doubt not only on his manliness but on his sexual orientation as well.

Philipsen also found that Teamsterville men avoided speaking to status superiors. If interacting with a boss or a government representative was necessary, the men would use surrogates, such as the local precinct captain, the Catholic parish priest, or the union steward. These "professional communicators" were considered perfect mediators. Their social status and training signified that they could speak easily with bosses, yet their ties to the neighborhood signified that they could be trusted.

In his second article, Philipsen reported on four places where the inhabitants of Teamsterville felt comfortable speaking: in the neighborhood, on the street, on the corner, and on the porch. All important social interaction took place in these locations. Philipsen noted a gender difference between corner and porch. The men and boys of Teamsterville tended to interact "on the corner." For men, the corner meant a neighborhood tavern, whereas for boys, it meant a street corner. The importance of the street as a source of identity was reflected in the fact that groups of boys referred to themselves by street names (for example, "the Wallace Street Boys" or "the 33rds"). Philipsen found that where a boy chose to hang out influenced how others saw him and how he saw himself.

The women and girls of Teamsterville congregated "on the porch." The porch served as a link between the woman's private domain in the kitchen or house and the public life of the street. The porch was a woman's principal setting for sociability. The porch also held deep cultural significance as a means of establishing community. An individual without a porch could never be fully accepted.

Philipsen concluded that when the people of Teamsterville look out at the world, they "see boundaries, social and physical, where others do not, and their vision serves as a major unifying perception in their world view."[14] Philipsen's research shows that talk is a highly rule-governed activity with its own set of values. Philipsen agrees with Dell Hymes's observation that in any community (ours as well as Teamsterville residents'), "speaking may carry different functional loads" and that unless we understand a given culture's communicative rules, we will have difficulty communicating across cultural borders.[15]

Survey Research

Perhaps the most direct and straightforward way to learn about other people is to ask them questions. Survey research does just that. In **survey research,** an investigator chooses a sample of people to question, decides what to ask and how to ask it, and administers the questions in either written or oral form. He or she then codes responses and looks for meaningful patterns. Finally, the survey researcher draws conclusions from the data.

> *Perhaps the most direct and straightforward way to learn about other people is to ask them questions. Survey research does just that.*

Surveys may be used to describe a population or to test a hypothesis. They may be used to build theories of social behavior or to solve practical problems. Surveys are part of public opinion research, marketing studies, and program evaluations. Because surveys are used in so many contexts, someday you will likely be asked to design and conduct a survey.

Steps in Conducting a Survey

Survey researchers are often interested in describing the attitudes and communication behaviors of large groups of people. A pollster's ideal is to know how every American will vote. Practically, however, he or she can question only a small fraction of the voting public. Luckily, it is not necessary to question every member of a **population** (the entire group a researcher wants to study) to get a good idea of what the population is like. By examining a **sample** (a small group of people representative of the population), the researcher can often draw very accurate conclusions about population characteristics.

There are good and bad ways to draw a sample; generalization is possible only if an unbiased sample has been chosen. To choose a representative sample, the researcher first chooses a **sampling plan,** a systematic method for choosing respondents for a study. Researchers use two general kinds of sampling plans: probability and nonprobability. **Probability sampling** allows generalizations because it assures the researcher that the sample is representative. In a probability sample, the researcher knows the exact probability that each member of a population will be included in a sample. For example, in **simple random sampling,** each member of the population has an equal chance of being in the sample. **Nonprobability sampling** does not give the researcher the same assurance. In nonprobability samples, some members of the population may have virtually no chance of being included, whereas others may be overrepresented. A common form of nonprobability sampling is **accidental sampling,** whereby the reseacher uses the most convenient people available.

Using nonprobability samples is risky. Imagine that you've been assigned to cover a presidential election for your college broadcasting station. Your task is to report the political views of students on your campus. With little time left before the election, you take the easy way out: you call all your friends and ask them how they intend to vote. The likelihood that this accidental sample will be accurate is very low. Because friends often share political views, your sample may be more likely to reflect your own opinions than to reflect those of the student body at large.

Simple random sampling, although costly in time and effort, significantly improves your chances of drawing a representative sample. If you were to use this method in our example, you would need a list of every student at your school as well as a computer-generated list of random ID numbers. You could then match the random numbers on your list to the student IDs, choosing for your survey only those students whose numbers came up. If you were to generate a sufficiently large sample (and if you could convince everyone in the sample to take part in the study), your results would closely approximate population figures.

Deciding whom to question is only the first step. A survey researcher must also frame questions and organize the survey. These steps are not as easy as they might seem. Like any other form of communication, questions can be misunderstood and misinterpreted. A researcher must take care that questions are answerable, unambiguous, and as nonthreatening as possible; that they focus on a single issue at a time; and that they do not lead the respondent to give a desired answer.

First, questions should be answerable; that is, they should avoid asking for information that the respondent does not know. "How many hours did you spend talking to friends last week?" is a difficult question; although some respondents might be able to give you a fairly accurate estimate, many would have no idea. Unfortunately, respondents often make up answers rather than admit their ignorance, making data from this kind of question suspect.

Questions should also be unambiguous; that is, what the researcher is asking should be clear. "How many channels of communication do you use in your job?" is ambiguous. "I am going to read off a number of ways people communicate on the job. As I mention each one, tell me whether you have used it during the last week: memo, telephone, fax . . ." is a much clearer way to ask the same question.

Questions should be as nonthreatening as possible; that is, they should avoid making the respondent feel guilty or incompetent. Questions about drug use, sexual behavior, or academic dishonesty are examples of topics that respondents may be unwilling to discuss. Explaining why these questions are necessary and assuring confidentiality may help respondents overcome their reluctance. Sometimes asking the question in an indirect form increases a respondent's willingness to respond. "Why do you think some students cheat?" may be more effective than "Why do you cheat?"

Double-barreled questions should be avoided. A double-barreled question asks several questions at once. "Do you believe that Governor Smith should be elected president because of her stand on the environment?" is really several questions rolled into one: "Do you believe that Smith should be elected?" is one question; "Do you approve of Smith's stand on the environment?" is another; and "Will Smith's environmental stand affect whether or not you vote for her?" is a third.

Another kind of question that should be avoided is the **leading question.** Leading questions are questions that indicate a preferred response. "Don't you think the depiction of women on MTV is shameful?" is a leading question. Generally, any question that starts with "Do you agree that . . ." is leading. A better phrasing would be "Consider the following statement. Do you agree or disagree with it?"

In addition to carefully considering the way a question is worded, the survey researcher is also concerned with the way questions are ordered. In general, easy-to-answer questions should be placed early in the questionnaire, and questions on sensitive topics should go toward the end. In addition, questions on a single topic should be grouped together.

Like other forms of communication, the survey interview should have a beginning, a middle, and an end. As Frey and colleagues point out, "how interviews are begun often determines whether, and then how fully, respondents cooperate."[16] In the beginning of a survey, the researcher must introduce himself or herself and state the purpose of the interview, the topic, how much time the survey will take, and whether the data will be confidential. At the end, he or she should thank the respondent for cooperating.

Researchers administer surveys in two general ways: through a face-to-face **interview** or through a self-administered **questionnaire.** Each method has advantages and disadvantages. Interviews allow the researcher to control what goes on during the survey and to clarify ambiguous questions. On the other hand, interviewers can inadvertently bias responses, and they are relatively expensive to train and use. Mailed questionnaires are cheap and have the advantage of being anonymous, but there is no way to control for distractions. In addition, response rate is often low.

Generally speaking, survey researchers convert responses into categories or numbers so that the responses can be statistically analyzed. Although this is relatively easy to do with responses to **closed-ended questions** (whereby respondents choose from a finite set of answers provided by the researcher) or **rating scales** (whereby the respondent rates an idea or an attitude on a numerical scale), it is more difficult to do with responses to **open-ended questions** (whereby the respondent is free to answer in his or her own words). With responses to open-ended questions, the researcher must find a way to categorize and compare responses. The researchers described in the next section used content analysis to categorize responses to open-ended questions.

Making the Love Connection:
An Example of Survey Research

In a movie you may remember, *The Lonely Guy,* comedian Steve Martin starred as a character who, no matter how hard he tried, couldn't manage to work out a relationship with the woman he loved. Robert Bell and Michael Roloff conducted a study to discover why lonely guys (and gals) have trouble building relationships.[17] Bell and Roloff argued that people who are successful at dating know how to "market" themselves. Lonely people, on the other hand, seem unable to advertise their good qualities. The authors predicted that when asked to advertise themselves, lonely people would fail to disclose relevant information about their personalities and interests, would describe themselves in unflattering ways, would set up unrealistic expectations for their partners and be quick to reject people who didn't meet their exacting standards, and would employ ineffective dating strategies.

To determine whether these hypotheses were correct and to collect descriptive data on how people go about advertising their romantic availability, the researchers administered a three-part questionnaire, which they presented to a sample consisting of 105 female and 73 male university students enrolled in communication courses. The mean age of the respondents was 19.5 years, and the average number of dates they reported was 3.9 per month.

In the first part of the questionnaire, respondents were asked to generate as many strategies as they could think of to advertise their romantic availability. In the second part, respondents were asked to write a script about themselves that could be used in a videotaped advertisement for a campus dating service. After writing the script, respondents were asked to judge its potential effectiveness. Finally, the respondents described their dating patterns and filled out a twenty-two-item scale that measured how often they experienced feelings of loneliness.

The researchers' first task in analyzing the data was to analyze the content of responses to the open-ended questions in parts one and two of the questionnaire. After unitizing the responses (i.e., reading them and deciding how many strategies were mentioned), the researchers developed a category system that described the strategies, and they placed each strategy into an appropriate category. They found that respondents used nine different methods to signal availability: (1) placing themselves in social situations in which potential partners might be found; (2) signaling, either directly or indirectly, that they were presently free to date; (3) contriving an encounter that would allow them to meet a potential partner again; (4) investigating whether a potential partner was currently seeing someone; (5) finding a way to make a potential partner more willing; (6) directly asking a potential partner for a future meeting; (7) making themselves more physically or psychologically attractive; (8) employing a professional dating service; or (9) getting a third party to set them up with a potential partner.

Analysis of the data from part one showed that the most popular strategies were making oneself more attractive and using third parties; the least popular strategies were trying to determine another's availability and using a professional service. Analysis of dating and loneliness scores showed that frequent daters were willing to place themselves in social situations, whereas lonely people avoided social situations and were unwilling to set up contrived encounters or to ask third parties for help. Analysis also showed that lonely people were more likely than nonlonely people to worry about other's availability.

The data from part two, the video-dating scripts, were also coded and analyzed. The researchers categorized the kind of information respondents offered about themselves, the ways they described themselves, their requirements for a potential date, and whether or not they gave excuses for participating in the dating service. Scripts, which had already been rated for effectiveness by their authors, were also rated by an independent set of judges.

Analyses showed that frequent daters were likely to provide information about their personality and interests and were unlikely to self-deprecate, to screen out potential partners, or to make excuses for participating. Loneliness was negatively associated with providing personality and interest information and positively associated with providing simple demographic information, making excuses, and screening out others on the basis of personality. Lonely people seemed to lack confidence in their scripts, as did the independent judges who rated them.

In interpreting the results, Bell and Roloff suggest that lonely people are unwilling to make themselves available to a wide range of romantic partners. They avoid social interaction and set up unrealistic demands that work to screen out others before they have a chance to develop a relationship. In contrast, nonlonely people are willing to give "tryouts" to a wide variety of people.

Lonely people also have trouble self-disclosing. As the authors put it, "when given the task of 'strutting their stuff' in a video-dating exercise, the [lonely] subjects . . . chose to focus on superficial demographic features to a greater extent than nonlonely people and gave less attention to social aspects of their personalities."[18] In closing, the authors acknowledge that one of the limitations of their study is that it employed hypothetical situations instead of real interaction. They also point out that a number of questions still need to be answered, including how lonely people gather information about others, how they engage in "audience adaptation," and how they maintain romantic attachments once they have made them. Despite these remaining questions, the researchers believe their results may be useful in helping lonely people make the behavioral changes necessary to overcome a serious social problem.

Experimental Research

In everyday life we frequently have hunches about cause and effect. To test these hunches, we run naive experiments: we manipulate what we think might be the cause and wait to see the effect of this manipulation. A parent, for example, may decide that arguing with a child simply reinforces the child's negative behavior. To test this idea, the parent may stop arguing and see what happens. If the child's bad behavior ceases, the parent will probably conclude that it was caused by too much attention. Although this conclusion may be questioned from a scientific point of view, this instance is an example of rudimentary experimentation.

> *In everyday life we frequently have hunches about cause and effect. To test these hunches, we run naive experiments: we manipulate what we think might be the cause and wait to see the effect of this manipulation.*

In **experimental research,** researchers are also interested in cause and effect. The effect they want to explain is called the **dependent variable,** whereas the suspected cause is called the **independent variable.** If, for example, a researcher believes that giving an employee praise will cause that employee to feel more satisfied with his or her work, praise is the independent variable, and satisfaction is the dependent variable.

All experiments involve manipulation, comparison, and control. To find out whether praise leads to satisfaction, for example, a researcher must **manipulate** the independent variable, praise. One way to do this is to choose two groups of workers, to praise one group and not the other, and then to **compare** the groups to see which group was most satisfied. If the researcher carefully **controls** the experiment by making sure no other independent variables are at work, then any change in satisfaction is necessarily due to the effects of praise.

Steps in Doing an Experiment

Like survey researchers, experimental researchers want to generalize their findings. They want to discover general laws of cause and effect that apply in many different situations. To do this, they must choose the best possible sampling plan. A probability sampling plan is best, but if this is impossible to implement, the researchers must devise a sampling strategy that controls for as much bias as possible.

The way the researcher sets up a study is called the **research design.** In designing a study, the researcher must decide how the independent variable, or **treatment,** is to be administered and when the dependent variable is to be measured. The measurement of the dependent variable before the treatment is called a **pretest;** the measurement after the treatment is called a **posttest.** Some research designs are faulty and allow no conclusions to be drawn. Others are logically valid and can be used to demonstrate causal relationships.

To see what constitutes a faulty design, let's return to the praise-satisfaction experiment. Assume, for a moment, that the researcher did the experiment on a single group of workers. The researcher measured workers' satisfaction level, praised the workers at least once a day for two weeks, and then measured their satisfaction again. Assume also that satisfaction was greater after the two-week period than before. Would the researcher be justified in concluding that the change in satisfaction was due to the praise? The answer is no. The change might well have been due to other factors—perhaps the workload lightened during that period or rumors of a wage increase circulated. Because this design (called a **one-group pretest-posttest design**) used only one group, it is impossible to rule out alternative explanations.

The research design can be improved by adding a second or **control group,** which is equivalent to the first group in every way except that it does not receive the experimental treatment. If the satisfaction level of the control group stays the same over the two weeks while the satisfaction level of the treatment group rises, then the researcher can rule out alternative explanations. To ensure that the control and treatment groups are equivalent, the researcher should not use existing groups, for they may be different to begin with. Instead, he or she should randomly assign subjects to the experimental and control groups. The design used in this example is called a **pretest-posttest control group design** and is one of the strongest and most popular of the experimental designs.

In any experiment the researcher must devise a way to measure the dependent variable. In the example we have been using, the researcher must measure satisfaction. To do so, he or she might use a simple yes-or-no question ("Are you satisfied with your job, yes or no?") and compare the percentages of workers in each group saying yes before and after the treatment. On the other hand, the researcher might use a more elaborate rating scale ("On a scale from one to ten, where ten indicates high satisfaction, how would you rate your feelings about your job?") and compare the average rating before and after the treatment. In any case, a measurement method must meet two criteria. It must be **reliable** (i.e., it must consistently yield the same results) and it must be **valid** (i.e., it must actually measure the dependent variable). If, for example, employees know that the boss will receive their answers to the satisfaction question, the results might not be valid; the results might reflect the employees' desire to please the boss and protect their jobs rather than the employees' actual degree of satisfaction.

Experimental researchers depend on statistical methods to help them analyze their data. They compute statistics that tell them whether their findings are due to random variation or to the presence of the independent variable. Although statistics provide an objective, numerical method for analyzing differences, it is still up to the researcher to interpret what these differences mean.

Thanks for Not Smoking:
An Example of a Field Experiment

Each day more than three thousand teenagers join the ranks of regular smokers, putting themselves at serious risk of illness or death. What, if anything, can be done to stop them? Persuasive theory presents one possible solution: inoculation. **Inoculation** is a form of communication designed to produce resistance to certain kinds of messages. It is used when a social influence agent wants to prevent an audience from succumbing to an undesirable message in the future. By warning audience members that they will be exposed to an undesirable message and by teaching them how to refute that message, the change agent tries to "immunize" the audience so that when they hear the expected message, they will be unaffected by it.

Research has shown that during the transition year from primary to middle or junior high school, adolescents are especially likely to be confronted with peer pressures to start smoking and to abandon previous negative attitudes about cigarettes and smokers. Michael Plau, Steve Van Bockern, and Jong Guen Kang reasoned that inoculation might protect vulnerable adolescents from peer messages urging them to smoke. They therefore undertook a field experiment to determine the relative effectiveness of inoculating adolescents against smoking by presenting groups of adolescents with a videotaped message that forewarned them of the peer pressure they would face and that taught them how to argue against that pressure.[19] Because previous studies had shown that people with low self-esteem have particular difficulty resisting pressures to conform and because some evidence suggests that females are more susceptible to social appeals than are males, the researchers thought that the success of the inoculation might be related to self-esteem and gender. They also wondered what the effect of giving a follow-up "booster" inoculation would be.

Thus, the researchers advanced four hypotheses: (1) that adolescents who received inoculations would be more resistant than those who did not; (2) that a follow-up reinforcement would strengthen resistance among those receiving inoculations; (3) that subjects with low self-esteem would be more affected by inoculations than would subjects with high self-esteem; and (4) that the inoculation would be more effective with females than with males.

The adolescents who served as subjects in the study were all seventh-grade students in junior high school in Sioux Falls, South Dakota. A total of 1,047 students began the study, and 948 completed it. Prior to the main manipulation, students' demographic characteristics, level of self-esteem, and attitudes to smoking were measured using standard scales that had shown themselves to be valid and reliable in previous studies.

At the beginning of the school year, students were randomly assigned to health classes, and the resulting thirty-eight health classes were randomly assigned to one of the following conditions: inoculation, inoculation plus reinforcement, or no treatment (the control group). The inoculation manipulation was accomplished by showing a video in class at the beginning of October. The reinforcement manipulation involved showing a second video on the same subject at the end of November. In February and again in May of the following year, attitudes and behavioral dispositions toward smoking were assessed.

The inoculation videos were professionally made and consisted of two parts. First, students were warned that their peers would put pressure on them to smoke and that despite their current attitudes, some of them would change their minds about smoking. Then, the kinds of arguments students were likely to hear were outlined ("Smoking is cool," "It's okay to experiment," "It won't hurt you"), and refutations of those arguments were presented.

Results showed qualified support for hypothesis one (that inoculation promotes resistance to smoking) and strong support for hypothesis two (that inoculation is most effective among adolescents with low self-esteem). For those adolescents who tested low in self-esteem, the inoculation had small, but significant, effects. In May, for example, low-self-esteem subjects in the control group estimated that the likelihood they would smoke was 29%; in comparison, low-self-esteem students in the inoculation group reported their likelihood of smoking to be only 19%. Similarly, on a seven-point scale measuring attitudes toward smoking, the low-self-esteem students in the control group rated smoking a 2.79, whereas low-self-esteem subjects in the experimental groups rated smoking a 2.27. No effect due to gender was observed, and, disappointingly, no effect due to reinforcement was found.

The researchers concluded that inoculation can stop some of the slippage in attitude that occurs in this transition period. They also concluded that, contrary to previous studies that portrayed video as an ineffective persuasive tool, a well-designed video can be a cheap and effective way to help promote smoking resistance. The researchers estimated that inoculation techniques could make attitudes more negative in up to 17% of adolescent receivers and could discourage as many as 10% of them from smoking, thus making an important contribution to efforts to combat this serious health problem.

TABLE 11-5

Subject Areas
in Speech
Communication

Interpersonal Communication

The study of verbal and nonverbal exchanges in everyday interaction. Specialists in interpersonal communication study topics such as interpersonal influence, relational development and maintenance, impression formation, interpersonal attraction, gender and communication, and communication and the development of the self.

Courses include Interpersonal Communication, Gender and Communication, Family Communication, Conflict Management, and Therapeutic Communication.

Small Group/Organizational Communication

The study of how communication helps people in groups accomplish goals and maintain group identity; the study of how communication operates in complex organizations. Specialists in small group/organizational communication study topics such as group problem solving, conflict resolution, leadership, mediation and negotiation, superior/subordinate relationships, and organizational culture.

Courses include Small Group Decision Making, Business and Professional Communication, Leadership, and Employment Interviewing, as well as courses in specialized professions, such as Health Communication or Legal Communication.

Public Communication

The study of communication in face-to-face, one-to-many communication settings. Specialists in the rhetoric of public communication study topics such as persuasion, propaganda, political communication, the history of public address, social movements, freedom of speech, and the ethics of speaking.

Courses include Public Speaking, Theories of Persuasion, Public Address, Rhetorical Theory, and Argumentation and Debate.

Learning More About Communication

The research methods we've looked at represent just a few of the ways scholars and critics gather new information and draw conclusions about communication. But experts in communication don't start out by doing research; they begin by taking the traditional courses that are the core of communication as an academic discipline.

Performance Studies

The study of the ways people perform personal, cultural, or artistic scripts before audiences. Specialists in performance studies study topics such as folklore and oral traditions; storytelling; performance art; the work of individual performers, such as stand-up comics or cultural icons; and the performance of literature.

Courses include Oral Interpretation, Readers' Theatre, Performance of Literature, and Folklore, as well as courses specializing in a given genre or author, such as Performing Joyce or Performance and Analysis of Prose.

Mass Communication

The study of mediated messages created for a wide public audience. Specialists in mass communication study topics such as the history of the media, prosocial effects of the media, television and the family, media law, nonfiction film, and politics and the media.

Courses include Advertising, Public Relations, Broadcast Production, Introduction to the Mass Media, Journalism, and Media Criticism.

Intercultural Communication

The study of communication across cultural boundaries. Specialists in intercultural communication study topics such as interethnic and interracial conflict, verbal and nonverbal differences across cultures, forms of talk unique to a given culture, and ways to increase cross-cultural understanding.

Courses include Cross-Cultural Communication and a variety of specialized courses examining given cultures.

Language and Semiotic Systems

The study of code systems used to create messages in any of the contexts listed above. Topics include nonverbal message systems, semantic and pragmatic rules and their effects, dialect differences and social class, bilingualism, gender differences in language use, and conversational structures.

Courses include Language and Social Action, The Psychology of Language, Language Development, American Dialects, and Phonetics.

Subject Areas in Speech Communication

If you're not familiar with the field of communication—if this is your first exposure to the study of human message making—you may not be aware of the range of topics routinely studied. Table 11-5 lists some of the major subject areas that make up this discipline, along with the kinds of courses offered at either the undergraduate or graduate level.

Although it may begin in the classroom, the study of communication is not limited to formal coursework. The world around us is a laboratory where the curious observer can continue to make discoveries.

As you can see, the types of courses offered in departments of communication are both theoretical and applied. Some, such as public speaking, argumentation, and group discussion, help you improve your organizational and delivery skills. Others, such as interpersonal, family, and gender communication courses, focus on understanding and analyzing everyday interaction. You may choose courses that explore the history of our field (e.g., Classical Theories of Rhetoric), courses that develop your critical and analytic skills (e.g., Rhetorical Theory, Analysis and Performance of Literature), or courses that prepare you for a specific communication-related career (e.g., Public Relations, Broadcast Production, Health Communication). The areas covered in departments of communication are far-reaching and varied.

Other Sources of Discovery

Although taking formal courses or reading books written by communication experts can increase your knowledge, you can learn more about communication in many other ways. One way is to explore other subject areas. Although colleges and universities are divided into separate departments and disciplines, these divisions are somewhat arbitrary. There are connections between all of the humanities and sciences. Psychology and sociology can offer insights into communication by illuminating human and group behavior, and anthropology can show us how communication practices differ from culture to culture. Literary criticism and linguistics can tell us more about how meanings are created and shared, whereas the study of music, art, and architectural design can help us see how different media transform expression. History and politics show us how events in the public sphere affect the subjects we communicate about as well as the ways we communicate about them. The list of cognate areas goes on and on. Indeed, it is difficult to think of any course in the humanities or social sciences that is not related to communication.

Another way you can understand communication more fully is through reading novels and viewing plays and films. Not only are these forms of expression examples of rhetorical acts in their own right, they also illuminate our understanding of human behavior and therefore make us more sensitive to one another.

Finally, you can gain insight into communication by observing human interaction. This takes a willingness to stand aside and to watch and wonder. Curiosity is at the heart of all discovery—a curiosity that is initially attracted by anything odd or different and that proceeds to celebrate regularities in the "life that flows beneath the surface of things." If you develop that curiosity, you cannot help but learn about communication theory and practice.

Summary

This chapter discusses methods of discovery: it describes the research process, examines four popular approaches to communication study, and outlines the structure of communication as an academic field.

Research is not exotic; it's something we do every day. Commonsense methods of discovery, however, are often biased. We privilege our own experiences, engage in wishful thinking, and rely too much on simple heuristics. Systematic research is more accurate and less biased; it is question-oriented, methodological, creative, replicable, self-critical, public, cumulative and self-correcting, and cyclical. Regardless of approach, researchers accomplish four tasks: they ask questions and define key concepts; they choose a method to guide their inquiry; they gather and analyze samples of communication acts; and they interpret these samples, sharing the results.

Four of the most popular research methods are rhetorical criticism, ethnographic inquiry, survey research, and experimental research. Rhetorical criticism is a systematic way of describing, analyzing, and evaluating rhetorical acts. In criticizing acts of influence, rhetorical critics use methods such as neo-Aristotelian criticism, genre criticism, Burkean analysis, fantasy theme analysis, social movement criticism, ideological criticism, and social value criticism. Rushing's analysis of the Western myth is an example of rhetorical criticism.

A second and very different kind of research is ethnography. Ethnographers try to understand how members of other cultures interpret their worlds. Ethnographers do this by observing behavior in natural surroundings to uncover rules that guide action. Ethnographers bracket their preconceptions and try to see the world without bias. Philipsen's study on male role-enactment in Teamsterville is an example of ethnographic research.

A third research method is survey research. Survey researchers describe populations by asking questions of systematically chosen samples. The questions must be answerable, unambiguous, and nonthreatening; researchers must avoid double-barreled and leading questions. Bell and Roloff's research on dating strategies is an example of survey research.

A final research method is experimental research. Experimental researchers manipulate independent variables to discover their effects on dependent variables. Experiments are controlled so that no unexpected factors invalidate conclusions about causal relationships. Measurement must be reliable and valid. Plau, Van Bockern, and Kang's study on ways to prevent adolescents from smoking is an example of experimental research.

The field of communication encompasses many interesting topics to study and many ways to study them. Whether your interest is in interpersonal, small group/organizational, public, mass, intercultural communication, or in performance studies or language, you will find large bodies of research available and a variety of courses to take. But taking a course in speech communication is not the only way to learn more about communication. By reading and studying related topics or by simply observing life around you, you can continue to make discoveries about human communication.

Key Terms

Listed below are the key terms used in this chapter, along with the number of the page on which each is explained.

Review Questions

1. What does the term *research* mean? What attitude should a researcher have?

2. What are the flaws in commonsense methods of discovery? What are heuristics?

3. What are the eight characteristics of systematic research? Explain each.

4. What are the four common research tasks? Give examples of research questions. What is a conceptual definition? an operational definition? Name some common research methodologies. What kinds of events might a rhetorical critic sample? What kind of sample might a survey researcher draw?

5. How does the critical impulse display itself in everyday life? What is rhetorical criticism, and how does it differ from everyday criticism? According to Rybacki and Rybacki, what three things must a rhetorical critic do?

6. What is a rhetorical act? What kinds of communication function as rhetorical acts? What does it mean to say that rhetorical criticism is a rhetorical act in its own right?

7. Describe the methods and results of Rushing's study of the myth of the American cowboy.

8. What is ethnographic research? What is its goal? What two roles might an ethnographer take? What is an informant? What does it mean to do presuppositionless research?

9. Describe the methods and results of Philipsen's study of Teamsterville.

10. What is survey research? How are sample and population related? What is a sampling plan? What is the difference between probability and nonprobability sampling? What are the advantages and disadvantages of each? Describe how a simple random sample is collected.

11. What are the characteristics of good questions? What kinds of questions should be avoided? What are the advantages and disadvantages of interviews and questionnaires? Give an example of an open- and a closed-ended question.

12. Describe the methods and results in Bell and Roloff's study of loneliness and dating strategies.

13. What is experimental research? What is the difference between dependent and independent variables? What three characteristics are found in all experiments? What kinds of decisions must one make in choosing a research design? What is wrong with a one-group pretest-posttest design? What is a better design? What are reliability and validity?

14. Describe the methods and result in Plau, Van Bockern, and Kang's field experiment on ways to prevent adolescents from smoking. What is inoculation?

15. Name some common subject areas in speech communication. What kinds of topics are studied in each area? In addition to formal course work in speech communication, what other sources can one turn to for information on human communication?

Suggested Readings

Ford, Julienne. (1975). *Paradigms and fairy tales: An introduction to the science of meanings* (Vol. 1). Boston: Routledge and Kegan Paul.

A whimsical and lively discussion of theory building and research. Ford touches on major issues in the philosophy of science with good humor and intelligence.

Frey, Lawrence R., Botan, Carl H., Friedman, Paul G., & Kreps, Gary L. (1991). *Investigating communication: An introduction to research methods.* Englewood Cliffs, NJ: Prentice-Hall.

An excellent introduction to research methods. This book contains everything you need to know to do communication research presented in a clear, intelligent, interesting way.

Rybacki, Karyn, & Rybacki, Don. (1991). *Communication criticism: Approaches and genres.* Belmont, CA: Wadsworth.

An excellent introduction to rhetorical criticism, especially useful for its annotated reading lists and examples of critical research.

Notes

1. Selltiz, Claire, Wrightsman, Lawrence S., & Cook, Stuart W. (1976). *Research methods in social relations* (3rd ed.). New York: Holt, Rinehart & Winston, 2.

2. For a good discussion of heuristic rules as they apply to persuasion, see Cialdini, Robert B. (1984). *Influence: How and why people agree to things.* New York: Morrow. For a more formal discussion, see Eagly, Alice H., & Chaiken, Shelly. (1986). Cognitive theories of persuasion. In Leonard Berkowitz (Ed.), *Advances in experimental social psychology* (Vol. 19). New York: Academic, 123–181.

3. Selltiz, Wrightsman, & Cook, 5.

4. Frey, Lawrence R., Botan, Carl H., Friedman, Paul G., & Kreps, Gary L. (1991). *Investigating communication: An introduction to research methods.* Englewood Cliffs, NJ: Prentice-Hall, 6–8.

5. Poole, Marshall Scott, & McPhee, R. D. (1985). Methodology in interpersonal communication research. In Mark L. Knapp & Gerald R. Miller (Eds.), *Handbook of interpersonal communication.* Newbury Park, CA: Sage, 100.

6. Frey, Botan, Friedman, & Kreps, 7–8.

7. Rybacki, Karyn, & Rybacki, Don. (1991). *Communication criticism.* Belmont, CA: Wadsworth, 16.

8. Rushing, Janice Hocker. (1983). The rhetoric of the American Western myth. *Communication Monographs, 50,* 14–32.

9. Ibid., 17.

10. Schwartz, Howard, & Jacobs, Jerry. (1979). *Qualitative sociology: A method to the madness.* New York: Free Press, 48.

11. Kirk, J., & Miller, M. L. (1986). *Reliability and validity in qualitative research.* Newbury Park, CA: Sage, 9.

12. Frey, Botan, Friedman, & Kreps, 247.

13. Philipsen, Gerry. (1975). Speaking "like a man" in Teamsterville: Cultural patterns of role enactment in an urban neighborhood. *Quarterly Journal of Speech, 61,* 13–22; and Philipsen, Gerry. (1976). Places for speaking in Teamsterville. *Quarterly Journal of Speech, 62,* 15–25.

14. Philipsen, 1976, 25.

15. Hymes, Dell. (1967). Models of the interaction of language and social setting. *Journal of Social Issues, 22,* 10.

16. Frey, Botan, Friedman, & Kreps, 199.

17. Bell, Robert A., & Roloff, Michael E. (1991). Making a love connection: Loneliness and communication competence in the dating marketplace. *Communication Quarterly, 39,* 58–74.

18. Ibid., 70.

19. Plau, Michael, Van Bockern, Steve, & Kang, Jong Guen. (1992). Use of inoculation to promote resistance to smoking initiation among adolescents. *Communication Monographs, 59,* 213–230.

Index

Author Index

Subject Index